Pro ASP.NET Extensibility

Jörg Krause

Apress®

Pro ASP.NET Extensibility

Copyright © 2009 by Jörg Krause

ISBN-13 (pbk): 978-1-4302-1983-5

ISBN-13 (electronic): 978-1-4302-1984-2

Printed and bound in the United States of America 9 8 7 6 5 4 3 2 1

Lead Editor: Jonathan Hassell
Technical Reviewer: Stefan Turalski
Editorial Board: Clay Andres, Steve Anglin, Mark Beckner, Ewan Buckingham, Tony Campbell, Gary Cornell, Jonathan Gennick, Jonathan Hassell, Michelle Lowman, Matthew Moodie, Jeffrey Pepper, Frank Pohlmann, Douglas Pundick, Ben Renow-Clarke, Dominic Shakeshaft, Matt Wade, Tom Welsh
Project Manager: Kylie Johnston
Copy Editor: Katie Stence
Associate Production Director: Kari Brooks-Copony
Production Editor: Laura Esterman
Compositor: Diana Van Winkle
Proofreader: Dan Shaw
Indexer: BIM Indexing & Proofreading Services
Artist: April Milne
Cover Designer: Kurt Krames
Manufacturing Director: Tom Debolski

Distributed to the book trade worldwide by Springer-Verlag New York, Inc., 233 Spring Street, 6th Floor, New York, NY 10013. Phone 1-800-SPRINGER, fax 201-348-4505, e-mail orders-ny@springer-sbm.com, or visit http://www.springeronline.com.

For information on translations, please contact Apress directly at 2855 Telegraph Avenue, Suite 600, Berkeley, CA 94705. Phone 510-549-5930, fax 510-549-5939, e-mail info@apress.com, or visit http://www.apress.com.

Apress and friends of ED books may be purchased in bulk for academic, corporate, or promotional use. eBook versions and licenses are also available for most titles. For more information, reference our Special Bulk Sales–eBook Licensing web page at http://www.apress.com/info/bulksales.

The source code for this book is available to readers at http://www.apress.com.

Contents at a Glance

About the Author xi

About the Technical Reviewer xiii

Acknowledgments xv

Introduction xvii

CHAPTER 1   Understanding ASP.NET 1

CHAPTER 2   Worker and Threads 53

CHAPTER 3   Modules and Handlers 107

CHAPTER 4   Providers and Configuration 153

CHAPTER 5   Extending the Resource Model 197

CHAPTER 6   Page and Session Management 245

CHAPTER 7   Security and User Management 273

CHAPTER 8   Site Management 341

CHAPTER 9   Control Extensibility 373

INDEX 395

Contents

About the Author xi

About the Technical Reviewer xiii

Acknowledgments xv

Introduction xvii

■CHAPTER 1   Understanding ASP.NET 1

A Promise in Advance 1

The Low-Level Architecture of Request Handling 1

    What Is ASP.NET? 2

    The Lifetime of a Request 2

    Request Comes In 7

    Getting into the .NET Runtime 8

    HttpContext and HttpApplication 13

    Flowing Through the ASP.NET Pipeline 18

    Modules and Handlers Using HttpModule and HttpHandler 19

    The Life Cycles 20

IIS7 Integrated Pipeline 21

The Application's Pipeline 21

    The Request Arrives 22

The Page's Life Cycle 25

    Page Request Stages 26

    Events Fired Within the Life Cycle's Stages 27

    Additional Page Life Cycle Considerations 29

Dynamic Controls and Data Binding Events 29

    Dynamic Control Events 29

    Data Binding Events for Data-Bound Controls 30

    Login Control Events 31

View State 31

Why Understanding View State Is Important 32

    A Word Regarding Control State 33

The Page Cycle from the View State Perspective 33

    Step One—Instantiation 34

    Step Two—Initializing 39

    Step Three—Loading the View State 39

    Step Four—Loading Postback Data 40

    Step Five—Loading Step 42

Step Six—Raising Postback Events 42

Step Seven—Storing the View State 43

Step Eight—Rendering the Page 43

The True Role of View State. 43

View State Anti-Patterns 44

Forcing a Default. 45

Persisting Constant Data 46

Persisting Cheap Data 46

Initializing Child Controls 48

Attaching Dynamic Controls 50

Initializing Dynamically Created Controls 51

Summary 52

▆CHAPTER 2   **Worker and Threads** 53

Managing the Worker Process. 53

Managing Worker Processes and AppDomains in IIS7 53

Understanding and Using Threads 70

ASP.NET Thread Usage on IIS 70

Tune the Threading. 73

Threading and Asynchronous Operations. 77

Summary 105

▆CHAPTER 3   **Modules and Handlers** 107

Module, Handlers, and IIS 107

Modules 108

IIS7 Architecture 108

The IIS7 Managed Module Starter Kit 113

Building a Module 115

Interaction Between Modules 119

Configuration and Deployment 120

Handlers. 122

Built-In Handlers 122

Extending ASP.NET Using Http Handlers 122

Building a Handler 124

Advanced Usage of Handlers. 136

Asynchronous Pages. 138

Prepare Pages for Asynchronous Operation. 138

Using a Public Web Service 140

Configuration and Deployment 143

Testing and Debugging Modules and Handlers 146

    Debug Using IIS. 147

    Set Up Tracing for Handlers. 151

Summary 152

■CHAPTER 4   **Providers and Configuration** 153

The Provider Model. 153

    Goals of the Provider Model. 154

    Default Provider 154

    Built-In Providers 156

    Extending Built-In Providers 156

The Anatomy of a Provider. 157

    Making the Provider Available. 158

    Configuring the Provider 158

General Considerations 160

    Initialization Procedure of a Provider 160

    Lifetime 161

    Thread Safety 161

Creating a Custom Provider-Based Service 163

    Limitations of the Code Samples. 163

    Creating a Service. 164

    Creating the Provider 165

    Configuring Providers. 170

    Using the Service 172

Extending the Configuration. 174

    How to Scaffold a Configuration Section 174

    Anatomy of a Configuration Section 174

    The Class Model 175

    Attributes to Control Elements' Behaviors 176

    Definition of a Simple Configuration Section 176

    Usage of a Custom Configuration Section 180

Accessing the Configuration Declaratively. 181

    Extending the Expression Binding Syntax 181

    Introduction to Expression Syntax. 181

    Creating an Expression Builder 183

    Accessing Settings for Non-Compiled Pages. 187

    Beyond Simple Expressions. 188

    Design-Time Support 189

    Implementing an Expression Builder with Design-Time Support 190

Summary 195

■CHAPTER 5   **Extending the Resource Model**..................................197

Principles of Resource Management 197
    The Fallback Strategy..197
    Using Global Resources 198
    Limitations of the Existing Provider...........................198
Programming a Custom Resource Provider...............................198
    Extending the Provider Model 198
    Prerequisites 200
    Implementing the Custom Provider...............................201
    Configure the Resource Provider................................208
    Using the Custom Resource Provider 208
Implementing Design-Time Support.....................................209
    Register the Design-Time Support 209
Edit Resources at Runtime..219
    How It Works...219
    Creating an Online Editor 223
Summary 243

■CHAPTER 6   **Page and Session Management**..............................245

The Page State Persister 245
    A Look Back..245
The Default Page State Persister.....................................246
    State Storage in ASP.NET.......................................246
Persisting Page State Information....................................247
    View State Explained 247
    Control State Explained 247
    The Default Providers..249
    Changing the Default Provider..................................251
Developing a Custom Page State Provider..............................251
    Choosing the Data Storage 252
    Analyzing a Provider...252
    Implementing the Provider......................................252
    Extending the Provider 254
    Maintaining the Storage by Using the Health Monitor............254
    Conclusion...256
Session State Providers 256
    The Session State Service 256
    Identifying the Session..258
    The Internal State Providers 260
    Improving the Session State 263
Implementing the Session State Store Provider 264
    The Session State Module 264

Preface. 266
Implementation of a File-Based Session State Persister 267
Summary. 272

■CHAPTER 7   Security and User Management. 273

Built-In Capabilities. 273
Authentication Modules 276
Authorization Modules 276
The User Management Interfaces 277
Extending Membership and Role Providers 281
Why Create a Membership Provider? 281
Solution Details 282
Developing Membership and Role Providers 282
Create Web Service–Driven Membership Provider 282
Create Web Service–Driven Role Provider 282
Configuring the Services 298
Implementing the Provider. 300
Configuring the Provider 308
Testing the Providers 308
Extending Profile Providers 310
The Profile Service 310
Understanding the Profile Provider 310
Configuring Custom Profile Providers. 314
Implementing a Custom Profile Provider 314
Preparation Steps 314
Implementing the Provider. 319
A Client Side–Driven Profile Provider 325
Extending Web Parts Personalization Providers. 329
Understanding the Web Parts Personalization Provider 329
Implementing a Custom Personalization Provider. 331
Testing the Custom Web Part Personalization Provider 339
Summary. 340

■CHAPTER 8   Site Management. 341

Site Map Providers 341
Internal Site Map Provider 341
Localization 343
Security Issues 343
Reasons to Write a Custom Sitemap Provider 343
Writing a Custom Sitemap Provider 344
Prerequisites 344
Learning About the Base Classes 344

Implementing a SQL Server–Based Navigation 348
Suggestions for Extending the Example 354
Extending the VirtualPathProvider 354
Using the VirtualPathProvider 354
Register the VirtualPathProvider 355
Prerequisites for a VirtualPathProvider 356
Helpful Classes for Path and File Operations 357
Creating a Virtual Path Provider to Get Themes from Database 358
Limitations of the VirtualPathProvider Approach .371
Summary 372

■CHAPTER 9   **Control Extensibility** 373

Adaptive Control Behavior 373
The Default Behavior 374
Using Control Adapters 376
Using Page Adapters 379
Device-Specific Filter for Adaptive Behavior 381
Using Control Adapters 385
Device Friendly Adapters 385
CSS Friendly Adapters 385
Other Adapter Ideas 385
Writing a Custom Control Adapter 385
Steps for Creating the Example 385
The Example Code 386
Why Use HtmlTextWriter? 390
Configure the Example 390
Writing a Custom Page Adapter 391
Steps for Creating the Example 391
Configure the Examples 393
Summary 394

■INDEX 395

About the Author

 **JÖRG KRAUSE** has been working with software and software technology since the early 1980s, beginning with a ZX 81 and taking his first steps as a programmer in BASIC and assembly language. He studied information technology at Humboldt University, Berlin, but in the 1990s he left early to start his own company. He has worked with Internet technology and software development since the early days when CompuServe and FidoNet dominated. He's been with Microsoft Technologies and Software since Windows 95. In 1998, he worked on one of the first commercial e-commerce solutions, and wrote his first book in Germany, *E-Commerce and Online Marketing*, published by Carl Hanser Verlag, Munich. Due to its wide success, he started working as a freelance consultant and author in order to share his experience and knowledge with others. He has written several books for Hanser, Addison-Wesley, and other major publishers in Germany—a total of more than 40 titles. He also publishes articles in magazines and speaks at conferences in Germany, including BASTA. Currently, Jörg works as a senior consultant for Microsoft Technologies at Computacenter AG & Co. oHG in Berlin.

In his occasional spare time, Jörg enjoys reading thrillers and science fiction, as well as playing badminton in the winter and golf in the summer.

About the Technical Reviewer

STEFAN TURALSKI is a nice chap who is capable of performing both magical and trivial things with a little help from code, libraries, tools, APIs, and servers. Wearing many hats, he has experience in almost all aspects of the software life cycle, and is especially skilled in business analysis, design, implementation, testing, and QA, as well as team management. His main areas of interest are quite wide but include emerging technologies with recent focus on RIA (Silverlight and AIR), cloud computing, functional programming, and software engineering at large.

Before he realized that he enjoys criticizing other people's work more, Stefan published several technical articles mainly about .NET technology, SOA, software engineering, and mobile development. For the last 10-plus years, he has been building solutions ranging from Perl scripts, integrations of SQLite, and Web sites, to highly scalable .NET and COM+ enterprise-class systems. Feel free to contact him at stefan.turalski@gmail.com.

Acknowledgments

I'd like to mention the people who helped me create this book and make it what it is. First, I'd like to thank David White and his daughter, Rebekah, for their amazing work smoothing my style and cajoling it into readable English. I know you had a challenging task. I can't forget the support from Jonathan Hassell for my first steps into the Apress world, as well as the continuing help from Kylie Johnston. Thanks for your frequent reminders about the deadline, Kylie. They really motivate lazy writers back to the keyboard. Thanks to our technical reviewer, Stefan, who opened my mind with his remarks and code style ideas, and pointed out the mistakes that I made in haste. His work greatly improved the quality of this book.

Last, but not least, I'd like to thank my family and friends for understanding when I went back to the computer to continue writing or fighting with Visual Studio, while they sat on the terrace for a barbeque. Believe me, it was much harder for me than for you.

Introduction

What Does This Book Cover?

ASP.NET is an established and well-known web application framework, and there are several books on the market with different emphases and at different levels. However, ASP.NET is becoming more and more a foundation technology upon which larger and larger projects are being built. Developers are facing increasing complexity and greater demands to fulfill in their daily tasks. This book examines in-depth the technology beyond the basic ASP.NET topics available elsewhere. It's full of practical tips and tricks from an experienced developer. You'll learn not only how things work, but also why. By adopting this knowledge, you will succeed in extending and adapting highly useful functionality in your own projects.

Extensibility is covered in great depth. Developers have a tendency to use a framework, language, or piece of software "as is." Even in the age of open source software, most developers don't look inside existing code or attempt to adapt it to fit their needs. Instead, they write their own code. For years, I've been asking developers why they avoid third-party code and go to such lengths in order to write essentially the same software. It's usually because if they've created it, they know that they can control, understand, and master it.

With .NET 2.0, Microsoft shifted the ASP.NET framework towards a new paradigm—the paradigm of extensibility. This allows developers to extend Microsoft's software and adapt the parts to behave exactly as you would have designed. Microsoft encourages you to change existing behaviors, add features, modify settings, and basically do whatever you want in order to get the most out of their framework. However, never ignore infrastructure parts of the framework or replace them completely with your own code.

Almost every ASP.NET book explains ASP.NET from the ground up—some are in-depth and some provide clear details, but ASP.NET is always treated "as is." Their failing is in treating ASP.NET like concrete—when, in fact, it's like Lego™. My underlying motivation for writing this book was to educate developers about this overlooked aspect of ASP.NET: the many ways it can be extended.

Conventions Used in This Book

We understand that you're eager to start reading and learning, but it is worth taking a few seconds to look over this section—it will help you to get the most out of this book. Several icons and font conventions are used throughout:

- Screen messages, code listings, and command samples appear in `monospace` type.

- The same `monospace font` is used for HTML, ASP.NET controls (declarative listings), and XML snippets.

- Important parts of a listing are highlighted in **`bold monospace`**.

- Code-related text includes many references to code, such as method names, class names, namespaces, members, and so on. This is a mixture of common framework names and the ones I've used in examples. To distinguish between them, all framework names (from the Microsoft world) are set in `monospace`, while all private names are set in *italics*.

- To emphasize or quote things, "quotes" are occasionally used.

Several icons highlight important definitions, cautions, and conclusions.

Tip This is a tip.

Note A note that explains a topic further but is not required for understanding the main topic.

Caution A warning to keep you from common pitfalls.

Who This Book Is For

This book is intended for advanced web developers interested in learning about the internal workings of ASP.NET. I assume that you already have some experience writing small web applications, that you've actively created some web projects, and you want to take your skills a step further. What if your next customer wishes to run a large server cluster, a site with thousands of pages, complex navigation, and heavy database access? ASP.NET can handle this, but its out-of-the-box features won't be adequate. This book covers situations such as these in detail and shows you what to do when ASP.NET reaches its limits. You'll learn how to extend, customize, and enhance this platform to get what you want. "No more compromise" is my motto.

Throughout my years of experience programming ASP.NET, I've noticed that developers often complain about incorrect behavior, supposed bugs, incomplete implementations, or missing features. In most of these situations, I don't agree that ASP.NET is deficient or faulty. I'll demonstrate that the key to success with ASP.NET is a deep understanding of the platform that goes beyond the basics. ASP.NET is not perfect—it has its rough edges, like any other piece of software. However, Version 3.5 is top-of-the-line, providing almost everything you need in order to get your professional projects functioning well. Really, really well. This is what I'd like to tell you: learn, explore, understand, and you will be *the* professional developer you want to be.

I also assume that you already have some basic knowledge of skills and technologies often required as a web developer:

- HTML, CSS, and JavaScript
- Visual Studio basics, such as creating a project, running, and debugging it
- ASP.NET basics, such as putting a control onto the page, customizing it, creating a user or custom control, and so on
- Basic knowledge of how to obtain database access, as well as using LINQ to query it and write data back
- Using XML as either a data source or storage

There is no information specific to the topics in this book, but I use all of these techniques with the example code.

Prerequisites

This book is based on ASP.NET 3.5. As a basic platform, I use Visual Studio 2008, running on Windows Server 2008 with IIS7. When a client is involved, I use Windows Vista SP1. A similar platform is helpful for getting samples running. Because the last radical change in IIS took place between IIS5 and IIS6, it's not possible to transform anything to IIS5 level. However, much of the information pertaining to IIS7 may also be true for IIS6—a bit of backward compatibility! Nevertheless, I'd encourage you to look to the future and work with the most current tools and platforms you can obtain.

How This Book Is Organized

There are many ways of structuring a book. From my long-term experience in writing and publishing books, I know that people read books very differently. Some read from beginning to end, just like a novel, while others start where they find an interesting topic. There is no book that can cover all reading styles! However, this book follows the same successful strategy I've used many times before. I start with the basics: low-level concepts and background information necessary to *really* understand a theme. Then I proceed systematically through all sections in an independent order. This allows you to read from beginning to end—or to dip into an interesting chapter and skip the others. The many references in the book, pointing to sections where related parts are described in more detail, will help you get the information you need.

This book is full of code and examples, which are all available for download at `www.apress.com` in the Downloads section of this book's home page. Included with the package are subfolders named after each chapter: "chapter01," "chapter02," etc. These folders contain several sample solutions or Web sites in separate folders. Almost all examples are fully functional. Smaller code snippets that can't run on their own aren't included to avoid confusion.

CHAPTER 1

Understanding ASP.NET

This chapter looks under the covers of ASP.NET. Many fundamentals of ASP.NET just scratch the surface, but to get the most out of the framework it is a good idea to look much deeper.

This chapter includes:

- How ASP.NET works internally and the relevant features needed for your everyday tasks
- The behind-the-scenes concepts: the application life cycle, the page life cycle, and the control creation process
- The steps taken to translate your `*.aspx` and `*.cs` files into compiled code
- The common ASP.NET features, such as form stickiness and view state, and beyond

A Promise in Advance

ASP.NET is a powerful and flexible architecture for building web applications. The high-level parts—WebForms and Web Services—are well known. However, as your applications scale up in real life, sooner or later you encounter performance issues, or find that things which seemed easy become challenging. That is what this book provides—a look beyond the big picture. The little details are harder to understand and sometimes more abstract, less fun for more work. But let me begin with a promise: it's worth the effort.

The Low-Level Architecture of Request Handling

Understanding the innermost parts of a platform is highly satisfying. You will feel confident knowing that you can write better applications and recognize why they work. In this section, you will examine the internals of ASP.NET in order to understand how requests flow through the processing pipeline. A processing pipeline is a chain of processing elements arranged so that the output of one is the input of the next. According to ASP.NET, these elements are the internal steps required to process a request. This is not aimed at those learning the basics or creating a simple interactive page. This is what you need to know when you write or build large sites that involve hundreds of pages handling requests from thousands of users.

WebForms and Web Services are both sophisticated, high-level implementations of HTTP handlers. HTTP handlers are parts of the processing pipeline that manage incoming requests that use the Hypertext Transfer Protocol by creating the required content. They are built on top of the ASP.NET framework and exposed as one of the default project templates in Visual Studio. Most developers are happy with these project types, and are ignorant of, or misunderstand, the additional potential that exists. The basic HTTP handlers are built with managed code. This means that you can get highly customized behavior processing requests through the pipeline by using your very own code.

What Is ASP.NET?

In general terms, ASP.NET is a request processing engine. It takes an incoming request and passes it through its internal pipeline to an end point, where you as a developer can attach code to process that request. This engine is completely separate from HTTP runtime and the Web Server. In fact, the HTTP runtime is a component that you can host in your own applications outside of Internet Information Services (IIS) or any server side application altogether. Visual Studio and the integrated development server is a good example of an implementation that is neither based on nor related to IIS.

The HTTP runtime is responsible for routing requests through this pipeline, a complex yet very elegant mechanism. Several interrelated objects, extensible via subclassing or through interfaces, are available for customization work. This makes the framework highly adaptable. In this book, I'll cover most of these extensibility points and show that there are virtually no limits when using ASP.NET.

Through this mechanism it's possible to hook into low-level interfaces, such as authentication, authorization, and caching. You can even filter content by routing incoming requests that match a specific signature directly to your code. Of course, there are a lot of different ways to accomplish the same thing—but all of the approaches are straightforward to implement.

The Internet Service API[1] (ISAPI) is a common Win32 API. The ASP.NET engine interfaces with IIS through an ISAPI extension. This extension hosts .NET through the ASP.NET runtime. The ASP.NET engine was written entirely in managed code, and all of the extensibility functionality is provided via "managed code extensions." The impressive part of ASP.NET is that it is very powerful but simple to work with. Despite its breadth and complexity, accomplishing your desired outcomes is easy. ASP.NET enables you to perform tasks that were previously the domain of ISAPI extensions and filters on IIS. ISAPI is a low-level Win32 API that has a very spartan interface. For .NET developers it could be very difficult to develop anything on top of this interface. Writing ISAPI filters in C++ is not included in most current application-level development. However, since ISAPI is low-level, it is likely very fast. Thus, for some time ISAPI development has been largely relegated to providing bridge interfaces to other application or platforms, such as PHP. But ISAPI did not become obsolete with the appearance of ASP.NET.

ISAPI provides the core interface from the Web Server, and ASP.NET uses the unmanaged ISAPI code portion to retrieve input and send output back to the client. The content that ISAPI provides is passed using common objects like `HttpRequest` and `HttpResponse` that expose the unmanaged data as managed objects. Back in the .NET world it becomes very easy to use these objects in your own code. I'll discuss later in the section "Getting into the .NET Runtime" how the unmanaged and managed world interoperate.

The Lifetime of a Request

The lifetime starts with an HTTP request. Whenever the user types in a URL, clicks on a hyperlink, or submits an HTML form on the browser, a request is sent to the server.

■**Note** It's essentially the same for Web Services. A client application calls an ASP.NET–based Web Service by sending a request. Therefore, I refer to the term Request and don't differentiate between Web Service and browser requests. You can assume that the examples given are intended to run in a browser environment.

For the sake of clarity, I left out the steps made behind the scenes in the browser and through the protocol stacks. This includes port assignment within the TCP/IP stack and name resolution using the DNS protocol. As long as we're talking about ASP.NET, there is no direct influence on DNS, so let's keep this in mind but not complicate the description with side effects.

---

1. API means Application Programming Interface.

DOMAIN NAME SYSTEM

The Domain Name System (DNS) is hierarchical naming system for internet resources. Mainly these are computers that get human readable names—the hostnames—the DNS translates into IP addresses. Beginning with some root servers, the DNS is a hierarchy of name resolution servers for particular levels of the hostname. The protocol running between the servers and clients is called DNS protocol.

.NET Framework supports DNS with several classes. However, for ASP.NET applications usually there is no need to program directly against this low-level protocol. The request focused on begins when the name resolution process is done.

On the server side the Web Server picks up the request. In this description, I'll focus mainly on IIS7 with some words for IIS6, which is still widely used. Additionally, I focus on preferred mode running ASP.NET on IIS7—the integrated mode. However, most parts will not refer to a specific version, so the term IIS covers all from IIS5 to IIS7 (and beyond, probably). Within IIS the request is usually routed to the aspx page. How this process works internally depends entirely on the HTTP handler that handles the request. The mapping between the .aspx extension and the ISAPI DLL, aspnet_isapi.dll, is responsible for this. Every request you want served by ASP.NET must be routed by its assigned application extension. This means that the extension is a pre-defined, yet voluntary, definition. Imagine if you mapped .html pages to be processed by ASP.NET as well—it wouldn't be obvious that ASP.NET was doing the trick. Hence, the extension is the basic mapping where the processing starts.

This means, too, that different extensions might route to different handlers. For instance, the .asmx extension is routed to the Web Service handler. Instead of opening a page and starting a page parser, this request does not open a file but a specially attributed class that identifies the implementation. Many other handlers are installed with ASP.NET, and you are also able to define your own. All of these handlers are mapped to the ASP.NET ISAPI extension and configured in *web.config* to get routed to a specific implementation. See the following example in Listing 1-1 from global definition *web.config* file that holds the majority of default mappings.

Listing 1-1. *Extract of Global web.config Showing Some of the Default Mappings*

```
<httpHandlers>
  <add path="trace.axd" verb="*" type="System.Web.Handlers.TraceHandler"➥
validate="true"/>
  <add path="WebResource.axd" verb="GET" ➥
      type="System.Web.Handlers.AssemblyResourceLoader" validate="true"/>
  <add path="*.axd" verb="*" type="System.Web.HttpNotFoundHandler" validate="true"/>
  <add path="*.aspx" verb="*" ➥
      type="System.Web.UI.PageHandlerFactory" validate="true"/>
  <add path="*.ashx" verb="*" ➥
      type="System.Web.UI.SimpleHandlerFactory" validate="true"/>
  <add path="*.asmx" verb="*" ➥
      type="System.Web.Services.Protocols.WebServiceHandlerFactory, ➥
          System.Web.Services, Version=2.0.0.0, Culture=neutral, ➥
          PublicKeyToken=b03f5f7f11d50a3a" validate="false"/>
  <add path="*.asax" verb="*" ➥
      type="System.Web.HttpForbiddenHandler" validate="true"/>
  <add path="*.ascx" verb="*" ➥
      type="System.Web.HttpForbiddenHandler" validate="true"/>
  <add path="*.master" verb="*" ➥
      type="System.Web.HttpForbiddenHandler" validate="true"/>
```

```
<add path="*.skin" verb="*"  ➥
     type="System.Web.HttpForbiddenHandler" validate="true"/>
<add path="*.browser" verb="*"  ➥
     type="System.Web.HttpForbiddenHandler" validate="true"/>
<add path="*.sitemap" verb="*"  ➥
     type="System.Web.HttpForbiddenHandler" validate="true"/>
<add path="*.config" verb="*"  ➥
     type="System.Web.HttpForbiddenHandler" validate="true"/>
<add path="*" verb="GET,HEAD,POST"  ➥
     type="System.Web.DefaultHttpHandler" validate="true"/>
<add path="*" verb="*"  ➥
     type="System.Web.HttpMethodNotAllowedHandler" validate="true"/>
</httpHandlers>
```

In the extract, you find a handler that services a request, like `PageHandlerFactory` for `*.aspx` pages, as well as some that suppress access to the extension, like `HttpForbiddenHandler` for `*.config` files. In coding terms the handler is a type, implemented by a .NET class that handles a specific extension. You can also attach your own handlers to existing extensions and route the request through both your own and the default implementation. A summary of all basic mappings already available are shown in Table 1-1.

Table 1-1. *Application Mappings Assigned to aspnet_isapi.dll*

Extension	Resource Type	Comments
.asax	ASP.NET application files	Usually the global.asax file only.
.ascx	ASP.NET user control files	Usually these files are not called directly.
.ashx	HTTP handlers	The managed counterpart of ISAPI extensions; see Chapter 3 for details.
.asmx	ASP.NET Web Services	Obsolete since the appearance of Windows Communication Foundation (WCF).
.aspx	ASP.NET web pages	The regular page handler.
.axd	ASP.NET internal HTTP handler	Used for embedded resources like JavaScript or images pulled from compiled code.
.svc	Web Service handler	WCF-based services now has its own extension.

Let's talk about the `*.asmx` extension shown in the table. With the introduction of .NET 3.0, Microsoft moved all the communication stuff like .NET remoting and Web Services to Windows Communication Foundation (WCF) base library.[2] This means that the ASP.NET-based Web Services are superseded. Even though they are still fully supported, it makes sense to consider moving Web Service projects from ASP.NET platform to WCF. It's not a significant change, as most classes are similar and WCF has some more powerful approaches. However, I don't cover WCF in this book, and therefore the following description is limited to the ASP.NET portion.

From ISAPI to ASP.NET

The purpose of ISAPI is to access a Web Server like IIS on a very low level. The interface is optimized for performance, but it's also very simple and straightforward. For most developers with .NET experience it's pretty hard to use, because the coding style you use in .NET to, say, create sophisticated infrastructure solutions, is the opposite of the style you see when coding ISAPI extensions in C++.

---

2.   The old assemblies and namespaces are still supported, of course.

Many high-level web development languages (such as PHP, Perl, and even ASP.NET) are built on top of ISAPI.

ISAPI is good for writing such environments. For application developers it's not the best way to write our sites on time and within budget. However, ISAPI is the layer the ASP.NET engine is built on, and a good understanding of the relation between ISAPI and ASP.NET is helpful for getting the most out of ASP.NET. For ASP.NET the ISAPI level is just acting as a routing layer. The heavy stuff, such as processing and request management, occurs inside the ASP.NET engine and is mostly done in managed code.

You can think of ISAPI as a sort of protocol. This protocol supports two flavors, ISAPI extensions and ISAPI filters. Extensions act as a transaction interface; they handle the flow of data into and out of the Web Server. Each request coming down the pipeline is going through the extensions and the code decides how they are treated. As you might imagine, ASP.NET is such an extension. ASP.NET has several ways to give you as much control as possible to hook into this extension and modify the default behavior. The low-level ISAPI interfaces are now available as high-level .NET interfaces, named `IHttpHandler` and `IHttpModule`. This is very powerful and still provides good performance, because it's a well-written balance between lean access to the lower level and an easy-to-use high-level API.

Like any other ISAPI extension, the code is provided as a DLL and is hooked into the IIS management. You can find this DLL here: `<.NET FrameworkDir>\aspnet_isapi.dll`.

If you have several versions of .NET framework installed, you may wonder why there is just one such DLL in the tree. I predict that you will find this in the v2.0.50727 folder or at least in one with v2.0 at the beginning. If you have .NET 1 installed, another version might reside in a folder named v1.1.*. The reason is that Microsoft has added a lot of features in .NET 3.0 and .NET 3.5 regarding ASP.NET, but its interfaces to the low-level portion are still the same. All new functionality is completely written in managed code. This is indeed a transition, as it shows that it's possible to write infrastructure components in managed code. With powerful hardware the performance loss is not that critical, whereas the benefits regarding security, reliability, and shorter development cycles matter.

■Note With the upcoming .NET 4.0, a new engine appears on the horizon that is closer to IIS7 and has several internal improvements. For now, it seems as though most of the techniques and internal behaviors described here have barely changed.

Extension Mapping

As you have already seen, the Web Server recognizes resource requests by analyzing the file extension. The first step to get the ASP.NET ISAPI extension running is a mapping between the several file types and the DLL I mentioned earlier. In IIS7 you can see this by following these steps:

1. Open Internet Information Services (IIS) Manager.

2. Choose the server node.

3. In the right pane scroll to the IIS table.

4. Double-click Handler Mappings.

In the table you will see a column Path with the extensions already assigned. In the column Handler you will see the assigned module. For the *.aspx extension you will see the following mappings:

- PageHandlerFactory-Integrated

- PageHandlerFactory-ISAPI-2.0

- PageHandlerFactory-ISAPI-2.0-64 (on a 64-bit system only)

Additionally, with .NET 4.0,[3] two additional mappings are installed (on a 32-bit machine):

- PageHandlerFactory-Integrated-4.0
- PageHandlerFactory-ISAPI-4.0_32bit

For the unmanaged side you will see the `IsapiModule` handler and for the managed one .NET types used to handle the pages. Figure 1-1 shows part of the mapping to ISAPI extension.

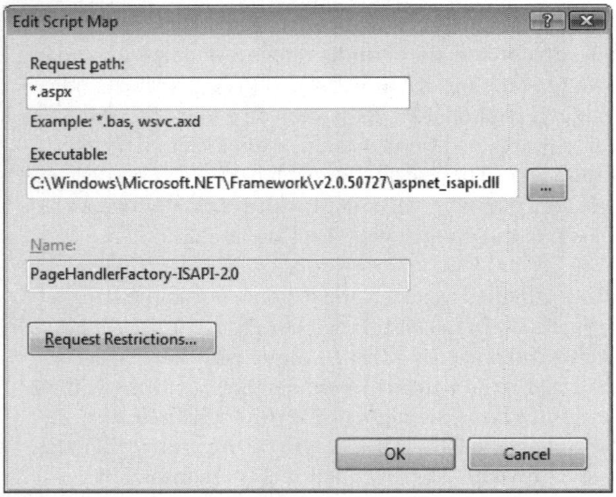

Figure 1-1. *IIS7 maps extensions like *.aspx to ISAPI extensions.*

If the mapping isn't there, ASP.NET is probably not correctly installed. Don't try to map this by hand. There is a lot of configuration that happens behind the scenes. Because you probably have several ASP.NET versions running parallel on the same machine, your application might fail to work just by complaining about wrong version. This does not require you to re-register the version needed. Applying the appropriate version is made in the application pool settings. In IIS6 the properties of a specific site of a Web Server let you choose the right framework. In IIS7 it has been moved to the application pool settings dialog. Each application pool can run only one version of the runtime. To set another framework for a specific site, you have to create another application pool, set the appropriate framework version, and assign the application pool to the site, as shown in Figure 1-2.

However, if the installation is destroyed or incomplete, a tool might help. To register or re-register the mappings, just invoke the following command:

```
cd <.NetFrameworkDirectory>
aspnet_regiis -i
```

Again, this command is not available for all .NET framework versions. The tools delivered with Version 2.0 will do the trick, even if you run 3.0 or 3.5. With ASP.NET 4.0, a new ISAPI DLL will be introduced—but backward compatibility is still guaranteed. If you still have Version 1.x sites running, another version is available. It's a bit tricky, but in order to run two different ASP.NET versions, just register with the highest available.

---

3. Naming not yet finalized at date of printing

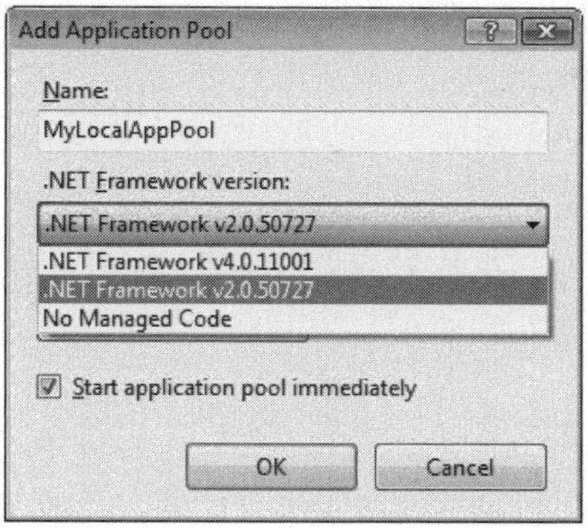

Figure 1-2. *Add a new application pool and get the right framework there.*

Request Comes In

When a request comes in, IIS checks for the script map and routes the request to the associated extension. In the case of ASP.NET let's assume that the request is something like Default.aspx, so it's being routed to aspnet_isapi.dll (see Figure 1-3).

I assume that you have already worked with and probably configured the application pool. The application pool was introduced with IIS6 and allows the complete isolation of applications from each other. This means that IIS is able to completely separate things happening in one application from those in another. Putting applications together in one pool could still make sense, because another pool would create its own worker process and could use up many resources. Each application pool is represented by separate worker process and seen on the list of processes as a separate entry. Separate applications make the Web Server more reliable. If an application hangs, consumes too much CPU time, or behaves unpredictably, it influences its entire pool. Other application pools (and the applications within them) will continue to run. Additionally, the application pools are highly configurable. You've already learned that the framework version can be different for each pool, which is very useful for migration scenarios. You can configure the security environment by choosing the impersonation level and customizing the rights given to a web application. Application pools are executables that run as any other program. This makes them easy to monitor and configure. Although this does not sound very "low level," application pools are highly optimized to talk directly to the kernel mode driver http.sys. Incoming requests are directly routed to the pool attached to the application. At this point, you might be wondering where InetInfo has gone. You may have heard of it in the context of previous versions of ASP.NET. If not, it's just a helper process mainly used for debugging purposes of Internet Information Services. It is still there, but it is basically just an administration and configuration service. The flow of data through the IIS system goes as directly and quickly as possible, straight down from http.sys to the application pools. This is one reason why IIS7 is much faster and more reliable than any other IIS before it.

An IIS7 application pool also has intrinsic knowledge of ASP.NET and in turn ASP.NET can communicate with the new low-level APIs that allow direct access to the HTTP Cache APIs. This can offload caching from the ASP.NET level directly into the Web Server's cache, which again will improve performance drastically.

In IIS7, ISAPI extensions run in the Application Pool's worker process. The .NET runtime also runs in this same process, and consequently communication between the ISAPI extension and the .NET runtime runs "in-process," which is inherently more efficient.

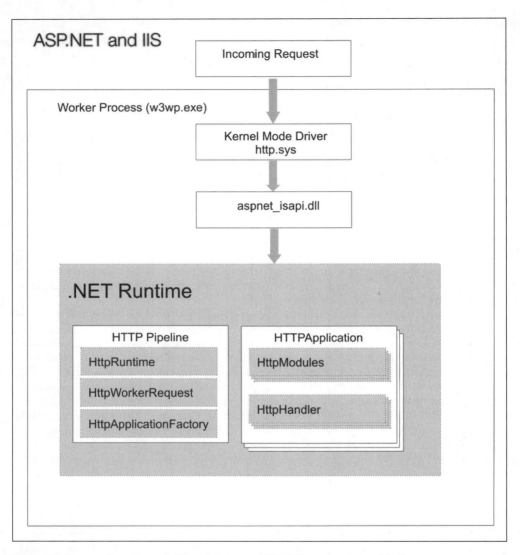

Figure 1-3. *Request flow through IIS and down to ASP.NET runtime (simplified)*

Getting into the .NET Runtime

Now let's look at what happens to the request when accessing the managed level. The worker process w3wp.exe hosts the .NET runtime, and the ISAPI DLL calls into a small set of unmanaged interfaces via low-level COM.[4] Unfortunately, not much information is available from Microsoft. Apart from a few blogs that one can't always trust, it's hard to say how the interaction between ASP.NET and ISAPI is made. Reading the manual doesn't help either. Microsoft states that the API "supports the .NET Framework infrastructure and is not intended to be used directly from your code," which confirms the existence of the interface but nothing more.

Using a disassembly tool like .NET Reflector (from red-gate.com) is one way to look into the details. Let's examine the System.Web DLL, which contains everything we'd like to know. First,

---

4. Component Object Model, an interface standard for software componentry

the entry point is the namespace System.Web.Hosting, where you'll see how the runtime interacts with the ISAPI part, as shown in Figure 1-4.

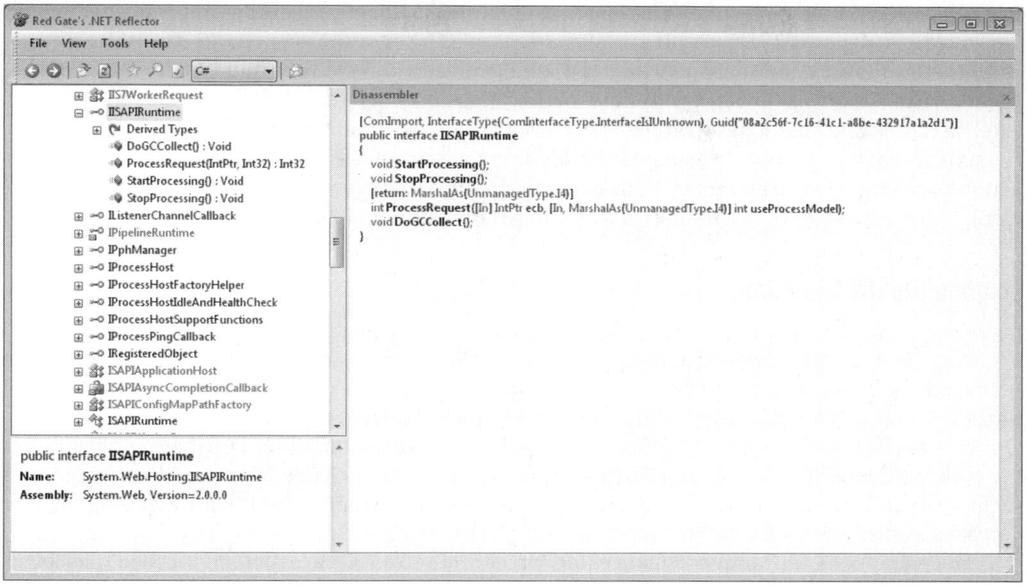

Figure 1-4. *If there is no information available, you can use Reflector to reveal the internal code.*

If the runtime handles a request, it calls the ProcessRequest method of the IISAPIRuntime interface. The interface is part of ISAPI and exposed as COM. The first parameter will return a pointer which gives access to the ISAPI module as shown in Listing 1-2.

Listing 1-2. *Definition of the ProcessRequest Method*

```
[return: MarshalAs(UnmanagedType.I4)]
int ProcessRequest([In] IntPtr ecb, ➥
                   [In, MarshalAs(UnmanagedType.I4)] int useProcessModel);
```

The parameter called "ecb" returns the ISAPI Extension Control Block (ECB, (Microsoft)) that is passed as an unmanaged resource. The method takes the ECB and uses it as the base input and output interface used with the Request and Response objects. An ISAPI ECB contains all low-level request information. This includes server variables, an input stream for form variables, as well as an output stream that is used to write data back to the client. The output is later accessible via the Response objects, but you can see the tight relation between incoming request and outgoing response. The ecb pointer basically provides access to the functionality of an ISAPI request. The ProcessRequest method is the entry and exit point where this resource initially enters the street up to our managed code world and where the managed processing ends.

Threads and Processes

So far things are not quite easy, but the flow of the request through the code is straight. However, in real life things tend to become more complex. The ISAPI extension runs requests asynchronously. This means that the ISAPI extension immediately returns on the calling worker process or IIS thread, but keeps the ECB for the current request alive. The ECB then includes a mechanism for letting ISAPI know when the request is complete. This asynchronous processing releases the

ISAPI worker thread immediately, and forwards processing to a separate thread that is managed by ASP.NET. We'll look into threading later to understand what ASP.NET is doing. For now, ASP.NET receives this ECB reference and uses it internally to retrieve information about the current request.

This includes such information as server variables, POST data, and output returning to the server. The ECB data block stays alive until the request finishes or times out in IIS. The ASP.NET engine continues to communicate with it until the request is done. Any output is written into the ISAPI output stream using the appropriate method call, and when the request is done, the ISAPI extension is notified of request completion. The extension will then free the ECB from memory. Just remember that in this cruel unmanaged world the code is responsible for handling all in-memory actions, and not releasing memory leads to memory leaks. However, the implementation is very efficient, as the .NET classes essentially act as a thin wrapper around ISAPI.

Loading the .NET Runtime

Again, not much information about the loading procedure is available. I assume that the runtime is loaded, if not yet present, when the first request to ASP.NET is made by a mapped extension. The managed ISAPIRuntime is then instantiated and starts talking to the unmanaged world. For isolation purposes, each virtual directory creates a new application domain (AppDomain). Within this App-Domain the ISAPIRuntime resides. Starting the application is also the beginning of the application's life cycle, which we'll look into later in the section called "The Life Cycles." It's also likely that the instantiation is made by the unmanaged part, because the wrapper interface is exposing the ComVisible attribute. This makes it available from the other side.

To create the ISAPIRuntime instance, the AppDomainFactory.Create method is called. The following code snippet in Listing 1-3, created with Reflector, shows how it's done internally.

Listing 1-3. *The Code of the AppDomainFactory.Create Method*

```
[return: MarshalAs(UnmanagedType.Interface)]
public object Create(string appId, string appPath)
{
  object obj2;
  try
  {
    if (appPath[0] == '.')
    {
        FileInfo info = new FileInfo(appPath);
        appPath = info.FullName;
    }
    if (!StringUtil.StringEndsWith(appPath, '\\'))
    {
        appPath = appPath + @"\";
    }
    ISAPIApplicationHost appHost = new ISAPIApplicationHost(appId, appPath, false);
    ISAPIRuntime o = (ISAPIRuntime) this._appManager.CreateObjectInternal(➥
                                appId, typeof(ISAPIRuntime), ➥
                                appHost, false, null);
    o.StartProcessing();
    obj2 = new ObjectHandle(o);
  }
  catch (Exception)
  {
      throw;
  }
  return obj2;
}
```

Even if it is not visible in this code snippet, internally the appId is used to cache the relation with the requested virtual directory. Therefore subsequent calls do not start the application again, but process the existing AppDomain. Finally, in this code StartProcessing forces ISAPI to process the request, and, because it is asynchronous, the call returns immediately and the method returns the ECB as type object, as shown in Figure 1-5.

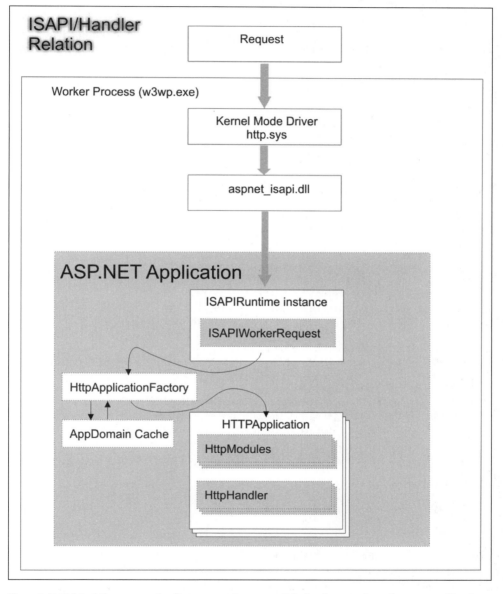

Figure 1-5. *Behind the scenes, the first request is responsible for the creation of a new application.*

Handle the Request Within the Runtime

The managed part is now alive, and ISAPI is able to call it whenever there is something available for processing. In basic ASP.NET terms, everything begins here. The AppDomain, the application life cycle, and the first page cycle are born here and live for varying lengths of time. From now on, we're back in the managed world. But there is a bit more you should know about the whole procedure. IIS is a multithreaded host and so is ISAPI. Each request is processed asynchronously, running in its own thread. Again, a look into the code using Reflector reveals what ASP.NET is doing here. The ProcessRequest method receives an ISAPI ecb object and server type as parameters. The method is thread safe, so multiple ISAPI threads can safely call this single returned object instance simultaneously.

```
public int ProcessRequest(IntPtr ecb, int iWRType)
{
    IntPtr zero = IntPtr.Zero;
    if (iWRType == 2)
    {
        zero = ecb;
        ecb = UnsafeNativeMethods.GetEcb(zero);
    }
    ISAPIWorkerRequest wr = null;
    try
    {
        bool useOOP = iWRType == 1;
        wr = ISAPIWorkerRequest.CreateWorkerRequest(ecb, useOOP);
        wr.Initialize();
        string appPathTranslated = wr.GetAppPathTranslated();
        string appDomainAppPathInternal = HttpRuntime.AppDomainAppPathInternal;
        if ((appDomainAppPathInternal == null)
            || StringUtil.EqualsIgnoreCase(appPathTranslated, ➥
                                    appDomainAppPathInternal))
        {
            HttpRuntime.ProcessRequestNoDemand(wr);
            return 0;
        }
        HttpRuntime.ShutdownAppDomain(➥
                    ApplicationShutdownReason.PhysicalApplicationPathChanged,
            SR.GetString("Hosting_Phys_Path_Changed", new object[] ➥
                    { appDomainAppPathInternal, appPathTranslated }➥
                    ));
        return 1;
    }
    catch (Exception exception)
    {
      // removed for sake of clarity
    }
}
```

The code is just a part of the complete method. I have removed the catch block to focus on the working code. The method receives the pointer to an ECB data block and passes it to the CreateWorkerRequest method. This method is responsible for creating the ISAPIWorkerRequest object. From now on there is a Request object available that is able to talk directly to the ISAPI layer.

The ISAPIWorkerRequest (defined in the System.Web.Hosting namespace) class is an abstract subclass of HttpWorkerRequest. This class holds all the knowledge to talk HTTP. It's a piece of cake, and although it would take too much time to go into here, it's worth a closer look if you like. I'd encourage you to go on and find out how things work under the hood. Just open the method

ProcessRequest in Reflector, click on ISAPIWorkerRequest and then on the HttpWorkerRequest subclass. At the end of the listing of signatures of either class, click on the link Expand Methods and there you have it. Since there is an abstract class, eventually there must be some implementation elsewhere. The factory method that creates the type using CreateWorkerRequest method is able to return one of the following four types available:

- ISAPIWorkerRequestInProcForIIS7
- ISAPIWorkerRequestInProcForIIS6
- ISAPIWorkerRequestInProc
- ISAPIWorkerRequestOutOfProc

It's a Bit in the ECB that drives the decision. This means that finally the ISAPI module controls the way ASP.NET handles requests. Because ASP.NET is not limited to IIS, it's simply the version of IIS that is responsible for the factory's selection. ISAPIWorkerRequestInProc type is for all IIS versions up to and including version 6, and ISAPIWorkerRequestInProcForIIS7type serves all versions from 7 and above. This sounds silly—there is no IIS8 in existence—but the ASP.NET engine would be robust against new versions as long as the ISAPI module is able to emulate IIS7 behavior.

Whenever you have trouble understanding what is going on in your application, whether it's with creating and sending headers, receiving weird stuff, or getting wrong data down the wire, it's worth taking a closer look here. HttpWorkerRequest is meant to provide a high-level abstraction around the low-level interfaces, regardless of the source of the data. However, reading and understanding are two different things. Let's take an example of how to deal with all the internals. The next listing shows you how the well-known QueryString is retrieved from the ECB. Moving down the class hierarchy, you'll find that it's partly implemented in the base class and partly in the ISAPIWorkerRequestInProc class. For IIS6 and IIS7 there is no distinct change here, so you can skip these classes for now.

```
internal override int GetQueryStringRawBytesCore(byte[] buffer, int size)
{
    if (base._ecb == IntPtr.Zero)
    {
        return 0;
    }
    return UnsafeNativeMethods.EcbGetQueryStringRawBytes(base._ecb, buffer, size);
}
[DllImport("webengine.dll")]
internal static extern int EcbGetQueryStringRawBytes(IntPtr pECB, byte[] buffer, ➥
                                                    int size);
```

Again, nothing is thrilling here. These classes are all very thin wrappers around native method calls. In fact, ASP.NET does not provide any significant overhead to the request procedure. That means ASP.NET is extremely fast—as fast as IIS with native code. If you feel (or know) that your application is slow, then you know that in most cases it will be a problem in your code. Let's focus on the managed side of the world and learn more about what's going on here.

HttpContext and HttpApplication

You're probably already familiar with the HttpContext and HttpApplication classes. Instances of these classes are created whenever a request hits the engine. At a glance, the steps are:

- Create a new HttpContext instance for the request.
- Retrieve an HttpApplication instance (or create one, if it's the first request).
- Call HttpApplication.Init to set up pipeline events.
- Call HttpApplication.ResumeProcessing to start the ASP.NET pipeline processing.

Wrapping the Request: HttpContext

The context of an HTTP request is available throughout the lifetime of the request. For ease of use it's always accessible through the static HttpContext.Current property. Because every request usually starts a new thread, or recycles a free one from the thread pool, your code runs in that thread. In Chapter 2 I'll explain in more detail the thread and processing behavior. For now, this isn't needed to understand the request processing on the context level. The current context has a one-to-one relation to the request for that thread. This context object is also the place where all other objects required to process the request are stored: Request, Response, Application, Server, and Cache. At any time during request processing HttpContext.Current gives you access to all these. There are several shortcuts, so you may use the Page's property Context instead, but it's exactly the same object.

You may already use several collections available in the Application, Session, and Cache objects. Even the HttpContext class contains a useful collection that provides a store for request specific data. The big difference to the other data collections is the life time. The HttpContext represents exactly the current request. If the processing is finished and the data sent to the server, which in turn sends it back to the client, then the collections are also disposed of. However, the Context exists before the page's life span begins and ends after it finishes. Technically it's an object and it ends when it gets disposed. This data storage is therefore a bit more powerful than simple page members.

Listing 1-4 shows how to use Context.Items to get information about the request processing elapsed time. At the BeginRequest event a timestamp is stored and retrieved later at EndRequest. Both events are part of the page's life cycle and are explained in more detail later in the section "The Page's Life Cycle."

Listing 1-4. *Get Request Information Using Events in global.ascx*

```
Application_BeginRequest(object sender, EventArgs e)
{
    if (Settings.Default.Logging)
    {
        Context.Items.Add("LogTime", DateTime.Now);
    }
}

protected void Application_EndRequest(object sender, EventArgs e)
{
    if (Settings.Default.Logging)
    {
        DateTime end = DateTime.Now;
        TimeSpan span = end.Subtract((DateTime) Context.Items["LogTime"]);
        System.Diagnostics.Debug.WriteLine(span.TotalMilliseconds, "RequestTime");
    }
}
```

This sample uses two events defined in the global.ascx code behind file. You might be thinking of how to put the results into a database or log file, but for now the output to a Visual Studio console window will do (see Figure 1-6).

If you feel that the values shown in the figure are too high, you need to be aware that I'm running the entire environment in a Virtual PC console, and that the timestamps shown are expressed in milliseconds.

Figure 1-6. *Get time information about the request while debugging.*

The Core Type: HttpApplication

The HttpApplicationFactory is responsible for creating an appropriate number of HttpApplication objects. The load and the number of threads required affect how it handles incoming requests. The size of the pool is limited to the MaxWorkerThreads setting in the ProcessModel key in the *machine. config*, which by default is 20. Since the days of .NET 2.0 it's still an auto-configured entry:

```
<processModel autoConfig="true" />
```

Change this to the following:

```
<processModel autoConfig="false" maxWorkerThreads="30" />
```

You can find more information about threading in Chapter 2.

The pool starts out with a smaller number—usually one—and it then grows as multiple simultaneous requests are processed. The pool is monitored so that under load it grows to a maximum number of instances. Later the pool is scaled back to a smaller number as the load drops. Once you have the right number of instances of HttpApplication, you have the real entry point within the managed world for an incoming request. HttpApplication is like an outer container for the whole application. For easy access the events related to the application are mapped in the global.asax file, which is the declarative expression of this class. This is true for all mapped requests handled by ASP.NET handlers. Other requests might be handled inside custom modules but would not appear in global.asax when running IIS7 integrated mode. The definition of global.asax in global.asax.cs reveals:

```
public class Global : System.Web.HttpApplication
```

During each request handling in the ASP.NET pipeline, several events let you control and intercept the various states of the application's life cycle. Listing 1-5 shows all of them, even if the majority is never used in an application. In the next few sections, I'll dig deeper into the world of application events.

Listing 1-5. *Events Available on Application Level (Pulled from HttpApplication)*

```
public event EventHandler BeginRequest;
public event EventHandler AuthenticateRequest;
public event EventHandler PostAuthenticateRequest;
public event EventHandler AuthorizeRequest;
public event EventHandler PostAuthorizeRequest;
public event EventHandler ResolveRequestCache;
public event EventHandler PostResolveRequestCache;
public event EventHandler MapRequestHandler;
public event EventHandler PostMapRequestHandler;
```

```
public event EventHandler AcquireRequestState;
public event EventHandler PostAcquireRequestState;
public event EventHandler PreRequestHandlerExecute;
public event EventHandler PostRequestHandlerExecute;
public event EventHandler UpdateRequestCache;
public event EventHandler PostUpdateRequestCache;
public event EventHandler LogRequest;
public event EventHandler PostLogRequest;
public event EventHandler EndRequest;
public event EventHandler Disposed;
public event EventHandler Error;
public event EventHandler PostReleaseRequestState;
public event EventHandler PreSendRequestCcntent;
public event EventHandler PreSendRequestHeaders;
public event EventHandler ReleaseRequestState;
```

By writing something like the following into the code-behind file, you attach an event to all requests against the dedicated handler:

```
protected void Application_BeginRequest(object sender, EventArgs e)
```

Avoiding an explicit delegate definition is just for the sake of convenience.

The whole handling of AppDomain, HttpApplication, and threads might look confusing. Remember that the server has to handle multiple incoming requests simultaneously. Each ASP.NET application runs in its own AppDomain, where several instances of HttpApplication can run in parallel, supplied from the pool managed by the factory. To get a better understanding of this, let's examine the information you can extract from related objects. Just to clarify typical usage scenarios, the following code samples run on IIS-based systems only. Other Web Servers does not support application pools.

In Listing 1-6, the values are written into Label controls named *appId*, *threadId*, *domainId*, *threadInfo*, and *threadApart*. Refer to Figure 1-7 to see the output.

Listing 1-6. *Retrieving Information About the Application (Excerpt)*

```
protected void Page_Load(object sender, EventArgs e)
{
    Guid id = (Guid)Application["AppId"];
    this.appId.Text = id.ToString();
    this.threadId.Text = Thread.CurrentThread.ManagedThreadId.ToString();
    this.domainId.Text = AppDomain.CurrentDomain.FriendlyName;
    this.threadInfo.Text = Thread.CurrentThread.IsThreadPoolThread ? ➥
                      "Pool Thread" : "No Thread";
    this.threadApart.Text = Thread.CurrentThread.GetApartmentState().ToString();
    Thread.Sleep(4000);
}
```

The Sleep call allows you to open several browser instances and hit F5 to refresh the page within the four-second period in order to see how it works. This simulates the behavior when several requests come in while previous requests are still running.

An application by definition has no internal id. To create one, add the following code to the global.asax code behind:

```
void Application_Start(object sender, EventArgs e)
{
    Application["AppId"] = Guid.NewGuid();
}
```

Figure 1-7 shows three screens made within the four-second period using three different browser windows.

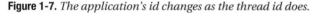

- **Application ID**: cf285d72-e8b4-43b8-8fba-2ee8bacc03da
- **Thread ID**: 8
- **Domain ID**: 58252b93-2-128846045806950000
- **Thread Pooling**: Pool Thread
- **Thread's Apartment**: MTA

    - **Application ID**: edb5d603-a9a4-485d-8c7f-6087bf1ac909
    - **Thread ID**: 3
    - **Domain ID**: 58252b93-2-128846045806950000
    - **Thread Pooling**: Pool Thread
    - **Thread's Apartment**: MTA

        - **Application ID**: c317acef-08b6-4782-afbf-3cc2329e007a
        - **Thread ID**: 12
        - **Domain ID**: 58252b93-2-128846045806950000
        - **Thread Pooling**: Pool Thread
        - **Thread's Apartment**: MTA

Figure 1-7. *The application's id changes as the thread id does.*

You can see that the application id and the thread id change. If you remove the `Sleep` command and request the pages one by one, the application id is always the same. Usually the thread is recycled from the pool and the id is also unchanged.

The abbreviation 'MTA' for the thread's apartment model stands for Multi Threaded Apartment. You can override this apartment state in ASP.NET pages with the `AspCompat="true"` attribute in the `@Page` directive. `AspCompat` is set to `true` means that COM components run within a safe environment. `AspCompat` uses special Single Threaded Apartment (STA) threads to service those requests. STA threads are set aside and pooled separately as they require special handling. As long as you have multi threaded COM component in your application only, you can simply ignore this. For single threaded components some additional work is required. Usually a well-developed COM component should support multiple threads.

It is a simple fact that all `HttpApplication` objects are in the same AppDomain. This has, however, some influence on their behavior. If you change something in the page's code or *web.config*, the application restarts. This is done automatically from the ASP.NET engine by watching those files for changes forcing the restart. To be more precise, it's actually the AppDomain which is being shut down and restarted. This ensures that all currently existing `HttpApplication` instances are also shut down and re-created. To see this behavior in action, open the example shown in Listing 1-6 and launch it. Hit F5 several times and notice that the Domain ID value is still the same. Now change something in the *web.config* file. This forces a shutdown and therefore the creation of a new AppDomain. The Domain ID value is now different.

Currently running requests are being processed properly, even if the new AppDomain is already up and running. To avoid old threads blocking resources, the request has a specific time out value. Once timed out, the threads are shut down and the request's "life" ends. However, for new requests a new application begins its life cycle. Application events are fired again, and subsequently application variables are deleted and restored again. This has an impact on the application's performance, too.

Flowing Through the ASP.NET Pipeline

You now have a good overview of what happens when a request comes in, and of how the HttpContext and HttpApplication objects start up as they wait to be used in your code. There are several steps following this startup sequence worth investigating further. In each step, you'll find events and callbacks to intercept the process and customize or optimize its behavior.

Figure 1-8 illustrates what happens during the various states. If you look into the code using Reflector, you can find the steps in subclass ApplicationStepManager and the additional steps for IIS7 in PipelineStepManager.

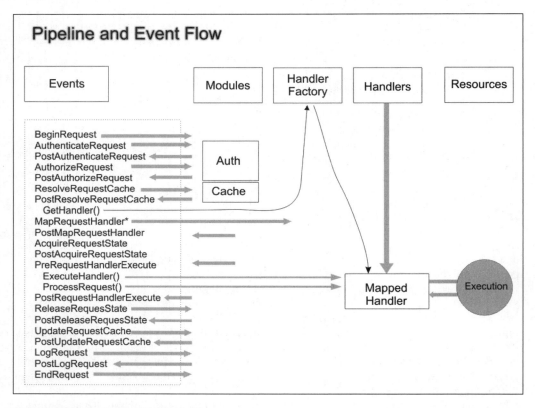

Figure 1-8. *Events that build the pipeline*

The most important information here is that modules precede handlers. Modules are responsible for all requests, whereas handlers support a specific extension, like *.aspx. You can find an in-depth explanation about both modules and handlers in Chapter 3. To have a brief overview let's recall the way ASP.NET handles each request through the pipeline. Modules and Handlers are the two processing points of this pipeline. Modules are just like a filter. The modules are called before and after the handler executes. Examples for related events in the pipeline are BeginRequest, AuthenticationRequest event, EndRequest event, etc. You may intercept, participate, and modify each request. Despite this, you may think of it as a program that executes some code for the request.

An .aspx page can be thought of as a handler, which implements specific functions. They are loaded and executed at the particular state of the processing pipeline, if configured properly in *web.config* file. The figure shows only the minimum number required to execute a page. You'll find a closer look at all these events in the next section. For now, it's enough to know when and why the modules and handlers get executed. This is the major part of the pipeline business, which I'll also discuss in the next section.

Modules and Handlers Using HttpModule and HttpHandler

`HttpApplication` and `HttpContext` are merely containers for incoming messages. They build the pipeline by forming a chain of events that commence in a defined order, and they hold together data related to the request in order to give other instances easy access to the information involved in the process. However, the real work is done in other processing units, particularly the modules and handlers. Modules are built on top of the `HttpModule` class. Handlers are built on top of the `HttpHandlers` class. Both are abstract classes and need concrete implementations. In addition, both are highly configurable and act as a chain of instances. This means that you can attach as many modules and handlers as you like and the request will flow through all of these instances.

Several tasks could be handled in both levels—however, there is a different intention behind them. Modules tend to control tasks on a lower level; their nature is more basic than that of handlers. Think of modules as the right place to prepare data being processed by handlers or modify data subsequently when the regular treatment by a handler is completed. IIS programming aficionados can think of modules as ISAPI filters. The good news is that programming ASP.NET modules using .NET is much easier than developing filters for IIS. Moving on from IIS, let's focus on the amazing things that become possible as ASP.NET is extended.

The natural order of modules and handlers is:

1. Use module to pre-process a request.

2. Use handler to process the request.

3. Use module again to post-process the request.

ASP.NET comes with several default handlers, such as the very basic ones for `*.aspx` pages or Web Services. Some default modules exist that are responsible for simple tasks like authentication and caching. In an ideal world, the modules are transparent to the handlers. This means that handlers don't know about the modules that work before or after their own processing. ASP.NET allows several easy ways to create your own modules and handlers.

This is usually the first approach of extending the standard behavior of ASP.NET. Let's take a closer look at this technique. Figure 1-9 shows how modules and handlers fit into the ASP.NET process model.

In Chapter 3, I'll discuss the process of developing custom modules and custom handlers with some clever examples. By now it's enough to know that several modules process the request one after another on both the request and the response path. Whereas only one handler processes the request finally, it's either an internal handler or a custom one.

However, all these techniques are based on the behavior of the pipeline. This pipeline fires the events that form the so-called life cycles.

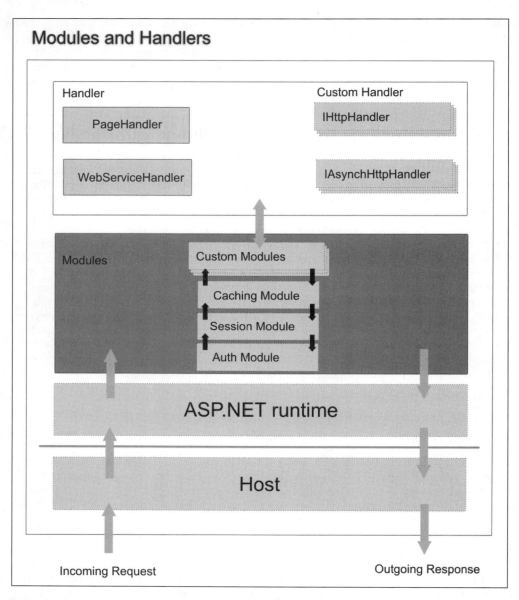

Figure 1-9. *Modules and handlers fit closely in the ASP.NET model.*

The Life Cycles

The life cycle is a term used in almost every introduction to ASP.NET. This term is absolutely crucial for a complete understanding and the correct usage of ASP.NET.

To break things down let's divide the different life cycles into three parts:

- The application's life cycle
- The page's life cycle
- The control's life cycle

The following sections cover this in-depth. The behavior of the cycles is slightly different between IIS versions, but the overall description is the same. The following explanations focus on IIS7 and Framework 3.5 behavior, which is valid for .NET 2.0 up to the upcoming 4.0.

IIS7 can run in two different modes. The IIS integrated mode is the new native one, whereas the classic mode mimics the behavior of IIS5 or IIS6. The integrated mode has several advantages and should be preferred if there is no explicit requirement to step down.

IIS7 Integrated Pipeline

The IIS7 integrated pipeline is a unified request processing pipeline. Each incoming request is handled by this pipeline and routed through the internal parts of IIS. The pipeline supports both managed and native code modules. You may already know about creating managed modules based on the IHttpModule interface. Once implemented and hooked into the pipeline, the module receives all events used to interact with the request passing through the pipe.

The term "unified request processing pipeline" needs some more investigation. IIS6 provided two different pipelines: one for native and one for managed code. This is obviously for historical reasons, because the managed world came after the IIS world. In IIS 7 both pipelines united to become the unified request processing pipeline. For ASP.NET developers this has several benefits:

- The integrated pipeline raises all exposed events, which enables existing ASP.NET modules to work in the integrated mode.

- Both native-code and managed-code modules can be configured at the Web Server, Web site, or Web application level.

- Managed-code modules can be invoked at certain stages in the pipeline.

- Modules are registered and enabled or disabled through an application's *Web.config* file.

The configuration of modules includes the built-in ASP.NET managed-code modules for session state, forms authentication, profiles, and role management. Furthermore, managed-code modules can be enabled or disabled for all requests, regardless of whether the request is for an ASP.NET resource like an .aspx file or a static file like an image.

Invoking modules at any stage means that this may happen before any server processing occurs for the request, after all server processing has occurred, or anywhere in between.

The Application's Pipeline

In more generic terms the pipeline describes the flow through several instances within the IIS. Each step processes the request in a distinct way and fires appropriate events. This forces interactions with the modules and applications attached by configuration. The variety of actions you can perform ranges from none to total control. However, doing nothing lets the built-in modules accomplish their job and handle the basic page processing. From the perspective of the extensibility of ASP.NET, "total control" is what we're looking for. Figure 1-10 shows the application life cycle events.

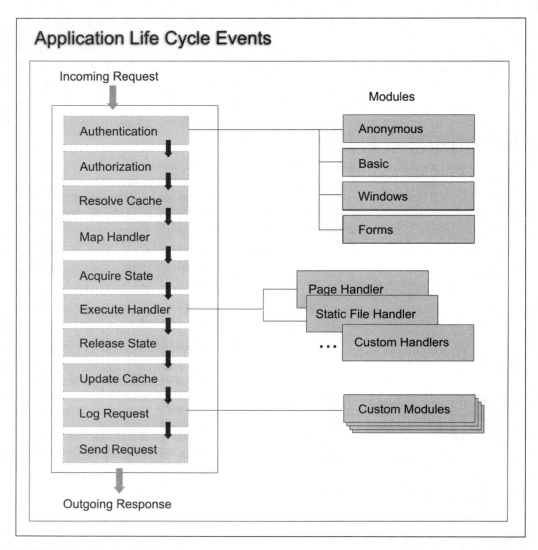

Figure 1-10. *Application's life cycle events*

Two states are new in IIS7: Map Handler and Log Request. This gives developers much more control over the request process. Some modules are managed, whereas others are written in native code. You can add your own modules in either way. However, as a .NET developer, you'd probably prefer writing in managed code and I would strongly recommend this. (Native code is an option if you need to create a high-performance module which performs simple functions.)

The Request Arrives

The application life cycle begins when a request is made for an application resource sent by a client application, such as a browser, to the Web Server. In integrated mode, the unified pipeline handles all requests. When the pipeline receives a request, it's being passed through stages that are common to all requests. These stages are represented internally by the RequestNotification enumeration. The enumeration is defined in the System.Web namespace. All request stages can be configured to allow developers to take advantage of ASP.NET functionality. That functionality is encapsulated in managed-code modules that have access to the request pipeline. For instance, even though the .htm filename extension is not mapped by default to ASP.NET, a request for an HTML page still invokes ASP.NET modules. This enables you to take advantage of ASP.NET authentication and authorization for all resources.

Unified Pipeline Receives the First Request

When the unified pipeline receives the first request for any resource in an application, an instance of the `ApplicationManager` class is created. Its core function is to build the application domain (AppDomain) in which the request is processed. Application domains provide isolation between applications for global variables and enable each application to be unloaded separately. In the application domain, an instance of the `HostingEnvironment` class is created, which provides access to information about the application, such as the name of the folder where the application is stored. You can find both types in the `System.Web.Hosting` namespace.

The first request has several additional tasks. You will notice this because the elapsed time for the page to be delivered is longer than all subsequent requests. During the first request, top-level items in the application are compiled, if required. This includes application code in the project. By the way, since the days of Visual Studio 2008, there is no longer a special code folder named App_Code. Even if you name a folder this, it will have no special function. Code that resides in any folder at any level is compiled in one assembly per project.

Response Objects Are Created for Each Request

After the application domain has been created and the `HostingEnvironment` object has been instantiated, application objects such as `HttpContext`, `HttpRequest`, and `HttpResponse` are created and initialized. These objects exist throughout the lifetime of the request and give developers full access to all related data.

The `HttpContext` class contains objects that are specific to the current application request, such as the `HttpRequest` and `HttpResponse` objects. The `HttpRequest` object contains information about the current request, which includes cookies and browser information. The `HttpResponse` object contains the response that is about to be sent to the client, which includes all rendered output and header data, such as cookies. `HttpContext.Current` gives you permanent access to the current context through a static method. For easy access the `Page` class has properties like `Request` and `Response` that return instances of the very same related objects.

Differences Between IIS6 and IIS7

We're currently in the transition period from IIS6 to IIS7. While IIS7 is the best choice for a Web Server on Microsoft platforms, there are still many servers with IIS6 in production. Because you may already have a deep understanding of processing ASP.NET based on IIS6, the following explanation focuses on the key differences between IIS6 and IIS7, running in both Integrated mode and with the .NET Framework 3.5 or later. The following properties are specific to IIS7 with Integrated mode. You must run IIS7 to take advantage of the following features.

The `HttpResponse` object has a new property `SubStatusCode`. This is useful for setting codes for tracking failed requests. The `Headers` property of the `HttpResponse` object provides access to response headers for the response. Two properties of the `HttpContext` object, `IsPostNotification` and `CurrentNotification`, are used when one event handler handles several `HttpApplication` events. This might happen when you try to simplify your code and use a `switch`-block to distinguish between concrete events. `CurrentNotification` returns a value from enumeration `RequestNotification`. This enum does not have specific values for the post events. To recognize the post event just read the Boolean value from `IsPostNotification`.

Both the `Headers` and `ServerVariables` property of the `HttpRequest` object are write-enabled.

An HttpApplication Object Is Assigned to the Request

After all application objects have been initialized, the application is started by creating an instance of the `HttpApplication` class. If the application has a `global.asax` file, ASP.NET instead creates an instance of the `global.asax` class that is derived from the `HttpApplication` class. It then uses the derived class to represent the application. This way you get access to the application events simply by overwriting the handlers within the `global.asax` code portion.

■**Note** The first time that an ASP.NET page or process is requested in an application, a new instance of the `HttpApplication` class is created. However, to maximize performance, `HttpApplication` instances might be reused for multiple requests.

Request Is Processed by the Pipeline

The `HttpApplication` class performs several tasks while the request is being processed. Each step fires a specific request to allow you to run code when the event is raised. Without any further action, all incoming requests will fire all events and the attached modules will be invoked in sequence. To take advantage of extensibility, some interfaces come into the scope. `IHttpModule` is the basic interface for custom modules. In IIS7's integrated mode you can use the module's `Init` method to attach the required events.

One step you're supposed to perform is the request validation. Imagine hackers trying to send malicious markup or other intrusions. The following list of events shows all steps you can run private code in. Validating the request should take place as early as possible, according to the following list in `BeginRequest`.

- Raise the `BeginRequest` event.
- Raise the `AuthenticateRequest` event.
- Raise the `PostAuthenticateRequest` event.
- Raise the `AuthorizeRequest` event.
- Raise the `PostAuthorizeRequest` event.
- Raise the `ResolveRequestCache` event.
- Raise the `PostResolveRequestCache` event.
- Raise the `MapRequestHandler` event. An appropriate handler is selected based on the file-name extension of the requested resource. The handler can be a native code module, such as the IIS7 `StaticFileModule,` or a managed module, such as the `PageHandlerFactory` class.
- Raise the `PostMapRequestHandler` event.
- Raise the `AcquireRequestState` event.
- Raise the `PostAcquireRequestState` event.
- Raise the `PreRequestHandlerExecute` event. Call either the `ProcessRequest` method for synchronous calls or the asynchronous version `IHttpAsyncHandler.BeginProcessRequest` of the appropriate `IHttpHandler` class.
- Raise the `PostRequestHandlerExecute` event.
- Raise the `ReleaseRequestState` event.

- Raise the `PostReleaseRequestState` event.

- Perform response filtering if the `Filter` property is defined.

- Raise the `UpdateRequestCache` event.

- Raise the `PostUpdateRequestCache` event.

- Raise the `LogRequest` event.

- Raise the `PostLogRequest` event.

- Raise the `EndRequest` event.

- Raise the `PreSendRequestHeaders` event.

- Raise the `PreSendRequestContent` event.

The Page's Life Cycle

After understanding the application's life cycle, you're now ready to move further along the path taken by the request. The request is now being processed until the resources are prepared and ready to be served. For static resources it's easy; the data is all ready to send to the client. (Examples of static resources include images, JavaScript files, and embedded objects.) The more exciting information is how dynamic resources are processed.

The basic steps in the page's life cycle include initialization, instantiating controls, restoring and maintaining state, running event handler code, and rendering. As you saw in the application's life cycle, you will be able to interact with the processing and change the handling for your intended effects. Some steps during the page's life cycle are more complex and require a closer look in order to take full advantage of their customization potential. One major portion is the view state handling. I'll dedicate a whole section to explaining view state later in section "View State."

It is also important for you to understand the page life cycle. As a developer creating custom controls, for instance, you must be familiar with the life cycle in order to correctly initialize controls, populate control properties with view state data, and run any control behavior code. You may have heard of a control life cycle, too. You may already know that a page in ASP.NET is a sort of specialized control, and therefore a control's life cycle is very similar. However, pages have more events available.

■**Tip** When an application operates in the context of Visual Studio while you run a debug session, the application starts with the launch of the integrated Web Server. When the debug session ends and you launch the application again using the F5 key, the integrated Web Server will run the same application domain. This means that between the debug sessions no new application life cycle is being started. To force the application to restart you can right click the notification icon in the system tray and stop the Web Server.

What About Master Page Life Cycle?

You might miss information regarding master pages here. The master page itself does not have any stages, because it's not an object created and run standalone. The master page hierarchy is used to resolve the final construct of the page requested, and then the page's life cycle begins. Therefore, the master page is treated like a control, with some events related to the page's life cycle events, but again, not with its own life cycle.

Page Request Stages

The page request occurs before the page life cycle begins. When the page is requested by a client, ASP.NET determines whether the page needs to be parsed and compiled, or whether a cached version of the page can be sent in response without executing the page. In each case the "life" of the page begins.

Start

In this step, page properties such as Request and Response are set. These properties give you access to the current HttpRequest and HttpResponse instances created through the application's life cycle.

You can access all information related to the request using this.Request. (In later stages you can modify the response created and stored in this.Response.) At this stage, the page also determines whether the request is a postback or a new request and sets the IsPostBack property. This involves two checks: whether the request is done as a POST, and whether it comes from the same ASP.NET page. Additionally, during the Start step, the page's UICulture property is set. At this point you can perform any action based on the automatically recognized page culture. Alternatively, you can force the culture property, so that the correct resources are obtained. (Forcing the culture doesn't work in other steps.)

Page Initialization

During page initialization step, controls on the page become available and each control's UniqueID property is set. The UniqueID is used later on postbacks to assign control state in order to make forms sticky. Any themes are also applied to the page. If the current request is a postback, the postback data has not yet been loaded and control property values have not been restored to the values from view state.

Load

During load, if the current request is a postback, control properties are loaded with information recovered from view state and control state. For a regular request via GET, view state and control state are set to their respective default states.

Validation

During this step the Validate method of all validator controls is called. The IsValid property of all validator controls is set, and as a summary the page's IsValid property is set, too.

Postback Event Handling

If the request is a postback, any event handlers are called, such as button click events.

Rendering

Before rendering, view state is saved for the page and all controls. Rendering is the process that creates the HTML that makes the page visible in a browser. Each control is responsible for rendering itself. This feature and the extensible design time support is a major opportunity for third-party control vendors. Their controls can encapsulate all the clever design time experience and runtime functionality within each control. That means during the rendering phase, the page calls the Render method for each control, providing a TextWriter instance that writes its output to the OutputStream of the page's Response property.

Unload

Unload is called after the page has been fully rendered, sent to the client, and is ready to be discarded. At this point, page properties such as `Response` and `Request` are unloaded and any cleanup is performed.

Events Fired Within the Life Cycle's Stages

Within each stage of the life cycle of a page, the page raises events that you can handle to run your own code. For control events, you bind the event handler to the event, either declaratively using attributes such as `onclick`, or in code.

When inheriting a class from the `Page` class, you can override methods from the page's base class. It's a common technique to create your own base page classes that derive from `Page` and to handle common tasks there. For example, you can override the page's `InitializeCulture` method to dynamically set culture information. Overriding event handlers or attaching events are two different methods to perform almost the same action. If you use the Page_<event> syntax, you don't need to handle the base implementation. However, if you override the method you must handle the base implementation and therefore call the base method. You can do this at the beginning, at the end, or anywhere in between. Despite this, a regular attach event handler can be used as well. Additionally, the `AutoEventWireup` attribute of `@Page` directive would route the event to the appropriate handler that has Page_<event> signature already mentioned.

Pages also support automatic event wire-up, meaning that ASP.NET looks for methods with particular names and automatically runs those methods when certain events are raised. If the `AutoEventWireup` attribute of the `@Page` directive is set to `true`, page events are automatically bound to methods that use the naming convention that follow the pattern Page_<event>, such as `Page_Load` and `Page_Init`.

The following sections list all the page events. Some events that do not map directly to the corresponding stages are less crucial but give you more control from the extensibility perspective—for example, when you create custom controls that require a very specific behavior.

PreInit Event

Use this event to check the `IsPostBack` property to determine whether this is the first time the page is being processed. Create or re-create dynamic controls. You may also set master pages and the `Theme` property dynamically. Read or set any profile property values.

If the request is a postback, the values of the controls have not yet been restored from view state during `PreInit` state. If you set a control property at this stage, its value might be overwritten in the next event.

Init Event

This event is raised after all controls have been initialized and any skin settings have been applied. Use this event to read or initialize control properties.

InitComplete Event

This event is raised by the Page object. Use this event for processing tasks that require all initialization be complete.

PreLoad Event

Use this event if you need to perform processing on your page or control before the Load event. Before the Page instance raises this event, it loads view state for itself and all controls, and then processes any postback data included with the Request instance.

Load Event

The Page calls the OnLoad event method on the Page, then recursively does the same for each child control, which does the same for each of its child controls until the page and all controls are loaded. Use the overridden OnLoad event method to set properties in controls and establish database connections.

In a postback request during Load event, if the page contains validator controls, check the IsValid property of the Page and of individual validation controls before performing any processing.

Control events

After Load the control events occur. Use these events to handle specific control events, such as a Button control's Click event or a TextBox control's TextChanged event.

LoadComplete Event

Use this event for tasks that require all other controls on the page be loaded.

PreRender Event

Before this event occurs, the Page object calls EnsureChildControls for each control and for the page itself. Each data bound control whose DataSourceID property is set calls its DataBind method. The PreRender event occurs for each control on the page. Use the event to make final changes to the contents of the page or its controls.

The render process itself does not have an event; it happens after PreRender and before UnLoad and can be intercepted by overwriting the Render method.

SaveStateComplete Event

Before this event occurs, view state has been saved for the page and for all controls. Any changes to the page or controls at this point will be ignored. See the section about view state later in this chapter to learn more about its specific behavior. Use this event to perform tasks that require view state to be saved, but that do not make any changes to controls.

Unload Event

This event occurs for each control and, when all control events are done, for the page. In controls, use this event to do final cleanup for specific actions, such as closing database connections. For the page itself, use this event to do final cleanup work, such as closing open files and database connections, finishing up logging or other request-specific tasks.

During the Unload stage, the page and its controls have been rendered, so you cannot make further changes to the response stream. If you attempt to call a method, such as the Response.Write method, the page will throw an exception.

Additional Page Life Cycle Considerations

Server controls have their own life cycle that is similar to the page life cycle. A control's Init and Load events occur during the corresponding page events. Due to the hierarchical nature of the page's controls, this happens recursively. For the event order this means in turn the events appear in reverse order. This is clearly the expected behavior, because the Init event on page level indicates that all subsequent Init events are completed. You may read the event as "Is Initialized." However, the Load event for a container occurs before the Load events for its child controls, which is the opposite behavior. This is so that you can have access to the process before any other processing takes place. From the perspective of the Init event, it doesn't make sense to do anything before it appears, because there is nothing you can access in your code.

You can change the properties of a control by handling the events for the control, such as the Click event for the Button control. Control events appear after the page's Load event has been fired.

Dynamic Controls and Data Binding Events

The page and control life cycles define a chain of events to give you maximum control over the creation and runtime of the control. However, the control handling has more possibilities than you can achieve with such a straightforward model. You will see a different behavior when adding controls dynamically. Furthermore, data-bound controls work internally slightly different due to the way data templates are parsed and executed.

Dynamic Control Events

The page life cycle and control life cycle are very similar because of the nature of a Page as a class derived from Control. However, you can add controls dynamically—a feature which doesn't make sense for pages. You might assume that adding controls is not very common in ASP.NET. However, imagine that declaratively authored controls within templates of data-bound controls are treated like dynamically added controls. Their events are not initially synchronized with the other controls on the page. The lifetime of such controls begins with their instantiation; they raise the life cycle events one after the other until the control has caught up to the event during which it was added to the Controls collection.

Usually this has no implications for developers. Unless you have nested data-bound controls, you don't need to be concerned about this. For nested data-bound controls, this behavior is a bit different. If a child control has been data bound, but its container control has not yet been bound, the data in the child control and the data in its container control can be out of sync.

Imagine that you have a GridView control and that each row contains a bound DropDownList control. Furthermore, assume that the DropDownList's data properties, such as DataSourceID, are set declaratively. The DropDownList will now bind to its datasource when the DataBinding event of the containing GridView row occurs. However, the GridView might not yet have raised its RowDataBound event. In that case the DropDownList and containing control are out of sync. To avoid this you simply put the data source control—the one you have set in the DataSourceID property—within the same template. Additionally, remove the declarative assignment and set it programmatically during the RowDataBound event. In this event the container's data are bound and both controls can stay in sync. See Listing 1-7 for a simplified scenario that fully supports a nested data-bound control within a template.

Listing 1-7. *Binding Nested Controls Within a Container's Template*

```
<html xmlns="http://www.w3.org/1999/xhtml">
<head runat="server">
    <title></title>
</head>
<body>
    <form id="form1" runat="server">
    <div>
        <asp:GridView ID="GridView1" runat="server" AutoGenerateColumns="False"
            DataSourceID="XmlDataSource1" ondatabinding="GridView1_DataBinding"
            ondatabound="GridView1_DataBound" oninit="GridView1_Init"
            onload="GridView1_Load" onprerender="GridView1_PreRender"
            onrowdatabound="GridView1_RowDataBound">
            <Columns>
                <asp:TemplateField HeaderText="ExecutionSymbol"
                    SortExpression="ExecutionSymbol">
                    <ItemTemplate>
                        <asp:DropDownList runat="server" id="ddCommand"
                            DataSourceID="ObjectDataSource1"
                            SelectedValue='<%# Bind("Default") %>' >
                        </asp:DropDownList>
                        <asp:ObjectDataSource ID="ObjectDataSource1" runat="server"
                                        SelectMethod="GetValues"
                                        TypeName="Data"></asp:ObjectDataSource>
                        <asp:Label ID="Label1" runat="server"
                            Text='<%# Eval("ExecutionSymbol") %>'></asp:Label>
                    </ItemTemplate>
                </asp:TemplateField>
                <asp:BoundField DataField="Name" HeaderText="Name"
                            SortExpression="Name" />
            </Columns>
            <EmptyDataTemplate>
                Empty
            </EmptyDataTemplate>
        </asp:GridView>
    </div>
    <asp:XmlDataSource ID="XmlDataSource1" runat="server"
        DataFile="~/App_Data/Data.xml"></asp:XmlDataSource>
    </form>
</body>
</html>
```

Moving the nested data source—the `ObjectDataSource` in the example—within the template assures that the events fires in the expected order.

Data Binding Events for Data-Bound Controls

To help you understand the relationship between the page life cycle and data binding events, Table 1-2 lists data-related events in data-bound controls. Remember that not all controls support all events shown in the table. Some data-bound controls do not have rows, for instance, which means that a RowDataBound event cannot occur.

■**Note** In the description of data-bound control's behavior, I often refer to the term "containing control." If there is no containing control, this assumes that the page is the container.

Table 1-2. *Relationship Between Life Cycle Events and Data-Bound Events*

Event	Typical Behavior	Usage Hints
DataBinding	Raised before `PreRender` of containing control. This is the beginning of binding procedure.	Open database connections here, if required.
RowCreated	Raised after each row gets bound.	Manipulate content that does not depend on data binding.
ItemCreated	Raised after each item gets bound.	Manipulate content that does not depend on data binding.
RowDataBound	Bound data is now available for the row.	Format data, get and filter child rows or related data.
ItemDataBound	Bound data is now available for the item.	Format data, pull and filter child rows or related data.
DataBound	Marks the end of binding operation. All rows are bound now.	Do any action that requires all data available.

Login Control Events

The login controls, which handle login and authentication, are highly sophisticated and powerful. They support—like the data-bound control's events—some special events related to their internal behavior. In most scenarios, the controls work well out of the box or just need some configuration using the *web.config* file. However, if you need to change or customize the behavior or extend the available features, you'll need to know the events fired during their life cycle (see Table 1-3). These events are additional to the regular events raised by all controls, as previously explained in the section "Dynamic Control Events."

Table 1-3. *Relationship Between Life Cycle Events and Logging-In Events*

Event	Typical Behavior	Usage Hints
LoggingIn	Raised during postback after LoadComplete.	Tasks required before the login procedure, such as opening a database connection, if required.
Authenticate	Raised next after LoggingIn.	Customize the authentication behavior itself.
LoggedIn	Raised after authentication.	Action required after successful authentication, such as redirect to another page.
LoginError	Raised after failed authentication.	Do any action to handle failed authentication, such as displaying instructions.

View State

The ASP.NET view state is a mechanism to track changes of the state of pages from one postback to the next. Postback occurs whenever a page sends the contents of a form back to the server. The name comes from the underlying HTTP command POST that is used here and the way that it takes the contents back to the server. View state is turned on by default and most developers don't care about it. It contains the values of properties of ASP.NET controls changed since the last page cycle and is stored in a serialized and encrypted format within the page, as shown in Figure 1-11. Each postback sends all the information stored in it back to the server. As you may know, using view state in the default manner can lead to huge pages that consume a lot of bandwidth. It's not easy to understand view state completely, and simply disabling it leads to controls not working or having fewer features.

The real internal behavior is confusing and hard to understand. As long as you deal with simple applications, a basic idea might be enough. But when it comes to your own controls, complex pages, or using AJAX, a good understanding is a prerequisite.

Why Understanding View State Is Important

Misunderstanding view state leads to leaking of sensitive data, being exploited by view state attacks, poor page performance, poor scalability, and headaches. Whatever you want to achieve with your application, Figure 1-11 shows the source of a page which you never want to see.

```
<input type="hidden" name="__VIEWSTATE" id="__VIEWSTATE"
value="/wEPDwUKLTUxNDE0ODExOA9kFgICAw9kFgICBw88KwANAgAPFgQeC18hRGF0YUJvdW5kZx4LXyFJdGVtQ291bnQCMmQMFCsAARYGHgRUeXB1GS±
CHgROYW11BQRJdGVtHg11bGQFASEWAmYPZB2mAgEPZBYCZg8PFgIeBFR1eHQFEmxqbGRramxramxramxrSmRkAgIPZBYCZg8PFgIfBQUSb
GpsZGtqbGtqbGtqbGtqbGtKZGQCAw9kFgJmDw8WAh8FBRJsamxka2psa2psa2psaOpkZAIED2QWAmYPDxYCHwUFEmxqbGRramxramxramxrSmF
kAgUPZBYCZg8PFgIfBQUSbGpsZGtqbGtqbGtqbGtqbGtKZGQCBg9kFgJmDw8WAh8FBRJsamxka2psa2psa2psaOpkZAIHD2QWAmYPDxYCHwUFEmxqk
GRramxramxramxrSmRkAggPZBYCZg8PFgIfBQUSbGpsZGtqbGtqbGtqbGtqbGtKZGQCCQ9kFgJmDw8WAh8FBRJsamxka2psa2psa2psaOpkZAI
KD2QWAmYPDxYCHwUFEmxqbGRramxramxramxramxrSmRkAgsPZBYCZg8PFgIfBQUSbGpsZGtqbGtqbGtqbGtqbGtKZGQCDA9kFgJmDw8WAh8FBRJsamxka
2psa2psa2psaOpkZAIND2QWAmYPDxYCHwUFEmxqbGRramxramxramxrSmRkAq4PZBYCZg8PFgIfBQUSbGpsZGtqbGtqbGtqbGtqbGtKZGQCDw5
kFgJmDw8WAh8FBRJsamxka2psa2psa2psaOpkZAIQD2QWAmYPDxYCHwUFEmxqbGRramxramxramxramxrSmRkAhEPZBYCZg8PFgIfBQUSbGpsZGtqk
GtqbGtqbGtqbGtKZGQCEg9kFgJmDw8WAh8FBRJsamxka2psa2psa2psaOpkZAITD2QWAmYPDxYCHwUFEmxqbGRramxramxramxrSmRkAhQPZBY
CZg8PFgIfBQUSbGpsZGtqbGtqbGtqbGtqbGtKZGQCFQ9kFgJmDw8WAh8FBRJsamxka2psa2psa2psaOpkZAIWD2QWAmYPDxYCHwUFEmxqbGRramxra
mxramxramxrSmRkAhcPZBYCZg8PFgIfBQUSbGpsZGtqbGtqbGtqbGtqbGtKZGQCGA9kFgJmDw8WAh8FBRJsamxka2psa2psa2psaOpkZAIZD2QWAmY
PDxYCHwUFEmxqbGRramxramxramxrSmRkAhoPZBYCZg8PFgIfBQUSbGpsZGtqbGtqbGtqbGtqbGtKZGQCGw9kFgJmDw8WAh8FBRJsamxka2psa2psa
2psa2psaOpkZAIcD2QWAmYPDxYCHwUFEmxqbGRramxramxramxramxrSmRkAhOPZBYCZg8PFgIfBQUSbGpsZGtqbGtqbGtqbGtqbGtKZGQCHg9kFgJmDwÊ
WAh8FBRJsamxka2psa2psa2psaOpkZAIfD2QWAmYPDxYCHwUFEmxqbGRramxramxramxramxrSmRkAiAPZBYCZg8PFgIfBQUSbGpsZGtqbGtqbGtqk
GtqbGtKZGQCIQ9kFgJmDw8WAh8FBRJsamxka2psa2psa2psa2psaOpkZAIiD2QWAmYPDxYCHwUFEmxqbGRramxramxramxramxrSmRkAiMPZBYCZg8PFgI
fBQUSbGpsZGtqbGtqbGtqbGtqbGtKZGQCJA9kFgJmDw8WAh8FBRJsamxka2psa2psa2psaOpkZAIlD2QWAmYPDxYCHwUFEmxqbGRramxramxramxrx
mxrSmRkAiYPZBYCZg8PFgIfBQUSbGpsZGtqbGtqbGtqbGtqbGtKZGQCJw9kFgJmDw8WAh8FBRJsamxka2psa2psa2psaOpkZAIoD2QWAmYPDxYCHwU
FEmxqbGRramxramxramxramxrSmRkAikPZBYCZg8PFgIfBQUSbGpsZGtqbGtqbGtqbGtqbGtKZGQCKg9kFgJmDw8WAh8FBRJsamxka2psa2psa2psa
OpkZAIrD2QWAmYPDxYCHwUFEmxqbGRramxramxramxramxrSmRkAiwPZBYCZg8PFgIfBQUSbGpsZGtqbGtqbGtqbGtqbGtKZGQCLQ9kFgJmDw8WAh8FBRJ
samxka2psa2psa2psaOpkZAIuD2QWAmYPDxYCHwUFEmxqbGRramxramxramxramxrSmRkAi8PZBYCZg8PFgIfBQUSbGpsZGtqbGtqbGtqbGtqbGtKZ
GQCMA9kFgJmDw8WAh8FBRJsamxka2psa2psa2psaOpkZAIxD2QWAmYPDxYCHwUFEmxqbGRramxramxramxramxrSmRkAjIPZBYCZg8PFgIfBQUSbGp
sZGtqbGtqbGtqbGtqbGtKZGQCMw8PFgIeB1Zpc21ibGVoZGQYAQUDZ3JkDzwrAAoBCAIBZHYfcLCtCZ26/bupXZd6b7EnFPWC" />
```

Figure 1-11. *The view state's form field could grow.*

Simply disabling view state will not help, however, because you will probably lose some features that you need and like. Especially complex data-bound controls hold their states for paging or sorting in the view state. In fact, nothing is wrong with view state; it's just the wrong or inappropriate usage of it that causes problems. Now let's move on by starting back at the beginning.

What View State Is Supposed to Do and Not Do

- Stores values of control's properties by keys, similar to a hash table
- Tracks changes to initial values
- Serializes and deserializes a saved dictionary in a hidden form field
- Restores stored values into control's properties

These features are well known. Much more important is what the view state does not do:

- Retain the state of class members without additional code
- Remember state information across page loads (page reloads by GET request)
- Avoid the need to repopulate data on every request
- Hold data in controls that are posted back—the so-called sticky form behavior

The last bullet point is probably the most confusing here. Many developers think that this is the only task that the view state has to do. Although the view state is involved in the process of holding the control's visible data, it is not the originator of the process. That would be the initializing phase that retrieves the form's data to set the control's state, often described as "retaining the control state" or short, "control state."

View state is held in a hidden field with the name __VIEWSTATE. "Hidden" means that the browser does not render the field, but the field itself and its content are visible in the page's source. It needs the bandwidth twice—the first time when the page is sent to the browser and the second time when the browser sends the page back (that is, when a postback happens). A postback occurs very frequently when a user navigates within the application; and unless you use hyperlinks almost all actions are based on a form being sent back.

A Word Regarding Control State

When talking about view state quite often the discussion includes the control state. The control state holds privately used control properties, especially for custom and complex controls in another serializable collection. Those data are stored within the view state storage that means by default the control state is part of the view state's hidden field. Disabling the view state disables the control state, too. However, there is no declarative way to control the control state separately. In this discussion, the control state is just a matter of fact and you shouldn't be worried about just another state of controls. Because it is essential for some controls, it is also not that critical because of the minimal amount of data well-developed controls might hold there.

The Page Cycle from the View State Perspective

The page cycle is very important to understanding view state completely, as several levels of the cycle treat view state explicitly. You can refer to the previous section to get an idea of the page cycle in a nutshell. In this section, I will repeat the major steps that actually handle view state.

Each time the server receives a request for an .aspx page it will be processed by the ASP.NET engine through a specific number of steps. These include checking access security and restoring the session state. The session state holds data related to the current session, like session variables or logon information. At the end of the process the engine creates a class that consists of the markup converted into code and code-behind. This step generates an instance of that class, which yields the content of the ProcessRequest method of the page's handler.

The page life cycle begins with the call to this method. Next, the initialization of the controls of the page occurs, followed by the life cycle phases of those controls. This includes the processing of the view state, handling of postback data and related events and finally the processing of HTML content.

The life cycle of the page ends when the HTML is completely rendered and handed over to the Web Server. The Web Server is responsible for sending the data over the wire to the browser. While the Web Server is sending the data, the garbage collector is already freeing up the released memory. This is true for all requests without any interaction or custom code required. However, within this cycle, view state has an extraordinary function and it makes your life as a control developer easier if you understand life cycles and their relation to view state.

Step One—Instantiation

The instantiation is the beginning of the life cycle of the page. The class built from markup and code, which represents the page, is instantiated and launched. But what actually happens and where does the page's code get stored? ASP.NET pages consist of HTML markup with controls and code. First, the ASP.NET engine converts the text portion of the page and all markup into web controls. That means the page is now completely made of code. Most parts that consist of HTML are replaced by LiteralControl controls. Literals contain text that doesn't need any further processing. This is required in order to avoid the extensive recognition process from ASP.NET engine. The ASP. NET engine is able to recognize changes made to either markup or code and re-runs the process, if required. The features provided for a page are inherited from the Page class (System.Web.UI.Page). If code behind is being used, one more step is required. Using the partial keyword this class is married with the code-behind class that is associated with the ASPX page.

Building the Hierarchy of Controls

The page is the top level of the hierarchy of controls. Because the Page class itself inherits from Control, it's a control, too. Each control has exactly one parent and none, one, or many children. The elements placed declaratively in the page are children of the highest level. There is no limit to nesting levels for the control hierarchy. This leads to vast trees made of complex controls.

One important control is HtmlForm (full name is System.Web.UI.HtmlControls.HtmlForm). It creates the <form> tag and determines the content sent during postback. The view state information is necessarily placed here. You can see this in the sample shown in Listing 1-8.

Listing 1-8. *Simple ASPX Page with Controls*

```
<html xmlns="http://www.w3.org/1999/xhtml">
<head runat="server">
    <title></title>
</head>
<body>
    <h1>
        Apress - ViewState</h1>
    <form id="form1" runat="server">
    <div>
        <asp:TextBox runat="server" ID="txtName" />
        <br />
        Are you called a
        <asp:DropDownList runat="server" ID="ddlWhat">
            <asp:ListItem Value="G" Selected="True">Geek</asp:ListItem>
            <asp:ListItem Value="N">Nerd</asp:ListItem>
            <asp:ListItem Value="W">Don't know</asp:ListItem>
        </asp:DropDownList>
        <br />
        <asp:Button runat="server" ID="btnSend" Text="Send!" />
    </div>
    </form>
</body>
</html>
```

Figure 1-12 shows how it will look like in the Visual Studio designer.

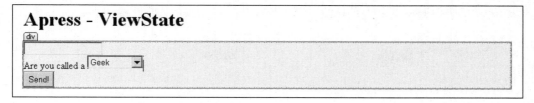

Figure 1-12. *Simple page in Visual Studio Designer*

The ASP.NET engine generates the output code, a fragment of which is shown in Listing 1-9.

Listing 1-9. *Simple ASPX Page from Last Listing Compiled into Code in Debug Mode*

```
public class default_aspx : _Default, IRequiresSessionState, IHttpHandler
{
    private static object __fileDependencies;
    private static bool __initialized;

    [DebuggerNonUserCode]
    public default_aspx()
    {
        base.AppRelativeVirtualPath = "~/Default.aspx";
        if (!__initialized)
        {
            string[] virtualFileDependencies = new string[] { "~/Default.aspx" };
            __fileDependencies = ➡
                    base.GetWrappedFileDependencies(virtualFileDependencies);
            __initialized = true;
        }
    }

    [DebuggerNonUserCode]
    private HtmlTitle __BuildControl__control2()
    {
        return new HtmlTitle();
    }

    [DebuggerNonUserCode]
    private void __BuildControl__control3(ListItemCollection __ctrl)
    {
        ListItem item = this.__BuildControl__control4();
        __ctrl.Add(item);
        ListItem item2 = this.__BuildControl__control5();
        __ctrl.Add(item2);
        ListItem item3 = this.__BuildControl__control6();
        __ctrl.Add(item3);
    }

    [DebuggerNonUserCode]
    private ListItem __BuildControl__control4()
    {
        ListItem item = new ListItem();
        item.Value = "G";
        item.Selected = true;
        item.Text = "Geek";
```

```
        return item;
    }

    [DebuggerNonUserCode]
    private ListItem __BuildControl__control5()
    {
        ListItem item = new ListItem();
        item.Value = "N";
        item.Text = "Nerd";
        return item;
    }

    [DebuggerNonUserCode]
    private ListItem __BuildControl__control6()
    {
        ListItem item = new ListItem();
        item.Value = "W";
        item.Text = "Don't know";
        return item;
    }

    [DebuggerNonUserCode]
    private Button __BuildControlbtnSend()
    {
        Button button = new Button();
        base.btnSend = button;
        button.ApplyStyleSheetSkin(this);
        button.ID = "btnSend";
        button.Text = "Send!";
        return button;
    }

    [DebuggerNonUserCode]
    private DropDownList __BuildControlddlWhat()
    {
        DropDownList list = new DropDownList();
        base.ddlWhat = list;
        list.ApplyStyleSheetSkin(this);
        list.ID = "ddlWhat";
        this.__BuildControl__control3(list.Items);
        return list;
    }

    [DebuggerNonUserCode]
    private HtmlForm __BuildControlform1()
    {
        HtmlForm form = new HtmlForm();
        base.form1 = form;
        form.ID = "form1";
        IParserAccessor accessor = form;
        accessor.AddParsedSubObject( ➥
                          new LiteralControl("\r\n    <div>\r\n        "));
        TextBox box = this.__BuildControltxtName();
        accessor.AddParsedSubObject(box);
        accessor.AddParsedSubObject( ➥
                          new LiteralControl("\r\n        <br />\r\n      ➥
                                       Are you called a \r\n        "));
```

```
        DropDownList list = this.__BuildControlddlWhat();
        accessor.AddParsedSubObject(list);
        accessor.AddParsedSubObject( ➡
                            new LiteralControl("\r\n        <br />\r\n          "));
        Button button = this.__BuildControlbtnSend();
        accessor.AddParsedSubObject(button);
        accessor.AddParsedSubObject( ➡
                            new LiteralControl("\r\n    </div>\r\n    "));
        return form;
    }

    [DebuggerNonUserCode]
    private HtmlHead __BuildControlHead1()
    {
        HtmlHead head = new HtmlHead("head");
        base.Head1 = head;
        head.ID = "Head1";
        HtmlTitle title = this.__BuildControl__control2();
        IParserAccessor accessor = head;
        accessor.AddParsedSubObject(title);
        return head;
    }

    [DebuggerNonUserCode]
    private void __BuildControlTree(default_aspx __ctrl)
    {
        this.InitializeCulture();
        IParserAccessor accessor = __ctrl;
        accessor.AddParsedSubObject( ➡
new LiteralControl("\r\n\r\n\r\n<!DOCTYPE html PUBLIC \"-//W3C//DTD XHTML 1.0 ➡
    Transitional//EN\" \"http://www.w3.org/TR/xhtml1/DTD/xhtml1- ➡
    transitional.dtd\">\r\n\r\n\r\n<html xmlns=\"http://www.w3.org/1999/xhtml\">\r\n"));
        HtmlHead head = this.__BuildControlHead1();
        accessor.AddParsedSubObject(head);
        accessor.AddParsedSubObject(new LiteralControl("\r\n<body>\r\n ➡
                <h1>\r\n        Apress - ViewState</h1>\r\n    "));
        HtmlForm form = this.__BuildControlform1();
        accessor.AddParsedSubObject(form);
        accessor.AddParsedSubObject(➡
                    new LiteralControl("\r\n</body>\r\n</html>\r\n"));
    }

    [DebuggerNonUserCode]
    private TextBox __BuildControltxtName()
    {
        TextBox box = new TextBox();
        base.txtName = box;
        box.ApplyStyleSheetSkin(this);
        box.ID = "txtName";
        return box;
    }

    [DebuggerNonUserCode]
    protected override void FrameworkInitialize()
    {
        base.FrameworkInitialize();
        this.__BuildControlTree(this);
```

```
        base.AddWrappedFileDependencies(__fileDependencies);
        base.Request.ValidateInput();
    }

    [DebuggerNonUserCode]
    public override int GetTypeHashCode()
    {
        return -1678387491;
    }

    [DebuggerNonUserCode]
    public override void ProcessRequest(HttpContext context)
    {
        base.ProcessRequest(context);
    }

    // Properties
    protected HttpApplication ApplicationInstance
    {
        get
        {
            return this.Context.ApplicationInstance;
        }
    }

    protected DefaultProfile Profile
    {
        get
        {
            return (DefaultProfile) this.Context.Profile;
        }
    }
}
```

The code is not very readable, but this is what generated code is supposed to look like, right? There is no need to do anything special with it, but rather to learn what is going on internally. Note two things here. First, the declarative assignment of attributes is being replaced with simple property assignments. See the following markup:

```
<asp:Button text="Send!">
```

It becomes this in the generated class:

```
button1.Text = "Send!"
```

Second, all literal stuff is placed in strings and copied into the final page "as is," which is shown in the following snippet:

```
new LiteralControl("\r\n</body>\r\n</html>\r\n"))
```

Once the class is complete, the engine proceeds to the next step.

Step Two—Initializing

After creating the control hierarchy, all the controls of the page are moved into the initialization state. This becomes apparent by raising the Init event. In this phase not only are the controls ready, but they also have their static, declarative properties assigned.

■**Note** "Declarative" is everything that's written within the markup and not in code fragments.

Whether or not a property has been declaratively assigned, you still can change the value any time before the render process is complete. However, because I'm talking about view state, the initialization step plays a special role regarding property values.

View State Tracks Changes

View state tracks changes of properties. This is a special function of the StateBag class defined in the System.Web.UI namespace, which holds the data behind the scenes. Tracking starts during the Initializing step of the page. In order to recognize the default value and the changed one, the StateBag compares the initialized value set by declarative markup with the current value set anytime later programmatically. Even if the results look the same, the view state treats the data in a different way.

View State and Dynamic Controls

Using dynamic controls, you'll know that technically it's possible to add controls any time before the page render process is complete. The view state is not that flexible. Adding controls using Controls.Add method must take place in the initializing phase. Otherwise, the StateBag class does not recognize the Init event at the right time and does not start tracking changes. You still can add controls anytime, but for those controls the view state will not work. You might find problems here occasionally, as the majority of controls being added dynamically—such as the Label control—don't require property value tracking.

The golden rule states that in order to "take care of the view state, whether it's required or not, add dynamic controls during the Initializing step."

Step Three—Loading the View State

View state data is saved into a hidden field called __VIEWSTATE. It's transmitted back to the server only during a POST operation, which forces a postback.

■**Note** You can completely ignore page requests that use GET for this step. Such requests do not interact with view state at all.

In this step the engine decodes values from the hidden field and assigns them to the controls, looping recursively through the control hierarchy. Also in this phase the validity of the view state is checked. There are several reasons why the view state could become invalid. One reason is that the control hierarchy has been changed during postback and the control is not at the expected place, or removed completely.

If everything is fine, the engine proceeds to the next step. See the section "View State Anti-Patterns" for an example of what's going on when it went wrong.

Step Four—Loading Postback Data

After loading and restoring the view state, the form data is processed. Not all controls can return data. To let the engine know whether it has to look for data sent back, the IPostBackDataHandler interface is recognized. Each control implementing this interface might send form data back. Form data is sent back in the HTTP protocol as id–value pairs:

```
Myclientid=value
```

The page class looks for a control with a ClientID that equals "Myclientid". When found, it checks whether the control implements the IPostBackDataHandler interface. If it does this, the page class calls the only method defined there—LoadPostData. That means that the control itself manages the loading of data, which opens up a great way of changing behavior and adding custom code.

Concerning view state, this behavior is very significant. The ability to get the values of controls back between postbacks is called "sticky form" behavior. It's one of the best features of ASP.NET. Let me explain this in more detail using the example of a TextBox control. The TextBox has a property Text. It also implements the IPostBackDataHandler interface. Once a page with the textbox control is posted back, the LoadPostData method reads the value of the control out of the view state and writes it into the Text property. The default value—that was probably set declaratively—is overwritten. You can easily check this with the following definition:

```
<asp:TextBox runat="server" ID="txtName" Text="" />
```

The render process transforms this markup into HTML form:

```
<input type="text" id="txtName" name="txtName" />
```

If the user now enters some text here, like "It's a geek", the form transmitted back to the server contains at least this line:

```
txtName=It's a geek
```

This data pair becomes part of the Request.Form collection. The key is "txtName" and the value is "It's a geek". The page class hands this data pair to the LoadPostData method. Internally there is nothing surprising here. Using Reflector, you can look into the relevant code inside System.Web.dll (see Listing 1-10).

Listing 1-10. *Disassembled Code of the LoadPostData Method*

```
protected virtual bool LoadPostData(string postDataKey, ➡
                                    NameValueCollection postCollection)
{
    base.ValidateEvent(postDataKey);
    string text = this.Text;
    string str2 = postCollection[postDataKey];
    if (!this.ReadOnly && !text.Equals(str2, StringComparison.Ordinal))
    {
        this.Text = str2;
        return true;
    }
    return false;
}
```

This code snippet is from TextBox, and the one and only property filled by a postback is Text. The control might have been set read-only and therefore this is checked first (this.ReadOnly). Also, as the code compares the old value and the new one, it's written only if the value has been changed. Why is this additional check required? You might assume that comparing takes more time than assigning a property—even if there is nothing to render at this stage. Well, the reason is view state. To understand this, take a look into the code for the Text property in Listing 1-11.

Listing 1-11. *Disassembled Code of Text Method of the TextBox Class*

```
public virtual string Text
{
    get
    {
        string str = (string) this.ViewState["Text"];
        if (str != null)
        {
            return str;
        }
        return string.Empty;
    }
    set
    {
        this.ViewState["Text"] = value;
    }
}
```

The value is not stored in a private field, but only in view state. The tracking feature of the underlying StateBag class handles changes as well. If nothing has changed, it's not recommended to assign the value to view state, or the StateBag class will start tracking. If there is nothing to track, it doesn't make sense to do so, and the LoadPostData method is clever enough to know.

One major aspect many developers overlook is the role of view state in the handling of postback data. The form data loading procedures do not involve view state. More than that, they try to avoid any interaction with view state. The form data handling and stickiness behavior has nothing to do with the view state. The stickiness is a feature that comes with the IPostBackDataHandler interface. Just for clarity, Listing 1-12 shows it in its entire glory.

Listing 1-12. *Code of IPostBackDataHandler Interface*

```
public interface IPostBackDataHandler
{
    bool LoadPostData(string postDataKey, ➥
                      NameValueCollection postCollection);

    void RaisePostDataChangedEvent();
}
```

You know now that view state tracks changes and stores these changes. You know, too, that the stickiness of the form has nothing to do with view state. The LoadPostData method just explores the values sent back to server and restores it into the appropriate properties.

Now, all the controls have been initialized, properly filled with declarative data, over-written with data posted back from the browser, and are ready to enter the next state.

Step Five—Loading Step

Most descriptions of ASP.NET put user code into the Load event. In the explanation of life cycles, you read about this important step because it signals to us that the control is now "ready." Even if you don't want to do anything else with the control, it's ready to be rendered. This is why the best step for adding custom code and modifying the behavior of the page is the load step. Internally, it's much easier, because there is nothing to do within the control. Anything that is supposed to happen here is up to you.

Step Six—Raising Postback Events

Several controls can fire events, depending on the form data posted back. After the loading step, the events are fired one by one. For example, the Button control can fire a Click event, whereas the DropDownList fires SelectedIndexChanged. This is another major feature that makes the dynamic portion of an ASP.NET page so powerful and easy to program.

There are two kinds of events fired during the page's postback.

One kind is responsible for changes, indicated by the suffix _Change. The implementation of IPostBackDataHandler is responsible for recognizing this and firing the appropriate event by calling the RaisePostDataChangedEvent method. In the case of the TextBox example, the event exposed by the class is OnTextChanged.

The other kind of event is the trigger event. For example, in the case of a Button this is a Click event. There is no special state required and no data to compare. As you can see in Listing 1-13, to handle trigger events the IPostBackEventHandler interface is used.

Listing 1-13. *Code of IPostBackEventHandler Interface*

```
public interface IPostBackEventHandler
{
    void RaisePostBackEvent(string eventArgument);
}
```

To understand what happens internally, we'll look into the RaisePostBackEvent method. Listing 1-14 is for a Button control.

Listing 1-14. *Code of Typical Implementation of IPostBackEventHandler Interface*

```
protected virtual void RaisePostBackEvent(string eventArgument)
{
    base.ValidateEvent(this.UniqueID, eventArgument);
    if (this.CausesValidation)
    {
        this.Page.Validate(this.ValidationGroup);
    }
    this.OnClick(EventArgs.Empty);
    this.OnCommand(new CommandEventArgs(
                    this.CommandName, this.CommandArgument));
}
```

As you can see, this method raises more than one event in a predefined and hard-coded order. Several other actions take place first—such as validation—but the events being fired are unconditional.

Again, all of these events can only happen during a postback. Calling the page using GET will do nothing. If you have a DropDownList, and if you change the current index programmatically, nothing will happen unless the page is posted back. This is different from the windows programming model, where the controls can fire events immediately and independently of a particular state.

Step Seven—Storing the View State

After all events have been fired, the current state of each control's property changes needs to be stored. The tracked changes are retrieved recursively through the controls hierarchy. To get the value back, the SaveViewState method of each control is called. The collection of data is then serialized and encoded using Base64.

In the next step, the string is saved to the hidden field with id __VIEWSTATE.

Step Eight—Rendering the Page

The render process runs through all the controls and allows them to render. This is done by a recursive call to all RenderControl methods. The HtmlForm control mentioned at the beginning is responsible for creating the __VIEWSTATE hidden field, which is the container for view state data.

The True Role of View State

The eight states of the life cycle are virtually all important for view state. There are several more steps the various life cycles could run through, but these steps don't affect view state, so I'll exclude them for now. To understand the view state, it's crucial to know what the purpose of view state is. As the name implies, view state stores status information. But what kind of status is it?

The hierarchy of controls and the default values of properties are defined in the declarative part of the page. Take a look at this markup:

```
<asp:Label runat="server" Text="We learn viewstate" Font-Bold="true" />
```

Neither the text "We learn viewstate" nor the value Bold of the Font property is stored in view state. The values are assigned during the initializing phase. View state, in contrast, tracks changes made *programmatically*. This leads to the first definition about view state.

■**Note** View state becomes important only if the page contains custom code.

However, if a page contains custom code, this does not necessarily mean that view state is required. Let's look into another code snippet. The following example in Listing 1-15 has two buttons. Both cause a postback, but only one has an OnClick event attached and handled to access properties in code.

Listing 1-15. *Markup of the View State Test*

```
<asp:Label ID="LabelMessage" runat="server" Text="We learn viewstate"></asp:Label>
<br />
<asp:Button ID="ButtonSubmit" runat="server" onclick="ButtonSubmit_Click"
    Text="Change Text" Width="150px" />
<br />
<asp:Button ID="ButtonEmpty" runat="server" Text="No Change"
    Width="150px" />
```

As shown in Listing 1-16, the code of the click handler is simple, too.

Listing 1-16. *Code of the Click Handler*

```
protected void ButtonSubmit_Click(object sender, EventArgs e)
{
    LabelMessage.Text = "Hello Geek!";
}
```

At the first call of the page the ASPX markup is processed and all values of properties are set, especially the text "We learn viewstate" for the Label. View state stores nothing and therefore contains only internal information without custom data:

```
<input type="hidden" name="__VIEWSTATE" id="__VIEWSTATE" ➥
    value="/wEPDwULLTExNjMzNDIxNjRkZGn5amjBsOOap6CvRbpUM5D9Mlgo" />
```

Now click on the button "No Change". This forces the page to postback and reload, but nothing more happens, because no custom code is involved. Now click on the other button "Change Text". Again a postback occurs, but now the handler processes the OnClick event. In the code, the text of the label gets a new value. View state is changed to this:

```
<input type="hidden" name="__VIEWSTATE" id="__VIEWSTATE" value= "/wEPDwULLTExNjMzNDIx
jQPZBYCAgMPZBYCAgEPDxYCHgRUZXhOBQtIYWxsbyBHZWVrIWRkZHTeN11LiTv5BJOxSdeyOLOQsnk8" />
```

As you see, the coded part is bigger and obviously contains more information. This is no surprise. If you click now on the other button "No Change", the page loads as expected and no custom code is run. However, the text of the label is still "Hello geek!" There is no custom code—the initializing phase has obviously passed and has set the declaratively assigned values. But the change made programmatically in an earlier postback is still there—it's persistent.

That's really the purpose of view state. During postbacks, it makes programmatic changes to control properties persistent. To check whether this behavior is really managed by view state, just disable it using the @Page directive:

```
<%@ Page Language="C#" EnableViewState="false" ...
```

The first click on "Change text" still works as expected. The new text appears. However, when you click on "No change", the postback forces the page to reload and the declarative part of the markup reloads the default values.

Imagine that the "no view state" behavior previously described is the intended behavior in most cases. If you have a label, you usually want it to show its default text. In case of an exception you might want to display a different text. But subsequent reloads usually store the state of such an exception by either overwriting the text again or letting the default text appear.

Globally disabling view state is not an option either, because several complex controls use it to handle their behavior properly, such as the GridView control.

View State Anti-Patterns

Improper use of view state is easily avoided once you really understand how it works. To make things clear, I'll explain the most frequent misuse scenarios. Examples of how *not* to use view state will help you understand how to use view state correctly:

- Forcing a default
- Persisting static data
- Persisting "cheap" data
- Initializing child controls
- Adding controls dynamically
- Initializing dynamically created controls

I'll explain each of these scenarios to make things as clear as possible.

Forcing a Default

Forcing a default value is a very common misuse. Fortunately, it's even easier to fix. It's also a good demonstration of the KISS[5] principle. The developers of ASP.NET did a tremendous job to give us a powerful and well-designed toolkit. The whole framework is an infrastructure thing and provides stable and reliable blocks of code for basic stuff. Doing too much infrastructure work is a signal that something is going wrong.

Assume that you want to store some private data used in a user control. The following code in Listing 1-17 uses the view state, which, in principle, is not a bad idea.

Listing 1-17. *DON'T TRY THIS AT HOME: a wrongly written user control*

```
public class MyControl : WebControl
{
  public string MyData
  {
    get { return ViewState["MyData"] as string;  }
    set { ViewState["MyData"] = value; }
  }

  protected override OnLoad(EventArgs e)
  {
     if (!IsPostBack)
     {
       this. MyData = Session["Control MyData"] as string;
     }
     base.OnLoad();
  }
}
```

You may have written code like this before. It's not a bad style; it's simply wrong. To understand my harsh judgment, let's examine the intent of the control. The developer wrote a user control with the public property MyData. This gives other developers access to it in order to put the control into a defined state using markup like this:

```
<alias:mycontrol runat="server" Text="Show this label" id="myControl1" />
```

This compiles and runs well without any exceptions. However, it doesn't work as expected because the MyData property is never set. Instead, the view state of the page starts growing because the view state field stores this private information. From that perspective, it's doing well; it holds some data. Also, remember the life cycle events. It's boring to repeat them again and again, but everything in ASP.NET is based on the life cycle. In Listing 1-17 the code is written into the OnLoad method. But the Load stage is too late. View state already tracks changes, and now it's being overwritten. That's why it doesn't make sense to write the data there. Let's improve our example (see Listing 1-18).

Listing 1-18. *Save to Be Used at Home: A Well-Written Control*

```
public class MyControl : WebControl
{
  public string MyData
  {
    get {
      if (ViewState["MyData"] == null)
```

---

5. Keep it Simple, Stupid

```
      return Session["Control MyData"] as string;
    else
    return ViewState["MyData"] as string;
  }
  set { ViewState["MyData"] = value; }
}

}
```

This involves less code and it's working well. The default value in the session is now used without touching view state. Simply putting the control onto the page does not increase the size of view state. OnLoad is out of the way here. The assignment of properties happens in the Initializing phase—early enough to set values properly. In case the user of the control sets the MyData property programmatically, view state is in full cry and stores the changes silently in the hidden field.

Persisting Constant Data

A lot of data used in a page's code never changes during the life of the page or during the user's session. Assume your application has some "My" section that is customizable by the user. After the user is logged on, his or her name appears at the top of each page. Assume further that a user control is being written to achieve this.

```
<asp:label id="lblUser" runat="server"/>
```

In the code-behind portion the name is set:

```
public class MyControl : WebControl
{
  protected override OnLoad(EventArgs e)
  {
    lbluser.Text = CurrentUser.Name;
    base.OnLoad();
  }
}
```

This is code that would work well. However, it's doing something under the hood that you don't want. The label has its own view state and, as a child control of the user control, it will store its changed properties in the parent's view state. The user control is going to recognize this and store the change of view state. Storing the label's text value in view state doesn't make sense as, each time it's loaded, the value is pulled from the CurrentUser class. The default behavior of controls is an implicit usage of view state. Either you assign it once, and hold data in view state, or you need to prevent it from using view state. The solution I would recommend looks very easy:

```
<asp:label id="lblUser" runat="server" EnableViewstate="false" />
```

Disable view state on the control level and it will work like a charm. The next pattern extends this solution by presenting an alternative solution.

Persisting Cheap Data

Sometimes you use data that changes frequently, depending on user action or external conditions. Assume you want to show a list of data on your page. It is a small list and it doesn't change frequently. But it could change or grow at any time. Your site is already using a database; it's fast and there is nothing wrong with pulling the data from a table.

```
<asp:dropdownlist runat="server" id="ddlMyData" DataTextField="Name" ➥
                  DataValueField="ID"/>
```

The (fictitious) code-behind portion could look like this:

```
public class MyControl : WebControl
{
  protected override OnLoad(EventArgs e)
  {
      if (!IsPostBack)
      {
        ddlMyData.DataSource = DAL.QueryDdlData();
        ddlMyData.DataBind();
      }
      base.OnLoad();
  }
}
```

This is, again, working well and nobody would see any issues here. However, there is something here that is easily overlooked. Databound controls need to remember their state, for instance, to hold the last selected option of a dropdownlist after postback. I discussed this previously and called this smart behavior "stickiness." You don't want to lose the form's sticky behavior. You might there-fore assume that switching view state off is not a solution either. But stickiness is part of the control state; it's made by checking the form data. It's not related to view state, as some developers think. The reason you run into trouble with view state is that it grows each time the page reloads.

This time the solution is not so simple. Switching off view state is only half of the answer:

```
<asp:dropdownlist runat="server" id=" ddlMyData" DataTextField="Name" ➥
                  DataValueField="ID" EnableViewState="false" />
```

The code-behind is almost the same, except you pull the data every time the control loads (note the missing if statement):

```
Public class MyControl : WebControl
{
  protected override OnLoad(EventArgs e)
  {
      ddlMyData.DataSource = DAL. QueryDdlData ();
      ddlMyData.DataBind();
      base.OnLoad();
  }
}
```

Now view state is as clean as possible. But the sticky form behavior has gone, too. Trying this, you might think you've found a bug in this book and that the author is wrong about view state.

The fault is not view state itself. It still has no function because the control state is restoring the data from postback values. However, let's overwrite this because the OnLoad event is fired after all states are restored. This is, again, a life cycle issue. Understanding the life cycle leads us to the solu-tion. Move the last code fragment as is to another step in the life cycle—OnInit:

```
public class MyControl : WebControl
{
  protected override OnInit(EventArgs e)
  {
      ddlMyData.DataSource = DAL. QueryDdlData ();
      ddlMyData.DataBind();
```

```
    base.OnInit();
  }
}
```

This solution is both clean and simple. OnInit fires before the control state restores the values. It pulls static data from a fast database, puts it directly into the control, forces the render process before the control restores its state, and everything is fine. The render process is an important step here, made by calling the DataBind method.

■Tip You'll probably want to avoid heavy database access whenever possible. Instead, you'll probably store small data portions in XML files and maintain changes there. I would recommend using a database anyway. Modern implementations, like Microsoft SQL Server™, hold frequently requested data in memory. The amount of data requested is small, and the connection is usually 1GB or 10GB Ethernet. A powerful data access layer will also cache the data locally, so that in reality nothing is transferred between the servers. The slowest part of the connection is from the Web Server to the user. He or she will have ISDN, DSL, or a mobile connection. Storing the small portion of data in view state sends the data three times over the wire: once when the user loads the page (as visible data in the dropdown control), once in view state, and the third time when the form is sent back (as view state is part of the form's field collection). Calling a database frequently is not torture; this is the reason for a database.

Initializing Child Controls

One paradigm you might hear frequently about ASP.NET is to do things declaratively. Whatever you can do directly within the ASPX page, do it! However, this has some implications and limitations, and eventually you must start doing some work programmatically. The trouble is that initializing controls programmatically is not straightforward. As shown before, you can do this in OnLoad, but this could cause the view state to grow and, in any case, it's not necessary to use view state when merely setting defaults. Even OnInit is not the best solution because view state will still track changes and catch the settings. If you need view state and can't disable it, you'll have to live with this behavior. Because the control's view state tracks changes from the bottom up—say, from the last leaf control in the control hierarchy up to the tree's root—the OnInit for child controls is done when the current OnInit is called.

```
<asp:label id="lblDate" runat="server"/>
```

In the code-behind portion, you set the text by assigning the current date:

```
public class MyControl : WebControl
{
  protected override OnInit(EventArgs e)
  {
    lblDate.Text = DateTime.Now.ToLongDate();
    base.OnInit();
  }
}
```

Even if this is the earliest event possible, it's already too late. The label is initialized before the user control, and view state is already tracking changes. This means that the date persists in view state, which doesn't make sense—this is the same situation faced in the current user name example.

Disabling view state has been discussed before, but this is not always a solution. Perhaps you have tried this:

```
<asp:label id="lblDat" runat="server" Text="<% =DateTime.Now.ToLongDateString()%>"/>
```

This is not possible, because ASP.NET doesn't allow the initializing of properties in that way. Using databinding syntax <%# %> is no solution, either.

Let's assume that for some reason you want to assign the value by code. And you want to use view state for some other reason as well. You may think about OnPreInit, but this event isn't recursive and appears only on the page level. So, what's going on here? It's interesting that the OnInit event behaves slightly different depending on how you get access to it. The obvious way is to override the event handler. This is easy, well-supported in IntelliSense, and the most common solution. You can attach events declaratively, too. As I said before, this is one of the major paradigms of ASP.NET.

```
<asp:label id="lblDate" runat="server" OnInit="lblDate_Init" />
```

This handler is fired before the internal initialization takes place—before the TrackViewState method is called and the view state starts tracking changes. Referring to the control's life cycle, there is a subtle difference between the declaratively attached event and overriding the method. Just set the text in the code-behind as you would before:

```
public class MyControl : WebControl
{
  public void lblDate_Init(object sender, EventArgs e)
  {
    lblDate.Text = DateTime.Now.ToLongDate();
  }
}
```

■Tip If you're wondering whether to use declarative events or just wire up to code—remember the basic rule: "Whatever we can do easily and safely the declarative way is our primary programming technique."

Another solution comes to mind if you're an experienced developer of object-oriented software. Each object starts its life with the call of the object's constructor. Usually the constructor is the place to initialize the object. However, in ASP.NET the life of controls begins some time later, in the initialization phase. You may subclass the control and override the constructor to invoke code there, but child controls are not yet present. The various events required are fired some time later. With a custom control it would work. This is indeed another powerful solution. By implementing your own label you can access the constructor without needing to do anything elsewhere:

```
public class MyLabel : Label
{
  public MyLabel()
  {
    this.Text = DateTime.Now.ToLongDate();
  }
}
```

This is a slightly modified label that simply initializes itself at the right time without any side effects. The constructor call assures that any tracking begins later.

■Note The internal "building steps" of an object, like the constructor call, are made before the lifetime of the object begins. By "lifetime," I mean the life of an object within the control's or page's life cycle—not the lifetime of an object within the runtime.

Attaching Dynamic Controls

All controls have a collection of child controls, represented by the property Controls. Some controls, such as Label, have an empty collection, because they can't render children. All controls inherit the collection from Control base class. This is the common way to access the hierarchy of controls. The class behind the collection is defined:

```
public class ControlCollection : ICollection, IEnumerable
```

There are no obvious limits preventing you from adding new controls at any time. With view state, it's not that easy. View state can track values only for existing controls. To handle dynamic controls, you need to add them on any page load, whether it's a postback or regular page load cycle. Attaching dynamic controls must happen in the initializing phase (OnInit event), because, at an earlier state, there is no hierarchy of controls to which you could attach anything. View state of those dynamically attached controls is then tracked automatically. Remember that this is done recursively through the whole hierarchy, so the StateBag class will never miss anything. However, this point is critical. You might experience the following exception loading the page after postback:

```
[Failed loading view state]
Failed to load view state. The control tree into which view state is being loaded must
match the control tree that was used to save view state during the previous request. For
example, when adding controls dynamically, the controls added during a post-back must
match the type and position of the controls added during the initial request.
```

Let's create an example so that you can figure out what is happening internally:

```
protected void Page_Init(object sender, EventArgs e)
{
  if (!IsPostBack)
  {
    Button myButton = new Button();
    form1.Controls.Add(myButton);
    myButton.Text = "Click here";
  }
  else
  {
    Label label = new Label();
    form1.Controls.Add(label);
  }
}
```

The intent of this code is obvious. The user has a Button to invoke some action, and, when the action is completed, the button is replaced by a Label control. You might argue that this is not good practice, but let's examine it for the moment. View state tries to recognize the elements solely by their index. In this example the control at index [0] is the Button. After postback it has been replaced by the Label, using the same index [0]. This does not lead to the exception previously shown, because the restoring code is fairly stupid. It just looks for the right property, and both Button and Label share the same Text property. While this works, the label now shows the text "Click here". Why? The exception appears even if this less-than-ideal method fails, probably because the control does not provide the expected property.

The first solution is simple. Turn off view state for the button control. Since you throw away the button anyway, view state is not required at all. If the view state is being saved, it can't disturb the next cycle—problem solved. Here is the solution in all its glory:

```
protected void Page_Init(object sender, EventArgs e)
{
```

```
  if (!IsPostBack)
  {
     Button myButton = new Button();
     myButton.EnableViewState = false;
     form1.Controls.Add(myButton);
     myButton.Text = "Click here";
  }
  else
  {
     Label label = new Label();
     form1.Controls.Add(label);
  }
}
```

Had you been using view state in the preceding sample, the problem would resolve itself—that is, if you had recreated the control after postback, which is one of the basic rules of dynamic controls creation. The ultimate solution looks like this:

```
protected void Page_Init(object sender, EventArgs e)
{
   Button myButton = new Button();
   myButton.EnableViewState = false;
   form1.Controls.Add(myButton);
   myButton.Text = "Click here";
   if (IsPostBack)
   {
      Label label = new Label();
      form1.Controls.Add(label);
      myButton.Visible = false;
   }
}
```

Here you are close to the best practice. Allow all controls on the page to remain untouched and switch the visibility on and off, as required, via code. The render method is smart enough to not render invisible controls. But that's another topic and would lead us away from view state.

Initializing Dynamically Created Controls

I discussed dynamic controls before and, reading the text, you might feel that there are some issues with them. This is indeed something you need to approach carefully, but there are no real issues.

The problem is very similar to the one described before. Because you create the control when you choose, you have more influence and this makes your life easier. It does, however, run against the paradigm that says that you should code in a declarative way whenever possible, because you leave the world of declarative definitions completely. In any case, let's look at how to handle another view state issue correctly.

```
public class MyCustomControl : Control
{
   protected override void CreateChildControls()
   {
     Label l =  new Label();
     Controls.Add(l);
     l.Text = DateTime.Now.ToLongDate();
   }
}
```

You can create child controls any time, but the CreateChildControls method is the best opportunity for fitting into the event sequence. The initialize event is called and the control doesn't miss the tracking of view state. The secret is the behavior of the Controls.Add call. This isn't just a collection; it does much more when the Add method is invoked. Even if all events of the parent hierarchy are complete, the control begins its regular life cycle and all events involved here are fired correctly. That means that the control starts tracking view state immediately after it's added to the collection. CreateChildControls always seems too late, as even though it is called at different points in time, it's always later than OnInit. Just for completeness, you need to know that it's based on EnsureChildControls call, which happens in OnPreRender at the latest. For some reasons the call might come much earlier. It depends on the control's parts being rendered due to specific conditions. This happens virtually in data-bound controls that can show different templates depending on actual state.

Now take a closer look at the solution:

```
public class MyCustomControl : Control
{
    protected override void CreateChildControls()
    {
        Label l =  new Label();
        l.Text = DateTime.Now.ToLongDate();
        Controls.Add(l);
    }
}
```

There is only a subtle difference. The control's properties are set before the control is added, which means that it's initialized before the OnInit is fired, and that subsequently it has not yet begun to track the view state.

You can also databind controls before they have been added to the parent control's control hierarchy. This is very powerful and flexible. So real developers write their own custom controls and know how they work internally.

Summary

In this chapter you learned about the internal processing of ASP.NET, especially the processing pipeline, which is running a single request and performs the steps required to create the content sent to the client finally. The pipeline forms the life cycle of application, pages, and controls. During the life cycle several states store current processing step's data. To rescue data from one request to another, the view state is used. You learned what the view state is for and how to overcome the quirks and traps the implementation has.

However, Web applications handle usually more than one request at a time. The next chapter extends the description by looking into threading, thread pools, and other stuff required to make an ASP.NET project fast and reliable even if it comes under pressure from multiple requests.

CHAPTER 2

■ ■ ■

Worker and Threads

In the first chapter I looked into the handling of a page request, and, in particular, the application life cycle and page life cycle. This is the fundamental process that runs when anyone requests a page resource. However, Chapter 1 was a simplification of the situation—I assumed that only one request comes in at a time. Reality is quite different.

Managing hundreds, or even thousands, of simultaneous requests requires advanced knowledge and skills. In this and subsequent chapters you will learn those skills.

This chapter includes:

- How ASP.NET handles multiple requests

- How to manage the worker processes and optimize the workload

- The thread model, thread pool behavior and how to optimize its usage

- How to build asynchronous handlers, pages, and tasks

Managing the Worker Process

In Chapter 1, you learned about the worker process, w3wp.exe, which executes a request and hosts the ASP.NET engine. Managing the worker process is the key to managing high server demand, and keeping your applications stable and reliable.

Managing Worker Processes and AppDomains in IIS7

One of the leading Windows application management tools is Windows Management Instrumentation (WMI). You have probably used WMI to administer basic ASP.NET-related parts of IIS. It's a well-known way to access worker processes while your application is running.

To accommodate today's managed-code world, Microsoft exposed the WMI and COM method calls via .NET. In previous programming environments, the access to properties and events of the model's components is based on untyped strings, like `getProperty("Name")`. Instead of invoking WMI directly, you can manage IIS using .NET typed classes, rather than using those untyped strings. These classes expose a direct interface to the IIS7 management level and appear to be easy to use and robust.

GOOD OLD DAYS: WINDOWS MANAGEMENT INSTRUMENTATION

Windows exposes the Windows Driver Model as a framework for device drivers. Windows Management Instrumentation (WMI) is a set of extensions that provides information about and notifications from instrumented components. Programming environments and tools use WMI to access the underlying hardware components using the driver model. You can find a good introduction in Wikipedia at: `http://en.wikipedia.org/wiki/Windows_Management_Instrumentation`.

It suggests that WMI is a good tool for automating the management of worker processes and application domains in IIS7. It can also help us find a better way to customize the ASP.NET environment. IIS7 worker processes are spawned by the Windows Process Activation Service (WAS), using w3wp.exe. A worker process can contain AppDomains that are typically created to handle a request.

Prerequisites

There are several prerequisites to writing sophisticated management applications using Visual Studio. First of all, IIS7 itself is a prerequisite. No other Web Server currently supports these interfaces. To test your application, it must run with elevated privileges. If you run the development environment on Windows Vista, you must launch Visual Studio with Administrator rights. An application built on such a system runs well on Windows Server 2008, as long as it runs with Administrator privileges. Once Visual Studio is running with the right account, you need to reference the administration assemblies in your project. There are several managed assemblies available in the IIS7 installation folder:

`<%WinDir%>\system32\inetsrv`

You will find several assemblies starting with the name "Microsoft.Web." Depending on what you're planning to do, you'll need one or another. For the moment, just reference all of them to ensure that all the examples in this chapter run properly. Here's the list of what you'll need:

- `Microsoft.Web.Administration`
- `Microsoft.Web.Management.Aspnet`
- `Microsoft.Web.Management.AspnetClient`
- `Microsoft.Web.Management`
- `Microsoft.Web.Management.Iis`
- `Microsoft.Web.Management.IisClient`

Tasks to Manage

There are several tasks you can manage using the techniques described in this chapter. They will allow you to extend the available toolkit and customize the management of the ASP.NET environment. I will focus here on some of the more common tasks, like:

- View the currently executing requests for a worker process.
- Get the state of all worker processes.
- Unload a specific AppDomain, or all AppDomains.
- Display all AppDomains and their properties.

There is almost unlimited scope for using the new management classes to extend the existing ASP.NET management capabilities. This includes, but is not limited to, the following:

- Notify when an unhandled exception occurs
- Watch long-lasting requests
- Watch the number of worker threads and status of thread pool
- Provide the number of users that match specific conditions
- Manage internal settings of ASP.NET and IIS

Back Up Your Configuration

It is possible that the following samples will destroy or damage your IIS7 configuration. As it's cumbersome to re-install your development environment after any undesirable side effects, you should test in a virtual machine or back up the IIS configuration of your production machine before you start. The AppCmd tool is very useful to make instant backups of the configuration. It has several options. The basic structure of the command is:

```
AppCmd Command ObjectType ID Parameter
```

The command parameter depends on the *ObjectType* parameter. For backup purposes the ObjectType is Backup. You can use the following commands:

- list: shows all available backups
- add: creates a new backup for the current configuration
- delete: delete a backup from disk
- restore: restore a backup and overwrite current configuration

The usage is straightforward. Again, remember to run this tool with Administrator privileges to access the IIS settings.

To make a backup of the configuration:

1. Open a command window with Administrator rights.
2. Navigate to %WinDir%\system32\inetsrv.
3. Enter the following command:

   ```
   AppCmd add backup IIS7backup
   ```

4. The backup is created in the folder %WinDir%\system32\inetsrv\backup\iis7backup.

You can use any name you like for the backup (see Figure 2-1).

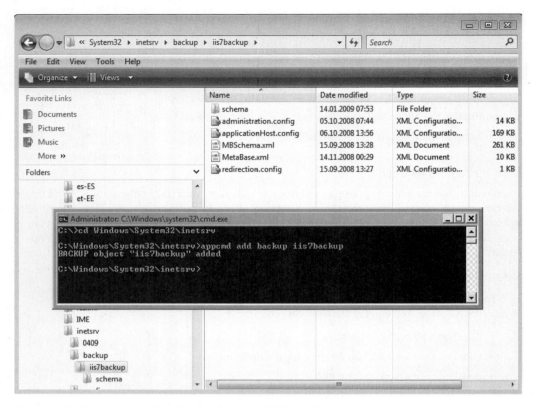

Figure 2-1. *Backup command and created Backup folder with IIS7 settings*

Basic Tasks

The code in Listing 2-1 shows the typical structure of an IIS7 management code snippet. You can use whatever client environment you prefer. You could use a simple WPF (Windows Presentation Foundation) client to display the data in a hierarchical format (such as a TreeView), or perhaps well-formatted in a RichTextBox control.

For the purpose of demonstrating sample code, a console application is a simple, satisfactory alternative. I will use the following generic test structure for the listing examples.

Listing 2-1. *Basic Code Structure for IIS7 Administration Code Snippets*

```
using System;
using System.Text;
using Microsoft.Web.Administration;

namespace Apress.AspNetExtensibility.IIS7Console
{
    static class IIS7Management
    {

        internal static string Method()
        {
            StringBuilder sb = new StringBuilder();
```

```
        // Code goes here
        return sb.ToString();
      }
   }
}
```

These static methods are invoked from the console's entry point. The basis for most operations is the `Microsoft.Web.Administration.ServerManager` class. From the `ServerManager` class there are several collections available via corresponding properties:

- Sites (SiteCollection)

- WorkerProcesses (WorkerProcessCollection)

- From Site class exposed by SiteCollection:

  - Applications (ApplicationCollection)

  - Bindings (BindingCollection)

- Form VirtualDirectories collection exposed by Application via Applications property:

  - VirtualDirectory (VirtualDirectoryCollection)

Through these collections you can reach the desired objects and properties for monitoring and managing IIS7. You always have read and write access. That means you can virtually change all configuration settings programmatically available using the Management Console. To save your changes, you need to explicitly call the `CommitChanges` method.

Get Information About the Worker Processes

In the next example, I show you how to loop through each worker process on a Web Server. You'll see then how to display the currently executing requests, process ID, and state of each worker process, as well as the application pool to which it belongs.

Get the State of a Worker Process

The `Microsoft.Web.Administration.WorkerProcess` object in the IIS7 administration has a `State` property that indicates whether a worker process is starting, running, or stopping. There are two more properties that particularly interest us: `AppPoolName` and `ProcessId`. The `ApplicationPool` property represents the application pool to which the worker process belongs. The `ProcessId` property contains the process' ID that uniquely identifies the worker process that is an integer value. The `ProcessGuid` method returns the particular Guid (see Listing 2-2).

Listing 2-2. *Getting Information About Worker Processes*

```
internal static string ShowWorkerProcesses()
{
    StringBuilder sb = new StringBuilder();
    try
    {
        ServerManager manager = new ServerManager();
        foreach (WorkerProcess proc in manager.WorkerProcesses)
        {
            sb.AppendFormat("WorkerProcess found: {0}\n", proc.ProcessId);
            sb.AppendFormat("\t|--AppPool : {0}\n", proc.AppPoolName);
            sb.AppendFormat("\t|--ProcGuid: {0}\n", proc.ProcessGuid);
            sb.AppendFormat("\t|--State   : {0}\n", proc.State.ToString());
```

```
        foreach (ApplicationDomain appDom in proc.ApplicationDomains)
        {
            sb.AppendFormat(
                "\t+--ApplicationDomain Found: {0}\n", appDom.Id);
            sb.AppendFormat(
                "\t\t|--AppDomPhysPath: {0}\n", appDom.PhysicalPath);
            sb.AppendFormat(
                "\t\t+--AppDomVirtPath: {0}\n", appDom.VirtualPath);
        }
    }
    return sb.ToString();
}
catch (Exception ex)
{
    return ex.Message;
}
}
```

The worker processes are exposed by the property WorkerProcesses. The value should match the number of w3wp.exe instances running in the Windows Task Manager.

■**Tip** If there are no worker processes but IIS7 is running, open a Web site to force the process to launch.

The properties used depend on the object you wish to investigate (see Figure 2-2). Refer to the documentation on MSDN to get full descriptions of all available values. See also http://msdn.microsoft.com/en-us/library/aa347649.aspx for more details.

Figure 2-2. *Watching worker processes*

To monitor your worker processes, check the State property. The state of a process can be one of the values defined in the WorkerProcessState enumeration:

- Starting
- Running
- Stopping
- Unknown

Why can't the worker process have a state of "Stopped"? After the process has been shut down, the executable is disposed of and removed from memory. The worker process then disappears from the list of processes. Therefore, the worker is first starting, then running, and, if there is nothing to do, stopping. There isn't a specific situation where the state Unknown appears, as the name implies. I assume that it occurs when the process dies unexpectedly and hangs.

Get Executing Requests

One exciting new feature of IIS7 is the ability to see the requests that are currently executing in a worker process. You do this with the WorkerProcess.GetRequests method in a manner very similar to the one shown before. Retrieve the worker process and invoke the GetRequests method to get the current requests.

The GetRequests method requires an int parameter to filter the results for requests that have run for at least the number of milliseconds specified. This is very useful for displaying only long-running requests. It's a good idea to set the value to zero initially in order to get all requests, as shown in Listing 2-3.

■**Tip** Capturing a request to test an application within the development environment can be tricky. Use the Thread.Sleep method to make the request last long enough to be caught. Use an editor to save the following text into a file called Sleep.aspx. The complete page for a request that will take a minute to execute:

```
<% System.Threading.Thread.Sleep(60000)
Response.Write ("I'm finally finished...") %>
```

Running the management code, as in Listing 2-3, shows that the request is running and displays various properties for the request. The code requires that IIS features like Request Monitor are properly installed. This is an option you can activate in the Windows Components installation feature of System Control Panel. Use *Internet Information Services* ➤ *WWW Services* ➤ *Health & Diagnostics* and check the Request Monitor option.

Listing 2-3. *Looping Through Some Properties of a Running Worker Process*

```
internal static string ShowRequest()
{
    StringBuilder sb = new StringBuilder();
    try
    {
        ServerManager manager = new ServerManager();
        foreach (WorkerProcess proc in manager.WorkerProcesses)
        {
            foreach (Request r in proc.GetRequests(0))
            {
                sb.AppendFormat("Request:\n");
                sb.AppendFormat(" Hostname = {0}\n", r.HostName);
                sb.AppendFormat(" Url = {0}\n", r.Url);
                sb.AppendFormat(" Verb = {0}\n", r.Verb);
                sb.AppendFormat(" IP = {0}\n", r.ClientIPAddr);
            }
        }
        return sb.ToString();
    }
    catch (Exception ex)
    {
        return ex.Message;
    }
}
```

The console (see Figure 2-3) shows all the requests currently running on available worker processes. Before running this on a production system, it would be advisable to add some filter conditions to avoid returning an excessive number of results.

```
Request:
  Hostname = localhost
  Url = /Index.aspx
  Verb = GET
  IP = 127.0.0.1
Request:
  Hostname = localhost
  Url = /
  Verb = GET
  IP = 127.0.0.1
Request:
  Hostname = localhost
  Url = /Content.aspx
  Verb = GET
  IP = 127.0.0.1
```

Figure 2-3. *Output shows detailed information about certain requests.*

Monitoring requests is not particularly suited to a console application. Imagine you have some requests that don't function as expected, but the errors are infrequent and not reproducible. In this situation, you could write an application to monitor a specific request and log all relevant data. When the error reappears, your log file should contain information enabling you to track down the error source.

Get Information About the Application Domains

The first time a request for an ASP.NET page is received, the IIS7 managed engine module creates an application domain (AppDomain) in memory, which I explained in Chapter 1. The AppDomain processes requests for aspx pages, or any page that uses managed code. Unloading and enumerating AppDomains is straightforward. This section shows you how to do both. Unloading an AppDomain implicitly unloads all assemblies in there. You may use this to save spaces occupied by assemblies no longer required. Another reason is the distribution of new versions of the related assemblies, which are required to be unloaded first and loaded again after an upgrade. Because the unloading of individual assemblies is not directly supported, the unloading of the AppDomain is quite often the only option.

Unloading a Specific AppDomain

To unload a specific `Microsoft.Web.Administration.AppDomain`, you must be able to uniquely identify it. AppDomains have three key properties: `Id`, `VirtualPath`, and `PhysicalPath`. One of these properties should be sufficient.

The code snippet in Listing 2-4 shows you how to obtain the desired AppDomain using a LINQ query. The nested `from` statements form a join to retrieve the `ApplicationDomains` property for each running `WorkerProcess` object. The `where` clause restricts the result to the single AppDomain defined by the given `Id`. For a real-life application, this value could be a variable. You saw the `ShowWorkerProcesses` method earlier in Listing 2-2. It's not required, but I've included it here for demonstration purposes (see Listing 2-4).

Listing 2-4. *Retrieve Information About the Application Domains*

```
internal static string UnloadAppDomain(string name)
{
    StringBuilder sb = new StringBuilder();
    string id = "/LM/W3SVC/1/ROOT";
    try
    {
        sb.Append(ShowWorkerProcesses());
        ServerManager manager = new ServerManager();
        var appDomains = from proc in manager.WorkerProcesses
                         from adc in proc.ApplicationDomains
                         where adc.Id == id
                         select adc;

        ApplicationDomain ad = appDomains.FirstOrDefault<ApplicationDomain>();

        if (ad != null)
        {
            ad.Unload();
            return name + " unloaded";
        }
        else
        {
            return "can't find " + name;
        }
    }
    catch (Exception ex)
    {
        return ex.Message;
    }
}
```

Incidentally, the AppDomain's `Id` property is a path that looks like this:

```
/LM/W3SVC/1/ROOT
```

The "1" in the path listed is the site's ID. "1" usually corresponds to the default Web site. You could find any number here, depending on how many webs you have on the machine you're currently investigating.

If you generate a list of your server's AppDomains and their properties first, you'll find the right one easily (see Listing 2-2 where you extracted the AppDomain instances from the currently running worker processes).

However, the purpose of the script was to unload a particular AppDomain. To understand what happens when you unload an AppDomain, run this scenario:

- Request a page from your server.

- Watch running processes and AppDomains and retrieve the properties.

- Launch the code and unload the domain.

- Request the page again.

- Retrieve the very same information from properties.

Unloading All AppDomains

The next example in Listing 2-5 unloads all AppDomains. Again, I use LINQ and generic features.
You don't have to do it this way, but it results in compact and highly readable code. The LINQ statement again uses a nested query.

Listing 2-5. *Unload All AppDomains*

```
internal static string UnloadAppDomains()
{
    try
    {
        ServerManager manager = new ServerManager();
        Func<ApplicationDomain, bool> unloadFunc = ➥
                        new Func<ApplicationDomain, bool>(Unload);
        var appDomains = from proc in manager.WorkerProcesses
                        from adc in proc.ApplicationDomains
                        where unloadFunc(adc) == true
                        select adc;
        return "Unloaded " + appDomains.Count() + " domain(s)";
    }
    catch (Exception ex)
    {
        return ex.Message;
    }
}

private static bool Unload(ApplicationDomain appDomain)
{
    try
    {
        appDomain.Unload();
        return true;
    }
    catch
    {
        return false;
    }
}
```

The unload method is encapsulated in the callback function Unload. It takes the AppDomain
as a parameter of type ApplicationDomain. As before, the query starts by retrieving the worker processes and the AppDomains joined to them. In the where clause, the inline method unloadFunc() is
used to unload the domain. The Func type is a predefined typed delegate used to pass a parameter
and retrieve a Boolean result flag. The clause forces the method call to Unload and the return value
decides whether the AppDomain becomes part of the result set. This leads to a direct usage of the
Count method that returns the number of successfully unloaded AppDomains (see Figure 2-4).

```
Unloaded 1 domain(s)
Hit enter to close console
```

Figure 2-4. *Number of successfully unloaded AppDomains*

Enumerating AppDomains

Dealing with AppDomains in a management environment often starts with showing all available properties. For learning purposes it makes sense to investigate the AppDomain's properties.
Listing 2-6 shows how to get this information. The helpful properties for an AppDomain are:

- `Id`
- `VirtualPath`
- `PhysicalPath`
- `Idle`

Id returns the current internal Id of the AppDomain. The `VirtualPath` is as defined in the IIS
settings; for the root path it is usually "/". Usually the physical location of a Web site is same as the
path used as the path part of the URL. A virtual path points to a location of content somewhere else
on the Web Server or even on a remote server. If there is no virtual directory the virtual path equals
the root ("/"). The `PhysicalPath` is the full path to the application on local disk. The `Idle` property
is a runtime value. It's defined as `int`; it returns either 0 or 1, where the latter is the value for an idle
application domain (see Listing 2-6).

Listing 2-6. *Show Properties of AppDomains*

```
internal static string ShowAppDomains()
{
    StringBuilder sb = new StringBuilder();
    try
    {
        ServerManager manager = new ServerManager();
        var appDomains = from proc in manager.WorkerProcesses
                         from adc in proc.ApplicationDomains
                         select
                             String.Format(@"Physical Path = {0}
                                            {4}Virtual Path = {1}
                                            {4}Process ID = {2}
                                            {4}Is Idle = {3}",
                             adc.PhysicalPath,
                             adc.VirtualPath,
                             adc.Id,
                             adc.Idle,
                             Environment.NewLine);

        if (appDomains.Count() == 0)
        {
            sb.Append("can't find AppDomains");
        }
        else
        {
            foreach (string ad in appDomains)
            {
                sb.AppendLine(ad);
            }
        }
        return sb.ToString();
    }
```

```
    catch (Exception ex)
    {
        return ex.Message;
    }
}
```

The LINQ query retrieves the worker processes and the attached AppDomains. In the select clause, the string is constructed to simplify output. You can alter this clause to retrieve the specific values you desire. With this, you can monitor your ASP.NET environment with your custom application, without requiring Internet Information Services Manager Console, as shown in Figure 2-5.

```
Physical Path = D:\Projects\Private\02 Visual Studio\08 Customer\11 Copyprint\www\
Virtual Path = /
Process ID = /LM/W3SVC/3/ROOT
Is Idle = 1
Hit enter to repeat, X + Enter to close
```

Figure 2-5. *Information About a Running AppDomain*

You can compare this information with that available in the IIS Manager Console. Open the IIS Manager Console, navigate to the site, and click on *Advanced Settings on Action List* to see the settings and check against the values retrieved using the code shown previously.

When working with the ApplicationDomain object, you might see many more properties than were shown in the last example. This is because all settings derive from the ConfigurationSettings type, which contains several common properties that you don't need.

Additional values about the worker process are helpful, too. You can add these easily by extending the select clause in this manner:

```
adc.WorkerProcess.ProcessId
```

The object adc is of the current ApplicationDomain type. By using a back reference to the WorkerProcess object, all property values available there can be retrieved directly.

Configuring the Worker Process

Unlike classic ASP, which runs in the same memory space as IIS, ASP.NET runs as a process of its own. This gives it more flexibility, stability, and power. You can use the configuration file *machine.config* to make the Webmaster's job a lot easier.

I'll take a closer look here at the ASP.NET process and the attributes that you can adjust. The *machine.config* file is plain XML and easy to read. As the name implies, it's a definition at the machine level. Several portions define the default values for the application and the folder-specific *web.config*. However, some parts can't be overwritten, and there's no point in attempting to alter others.

The machine.config File

As mentioned earlier, version 3.5 of the .NET framework augments, rather than replaces, .NET Framework 2.0. This explains why the *machine.config* file is stored under the 2.0 hive. The path on your machine should look similar to:

```
%WinDir%\Microsoft.NET\Framework\v2.0.50727\CONFIG
```

There are several other configuration files, but we're only examining *machine.config*. Because it's XML, you can use Visual Studio to edit it. The worker process settings are stored in the `<processModel>` tag. It's located under `<system.web>` and usually looks like this:

```
<processModel autoConfig="true" />
```

Microsoft sets all common values using the auto configuration option. This is good for most installations, but not all. To optimize the settings, you can set the value of this attribute to `false` and change whatever you like:

```
<processModel autoConfig="false" />
```

However, changing basic settings is not simple and may lead to servers not responding or performing poorly. Before going on, let me explain the various settings.

■**Note** Changes made to the `<processModel>` tag do not have immediate effect. You must restart a worker process to force it to re-read the settings. To restart a worker process, you can open Task Manager, right-click the w3wp.exe found in the task list, and kill the process. The worker process will start again automatically.

Why Customize the machine.config Settings?

You may wonder why and when you're supposed to change the *machine.config* settings and the `<processModel>` settings. Let's consider the following scenario:

- Your network supports only one application domain (AppDomain).
- Each page causes one request (no subsequent AJAX calls).
- All requests go to the same IP address.

In this case, the default settings are very good and there is no reason to change anything. However, other specific scenarios could be problematic:

- Requests to many IP addresses
- Frequent redirects (HTTP status code 302)
- Using authentication
- Using more than one AppDomain

The following section describes all the `processModel` parameters. (In a later section in this chapter, "Configuring the Thread Pool," I'll explain this in even greater depth.)

Keep in mind that, behind the scenes, IIS must handle the available resources to manage all incoming requests. If the rate of incoming page requests is such that the fraction of memory in use or CPU power exceeds certain levels, the default values for the `processModel` parameters may not be optimal. However, setting higher values is not always better, as this can lead to higher resource consumption and slow down even a lightly-loaded server handling simple requests. Finding the most appropriate options in the parameter jungle is a challenge.

A First Look into the Attributes

Table 2-1 lists the `processModel` attributes available. The description column indicates the purpose of each attribute and where to find more information.

Table 2-1. *Settings Available for the <processModel> Tag (Excerpt)*

Attribute	Default	Description
clientConnectedCheck	00:00:05 (five seconds)	Once a request has been waiting in the queue for this long, ASP.NET checks whether the client is still connected.
cpuMask	0xffffffff	Specifies which CPU of a multiprocessor system runs ASP.NET processes. The value is a bitmask where each bit represents a CPU. Assume you set the value to 0xa, which is 1010 in binary form. CPUs are numbered beginning with 0, and read from right to left. For this value, CPUs 1 and 3 are qualified to run ASP.NET threads and CPUs 0 and 2 are not.
enable	true	Enables or disables the process model.
idleTime	Infinite	The period of inactivity (in time format hh:mm:ss), after which the worker process ends. (For example, a value of "00:20:00" will cause the worker process to shut down 20 minutes after the last request is concluded.) "Infinite" prevents the worker process from stopping at all.
logLevel	Errors	The quantity of errors written to the event log. Choose from "All," "Errors," or "None."
maxAppDomains	2000	The number of application domains in one process. The default value, 2000, is the maximum allowed. Lower values are appropriate for hosting providers, for instance.
maxIoThreads	20	The maximum number of threads for I/O operations, counted on a per-CPU basis. Must be greater than or equal to minFreeThreads in <httpRuntime> settings. Allowed range is between 5 and 100. See the section "Understanding and Using Threads" in this chapter for more information.
maxWorkerThreads	20	The maximum number of worker threads, counted on a per-CPU basis. Must be greater than or equal to minFreeThreads in <httpRuntime> settings. Allowed range is between 5 and 100. See the section "Understanding and Using Threads" in this chapter for more information.
memoryLimit	60	The maximum allowed memory size as a percentage of total system memory that one worker process is allowed to consume. Beyond this limit, a new worker process is launched and subsequent requests are redirected to this one.
minIoThreads	1	The minimum number of I/O threads. See the section "Understanding and Using Threads" in this chapter for more information.
minWorkerThreads	1	The minimum number of worker threads. See the section "Understanding and Using Threads" in this chapter for more information.

Attribute	Default	Description
username, password	AutoGenerate	The account used to run the worker process.
pingFrequency	Infinite	The time interval in hh:mm:ss format used to ping the worker process to get its state. If the worker process is not running, it is restarted.
pingTimeout	Infinite	The time, also in hh:mm:ss format, waiting for a response to a ping request. After a ping timeout is detected, the process is restarted.
requestLimit	Infinite	The number of requests a single worker process can handle. Beyond this value a new worker process starts.
requestQueueLimit	5000	The number of requests allowed in the queue. Any request beyond this limit receives the HTTP error 503 "Server Too Busy" response.
responseDeadlockInterval	00:03:00	The time period (again in hh:mm:ss format) allowed for the worker process to respond to a queued request. After the time period expires, the worker process is restarted. The default is three minutes.
restartQueueLimit	10	After a nonstandard (unexpected) termination of the worker process, incoming requests are queued, waiting for the worker process to become available. The value specifies the number of requests queued.
serverErrorMessageFile	-	A file path (either absolute or relative to the *machine.config* file path) for a file containing the error message to send to the client when a fatal error occurs. If no file is present or the attribute is not set, the string "Server unavailable" is sent. This is the default setting.
shutdownTimeout	00:00:05	The time the worker process is allowed to take when shutting the process down. If this time interval is exceeded, the worker process is forcibly terminated.
timeout	Infinite	If a worker process is not responding, ASP.NET launches a new one after the specific period is elapsed.
webGarden	False	A flag which indicates that the attribute cpuMask is being used. If False (default), this means that all CPU cores are available for worker processes and the operating system decides which CPU will handle the next request.

Additional Settings Outside the ProcessModel Tag

The `<processModel>` tag attributes control most of the relevant settings. However, there are more tags where you can refine the configuration. One important setting is shown in the following:

```
<system.net>
  <connectionManagement>
    <add address="*" maxconnection="100" />
  </connectionManagement>
</system.net>
```

This does not impact your client connections but controls the connections you make from your application to other servers, such as fetching RSS feeds or using Web Services on another server. The default for the attribute `maxconnection` is 2, which is obviously too low. It means you cannot make more than two simultaneous connections to an IP address, from your web application. In the preceding sample the value is set to 100.

Specific Tasks

Using these settings, you can perform specific tasks. The following sections explain how to use the attributes to:

- Recycle the worker process.
- Shut down the worker process.
- Check if the client is still connected.

Recycling the Worker Process

A common task configured in this manner is the recycling of the process. This generally improves the stability and reliability of your web application. There are five ways to recycle a process using the attributes `timeout`, `requestLimit`, `memoryLimit`, `responseDeadlockInterval`, and the pair `pingFrequency`/`pingTimeout`. In the following list, they are explained one by one:

- `timeout="48:00:00"`

  This involves the `timeout` attribute, which simply creates a new process after the specified time interval elapses. For example, the preceding setting will start a new process after 48 hours, or two days. The first request causes the timer to start.

- `requestLimit="1000"`

  Another way is to use the `requestLimit` attribute and an Integer value. A value of 1,000 will start a new worker process after 1,000 requests have been made. This can be useful if your web server's performance degrades after a set number of requests. This could happen if your application or components in it doesn't free all memory.

- `memoryLimit="30"`

  A third way is to let your system watch how much memory the process is consuming. In the preceding example, the attribute `memoryLimit` is set to 30% of the total system memory. Once the limit is reached, the process is killed, a new one is created, and all existing requests are reassigned to the new process. This is helpful when you have a memory leak. Usually you set this option if you have no influence on the application or parts of it, for example, if your applications suffer from a third-party component of that you can't surrender.

- `responseDeadlockInterval="00:02:00"`

  A fourth approach is to use the `responseDeadlockInterval` attribute. The time setting of two minutes will restart the process if there are requests in the queue and if there have been no responses for the last two minutes.

- `pingFrequency="00:00:30"`

- `pingTimeout="00:00:05"`

The final method for recycling the process is to use the `pingFrequency` and `pingTimeout` attributes in tandem. The ISAPI extension pings the process at the `pingFrequency` interval, and restarts it if there is no response within the `pingTimeout` time interval.

IMPACT OF RECYCLING THE WORKER PROCESS

Recycling the worker process might have an impact on current state of application and sessions. By default, you will have an "overlapping" recycle. A new worker process will be created, and will start serving new requests. The old worker process will continue serving existing requests. When all existing requests have been services, the old worker process is shut down. Your Web site should experience no down-time. The actual time it takes for the old worker process to finish servicing all requests depends on what the requests are doing. Most requests are served in a short period of time, but suppose one is performing a long-running database query that takes more time. If so, then the old worker process will hang around for a couple of seconds.

Be aware that if your web application is using in-process session state, then you will lose all sessions during a recycle. Using ASP.NET you can configure your applications to use the ASP.NET session state service, or an SQL Server to store session state, in which case you will not lose session state.

Shutting Down the Process

There are two ways of shutting down the worker process.

- `idleTimeout="00:20:00"`

  The first way uses the `idleTimeout` attribute. If the server has not served any requests for 20 minutes (in this example), then it automatically shuts down the process. If a new request comes in, a new process is started automatically. This might be useful if you experience long periods of inactivity. The server can then handle other tasks better because there is more free memory.

- `shutDownTimeout="00:00:10"`

  The second way is by using the `shutDownTimeout` attribute. This is used as a last resort after the worker process tries to shut down gracefully and fails. In this case, after the time set here has passed, a low-level kill command is performed on the process to ensure its termination. This is useful in situations where the process has crashed and is no longer responding. The setting shown will force a kill after ten seconds.

Checking Whether the Client Is Still Connected

This is useful for eliminating unwanted requests from the queue.

- `clientConnectedCheck="00:00:10"`

    Users can become impatient. If your web server is slow to respond to their requests, they might click on the same link many times. Even if only the last request is returned to them, the server will process all the previous ones. Furthermore, if the user abandons their session with your server, the queue from that user will remain. In the preceding example, the server will check each request at ten seconds intervals after it has entered the queue, to ensure that the user who made it is still connected. If he or she is not, the server discards that request. The request is discarded always before it's passed to the worker process.

Understanding and Using Threads

In ASP.NET, threads are like magic.

Threads are well-known and easy to program using .NET techniques. However, in ASP.NET, threading is handled behind the scenes and consequently regarded by some developers as unimportant. This common misunderstanding of threading can cause poor performance, unpredictable behavior, and, in the end, unreliable applications.

ASP.NET Thread Usage on IIS

Threading in ASP.NET is complicated by the various changes Microsoft applied over the years with each new version of IIS. As you saw in Chapter 1, IIS plays a major part in ASP.NET's request processing. Because of the co-existence of IIS6 and IIS7, I will first explain how threads are handled in IIS6, and then the changes in threading introduced with IIS7.

You may also think of other hosting capabilities ASP.NET supports. Because threading has a direct and explicit relation to multiple requests and high workload, other environments, such as Visual Studio's integrated Web Server, do not handle threads in any special way worth discussing. That's the reason why applications might behave differently when running in either IIS or another Web Server.

Thread Usage with IIS6

Each request from the outside world to the Web Server running ASP.NET engine is handed over to an I/O thread on IIS. This thread comes from the CLR (Common Language Runtime) ThreadPool and returns the status "Pending" to IIS. Having passed the work on to the new thread, IIS is now free to service other requests, such as requests for static resources.

The CLR ThreadPool works like a queue. It can adjust itself according to the actual workload. This means that the situation depends on the frequency of incoming requests and the ability of the processor workload to respond to each request. There are two extreme situations you need to take care of.

First, you might receive many simultaneous requests that are processed quickly. In this case, the ThreadPool will attempt to run only one or two threads per CPU to ensure a very low latency (waiting time).

Second, you might receive a few requests where one is processor intensive and somewhat long-running. Additional incoming requests will cause more threads to be spawned per CPU. The processing time will always be longer in this scenario.

A queue is a clever way to avoid allocating a lot of memory for each request, before processing starts and memory-expensive objects such as HttpRequest are created. Keep in mind that the thread queue is in native memory and has no overhead caused by managed code components. Once a thread is ready for processing, you leave the unmanaged world and start working completely within the managed code realm.

The ThreadPool queue is not the only way to handle a lot of incoming requests. Within each AppDomain there are ways to handle requests that exceed the number of available threads. If there is lot of latency, the ThreadPool starts growing and launches more active threads. However, there are physical limitations; either the system runs out of threads, or the available memory restricts the number of threads.

■**Note** By default the ThreadPool has a limitation of 25 worker threads per CPU and 1000 I/O completion threads.

ASP.NET sets its own limits to ThreadPool usage. If this limit is exceeded, incoming requests are still handled, but another queue is now built on the application level and performance becomes significantly worse. You can control the settings with the following parameters of the `<httpRuntime>` tag:

- `minFreeThreads`: This parameter specifies the minimum number of free threads for new requests. That's used to assure that requests that need additional threads internally are handled properly. The default value is 8.

- `minLocalRequestFreeThreads`: This parameter specifies the number of free threads for local requests. These are requests from a local host in case of child requests issued during processing. This helps prevent deadlocks caused by recursive re-entries. The default value is 4.

Performance Counters are widely used in Windows to monitor a system running with high workload. To observe the internal behavior of the ThreadPool, you can use the following counter: "ASP.NET Applications\Requests in Application Queue."

Any value but zero shows that there is a performance problem on that system, as it indicates that the ThreadPool has at some time run out of threads.

Managing the ThreadPool

Usually the ThreadPool does not require managing, because few sites exceed the default limitations. Additionally, the `autoConfig` settings allow the ASP.NET engine to optimize behavior as much as possible. However, maintaining an ASP.NET system that is running near its limits is the goal of this book. If you experience performance issues, it's time to explore manual intervention. The auto settings assume that the number of concurrently executing requests per CPU is 12. An application with high latency might require higher values.

Thread Usage with IIS7

In Chapter 1, I discussed IIS7 and integrated mode several times. As mentioned earlier, the differences between IIS7 and IIS6 are significant for basic page request processing.

First of all, the queues built on the application level are gone, due to poor performance. The biggest difference is that IIS6 restricts the number of threads, while IIS7 restricts the number of requests. Each thread in IIS6 handles a request, and this—indirectly—limits the number of requests handled in parallel. IIS7 is able, due to the tight integration of ASP.NET within IIS7, to directly restrict the number of requests. It is when you employ asynchronous processing that this makes a difference. Although the processing pipeline is usually synchronous (see Chapter 1), both handlers and modules, can be set up to run asynchronously. I explain this, with examples, in Chapter 3.

For requests that are processed synchronously, the number of threads equals the number of requests, as each request runs in a single thread. If the processing is asynchronous, the number of threads may differ from the number of requests. Imagine that an incoming request starts processing and is running a long-lasting action. The thread is handed over to ASP.NET, and IIS accepts the next incoming request. This leads eventually to more concurrently running requests than threads. ASP.NET gets the request as incoming IIS I/O thread. The CLR ThreadPool is immediately asked to create and start a new thread, and this thread becomes responsible for this very request. As quickly as it starts, it returns with status of "Pending." After this, IIS checks the number of requests currently executing. If this value is too high, the next request is put in a process-wide global queue. This queue is in native code within IIS7.

Configuring the ThreadPool

In the `<processModel>` configuration settings are the following parameters:

- `autoConfig`
- `maxWorkerThreads`
- `maxIoThreads`
- `minWorkerThreads`
- `minIoThreads`

The settings for IIS6 `minFreeThreads` and `minFreeThreads` in the `httpRuntime` tag are still there, but they do nothing. They are there merely for backwards compatibility. But where can you find the settings for IIS7? With .NET 3.5 SP1 the settings become available[1] in *web.config*, as the following shows:

```
<system.web>
  <applicationPool maxConcurrentRequestsPerCPU="12"
                   maxConcurrentThreadsPerCPU="0"
                   requestQueueLimit="5000"/>
</system.web>
```

The *web.config* settings override the settings in the Registry mentioned in the footnote.

They are not values that you would change frequently. You might experiment with different quantities, but the default is usually appropriate. The current settings are a compromise between requests for static resources such as images, and dynamic resources such as aspx pages.

In Chapter 6, I'll explain the extensibility concepts of resource management. This includes the creation of design time expressions to retrieve resources. It's possible to suppress code compilation when your aspx pages consist solely of declarative markup, resources, and expressions. This is a way to optimize overall system performance under particular circumstances.

Now, you could try setting the number of threads per request to 0. If you have only static requests and no (or very few) dynamic ones, and if these dynamic requests are fast due to such techniques like caching, this might improve performance. Imagine that the requests are now being executed within the IIS I/O thread and that there is no handover procedure to the CLR ThreadPool. Less overhead leads to faster resource processing.

The opposite scenario appears when you have many heavily asynchronous operations. In this case, the limit of 12 threads might be too low. Imagine a scenario you'll probably work with: Ajax-enabled applications. These applications have fewer page requests but many background tasks created by JavaScript/web service pairs. This is heavily asynchronous, and a single web page can

---

1. Before the appearance of .NET 3.5 SP1, the settings can be found in the Registry under the path HKEY_LOCAL_MACHINE\SOFTWARE\Microsoft\ASP.NET\2.0.50727.0. A DWORD value named MaxConcurrentRequestsPerCpu limits the number of concurrent requests per CPU. The default is 12.

send large numbers of such requests. If you look into browser-based Outlook clients or Word-like text processing interfaces, you'll see that a lot of background work happens even when the user merely moves the mouse pointer. Settings of up to several thousand are possible in order to handle many simple requests. 5,000 is the limit, without making changes elsewhere in the system.

Server Too Busy

You might be wondering when and why the "Server Too Busy" status is sent to the client. This is HTTP status error 503 and appears among other reasons when the limit of concurrent requests exceeds the default value of 5,000, which could be changes by the requestQueueLimit parameter mentioned before. The actual value is exposed by the "ASP.NET/Requests Current" performance counter.

See the section "Install a Performance Counter" for details on how to monitor and log such values and discover what is happening to your server at any given moment.

Tune the Threading

The previous explanations might discourage you from changing the settings. However, they're worth exploring when performance issues arise or strange errors occur. This section shows some solutions for the following error messages:

- A process serving application pool "name" exceeds time limits during shutdown.
- System.InvalidOperationException: There are not enough free threads in the ThreadPool object to complete the operation.
- HttpException (0x80004005): Request timed out.

To solve the preceding problems, try the following:

- Limit the number of requests that can execute at the same time to approximately 12 per CPU. This limit works well for most applications.
- Permit Web Service callbacks to freely use threads in the ThreadPool.
- Select an appropriate value for the maxconnections attribute. Base your selection on the number of IP addresses and AppDomains that are used (more details follow in the section "Set maxconnection").

Tuning Task by Task

This section gives some examples of how and when to change the default settings of the following values:

- maxWorkerThreads
- minWorkerThreads
- maxIoThreads
- minFreeThreads
- minLocalRequestFreeThreads
- maxconnection
- executionTimeout

Set maxWorkerThreads and maxIoThreads

ASP.NET uses the following two configuration settings to limit the number of worker threads and completion threads used:

```
<processModel maxWorkerThreads="20" maxIoThreads="20">
```

The `maxWorkerThreads` attribute and the `maxIoThreads` attribute are implicitly multiplied by the number of CPUs. In the example, the maximum number of worker threads is 40 if you have a dual-core processor.

Set minFreeThreads and minLocalRequestFreeThreads

ASP.NET also contains the following configuration settings, which determine how many worker threads and completion port threads must be available to start a remote request or a local request:

```
<httpRuntime minFreeThreads="8" minLocalRequestFreeThreads="8">
```

If there are insufficient threads available, the request is queued until sufficient threads are free to handle the request. Therefore, ASP.NET will not execute more than the following number of requests at the same time:

```
(maxWorkerThreads * numCPUs) - minFreeThreads
```

The `minFreeThreads` parameter and the `minLocalRequestFreeThreads` attributes are not implicitly multiplied by the number of CPUs. Assuming you have four CPUs, the formula given equals 24 parallel requests $((8 \times 4) - 8)$.

Set minWorkerThreads

ASP.NET also contains a configuration setting for the number of worker threads to be made available immediately to service a remote request.

```
<processModel minWorkerThreads="1">
```

The specified number of threads that are controlled by this setting can be created at a much faster rate than worker threads that are created from the CLR's default capabilities. These are still regular threads, but they are prepared and ready to use anytime. Requests may suddenly fill the request queue due to a slow-down on a back-end server, a sudden burst of requests from the client end, or something similar that would cause a sudden rise in the number of requests in the queue.

The default value for the `minWorkerThreads` parameter is 1. Microsoft recommends that you set the value for the `minWorkerThreads` parameter to half of the `maxWorkerThreads` value. By default, the `minWorkerThreads` parameter is implicitly multiplied by the number of CPUs.

Set maxconnection

The `maxconnection` attribute determines how many connections can be made to a specific IP address. The setting was mentioned before, but here is a more complex scenario:

```
<connectionManagement>
    <add address="*" maxconnection="2">
    <add address="10.6.205.84" maxconnection="20">
</connectionManagement>
```

The `maxconnection` setting applies at the AppDomain level. Consequently, only two connections (by default) can be made to a specific IP address from each AppDomain in your process.

In this example, all IP addresses accept two connections, except for the specified one at 10.6.205.84, which accepts 20.

Set executionTimeout

ASP.NET uses the following configuration setting to limit the request execution time (in seconds):

```
<httpRuntime executionTimeout="90"/>
```

This refers to the `Server.ScriptTimeout` property exposed by the `HttpServer` object. If you increase the value of the `executionTimeout` attribute, you may have to also modify the `responseDeadlockInterval` attribute of the `<processModel>` tag.

Install a Performance Counter

To monitor the current workload, you can use a Performance Counter. Open the *Reliability and Performance Monitor* tool (PerfMon) by entering *PerfMon* in the *Run* window. Install the counter using these steps:

1. Click on Performance Monitor in the tree view.

2. Right-click and choose New and then Data Collector Set.

3. Give the collection an appropriate name (such as "MonitorIIS") and click Next (see Figure 2-6).

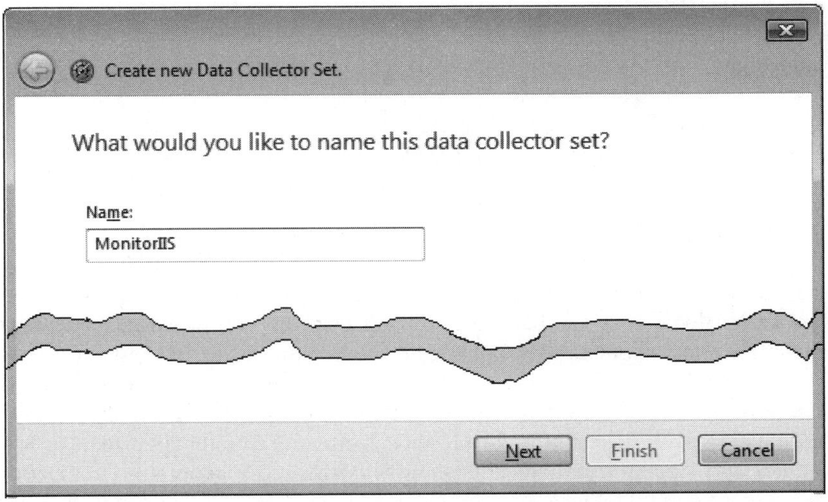

Figure 2-6. *Install new data collection using the Performance Monitor tool.*

4. Choose a directory in which the data is to be saved. The default path is %systemdrive%\PerfLogs\Admin\MonitorIIS, if you have named the collection "MonitorIIS." Click Next.

5. In the last step, you can choose an account with which to run the counter. This is, by default, the current account. If you're logged on as Administrator, it's fine. Otherwise, select an appropriate account by clicking on Change.

6. Finish the wizard with the Finish button.

You can now open your collection within the object's tree view at the left and navigate the path to Reliability and Performance ➤ Data Collector Sets ➤ User Defined ➤ MonitorIIS. There is a default entry here named "System Monitor Log". You can modify this or add a new data collector. Let's add a new one to demonstrate the process. Right-click on the leaf entry in the tree named MonitorIIS and choose New ➤ Data Collector. A wizard launches and asks for a name and collection type. Name it "IISRequest" and choose Performance counter data collector as the type (see Figure 2-7).

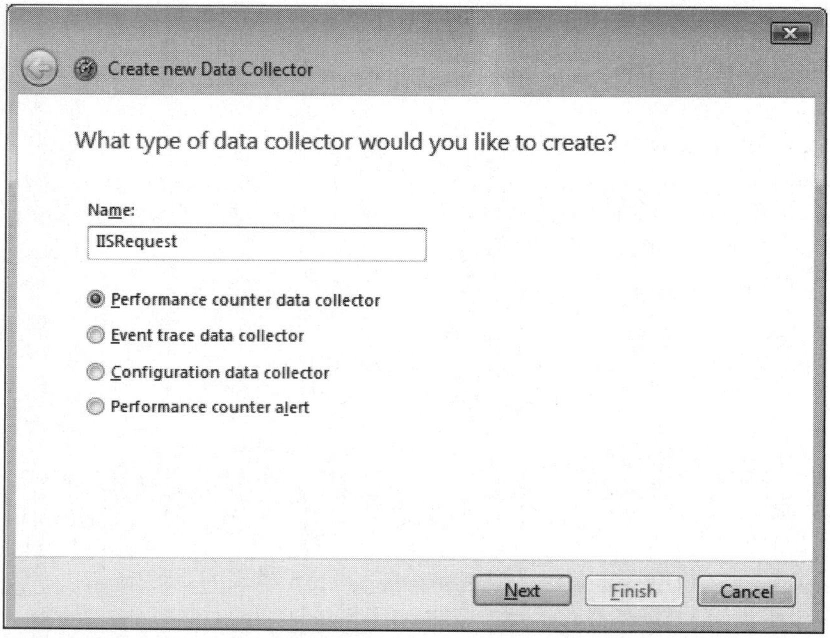

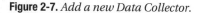

Figure 2-7. *Add a new Data Collector.*

Click on Next to add the counter. On the wizard's next screen, choose Add . . . and search for the counter. In the left-hand area you'll find the Available counters group. Search for the section "ASP.NET Application" and expand it. The list is sorted alphabetically. Scroll down to "Requests In Application Queue". In the "Instances of selected object" group, you'll find all applications. Accept the default selection __Total__ to view all requests. Click Add>> and OK. The monitor begins to watch the counter and saves the results in the file chosen after the counter is started.

To view the results, open the path Reliability and Performance ➤ Reports ➤ User Defined ➤ MonitorIIS ➤ IISRequest. It might take some time to load the results, depending on workload and settings. There are several ways to modify the counter to bind it to specific events. For example, you could add a scheduler to run the counter at a specific time. For instance, if you experience problems between 1 and 2 a.m. on your server, it doesn't make sense to run the tool the whole day and collect an unnecessarily large amount of data.

You can define stop conditions based on time frame or the size of the log file. You can also launch a task when the scheduler stops. Depending on the resources of the server, you could run an application that automatically analyzes the content, sending the log file to an email address, or just copying it to another location.

This short description does not cover the Reliability and Performance Monitor tool in all its glory. It's just a "teaser" so that you know there are powerful tools available to monitor a server and find bottlenecks, failures, and performance loss easily. You can also gather hard data to confirm a problem, find a solution, and validate that your solution fixes the problem. Start here reading more about the tool regarding Windows Server operating system: `http://technet.microsoft.com/en-us/library/cc755081.aspx`.

Threading and Asynchronous Operations

For most scenarios, the internal thread handling is well-designed and functional. However, there are situations where you reach the limits of the default settings. In particular, if a site comes under pressure from too many requests, the internal thread pool can run out of threads and the server will no longer respond as expected. I'll discuss several techniques for overcoming this. I'll consider how the common language runtime thread pool is used by ASP.NET to service requests, as well as looking into the pooling mechanisms used for handlers, modules, and applications.

I'll also show the threading usage independent of other techniques and the asynchronous processing of requests using internal features to solve common issues.

Threading in ASP.NET

To efficiently service multiple client requests, Web Servers make extensive use of concurrency by launching multiple processes and spawning multiple threads to service requests. Considering the construction and behavior of the ASP.NET engine, it seems that developers need not concern themselves with threading at all, as the challenging aspects are handled internally. This is correct for most scenarios; page requests are serviced on the same thread, and a separate instance is created to service each new request. However, there are scenarios where you reach the limits of this model—as every model has limits—and need to extend the behavior.

First of all, a clear understanding of the internal behavior is required. Some parts have been explained in the previous sections but I will repeat it from the perspective of threading. The process-wide CLR thread pool services requests. The thread pool size is set to 25 worker threads and 25 I/O threads by default. Recall the `<processModel>` settings explained already:

```
<processModel enable="true"
            maxWorkerThreads="25"
            maxIoThreads="25" />
```

As explained in Chapter 1, for each incoming request an instance of the type `HttpApplication` is created. To avoid reallocating applications and modules, each AppDomain holds a pool of application instances and HTTP modules. The size of this pool is also 25—that means that 25 requests can be handled per worker process.

The Need for Asynchrony

Imagine that you need to exclusively request a resource. As long as one person is using an application, this is not a problem. However, web applications are typically employed by many, if not thousands, of concurrent users. The thread pool and thread handling design allows several requests to be executed in parallel to improve the user's experience when using a web application. Limiting the number of threads is important in order to allow more than one request per CPU or core. Creating a vast number of threads can cause a system to a grind to a halt.

However, a request can launch different kinds of tasks. Processing a page and sending resources to the client is the most common action. Requesting data from a database, RSS feed, or Web Service is another. Requesting data can be time consuming, rather than processor intensive. What happens then? The number of threads in the thread pool quickly reaches its limit and subsequent requests are not handled as expected. Despite this, the CPU is only idling. As you learned in the previous sections, the settings allow you to change the number of concurrent threads. But this is not a solution either, as your system has to handle both kinds of requests: short-lived requests for resources and long-running queries against other servers.

To make things clearer, look at Listing 2-7. It delays a request while demanding little from the CPU. It displays the thread ID to show whether or not a new thread is created to handle the request.

Listing 2-7. *A Simple Page That Slows Down a Request*

```
<%@ Page Language="C#" %>
<%@ Import Namespace="System.Reflection" %>
<%@ Import Namespace="System.Threading" %>

<script runat="server">
  protected void Page_Load(object src, EventArgs e)
  {
    Thread.Sleep(3000);
    Response.Output.Write("Slow Response, Thread ID={0}", ➥
                AppDomain.GetCurrentThreadId());
  }
</script>
```

To test it, open the page in a browser. Open the page in more browser windows and refresh all the pages within the three-second (3000 millisecond) period. You'll see that the thread ID exposed by the script changes for each request. Once the period is over, the next request receives a recycled thread from a previous request. Several long-running requests can fill the thread pool and easily reach the limit of 25 concurrent threads.

Removing the Sleep call (Listing 2-7) will result in a faster running page. You won't be able to request the page again while the server is handling the previous one. The thread IDs demonstrate that all requests run on the same thread and the thread pool is never filled up to its limit (see Listing 2-8).

Listing 2-8. *A Simple Page That Performs Well (Threading/FastThread.aspx)*

```
<%@ Page Language="C#" %>
<%@ Import Namespace="System.Reflection" %>

<script runat="server">
  protected void Page_Load(object src, EventArgs e)
  {
    Response.Output.Write("Fast Response, Thread ID={0}",
                AppDomain.GetCurrentThreadId());
  }
</script>
```

Microsoft offers a stress test tool for simulating multiple concurrent requests even in the development environment. See the sidebar about the Web Stress Tool for more information.

WEB STRESS TOOL

The web application stress tool can be downloaded from: `http://www.microsoft.com/downloads/details.aspx?familyid=e2c0585a-062a-439e-a67d-75a89aa36495&displaylang=en`.

Unfortunately, the tool is quite old and Microsoft has not refreshed it to support newer environments. So if you run it on Vista, a DLL named msvcp50.dll is missing. You may find the file on the Web or you can safely copy it from the support files section provided with this book. Perform these steps to install the stress test tool:

- Download the setup.exe from the address previously shown.
- Download msvcp50.dll from the Apress support Web site.
- Copy the unzipped file to folder %WinDir%\system (you must run with higher privileges to do this). Note that this is really system, not system32!
- Install the stress test tool.
- Run it once to check that it's working. Start it as an Administrator.

Now you can use the tool as outlined in the following sections.

There are few alternative tools out there you might consider for your own stress testing. See Alik Levin's WCAT at `http://blogs.msdn.com/alikl/archive/2008/03/09/stress-test-asp-net-web-application-with-free-wcat-tool.aspx` or the Fiddler Add-in neXpert, available at `http://www.microsoft.com/downloads/details.aspx?familyid=5975da52-8ce6-48bd-9b3c-756a625024bb&displaylang=en`.

Working with the Stress Test Tool

A stress test is what the name implies—your application is forced to handle as many requests as necessary to feel stressed. To walk through this stress test, you'll need to set up the pages previously shown (see Listings 2-8 and 2-9 later in this chapter) within your IIS environment, which you're able to run from a browser manually. Follow these steps to set up the script in the stress test tool. I have set IIS to use this path:

```
http://localhost/Threading/SlowThread.aspx
http://localhost/Threading/FastThread.aspx
```

First, set up the script by adding the content tree—the pages requested from the tool (see Figure 2-8).

The content tree allows you to set the actions the tool performs several times. Alternatively, you can record a session to save the page load action. However, in this script, only one page is called using a GET command, so recording is not necessary.

The settings define how the tool operates on the server. In Figure 2-9, I set 30 threads, which create 30 concurrent requests. This runs for 20 seconds as quickly as possible. There is no throttling and no other options are used. This is the configuration that should cause the server to create 25 threads and bring the thread pool to its limit.

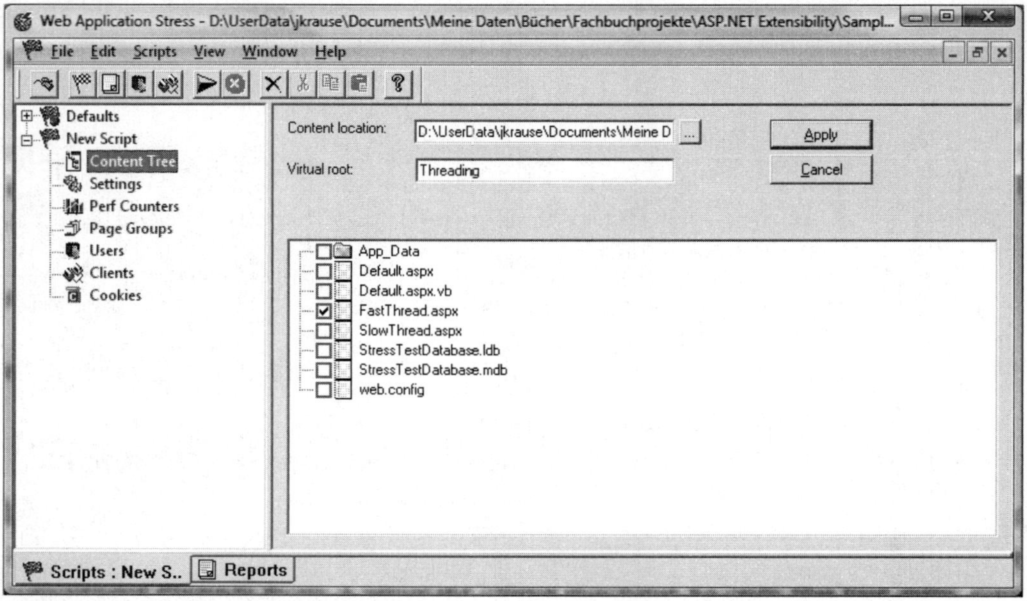

Figure 2-8. *Set the content for a stress test.*

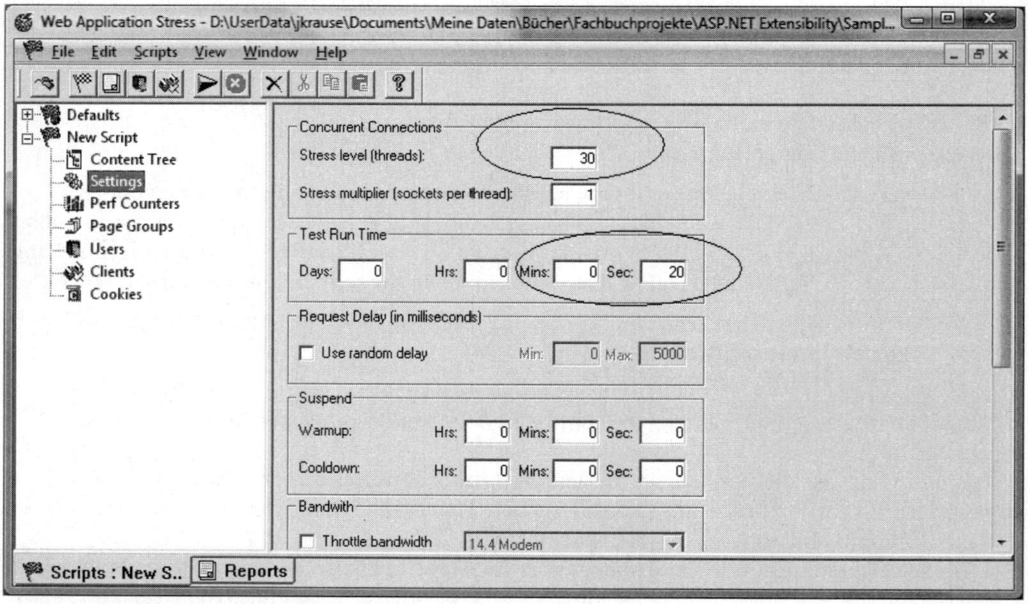

Figure 2-9. *Settings used to force the test*

Table 2-2 shows the results of some stress tests. Remember that there is a wide range of possible values for response time, depending on your machine, its configuration, and what other applications and services are currently running. It's the relative values that are significant here.

Table 2-2. *Test Results Using a Web Stress Test Tool*

Threads	File	Hits	Average Response Time
100	FastThread.aspx	21093	45 ms
20	FastThread.aspx	21034	8.3 ms
100	SlowThread.aspx	33	6,108 ms
20	SlowThread.aspx	32	4,654 ms
100	Both (see the following)	98	2,050 ms (FastThread.aspx)

These results are not surprising. The server is less able to handle the requests as the number of parallel threads increases. Because we're forcing IIS to queue the requests, this causes additional overhead. Running the client against both FastThread.aspx and SlowThread.aspx, however, increases the average response time for FastThread.aspx requests to 2.05 seconds and only 98 hits being handled. For SlowThread.aspx, the number of threads makes no significant difference. This is the worst case—because of long-running requests, fast ones are not served quickly. Increasing the CPU power will not help. The slow page does not consume any CPU power because there is nothing to calculate. The delay you see is due to the saturation of the thread pool. Even the fast requests are queued until a thread is released.

This demonstrates that some pages can influence the performance of other requests even if they have nothing to do with each other. What is the solution?

I discussed previously the various settings available for improving the system's behavior. In the stress test I used 100 threads. Increasing the thread pool limits might help. However, the real world does not have a defined number of requests regularly arriving. Finding the right value is anything but easy. It could change depending on user behavior, server settings, network connection, and application code—which means that there is no right answer.

The solution we're looking for should free the threads in the thread pool to hold the utilization low and have enough threads available at any time. In other words, each page should behave like a fast-running page. This brings us to asynchronous handlers.

■**Note** Chapter 3 is dedicated to the world of handlers and modules. Here I discuss only the portion directly related to threading issues. For more information about handlers, refer to the next chapter.

Custom Thread Pool and Asynchronous Handlers

While most ASP.NET pages and handlers are serviced synchronously on threads drawn from the thread pool, it is possible to create handlers and pages that service requests asynchronously.

Asynchronous handlers implement the `IHttpAsyncHandler` interface, which derives from `IHttpHandler` (see Listing 2-9).

Listing 2-9. *Definition of the IHttpAsynchHandler Interface*

```
public interface IHttpAsyncHandler : IHttpHandler
{
  IAsyncResult BeginProcessRequest(HttpContext ctx,
                                   AsyncCallback cb,
                                   object obj);
  void EndProcessRequest(IAsyncResult ar);
}
```

The interface follows the typical pattern for asynchronous actions—it has a method for indicating the beginning and one for indicating the end of a process. Handlers must have a method named ProcessRequest due to the implemented IHttpHandler interface. Instead of calling this method, the asynchronous handler calls the BeginProcessRequest method. In this method, you launch a new thread and manage things, which can take some time. The method returns immediately, providing a reference to an IAsyncResult instance. This frees the thread from the thread pool. A new thread is then used to perform the long-running action. When the internal (or private) thread returns, the EndProcessRequest method is called. The IAsyncResult instance is handed over in order to parameterize the call. Cleanup actions, such as closing a database connection, are best placed here.

Asynchronous Handler with a Delegate

Creating an asynchronous handler with a delegate is the most common approach. Delegates called with BeginInvoke implicitly create a new thread (see Listing 2-10).

Listing 2-10. *A Handler Using IHttpAsyncHandler*

```
<%@ WebHandler Language="C#" Class="Apress.Threading.AsyncHandlers.AsyncHandler" %>

using System;
using System.Web;
using System.Threading;
using System.Diagnostics;
using System.Reflection;

namespace Apress.Threading.AsyncHandlers
{

    public delegate void ProcessRequestDelegate(HttpContext ctx);

    public class AsyncHandler : IHttpAsyncHandler
    {
        public void ProcessRequest(HttpContext ctx)
        {
            System.Threading.Thread.Sleep(2000);
            ctx.Response.Output.Write(
                    "Async Delegate, Thread ID={0}",
                    AppDomain.GetCurrentThreadId());
        }

        public bool IsReusable
        {
            get { return true; }
        }
```

```
        public IAsyncResult BeginProcessRequest(HttpContext ctx, ➡
                                                AsyncCallback cb, ➡
                                                object obj)
        {
            ProcessRequestDelegate prg = new ProcessRequestDelegate(ProcessRequest);
            return prg.BeginInvoke(ctx, cb, obj);
        }

        public void EndProcessRequest(IAsyncResult ar)
        {
        }
    }
}
```

Call this handler by using a browser, as before, to test that it's running properly. The following URL assumes that you have the project configured in IIS using a virtual directory named "Threading":

```
http://localhost/Threading/AsyncThreadDelegate.ashx
```

The process starts with the method `BeginProcessRequest`. Using the delegate and its `BeginInvoke` method, the method `ProcessRequest` is called. Then the `Sleep` method simulates something long running without performing anything on the CPU. Because there is nothing to clean up, no code is required in `EndProcessRequest`.

Now it's time to see what the stress test tool is reporting.

If you run the test as before, you can see that the results are nearly identical. What is going on here? Why write asynchronous delegates if there is no speed improvement at all? The reason is in the way ASP.NET internally handles the threading.

Recall that when I first introduced the term "thread pool," it was called a "process wide thread pool." The asynchronous handler still runs in the very same process, which leads to a lack of improvement. The original thread is freed, but the new one is taken from the same thread pool. The same thing would happen if you used `ThreadPool.QueueUserWorkItem` from the `System.Threading` namespace. You need to find from what other thread source you can get a new thread.

Asynchronous Handler with Custom Threads

Before you can implement the whole solution, another interface is required—`IAsynchResult`—as the return result is now essential. The definition is short—just four properties (see Listing 2-11).

Listing 2-11. *The Definition of IAsyncResult*

```
public interface IAsyncResult
{
    public object     AsyncState             { get; }
    public bool       CompletedSynchronously { get; }
    public bool       IsCompleted            { get; }
    public WaitHandle AsyncWaitHandle        { get; }
}
```

Our actual implementation of the `IAsynchResult` interface (Listing 2-12) has two additional properties: a reference to the `HttpContext` object, and a reference to the callback object. The callback method is invoked later, when processing is complete. The `AsyncState` object is optional; you can use it to store private data. `AsyncWaitHandle` returns a `WaitHandle` object, which is used to signal when the request is complete. Using the `CompleteRequest` method implemented additionally to the requirements of the interface, the calling class can execute the `EndProcessRequest` method. In this routine, the `WaitHandle` object is triggered. Either way, the `IsCompleted` property shows that the object has reached the completed state.

Listing 2-12. *The Implementation of IAsyncResult (from AsyncThreadCallback.ashx)*

```
class AsyncRequestState : IAsyncResult
{

    internal HttpContext _ctx;
    internal AsyncCallback _cb;
    internal object _data;
    private bool _isCompleted;
    private ManualResetEvent _ completeEvent;

    public AsyncRequestState(HttpContext ctx, ➡
                             AsyncCallback cb, ➡
                             object data)
    {
      _ctx = ctx;
      _cb = cb;
      _data = data;
    }

    internal HttpContext CurrentContext
    {
        get
        {
          return _ctx;
        }
    }

    internal void EndRequest()
    {
        _isCompleted = true;
        lock (this)
        {
            if (_completeEvent!= null)
                _ completeEvent.Set();
        }
        // invoke registered callback, if any
        if (_cb != null)
            _cb(this);
    }

    public object AsyncState
    {
        get
        {
            return (_data);
        }
    }

    public bool CompletedSynchronously
    {
        get
        {
            return (false);
```

```
        }
    }

    public bool IsCompleted
    {
        get
        {
            return (_isCompleted);
        }
    }

    public WaitHandle AsyncWaitHandle
    {
        get
        {
            lock (this)
            {
                if (_completeEvent == null)
                    _ completeEvent = new ManualResetEvent(false);

                return _completeEvent;
            }
        }
    }
}
```

The next step is to spawn a new thread to process the request. The method called on this new thread will need access to the state cached in the AsyncRequestState class previously shown. To pass necessary data to this object, a parameterized thread is used, based on ParameterizedThreadStart class.

The handler itself is similar to the one already introduced. The definition for the ashx page looks like this:

```
<%@ WebHandler Language="C#" ➥
            Class="Apress.Threading.AsyncHandlers.CustomAsyncHandler" %>
```

The ProcessRequest method must be present, as it is required by the interface IHttpAsyncHandler, but you don't use it. The whole work is split between the BeginProcessRequest and EndProcessRequest methods. In the BeginProcessRequest method the AsyncRequestState object is created, along with the reference to the context and callback (see Listing 2-13).

Listing 2-13. *The Implementation of AsyncResult (AsyncThreadCallback.ashx)*

```
public class CustomAsyncHandler : IHttpAsyncHandler
{
    public void ProcessRequest(HttpContext ctx)
    {
        // not used
    }

    public bool IsReusable
    {
        get { return false; }
    }

    public IAsyncResult BeginProcessRequest(HttpContext ctx, ➥
                                            AsyncCallback cb, ➥
                                            object obj)
```

```
    {
        AsyncRequestState reqState = ➡
                        new AsyncRequestState(ctx, cb, obj);
        ParameterizedThreadStart ts = new ParameterizedThreadStart(ProcessThread);
        Thread t = new Thread(ts);
        t.Start(reqState);

        return reqState;
    }

    public void EndProcessRequest(IAsyncResult ar)
    {
        AsyncRequestState ars = ar as AsyrcRequestState;
        if (ars != null)
        {
            ars.CurrentContext.Response.Write("End Request reached");
        }
    }

    private void ProcessThread(object obj)
    {
        Thread.Sleep(2000);
        AsyncRequestState asr = obj as AsyncRequestState;
        asr.CurrentContext.Response.Output.Write( ➡
                "Async Thread, Thread ID = {0}", ➡
                AppDomain.GetCurrentThreadId());
        // signal end of processing
        asr.EndRequest();
    }

}
```

Let's look at the code to understand how it's working. Figure 2-10 shows the thread usage during internal processing. Initiated by the request, the process starts by calling the BeginProcessRequest method. The AsyncHandler creates the helper objects required and launches the new custom thread independent of the thread pool. The custom thread runs and the thread pool thread is released. Once the process is completed, the end is signaled via the callback method and the request is finished.

The response held in memory is waiting for the thread to complete. This might seem disappointing, because it doesn't make anything faster. The page is still waiting for the slow operation to finish, and so is the user. Remember the thread pool issue, however; once the pool runs out of threads, the performance of the whole server is reduced and no more requests are handled properly. The advantage of custom threads is not a faster response for one user but for all users.

In step 2, as shown in Figure 2-11, the call to EndRequest indicates the end of the process and terminates the request. Once called, the response is complete and sent to the browser. This means that you can add content to the response at any time before the EndProcessRequest method is called. In the example code (Listing 2-14) the Response.Output.Write method demonstrates this.

Run the stress test again to see whether you find an improvement. Under pressure it performs better, and the thread pool no longer runs out of threads. This allows the site to accept incoming requests at any time, and the whole server appears to be more responsive. Again, the processing time for a single page is the same.

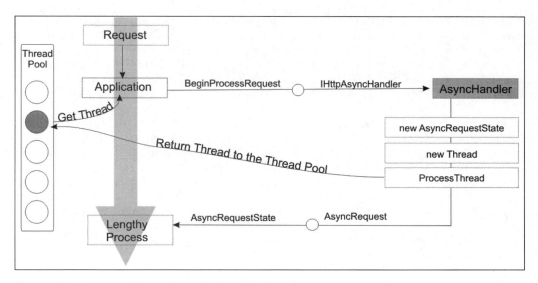

Figure 2-10. *First step of the processing using an asynchronous handler*

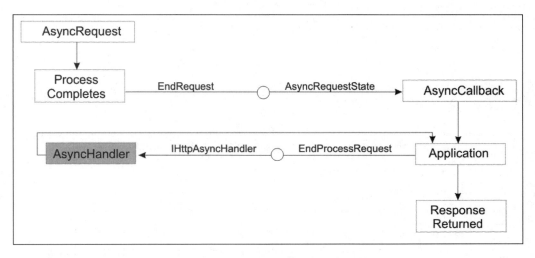

Figure 2-11. *Second step of the processing using an asynchronous handler*

Creating a Custom Thread Pool

This technique is useful for many extensibility projects. In Chapter 3, I'll show more examples of practical implementations that solve common issues. All handlers explained there use simple synchronous operations. You can implement them all as asynchronous counterparts using the techniques described here. Using asynchronous handlers, you'll see how to improve the overall performance of an ASP.NET site drastically. The thread issues and handlers that I discuss here are just one solution.

There is another issue that can be found easily using the stress test tool. In one of the previous paragraphs I wrote "accept incoming requests at any time." This is quite a claim, as it assumes that the server will respond no matter how many requests arrive, just by creating new threads. However, the operating system, CPU power, available memory, and architectural restrictions of the hardware may stop the code from creating new threads. It is possible for too many threads to be created, in which case they will block each other and make the system slow and unresponsive.

You might ask "Why not use a thread pool?" Unfortunately, .NET has only one thread pool internally and it is used by ASP.NET. That's why using `ThreadPool.QueueUserWorkItem` does not work. Our task now is the creation of our own thread pool. Several people have done this successfully. Mike Woodring wrote a version which is useful and fits our needs, using the code in an asynchronous handler. The original version can be found on his page: `http://www.bearcanyon.com/`.

I have adapted his code to suit our needs for a handler. There are several clever aspects to this code. The usage of `HttpContext` is much simpler. In the previous example, a reference to the context object was stored and the use of `HttpContext.Current` was forbidden. It is not good programming practice to change well-known method calls. Apart from this example there are several other implementations out there that might help as well. Alternatively you may have a look at Jon Skeet's CustomThreadPool that's part of his "Miscellaneous Utility Library": `http://www.yoda.arachsys.com/csharp/miscutil/`

However, the custom thread pool explained here is just an example of where ASP.NET extensibility approaches can go and how to deal with very specific conditions.

Overview

A custom thread pool is not a trivial piece of code. It consists of several classes, delegates, and an interface as well. First, have a look at the types defined in the project:

- CustomThreadPool
- IWorkRequest
- WorkRequest
- ThreadInfo
- ThreadWrapper

The CustomThreadPool class is the core implementation. It supports a bunch of characteristics. Apart from the features provided by the CLR's thread pool, those are the crucial ones:

- It can be explicitly started and stopped (and restarted).
- It has configurable thread priority.
- It has configurable foreground/background characteristic.
- It has configurable minimum thread count (called "static" or "permanent" threads).
- It has configurable maximum thread count (threads added over the minimum are called "dynamic" threads).
- It has configurable dynamic thread creation trigger (the point at which the pool decides to add new threads).
- It has configurable dynamic thread decay interval (the time period after which an idle dynamic thread will exit).
- It supports configurable limit (optional) to the request queue size (by default unbounded).
- The pool extends WaitHandle that becomes signaled when last thread exits.
- Operations enqueued to the pool are cancellable.
- Enqueue operation supports early bound approach (like the `ThreadPool.QueueUserWorkItem` type) as well as late bound approach (like the `Control.Invoke/BeginInvoke` approach) to posting work requests.

- Optional propagation of calling thread call context to target.
- Optional propagation of calling thread principal to target.
- Optional propagation of calling thread HttpContext to target.
- It has support for started/stopped event subscription and notification.

This all makes it a well-designed tool to extend the thread pool behavior where necessary.

The Implementation of the Custom Thread Pool

The next code listings show the implementation in several steps. The core functionality is explained in-line (see Listing 2-14).

Listing 2-14. *The Basic Thread Pool Implementation*

```
public sealed class CustomThreadPool : WaitHandle
{
    // Default parameters
    // Decay time in ms made of minutes * sec * ms
    const int DEFAULT_DYNAMIC_THREAD_DECAY_TIME = 5 * 60 * 1000;
    // milliseconds
    const int DEFAULT_NEW_THREAD_TRIGGER_TIME = 500;
    const ThreadPriority DEFAULT_THREAD_PRIORITY = ThreadPriority.Normal;
    // unbounded
    const int DEFAULT_REQUEST_QUEUE_LIMIT = -1;

    public CustomThreadPool( int initialThreadCount, int maxThreadCount, ➥
                             string poolName )
        : this( initialThreadCount, maxThreadCount, poolName,
                DEFAULT_NEW_THREAD_TRIGGER_TIME,
                DEFAULT_DYNAMIC_THREAD_DECAY_TIME,
                DEFAULT_THREAD_PRIORITY,
                DEFAULT_REQUEST_QUEUE_LIMIT )
    {
    }

    public CustomThreadPool(int initialThreadCount, int maxThreadCount, ➥
                            string poolName, ➥
                            int newThreadTrigger, int dynamicThreadDecayTime, ➥
                            ThreadPriority threadPriority, int requestQueueLimit )
    {
        Handle = stopCompleteEvent.Handle;
        if( maxThreadCount < initialThreadCount )
        {
            throw new ArgumentException("Maximum thread count must be >=
                                        initial thread count.", "maxThreadCount");
        }
        if( dynamicThreadDecayTime <= 0 )
        {
            throw new ArgumentException("Dynamic thread decay time cannot be <= 0.",
                                        "dynamicThreadDecayTime");
        }
        if( newThreadTrigger <= 0 )
        {
            throw new ArgumentException("New thread trigger time cannot be <= 0.",
                                        "newThreadTrigger");
```

```
        }
        this.initialThreadCount = initialThreadCount;
        this.maxThreadCount = maxThreadCount;
        this.requestQueueLimit = (requestQueueLimit < 0 ?
                            DEFAULT_REQUEST_QUEUE_LIMIT : requestQueueLimit);
        this.decayTime = dynamicThreadDecayTime;
        this.newThreadTrigger = new TimeSpan(➡
                            TimeSpan.TicksPerMillisecond * newThreadTrigger);
        this.threadPriority = threadPriority;
        this.requestQueue = new Queue(➡
                            requestQueueLimit < 0 ? 4096 : requestQueueLimit);

        if( poolName == null )
        {
            throw new ArgumentNullException("poolName", ➡
                                    "Thread pool name cannot be null");
        }
        else
        {
            this.threadPoolName = poolName;
        }
    }

    // The Priority & DynamicThreadDecay properties are not thread safe
    // and can only be set before Start is called.
    public ThreadPriority Priority
    {
        get { return(threadPriority); }

        set
        {
            if( hasBeenStarted )
            {
                throw new InvalidOperationException("Cannot adjust thread ➡
                        priority after pool has been started.");
            }

            threadPriority = value;
        }
    }

    public int DynamicThreadDecay
    {
        get { return(decayTime); }

        set
        {
            if( hasBeenStarted )
            {
                throw new InvalidOperationException("Cannot adjust dynamic ➡
                        thread decay time after pool has been started.");
            }
            if( value <= 0 )
            {
                throw new ArgumentException("Dynamic thread decay time ➡
                                    cannot be <= 0.", "value");
            }
```

```
            decayTime = value;
        }
}

public int NewThreadTrigger
{
    get { return((int)newThreadTrigger.TotalMilliseconds); }

    set
    {
        if( value <= 0 )
        {
            throw new ArgumentException("New thread trigger time cannot ➥
                                be <= 0.", "value");
        }
        lock( this )
        {
            newThreadTrigger = new TimeSpan(➥
                                TimeSpan.TicksPerMillisecond * value);
        }
    }
}

public int RequestQueueLimit
{
  get { return(requestQueueLimit); }
  set { requestQueueLimit = (value < 0 ? DEFAULT_REQUEST_QUEUE_LIMIT : value);}
}

public int AvailableThreads
{
    get { return(maxThreadCount - currentThreadCount); }
}

public int MaxThreads
{
    get { return(maxThreadCount); }

    set
    {
        if( value < initialThreadCount )
        {
            throw new ArgumentException("Maximum thread count must ➥
                    be >= initial thread count.", "MaxThreads");
        }

        maxThreadCount = value;
    }
}

public bool IsStarted
{
    get { return(hasBeenStarted); }
}

public bool PropogateThreadPrincipal
{
```

```csharp
        get { return(propogateThreadPrincipal); }
        set { propogateThreadPrincipal = value; }
    }

    public bool PropogateCallContext
    {
        get { return(propogateCallContext); }
        set { propogateCallContext = value; }
    }

    public bool PropogateHttpContext
    {
        get { return(propogateHttpContext); }
        set { propogateHttpContext = value; }
    }

    public bool PropogateCASMarkers
    {
        get { return(propogateCASMarkers); }
    }

    public bool IsBackground
    {
        get { return(useBackgroundThreads); }

        set
        {
            if( hasBeenStarted )
            {
                throw new InvalidOperationException("Cannot adjust background ➥
                        status after pool has been started.");
            }

            useBackgroundThreads = value;
        }
    }

    public event ThreadPoolDelegate Started;
    public event ThreadPoolDelegate Stopped;

    public void OnStopped()
    {
        if (this.Stopped != null)
        {
            this.Stopped();
        }
    }

    public void OnStarted()
    {
        if (this.Started != null)
        {
            this.Started();
        }
    }

    public void Start()
```

```
{
    lock( this )
    {
        if( hasBeenStarted )
        {
            throw new InvalidOperationException("Pool has already ➥
                                     been started.");
        }

        hasBeenStarted = true;

        // Check to see if there were already items posted to the queue
        // before Start was called.  If so, reset their timestamps to
        // the current time.
        if( requestQueue.Count > 0 )
        {
            ResetWorkRequestTimes();
        }

        for( int n = 0; n < initialThreadCount; n++ )
        {
            ThreadWrapper thread = ➥
                new ThreadWrapper(this, true, threadPriority, ➥
                              string.Format("{0} (static)", threadPoolName));
            thread.Start();
        }
        OnStarted();
    }
}

public void Stop()
{
    InternalStop(false, Timeout.Infinite);
}

public void StopAndWait()
{
    InternalStop(true, Timeout.Infinite);
}

public bool StopAndWait( int timeout )
{
    return InternalStop(true, timeout);
}

private bool InternalStop( bool wait, int timeout )
{
    if( !hasBeenStarted )
    {
        throw new InvalidOperationException("Cannot stop a thread pool ➥
                                     that has not been started yet.");
    }
    lock(this)
    {
        stopInProgress = true;
        Monitor.PulseAll(this);
    }
```

```
        if( wait )
        {
            bool stopComplete = WaitOne(timeout, true);

            if( stopComplete )
            {
                // If the stop was successful, we can support being
                // restarted.  If the stop was requested, but not
                // waited on, then we don't support restarting.
                hasBeenStarted = false;
                stopInProgress = false;
                requestQueue.Clear();
                stopCompleteEvent.Reset();
            }
            return(stopComplete);
        }
        return(true);
    }

    // Overloads for the early bound WorkRequestDelegate-based targets.
    public bool PostRequest( WorkRequestDelegate cb )
    {
        return PostRequest(cb, (object)null);
    }

    public bool PostRequest( WorkRequestDelegate cb, object state )
    {
        IWorkRequest notUsed;
        return PostRequest(cb, state, out notUsed);
    }

    public bool PostRequest( WorkRequestDelegate cb, object state, ➡
                             out IWorkRequest reqStatus )
    {
        WorkRequest request = ➡
            new WorkRequest( cb, state, ➡
                             propogateThreadPrincipal, propogateCallContext, ➡
                             propogateHttpContext, propogateCASMarkers );
        reqStatus = request;
        return PostRequest(request);
    }

    // Overloads for the late bound Delegate.DynamicInvoke-based targets.
    public bool PostRequest( Delegate cb, object[] args )
    {
        IWorkRequest notUsed;
        return PostRequest(cb, args, out notUsed);
    }

    public bool PostRequest( Delegate cb, object[] args, ➡
                             out IWorkRequest reqStatus )
    {
        WorkRequest request = ➡
            new WorkRequest( cb, args, ➡
                             propogateThreadPrincipal, propogateCallContext, ➡
                             propogateHttpContext, propogateCASMarkers );
        reqStatus = request;
```

```
        return PostRequest(request);
}

// The actual implementation of PostRequest.
bool PostRequest( WorkRequest request )
{
    lock(this)
    {
        // A requestQueueLimit of -1 means the queue is "unbounded"
        // (subject to available resources).  IOW, no artificial limit
        // has been placed on the maximum # of requests that can be
        // placed into the queue.
        if( (requestQueueLimit == -1) || ➡
            (requestQueue.Count < requestQueueLimit) )
        {
            try
            {
                requestQueue.Enqueue(request);
                Monitor.Pulse(this);
                return(true);
            }
            catch
            {
            }

        }
    }

    return(false);
}

internal void ResetWorkRequestTimes()
{
    lock( this )
    {
        DateTime newTime = DateTime.Now;
        foreach( WorkRequest wr in requestQueue )
        {
            wr.workingTime = newTime;
        }
    }
}

private bool hasBeenStarted = false;
private bool stopInProgress = false;

internal bool StopInProgress
{
    get { return stopInProgress; }
}
private readonly string threadPoolName;

public string ThreadPoolName
{
    get { return threadPoolName; }
}
// Initial # of threads to create (called "static threads" in this class).
```

```csharp
private readonly int         initialThreadCount;
// Cap for thread count.
// Threads added above initialThreadCount are called "dynamic" threads.
private int maxThreadCount;
public int MaxThreadCount
{
    get { return maxThreadCount; }
}
// Current # of threads in the pool (static + dynamic).
private int currentThreadCount = 0;
public int CurrentThreadCount
{
    get { return currentThreadCount; }
    set { currentThreadCount = value; }
}
// If a dynamic thread is idle for this period of time w/o processing
// work requests, it will exit.
private int decayTime;

public int DecayTime
{
    get { return decayTime; }
}
// If a work request sits in the queue this long before being processed,
// a new thread will be added to queue up to the max.
private TimeSpan newThreadTrigger;
public TimeSpan NewThreadTriggerTimeSpan
{
    get { return newThreadTrigger; }
    set { newThreadTrigger = value; }
}
private ThreadPriority       threadPriority;
// Signaled after Stop called and last thread exits.
private ManualResetEvent stopCompleteEvent = new ManualResetEvent(false);
public ManualResetEvent StopCompleteEvent
{
    get { return stopCompleteEvent; }
}
private Queue requestQueue;

public Queue RequestQueue
{
    get { return requestQueue; }
}
// Throttle for maximum # of work requests that can be added.
private int requestQueueLimit;
private bool useBackgroundThreads = true;

public bool UseBackgroundThreads
{
    get { return useBackgroundThreads; }
}
private bool                 propogateThreadPrincipal = false;
private bool                 propogateCallContext = false;
private bool                 propogateHttpContext = false;
private bool                 propogateCASMarkers = false;

}
```

Before looking into the implementation details of the usage scenario, it is helpful to understand how it works:

```
CustomThreadPool tp1 = new CustomThreadPool(2, 6, "Pool1");
tp1.Priority = System.Threading.ThreadPriority.BelowNormal;
tp1.NewThreadTrigger = 400;
tp1.DynamicThreadDecay = 5000;
tp1.Start();
```

This starts a new thread pool using two initial threads and defines a maximum of six with low priority. The decay time is five seconds for testing purposes—the default is five minutes. The new thread trigger is set to 400 milliseconds.

The code used to test the thread pool requires an interface and a delegate, as defined in Listing 2-15.

Listing 2-15. *Delegates and Base Interface for the Thread Pool*

```
public delegate void WorkRequestDelegate(object state, ➥
                                DateTime requestEnqueueTime );
public delegate void ThreadPoolDelegate();

#region IWorkRequest interface
public interface IWorkRequest
{
    bool Cancel();
}
#endregion
```

Once the pool is up and running, you can issue requests to get threads out of it. Doing so requires a callback that's responsible to handle the workload.

```
WorkRequestDelegate cb1 = new WorkRequestDelegate(CallbackOne);
string arg = "";
```

Then a request internally starts the thread, using the callback to handle the worker method:

```
tp1.PostRequest(cb1, arg);
```

Once the threads are no longer required, the pool can be stopped:

```
tp1.StopAndWait();
```

This method call assures that the currently running threads can properly end its work before the thread pool is going down (see Listing 2-16).

Listing 2-16. *The ThreadInfo Class That Provides the Thread-Specific HttpContext*

```
internal class ThreadInfo
{
    public static ThreadInfo Capture(bool propogateThreadPrincipal, ➥
                                bool propogateCallContext, ➥
                                bool propogateHttpContext, ➥
                                bool propogateCASMarkers)
    {
        return new ThreadInfo(propogateThreadPrincipal, propogateCallContext, ➥
                            propogateHttpContext, propogateCASMarkers);
    }

    public static ThreadInfo Impersonate(ThreadInfo ti)
```

```
    {
        if (ti == null) throw new ArgumentNullException("ti");

        ThreadInfo prevInfo = Capture(true, true, true, true);
        Restore(ti);
        return (prevInfo);
    }

    public static void Restore(ThreadInfo ti)
    {
        if (ti == null) throw new ArgumentNullException("ti");

        // Restore call context.
        if (miSetLogicalCallContext != null)
        {
            miSetLogicalCallContext.Invoke(Thread.CurrentThread, ➥
                                new object[] { ti.callContext });
        }

        // Restore HttpContext with the moral equivalent of
        // HttpContext.Current = ti.httpContext;
        CallContext.SetData(HttpContextSlotName, ti.httpContext);

        // Restore thread identity.  It's important that this be done after
        // restoring call context above, since restoring call context also
        // overwrites the current thread principal setting. If
        // propogateCallContext
        // and propogateThreadPrincipal are both true, then the
        // following is redundant.
        // However, since propogating call context requires the use
        // of reflection to capture/restore call context, I want
        // that behavior to be independently
        // switchable so that it can be disabled; while still allowing
        // thread principal to be propogated.
        // This also covers us in the event that call context
        // propagation changes so that it no longer propogates thread principal.
        Thread.CurrentPrincipal = ti.principal;
    }

    private ThreadInfo(bool propogateThreadPrincipal, bool propogateCallContext, ➥
                    bool propogateHttpContext, bool propogateCASMarkers)
    {
        if (propogateThreadPrincipal)
        {
            principal = Thread.CurrentPrincipal;
        }

        if (propogateHttpContext)
        {
            httpContext = HttpContext.Current;
        }

        if (propogateCallContext && (miGetLogicalCallContext != null))
        {
            callContext = (LogicalCallContext) ➥
                miGetLogicalCallContext.Invoke(Thread.CurrentThread, null);
            callContext = (LogicalCallContext)callContext.Clone();
```

```
        }
    }

    IPrincipal principal;
    LogicalCallContext callContext;
    // Always null until Get/SetCompressedStack are opened up.
    CompressedStack compressedStack = null;
    HttpContext httpContext;

    // Cached type information.
    const BindingFlags bfNonPublicInstance = BindingFlags.Instance | ➥
                                    BindingFlags.NonPublic;
    const BindingFlags bfNonPublicStatic = BindingFlags.Static | ➥
                                    BindingFlags.NonPublic;

    static MethodInfo miGetLogicalCallContext = ➥
            typeof(Thread).GetMethod("GetLogicalCallContext", bfNonPublicInstance);

    static MethodInfo miSetLogicalCallContext = ➥
            typeof(Thread).GetMethod("SetLogicalCallContext", bfNonPublicInstance);

    static string HttpContextSlotName;

    static ThreadInfo()
    {
        // Lookup the value of HttpContext.CallContextSlotName (if it exists)
        // to see what the name of the call context slot is
        // where HttpContext.Current
        // is stashed.  As a fallback, if this field isn't present anymore, just
        // try for the original "HttpContext" slot name.
        FieldInfo fi = typeof(HttpContext).GetField("CallContextSlotName", ➥
                                            bfNonPublicStatic);

        if (fi != null)
        {
            HttpContextSlotName = (string)fi.GetValue(null);
        }
        else
        {
            HttpContextSlotName = "HttpContext";
        }
    }
}
```

The ThreadInfo class handles logical information regarding the current thread. This includes the HttpContext object of current request. The idea is that several parallel running threads handle different contexts and need to restore the one currently being executed. The data are held in the LogicalCallContext class that holds a set of serializable properties (see Listing 2-17).

Listing 2-17. *The ThreadWrapper Class That Wraps the Actual Thread*

```
internal class ThreadWrapper
{
    private CustomThreadPool pool;
    private bool isPermanent;
    private ThreadPriority priority;
    private string name;
```

```
public ThreadWrapper(CustomThreadPool pool, bool isPermanent, ➥
                        ThreadPriority priority, string name)
{
    this.pool = pool;
    this.isPermanent = isPermanent;
    this.priority = priority;
    this.name = name;

    lock (pool)
    {
        // Update the total # of threads in the pool.
        pool.CurrentThreadCount++;
    }
}

public void Start()
{
    Thread t = new Thread(new ThreadStart(ThreadProc));
    t.ApartmentState = ApartmentState.MTA;
    t.Name = name;
    t.Priority = priority;
    t.IsBackground = pool.UseBackgroundThreads;
    t.Start();
}

void ThreadProc()
{
    bool done = false;
    while (!done)
    {
        WorkRequest wr = null;
        ThreadWrapper newThread = null;
        lock (pool)
        {
            // As long as the request queue is empty and a shutdown hasn't
            // been initiated, wait for a new work request to arrive.
            bool timedOut = false;
            while (!pool.StopInProgress && !timedOut && ➥
                (pool.RequestQueue.Count == 0))
            {
                if (!Monitor.Wait(pool, ➥
                    (isPermanent ? Timeout.Infinite : pool.DecayTime)))
                {
                    // Timed out waiting for something to do.
                    // Only dynamically created
                    // threads will get here, so bail out.
                    timedOut = true;
                }
            }

            // We exited the loop above because one of the
            // following conditions was met:
            // - ThreadPool.Stop was called to initiate a shutdown.
            // - A dynamic thread timed out waiting for a work request
            // - There are items in the work queue to process.

            // If we exited the loop because there's work to be done, a
```

```
// shutdown hasn't been initiated, and it isn't a dynamic thread
// that timed out, pull the request off the queue and prepare to
// process it.
if (!pool.StopInProgress && !timedOut && ➥
    (pool.RequestQueue.Count > 0))
{
    wr = (WorkRequest)pool.RequestQueue.Dequeue();
    Debug.Assert(wr != null);

    // Check to see if this work request languished in the queue
    // very long.  If it was in the queue >= the new thread
    // trigger time, and if we haven't reached the max thread
    // count cap, add a new thread to the pool.
    // If the decision is made, create the new thread object
    // (updating the current # of threads in the pool),
    // but defer starting the new
    // thread until the lock is released.
    TimeSpan requestTimeInQ = DateTime.Now.Subtract(wr.workingTime);

    if ((requestTimeInQ >= pool.NewThreadTriggerTimeSpan) && ➥
        (pool.CurrentThreadCount < pool.MaxThreadCount))
    {
        newThread = ➥
            new ThreadWrapper(pool, false, priority, ➥
                                string.Format("{0} (dynamic)", ➥
                                pool.ThreadPoolName));

        // Since the current request we just dequeued is stale,
        // everything else behind it in the queue is also stale.
        // So reset the timestamps of the remaining pending work
        // requests so that we don't start creating threads
        // for every subsequent request.
        pool.ResetWorkRequestTimes();
    }
}
else
{
    // Should only get here if this is a dynamic thread that
    // timed out waiting for a work request, or if the pool
    // is shutting down.
    pool.CurrentThreadCount--;

    if (pool.CurrentThreadCount == 0)
    {
        // Last one out turns off the lights.
        pool.OnStopped();
        pool.StopCompleteEvent.Set();
    }

    done = true;
}
} // lock

// No longer holding pool lock here...

if (!done && (wr != null))
{
```

```
              // Check to see if this request has been cancelled while
              // stuck in the work queue.
              // If the work request was pending, mark it processed and
              // proceed to handle.  Otherwise, the request must have been
              // cancelled before we plucked it off the request queue.
              if (Interlocked.CompareExchange(ref wr.state, ➡
                  WorkRequest.PROCESSED, ➡
                  WorkRequest.PENDING) != WorkRequest.PENDING)
              {
                  // Request was cancelled before we could get here.
                  // Bail out.
                  continue;
              }

              if (newThread != null)
              {
                  newThread.Start();
              }

          // Dispatch the work request.
          ThreadInfo originalThreadInfo = null;

          try
          {
              // Impersonate (as much as possible) what we know about
              // the thread that issued the work request.
              originalThreadInfo = ThreadInfo.Impersonate(wr.threadInfo);

              WorkRequestDelegate targetProc = wr.targetProc as ➡
                                        WorkRequestDelegate;

              if (targetProc != null)
              {
                  targetProc(wr.procArg, wr.timeStampStarted);
              }
              else
              {
                  wr.targetProc.DynamicInvoke(wr.procArgs);
              }
          }
          catch (Exception e)
          {
          }
          finally
          {
              // Restore our worker thread's identity.
              //
              ThreadInfo.Restore(originalThreadInfo);
          }
      }
    }
  }
}
```

While the thread is there to do the work, another piece in the puzzle is required—the WorkRequest. This type contains the reference between the callback method that is handling the workload and the thread (Listing 2-18).

Listing 2-18. *The WorkRequest Class That Associates Request and Thread*

```
internal class WorkRequest : IWorkRequest
{
    internal const int PENDING = 0;
    internal const int PROCESSED = 1;
    internal const int CANCELLED = 2;

    public WorkRequest(WorkRequestDelegate cb, object arg,
                       bool propogateThreadPrincipal, bool propogateCallContext,
                       bool propogateHttpContext, bool propogateCASMarkers)
    {
        targetProc = cb;
        procArg = arg;
        procArgs = null;

        Initialize(propogateThreadPrincipal, propogateCallContext,
                   propogateHttpContext, propogateCASMarkers);
    }

    public WorkRequest(Delegate cb, object[] args,
                       bool propogateThreadPrincipal, bool propogateCallContext,
                       bool propogateHttpContext, bool propogateCASMarkers)
    {
        targetProc = cb;
        procArg = null;
        procArgs = args;

        Initialize(propogateThreadPrincipal, propogateCallContext,
                   propogateHttpContext, propogateCASMarkers);
    }

    void Initialize(bool propogateThreadPrincipal, bool propogateCallContext,
                    bool propogateHttpContext, bool propogateCASMarkers)
    {
        workingTime = timeStampStarted = DateTime.Now;
        threadInfo = ThreadInfo.Capture(propogateThreadPrincipal, ➥
                                        propogateCallContext, ➥
                                        propogateHttpContext, ➥
                                        propogateCASMarkers);
    }

    public bool Cancel()
    {
        // If the work request was pending, mark it cancelled.  Otherwise,
        // this method was called too late.  Note that this call can
        // cancel an operation without any race conditions.  But if the
        // result of this test-and-set indicates the request is in the
        // "processed" state, it might actually be about to be processed.
        return (Interlocked.CompareExchange(ref state, CANCELLED, PENDING) ➥
            == PENDING);
    }
    // Function to call.
    internal Delegate targetProc;
    // State to pass to function.
    internal object procArg;
    // Used with Delegate.DynamicInvoke.
```

```
          internal object[] procArgs;
          // Time work request was originally enqueued (held constant).
          internal DateTime timeStampStarted;
          // Current timestamp used for triggering new threads (moving target).
          internal DateTime workingTime;
          // Everything we know about a thread.
          internal ThreadInfo threadInfo;
          // The state of this particular request.
          internal int state = PENDING;
}
```

The goal is the function that contains the worker code stored in `targetProc`. The field `procArgs` held the particular arguments. The field `threadInfo` contains the associated information, especially the `HttpContext` object.

This all creates the necessary functions to have threads ready to be used any time and independent of the internal thread pool. Now that you have a custom thread pool implementation, it's time to use it.

Using the Custom Thread Pool with ASP.NET's Asynchronous Handler

The following example is simply an extended version of the previous one. Instead of using single threads, however, and risk having too many of them, you can use the custom thread pool and set some limitations (see Listing 2-19).

Listing 2-19. *Using the Thread Pool*

```csharp
<!-- File: AsyncPool.ashx -->
<%@ WebHandler Language="C#"
    Class="Apress.Threading.HttpPipeline.AsyncHandler" %>

namespace Apress.Threading.HttpPipeline
{

  public class AsyncHandler : IHttpAsyncHandler
  {
    static Apress.Extensibility.Threading.CustomThreadPool _threadPool;

    static AsyncHandler()
    {
      _threadPool = ➥
        new Apress.Extensibility.Threading.CustomThreadPool (2, 25, "AsyncPool");
      _threadPool.PropogateCallContext = true;
      _threadPool.PropogateThreadPrincipal = true;
      _threadPool.PropogateHttpContext = true;
      _threadPool.Start();
    }

    public void ProcessRequest(HttpContext ctx)
    {
     // not used, for sync only
    }

    public bool IsReusable
    {
      get { return false;}
    }
```

```
public IAsyncResult BeginProcessRequest(HttpContext ctx, ➥
                                        AsyncCallback cb, object obj)
{
  AsyncRequestState reqState = ➥
                new AsyncRequestState(ctx, cb, obj);
  _threadPool.PostRequest(new WorkRequestDelegate(ProcessRequest),reqState);

  return reqState;
}

public void EndProcessRequest(IAsyncResult ar)
{
}

void ProcessRequest(object state, DateTime requestTime)
{
  AsyncRequestState reqState = state as AsyncRequestState;

  // Take some time to do it
  Thread.Sleep(2000);

  reqState._ctx.Response.Output.Write( ➥
            "AsyncThreadPool, {0}", ➥
            AppDomain.GetCurrentThreadId);

  // tell asp.net you are finished processing this request
  reqState.CompleteRequest();
  }

 }
}
```

In theory, this thread pool will not run out of threads unless it does not reach the limit of 4,096 threads allowed. However, there are some limitations, such as available memory, CPU power, and operating system restrictions. This is why the pool was designed, so that you can optionally specify limits. The previous code is a good platform for experimenting with threads and thread pools, and for monitoring the number of threads for your application. If you want to replace the internal thread pool, try out the custom pool to learn how ASP.NET requests threads, and find out where to improve performance.

Summary

This chapter covered in-depth information about the internal request processing and how to tweak the worker process and the threading. You were given an idea of how the thread pool works and how to extend the behavior. Using asynchronous processing might increase performance and handle high workload. A custom thread pool was introduced to demonstrate how to change internal parts of the processing pipeline transparently. In anticipation of Chapter 3, you had a first look into asynchronous handlers and their usage.

CHAPTER 3

■■■

Modules and Handlers

In this chapter, you will look more closely at the extensibility of ASP.NET through the addition of custom modules and handlers. Handlers and modules are integrated into IIS so that your web applications can perform and scale well. In Chapter 2, you learned how to use asynchronous handlers to handle custom threads. Here, you'll learn more about how ASP.NET can extend using handlers. This chapter includes:

- What internal modules are for
- How to create, activate, and debug custom modules
- The handlers included in ASP.NET
- How to extend, customize, and replace handlers
- Writing your own handlers with both synchronous and asynchronous behavior

Module, Handlers, and IIS

IIS7 Web Server features fit into one of two categories:

- Modules
- Handlers

Similar to the *ISAPI filter* in previous IIS versions, a module participates in the processing of each request. Its role is to change or add content to the request. Examples of some out-of-the-box modules in IIS7 include authentication modules, compression modules, and logging modules. The names indicate the function of each module.

A module is a .NET class that implements the System.Web.IHttpModule interface and uses APIs in the System.Web namespace to participate in one or more of ASP.NET's request-processing stages. I explained the stages of this "pipeline" in Chapter 1.

By contrast, a handler, similar to the *ISAPI extension* in previous IIS versions, is responsible for handling requests and creating responses for specific content types. The main difference between modules and handlers is that handlers typically map to a particular request path or extension. They also support the processing of a specific resource to which that path or extension corresponds. Handlers provided with IIS7 include ASP.NET's PageHandlerFactory, which processes .aspx pages, among others. This kind of a handler is a .NET class that implements the ASP.NET System.Web. IHttpHandler or System.Web.IHttpAsyncHandler interface. It uses APIs in the System.Web namespace to produce an HTTP response for the specific content it creates.

When developing an IIS7 feature or ASP.NET extension, you'll need to decide whether a module or a handler is appropriate. No common task requires both. If your feature is responsible for serving requests to a specific URL or file extension, like *.png, then a handler is the right choice, as handlers are primarily for specific tasks. Alternatively, if you want to respond to some or all requests, a module is appropriate.

Creating images on the fly corresponds to a specific file type—use a handler to achieve this. Adding footers to all your pages from one location is a good idea—implement a module to do that.

Modules

This section explains how to create internal modules and gives some examples that you can use in your own applications.

IIS7 Architecture

ASP.NET is tightly integrated with IIS7. Even though it is possible to run ASP.NET with any host, thanks to its modular architecture, you should keep in mind that IIS is the best platform "by design." Extending and customizing ASP.NET is only possible with a good understanding of IIS and its parts.

Microsoft changed large parts of the architecture of IIS7 compared to previous versions. One of the major changes was the greatly enhanced extensibility. Instead of a powerful yet monolithic Web Server, IIS7 now has a Web Server engine to which you can add or remove components. These components are called modules.

Modules build the features offered by the Web Server. All modules have one primary task—processing a request. This can become complicated, however, as a request is not just a call to static resources. Consider requests involving the authentication of client credentials, compression and decompression, or cache management.

Assuming that IIS7 is the primary platform for running ASP.NET, any discussion about extensibility does not make sense without understanding what accompanies IIS7. IIS7 comes with two module types:

- Native Modules
- Managed Modules

Native Modules

Native modules perform all the basic tasks of a Web Server. However, not all modules manage common requests. It depends on your installation and configuration as to whether a module is available and running. Inside IIS7 are:

- HTTP Modules
- Security Modules
- Content Modules
- Compression Modules
- Caching Modules
- Logging and Diagnosing Modules
- Integration of Managed Modules

You can find all modules—apart from those whose full path follow—in the following directory:

`%WinDir%\System32\InetSrv`

As shown in Table 3-1, the HTTP modules perform tasks specific to Hypertext Transfer Protocol.

Table 3-1. *HTTP Modules*

Module Name	DLL	Description
CustomErrorModule	Custerr.dll	Its purpose is to send default or configured HTTP error messages when the response contains an error status.
HttpRedirectionModule	Redirect.dll	Module supports configurable redirection for HTTP requests.
ProtocolSupportModule	Protsup.dll	This module executes protocol-related actions, such as setting response headers and redirecting headers.

Security is essential for a Web Server, as shown by the number of modules in Table 3-2.

Table 3-2. *Security Modules*

Module Name	DLL	Description
AnonymousAuthenticationModule	Authanon.dll	Accomplishes anonymous authentication in case other authentication methods fail.
BasicAuthenticationModule	Authbas.dll	Performs Basic authentication.
CertificateMappingAuthenticationModule	Authcert.dll	Performs Certificate Mapping authentication using Active Directory.
DigestAuthenticationModule	Authmd5.dll	Performs Digest authentication.
IISCertificateMappingAuthenticationModule	Authmap.dll	Performs Certificate Mapping authentication using IIS certificate configuration.
RequestFilteringModule	Modrqflt.dll	Performs tasks such as configuring allowed verbs and file extensions, setting limits, and scanning for bad character sequences by scanning the URL.
UrlAuthorizationModule	Urlauthz.dll	Executes URL authorization.
WindowsAuthenticationModule	Authsspi.dll	Performs NTLM integrated authentication.
IpRestrictionModule	iprestr.dll	The purpose is to restrict IPv4 addresses listed in the IpSecurity list.

Once the request is accepted and authorized, the requested resources are handled. Several modules perform these specific tasks. Table 3-3 shows the modules that handle content directly, like static files.

Table 3-3. *Content Modules*

Module Name	DLL	Description
CgiModule	Cgi.dll	Executes Common Gateway Interface (CGI) processes to build response output.
DefaultDocumentModule	Defdoc.dll	Attempts to return a default document for requests made to the parent directory.
DirectoryListingModule	dirlist.dll	Lists the contents of a directory and builds a HTML response of the listing.
IsapiModule	Isapi.dll	This modules hosts other ISAPI extension DLLs.
IsapiFilterModule	Filter.dll	This module supports ISAPI filter DLLs.
ServerSideIncludeModule	Iis_ssi.dll	This module is responsible for server-side include code, a former modularization technique.
StaticFileModule	Static.dll	This module serves static files, such as images.
FastCgiModule	iisfcgi.dll	Supports FastCGI, which provides a high-performance alternative to CGI. Used to support web development environments like PHP.

Compression is a common way to save bandwidth and transfer large files more efficiently (see Table 3-4).

Table 3-4. *Compression Modules*

Module Name	DLL	Description
DynamicCompressionModule	Compdyn.dll	Used to compress responses using *gzip* compression transfer coding on the fly
StaticCompressionModule	Compstat.dll	Performs the pre-compression of static content

Caching is another way to improve performance. Several modules store files so that the delivery process is either accelerated or eliminated altogether (see Table 3-5).

Table 3-5. *Caching Modules*

Module Name	DLL	Description
FileCacheModule	Cachfile.dll	Provides user mode caching for files and file handles
HTTPCacheModule	Cachhttp.dll	Provides kernel mode and user mode caching in HTTP.sys driver
TokenCacheModule	Cachtokn.dll	Provides user mode caching of user name and token pairs for modules that use Windows user principals
UriCacheModule	Cachuri.dll	Provides user mode caching of URL information

Knowing what is happening is essential for Web Server administrators. There are several steps from the code on your server—where you probably have debug capabilities—to the browser, where you might miss seeing the desired output. Even production systems do not always behave as expected. Table 3-6 shows logging and diagnostic modules, which help you understand the internal processing of requests and responses.

Table 3-6. *Logging and Diagnostic Modules*

Module Name	DLL	Description
CustomLoggingModule	Logcust.dll	Loads additional custom logging modules.
FailedRequestsTracingModule	Iisfreb.dll	This module supports the "Failed Request Tracing" feature.
HttpLoggingModule	Loghttp.dll	This module passes information and processing status to the HTTP.sys driver for logging purposes.
RequestMonitorModule	Iisreqs.dll	This module tracks requests currently executing in worker processes and reports information using the Runtime Status and Control Application Programming Interface (RSCA).
TracingModule	Iisetw.dll	Reports events to Microsoft Event Tracing for Windows (ETW).

Finally, you need an interface to the managed world. In Chapter 1, you saw how modules interacted. Table 3-7 shows which modules are involved in this interaction.

Table 3-7. *Integration of Managed Modules*

Module Name	DLL/Assembly	Description
ManagedEngine	Microsoft.NET\Framework\ v2.0.50727\webengine.dll	Provides integration of managed code modules in the IIS request-processing pipeline. The version number might change.
ConfigurationValidationModule	validcfg.dll	Validates configuration issues, such as if an application is running in Integrated mode but has handlers or modules declared in the system.web section of *web. config* file.

Managed Modules

While extending IIS7 via native modules is one method of writing high-performance applications, for most projects, this is not necessary or desirable. Extending ASP.NET using managed modules has significant advantages in development time and reliability. IIS7 includes several built-in, managed modules, which show that it is possible to write low-level infrastructure components in managed code.

You can find the definition of security modules in the `System.Web.Security` namespace (see Table 3-8).

Table 3-8. *Managed Code Security Modules Shipped with IIS7*

Module Name	Class	Description
AnonymousIdentification	AnonymousIdentificationModule	Manages anonymous identifiers, which are used by features to support anonymous identification such as the ASP.NET profile.
DefaultAuthentication	DefaultAuthenticationModule	Ensures that a default authentication object is present in the context.
FileAuthorization	FileAuthorizationModule	Verifies that a user has permission to access the requested file based on file security.
FormsAuthentication	FormsAuthenticationModule	Supports authentication using the Forms authentication technique.
RoleManager	RoleManagerModule	Manages a RolePrincipal instance for the current user and therefore the role management. This is extensible through providers.
UrlAuthorization	UrlAuthorizationModule	Determines whether the current user is permitted to access the requested URL, based on the user's name or his or her membership of a suitable role.
WindowsAuthentication	WindowsAuthenticationModule	Supports the identity of a user when Windows authentication is enabled for the application.

Table 3-9 shows some more modules for particular usage. The definition of the cache module is stored in `System.Web.Caching`. This module is declared as `internal` and is not accessible by user code. The other ones are declared `public`. The module for profile handling is in the `System.Web.Profile` namespace. For session handling modules, look into the `System.Web.SessionState` namespace. The modules for URL handling are stored in the root namespace `System.Web`.

Table 3-9. *Managed Code Modules Shipped with IIS7*

Module Name	Class	Description
OutputCache	OutputCacheModule	This module supports output caching.
Profile	ProfileModule	Manages user profiles by using ASP.NET profiles, which store and retrieve user settings in a data source such as a database. This is extensible through providers.
Session	SessionStateModule	Supports the maintenance of the session state, which enables the storage of data specific to a single client on the server. This is extensible through providers.
UrlMappingsModule	UrlMappingsModule	Supports the mapping of a real URL to a more user-friendly or even a search-engine friendly URL.

Given this list of modules, you might feel that there is no need to write custom modules to perform standard tasks. This is true; the developers of ASP.NET and IIS have delivered everything you need for common infrastructure work. However, if you'd like to program an application-specific task, writing your own module is an excellent way to extend ASP.NET and add sophisticated features of your choice.

The IIS7 Managed Module Starter Kit

Microsoft provides a starter kit to make it easy to write your first module for the new IIS7 managed API. This Visual Studio Content Installer contains a project template for building IIS7 Modules using the .NET Framework.

Get the Starter Kit

The Starter Kit is available at no cost from Microsoft at the www.iis.net Web site: http://www.iis.net/downloads/default.aspx?tabid=34&i=1302&g=6.

Click on Download, save the file, and unzip to a current folder. The kit is a Visual Studio template installer, provided as a .vsi file.

Benefits of Module Development Kit

Since IIS7 supports development using managed code, it means you can program HTTP request processing in managed code. The entire event structure of IIS7, written in native API (C/C++), is also available to managed code developers. Figure 3-1 shows the start screen of the installation wizard.

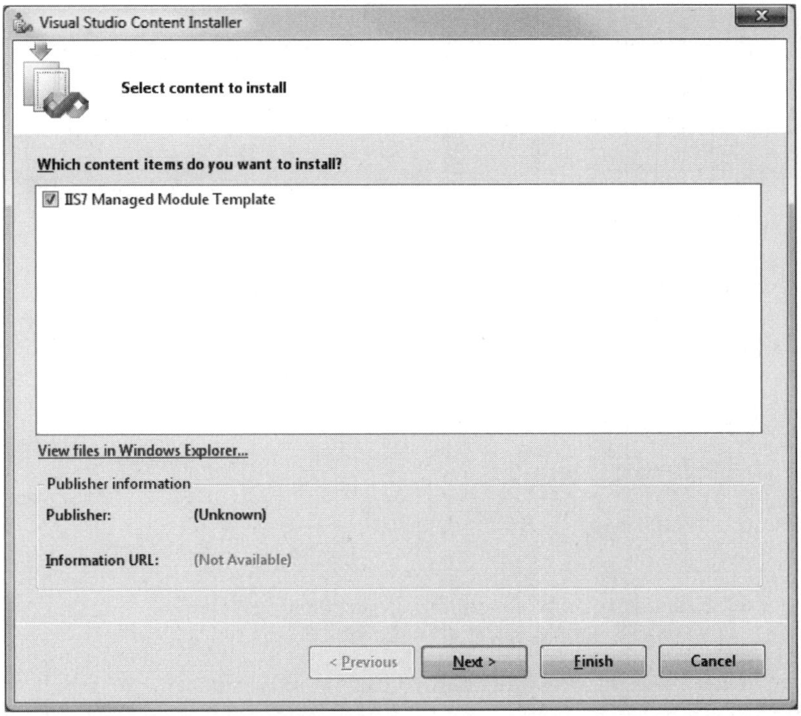

Figure 3-1. *Installing the template*

■**Note** Using the Starter Kit simplifies the first steps. However, you don't need it to run the samples provided in this chapter.

Once you install the template, you can add new modules by using the right item for your project. Additionally, you can use the "IIS7 Managed Module" project template to create a new project with a predefined module class already there. The project template provides a comprehensive instruction, too (see Figure 3-2).

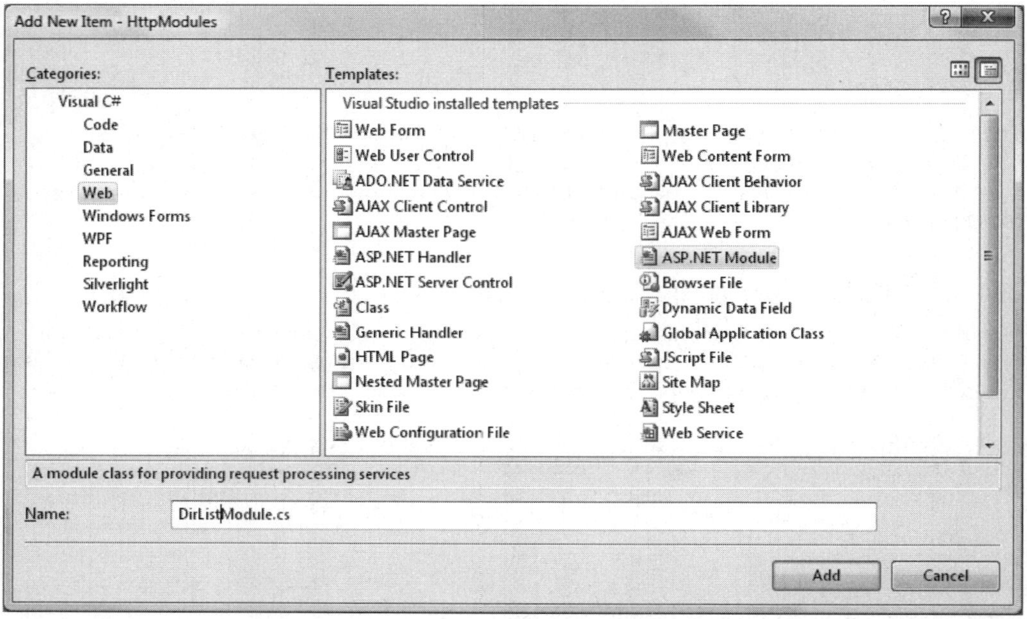

Figure 3-2. *Adding a new module code item to a current project*

This item creates a class skeleton, as shown in Listing 3-1.

Listing 3-1. *Skeleton of a Module Class*

```csharp
using System;
using System.Web;

namespace Apress.Extensibility.HttpModules
{
    public class MyModule : IHttpModule
    {
        /// <summary>
        /// You will need to configure this module in the web.config file
        /// and register it with IIS before being able to use it.
        /// For more information
        /// see the following link: http://go.microsoft.com/?linkid=8101007
        /// </summary>
        #region IHttpModule Members
```

```
// Disposes of the resources (other than memory) used by the module.
public void Dispose()
{
    //clean-up code here.
}

// Initializes the module, and registers for application events.
public void Init(HttpApplication application)
{
    // What follows is an example of how you can handle LogRequest
    // event and provide
    // custom logging implementation for it
    application.LogRequest += new EventHandler(OnLogRequest);
}

#endregion

public void OnLogRequest(Object source, EventArgs e)
{
    //custom logging logic can go here
}
    }
}
```

For the sake of clarity and space, I will not repeat this part of the module code in the following sections when examining the various examples.

Building a Module

As requests move through the pipeline, a number of events fire on the HttpApplication object. As you've seen already, these events publish as event methods in *Global.asax*. This approach is application-specific, but not always ideal. If you want to build generic HttpApplication event hooks that can plug into any Web application, you can use HttpModules. These are reusable and require an entry in *web.config* instead of application-specific code.

Define the Modules

Modules allow you to hook events for any request that passes through the ASP.NET HttpApplication object. These modules are stored as classes in external assemblies configured in *web.config*, which causes them to load when the application starts. By implementing specific interfaces and methods, the module hooks up to the HttpApplication event chain. Multiple HttpModules can hook the same event. Their order is determined by appearance in *web.config*. Listing 3-2 shows a handler definition in *web.config*.

Listing 3-2. *Register a Module in web.config*

```
<configuration>
  <system.web>
    <httpModules>
      <add name="MyModule" ➥
           type="Apress.Extensibility.HttpModules.Modules,MyModule" />
    </httpModules>
  </system.web>
</configuration>
```

Note that you need to specify both a full type name and an assembly name without the DLL extension.

Modules allow you to observe each incoming request and perform an action based on the events that fire. Modules are excellent for modifying a request or responding to particular content in order to provide custom authentication or pre- or post-processing to each request that arrives.

Many of ASP.NET's features, such as the Authentication and Session engines, are implemented as HTTP Modules. While HttpModules might feel similar to *ISAPI Filters* in that they examine every request that arrives through an ASP.NET application, in reality they are limited to scrutinizing requests mapped to a single specific ASP.NET application or virtual directory.

Therefore, you can inspect all .aspx pages or any other custom extensions that map to this application. However, you cannot look at standard .html or image files unless you explicitly map the extension to the ASP.NET ISAPI.dll.

Example—Write a Simple Authentication Module

This first example shows how to intercept the authentication procedure of the request pipeline. It also demonstrates how to add your own authentication module to handle tasks independently of the existing code.

Implementing an HTTP Module is very easy. Implement the IHttpModule interface, which contains two methods: Init and Dispose.

■**Note** The Starter Kit item additionally creates a LogRequest handler, if you add the module using the ASP.NET module item. If you use the IIS7 Managed Module project with the first module item predefined, the PreRequestHandlerExecute event is already hooked. You can safely remove these handlers and their event assignment if you don't need them.

The event parameters passed include a reference to the HTTPApplication object, which in turn gives you access to the HttpContext object. Using the Init method, you can hook up to HttpApplication events. For example, if you want to hook the AuthenticateRequest event to a module, you would do so as shown in Listing 3-3.

Listing 3-3. *Simple Implementation of an HTTP Module*

```
public class BasicAuthCustomModule : IHttpModule
{
  public void Init(HttpApplication application)
  {
    application.AuthenticateRequest += ➡
      new EventHandler(this.OnAuthenticateRequest);
  }

  public void Dispose() { }

  public void OnAuthenticateRequest(object source, Even-tArgs eventArgs)
  {
    HttpApplication app = (HttpApplication) source;
    HttpContext Context = HttpContext.Current;
    // and action
}
```

Remember that your module has access to the HttpContext object and from there to all other intrinsic ASP.NET pipeline objects, such as Response and Request. From here, you can retrieve input, create content, and so forth. However, keep in mind that certain things may not be available until further down the chain.

You can hook as many events as you like in the Init method so that your module is able to manage multiple operations with different functions. It is tidier to separate differing logic into separate modules. This ensures that the modules are, indeed, modular, as their name implies. In many cases, any functionality that you implement could require hooking multiple events. For example, a logging filter might log the start time of a request in BeginRequest and then write the request completion into the log in EndRequest.

■**Caution** Modules work deep inside the processing pipeline. Calling certain methods can prevent the pipeline from proceeding to the next step. In particular, Response.End and Application.CompleteRequest complete the request and force the pipeline to end, thus skipping all subsequent steps. The pipeline will return control to the Web Server and no further modules will be invoked. A better practice is to leave the pipeline running, but use a context variable to inform subsequent modules not to execute.

The purpose of the Dispose method is to clean up any resources when the module unloads and to release other resources before the garbage collector finalizes the module instance. If there is nothing to dispose, leave the method body blank.

The Init method is the main method of interest. Here, you can initialize your module and wire it up to one or more request-processing events available on the HttpApplication class. Keep in mind that events fire when the appropriate step in the pipeline is reached, in a defined order, and in conjunction with other modules. Without a clear understanding of the pipeline architecture explained in Chapter 1, you'll have difficulty writing sophisticated modules that perform well.

Example—Check for a Specific Header

The following example checks for a specific header, called a referrer, which provides information about the referring page. Paradoxically, the referrer is named "referrer." Don't worry about the misspelled word (the sidebar explains more).

WIKIPEDIA ON THE WORD *REFERER*

Referer is a common misspelling of the word *referrer*. It is so common, in fact, that it made it into the official specification of HTTP—the communication protocol of the World Wide Web—and has therefore become a widely used industry spelling when discussing HTTP referrers. The misspelling usage is not universal; the correct spelling of "referrer" occurs in some web specifications, such as the Document Object Model.

[Source: http://en.wikipedia.org/wiki/Referer]

I advise you to pay attention to which word you're using!

In this example, you'll look for a specific referrer or referring page—the URL of the previous page. (It's the page containing the link to the page you're currently processing.) The usage of the header is voluntary, according to HTTP standards, but most sites use it to track users or manage logging. However, some pages are not intended to be called from outside our site. If linked from another page within our application, such pages will execute correctly, but if linked from anywhere else, you'll treat that as an exception. Such external links typically occur when a user bookmarks a specific page deep within your application. When attempting to open one of these pages, it is not possible, because there are several prerequisite steps to complete beforehand. Using a module like the one in Listing 3-4, you can capture these requests outside the common page code and redirect users to a suitable page, such as one that explains appropriate usage of bookmarks.

Listing 3-4. *An HTTP Module That Looks for the Referer Header*

```
public class ReferrerModule : IHttpModule
{
    #region IHttpModule Members

    public void Dispose()
    {
        //clean-up code here.
    }

    public void Init(HttpApplication context)
    {
        context.PreRequestHandlerExecute += ➥
            new EventHandler(context_PreRequestHandlerExecute);
    }

    void context_PreRequestHandlerExecute(object sender, EventArgs e)
    {
        HttpApplication app = (HttpApplication)sender;
        HttpRequest request = app.Context.Request;
        if (!request.Url.LocalPath.EndsWith("Default.aspx"))
        {
            if (String.IsNullOrEmpty(request.Headers["Referer"]))
            {
                throw new HttpException(403, "Bookmarking is not allowed");
            }
        }
    }

    #endregion
}
```

This code assumes that you have a page called or at least ending with "Default.aspx" linking to another page in your application. The name of the other page doesn't matter.

To test this module:

1. Configure *web.config* to activate the module.

2. Create two pages, Default.aspx and RefererTest.aspx. Default.aspx has a hyperlink to RefererTest.aspx.

3. Compile and start the application by launching the Default.aspx page.

4. Click the hyperlink on Default.aspx—the RefererTest.aspx page is displayed.

5. Bookmark the RefererTest.aspx page.

6. Close your browser, reopen it, and load the bookmark, then press F5 to force a refresh of the page from the server.

7. An exception occurs and the browser shows a 403 error.

You might insist that all of this can be accomplished on the page level using conventional code. This is correct, but fundamental tasks are best handled on a fundamental level. In addition, intercepting low-level events to handle low-level action is faster, more secure, and more reliable. Adding more pages with the same behavior does not require any change to the code. It simply works because the module tests all pages in the application.

Interaction Between Modules

Writing private modules is a powerful technique for extending ASP.NET. However, extending can mean replacing existing functionality. Sometimes a smart solution results simply from using the internal modules and your own module together.

To begin, you'll need access to the internal modules at runtime. You should make connections in the Init event in order to have access at an early stage. Listing 3-5 shows you how to retrieve information about internal modules, and other kinds of modules, attached to the pipeline so far.

Listing 3-5. *Retrieving Information About Modules*

```
public class SessionLogModule : IHttpModule
{
    #region IHttpModule Members

    public void Dispose()
    {
    }

    public void Init(HttpApplication application)
    {
        HttpContext context = HttpContext.Current;
        foreach (string key in application.Modules.AllKeys)
        {
            context.Response.Write(String.Format("{0}= {1} {2}<br>",
                key,
                application.Modules[key].GetType().IsPublic ? "public" : "internal",
                application.Modules[key].GetType().AssemblyQualifiedName));
        }
    }

    #endregion
}
```

The current context is used to output the text directly into the current page where the request is handled. You can use the `Modules` property to get a list of the modules and where they are defined (see Figure 3-3).

```
OutputCache= internal System.Web.Caching.OutputCacheModule, System.Web, Version=2.0.0.0, Culture=neutral, PublicKeyToken=b03f5f7f11d50a3a
Session= public System.Web.SessionState.SessionStateModule, System.Web, Version=2.0.0.0, Culture=neutral, PublicKeyToken=b03f5f7f11d50a3a
WindowsAuthentication= public System.Web.Security.WindowsAuthenticationModule, System.Web, Version=2.0.0.0, Culture=neutral, PublicKeyToken=b03f5f7f11d50a3a
FormsAuthentication= public System.Web.Security.FormsAuthenticationModule, System.Web, Version=2.0.0.0, Culture=neutral, PublicKeyToken=b03f5f7f11d50a3a
PassportAuthentication= public System.Web.Security.PassportAuthenticationModule, System.Web, Version=2.0.0.0, Culture=neutral, PublicKeyToken=b03f5f7f11d50a3a
RoleManager= public System.Web.Security.RoleManagerModule, System.Web, Version=2.0.0.0, Culture=neutral, PublicKeyToken=b03f5f7f11d50a3a
UrlAuthorization= public System.Web.Security.UrlAuthorizationModule, System.Web, Version=2.0.0.0, Culture=neutral, PublicKeyToken=b03f5f7f11d50a3a
FileAuthorization= public System.Web.Security.FileAuthorizationModule, System.Web, Version=2.0.0.0, Culture=neutral, PublicKeyToken=b03f5f7f11d50a3a
AnonymousIdentification= public System.Web.Security.AnonymousIdentificationModule, System.Web, Version=2.0.0.0, Culture=neutral, PublicKeyToken=b03f5f7f11d50a3a
Profile= public System.Web.Profile.ProfileModule, System.Web, Version=2.0.0.0, Culture=neutral, PublicKeyToken=b03f5f7f11d50a3a
ErrorHandlerModule= public System.Web.Mobile.ErrorHandlerModule, System.Web.Mobile, Version=2.0.0.0, Culture=neutral, PublicKeyToken=b03f5f7f11d50a3a
ServiceModel= internal System.ServiceModel.Activation.HttpModule, System.ServiceModel, Version=3.0.0.0, Culture=neutral, PublicKeyToken=b77a5c561934e089
ScriptModule= public System.Web.Handlers.ScriptModule, System.Web.Extensions, Version=3.5.0.0, Culture=neutral, PublicKeyToken=31bf3856ad364e35
SessionLogModule= public Apress.AspNetExtensibility.HttpModules.SessionLogModule, Apress.AspNetExtensibility.HttpModules, Version=1.0.0.0, Culture=neutral,
PublicKeyToken=null
ReferrerModule= public Apress.AspNetExtensibility.HttpModules.ReferrerModule, Apress.AspNetExtensibility.HttpModules, Version=1.0.0.0, Culture=neutral,
PublicKeyToken=null
DefaultAuthentication= public System.Web.Security.DefaultAuthenticationModule, System.Web, Version=2.0.0.0, Culture=neutral, PublicKeyToken=b03f5f7f11d50a3a
```

Figure 3-3. *Modules already available*

You probably need to use this method of getting access to an embedded module, as not all modules offer direct access to their states and events. Once you know the name and type of a specific module, you can cast the type and get the object you need.

Configuration and Deployment

Now that the module is implemented, you can compile it into an assembly that ASP.NET is able to load at runtime. This is straightforward as long as the module is in the web application. No special action is required. You will probably want to create several modules and have them in different assemblies for easy reuse. The assemblies will need to be referenced by your web project. To construct such a module, choose "Class Library" as the project template. Remove the default class created by the template, and add an object of type "ASP.NET Module" as shown in Figure 3-4.

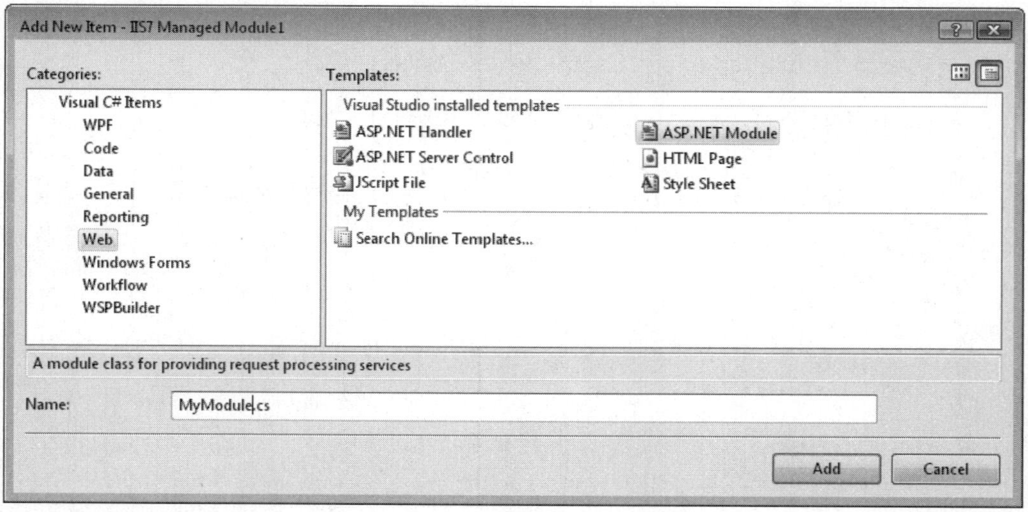

Figure 3-4. *Add a module to current project.*

Configuring the Default Web Server and Development Environment

To test the module, you'll need to configure the settings in *web.config*. Place the appropriate lines in the <system.web> section:

```
<httpModules>
  <add name="ReferrerModule"
       type="Apress.Extensibility.HttpModules.ReferrerModule "/>
</httpModules>
```

The settings for the development environment also apply for IIS5, IIS6, and IIS7 in classic mode. There are several advantages to running the IIS7 integrated pipeline; however, that requires different settings, as shown in Table 3-10.

Table 3-10. *Options of the httpModule Settings*

Attribute	Typical Values	Description
name	any string	The module name that appears in settings dialogs
type	class, assembly	Module type

Configuring IIS7 Settings

In the main (web) project, add a reference to the project containing the module. Assuming the namespace of the external project is Apress.Extensibility.HttpHandler.MyHandler, add the following to *web.config*:

```
<system.webServer>
  <modules>
    <add name="ReferrerModule"
         type="Apress.Extensibility.HttpHandler.MyHandler" resourceType="File"
         requireAccess="Read" preCondition="integratedMode" />
  </modules>
</system.webServer>
```

Compile both the project containing the module and the web project. Add the mapping in Internet Information Services Manager. The mapping will now function perfectly for both the development environment and direct usage from the local IIS7 (see Table 3-11).

Table 3-11. *Options for the Module Settings for IIS7 Integrated Mode*

Attribute	Typical Values	Description
name	any string	The module name that appears in settings dialogs.
precondition	string	Specifies conditions under which the module will run. This is usually the name of another handler or module required to run before this one.
type	class, assembly	Type information of the handlers definition.

Configure Using IIS Management Console

Rather than adding the IIS7 integrated mode settings to *web.config*, you can simply use the IIS Management Console. The settings correspond directly. Altering *web.config* will result in an immediate change to the Management Console settings, and vice versa. To configure using the IIS Management Console:

1. Open Internet Information Service Manager.

2. Open the web you want to change.

3. In the IIS section, double-click on the Modules icon.

4. Click on Add Managed Module in the task list to the right.

5. Enter these values in the dialog and close the dialog by clicking OK, then:

   a. Give the module an appropriate name.

   b. Open the type drop-down and select the module's type.

6. Close the main dialog by pressing OK.

No restart is required to activate the new settings.

Handlers

This section focuses on developing HTTP handlers for IIS7, using the .NET Framework. You'll look at when it is appropriate to develop an IIS7 handler rather than a module.

Built-In Handlers

ASP.NET offers several default HTTP handlers:

- Page Handler (.aspx): Handles web pages
- User Control Handler (.ascx): Handles Web user control pages
- Web Service Handler (.asmx): Handles Web Service pages
- Trace Handler (trace.axd): Handles trace functionality
- Assembly Resource Loader (WebResource.axd): Handles embedded resources in assemblies
- Script resource handler (ScriptResource.axd): Handles the scripting support for AJAX-enabled projects
- Forbidden Handler (.config): Denies access to files that contain confidential information

The IIS configuration defines the assignments. You will also find other assignments there. Extensions such as .xoml, .rem, .soap, and .svc relate to the capabilities provided by Windows Communication Foundation (WCF) and its predecessor, .NET remoting.

Extending ASP.NET Using Http Handlers

While modules are low level, and run against every inbound request to the ASP.NET application, HTTP handlers focus more on a specific request mapping. This is usually a mapping of a file extension.

HTTP handler implementations are very simple in their concept, but having access to the `HttpContext` object enables enormous versatility. Handlers are implemented through the `IHttpHandler` interface, or its asynchronous counterpart, `IHttpAsyncHandler`. The interface consists of a single method, `ProcessRequest`, and a single property, `IsReusable`. The asynchronous version has a pair of methods (`BeginProcessRequest` and `EndProcessRequest`) and the same `IsReusable` property. The vital ingredient is `ProcessRequest`, which receives an instance of the `HttpContext` object. This single method is responsible for handling a Web request from start to finish.

However, simple does not imply simplistic. As you may know, the regular page processing code and the Web Service processing code are implemented as handlers. Both are anything but simple. Their power originates from the `HttpContext` object, which has access to both the request information and the response data. This means that, like a Web Server, a handler can control the whole process on its own. Whatever you want to implement on the level of specific mapping is achievable using handlers.

Scenarios to Use HTTP Handlers

To better understand the power of handlers, let's take a look at what others have implemented on top of `IHttpHandler`:

- Creating dynamic images
- Watermarking existing images
- "Pretty printing" of the page's source code
- Generating dynamic content pulled from a database or external resource
- Transforming content from other resources, such as XML into HTML
- Extracting resources from assemblies on the fly
- Redirecting to/from SSL
- Implementing Pingback and Trackback capabilities, even if the site is not a blog

Additionally, you can implement handlers asynchronously. This vastly extends the potential usage scenarios. Since asynchronous calls are closely related to threading and performance, you looked at threading and how it could benefit from asynchronous programming in Chapter 2. In this section, I will focus more on common usages of basic HTTP handler implementations.

Getting Started

For an HTTP handler, all the action occurs through a single call to `ProcessRequest`. This can be as simple as:

```
public void ProcessRequest(HttpContext context)
{
    context.Response.Write("Hello World");
}
```

Using the `HttpContext` object, you have access to the `Request`, `Response`, `Session`, and `Cache` objects. You have all the key features of an ASP.NET request at your disposal, and you can use this to determine what users submitted and to return content back to the client. (Refer to Chapter 1 to see why `HttpContext` plays such an important role in the request-processing process.)

The key operation of the handler is to write output into the Response object—or, more specifically, the Response object's OutputStream. This output is sent back to the client. Behind the scenes—for IIS6 or classic mode—the ISAPIWorkerRequest sends the OutputStream back to the ISAPI ecb.WriteClient method, which actually performs the IIS output generation. For IIS7 Integrated Mode the pipeline is responsible to handle the OutputStream object. Again, refer to Chapters 1 and 2 to learn more about these steps.

Building a Handler

Now, let's build a simple handler. To do this, you define a class, which implements the System.Web.IHttpHandler interface.

Despite the prominence of the ProcessRequest method, you'll also need to implement a property—IsReusable. This property, which returns a Boolean value, indicates whether the instance can be reused for subsequent requests. In some cases, after processing a request, your handler may not be in a valid state for processing further requests—especially if data about the previous request was stored in member variables. This is because the ASP.NET runtime can handle many requests at the same time. As long as there are threads available in the thread pool, a new request will be processed even if another one is still running. Each thread requires a new instance of the handler, even if the handler is marked "is reusable." When a request is complete, the current handler instance is retained in memory and reused for the next request. This can lead to odd behavior, depending on the workload and on the existence of other instances of the handler. Such problems can be unpredictable and difficult to simulate or recognize in a development environment.

For stable and reliable behavior, you might assume that setting the IsReusable property to false is the solution. After all, this would create a new instance of the object any time a request is about to be processed. However, depending on how "intensive" your code is, this can lead to higher memory consumption, more CPU workload, and less throughput. There is no strict rule about it, but reusing the instances is the preferred solution. Keep in mind that access to members is not exactly what you might expect. Therefore, it is advisable to avoid private members that hold data, if possible. If you still wish to use member variables, remember that they need to be thread safe. When replacing regular members with static methods, you'll have to implement thread safe code. If any of these requirements cannot be fulfilled, you should set IsReusable to false. Otherwise, the implementation will look like the following:

```
public bool IsReusable
{
    get
    {
      return true;
    }
}
```

IsReusable should be a constant. Changing the value during processing would not have any effect, as the value is read once the handler is instantiated.

The Entry Point

The ProcessRequest method is the main entry point for the handler. Its role is to work off the request specified by the HttpRequest instance, from the provided HttpContext instance, and generate an appropriate response using the HttpResponse instance. The ProcessRequest method is invoked by the .NET runtime during the ExecuteRequestHandler request processing stage, assuming that the mapping is able to route the request to the specific handler. This is in contrast to modules, which receive all requests passing through the pipeline.

Finally, let's implement the ProcessRequest method, so that our handler has something to do. To keep things simple, our handler will return the current time of the server. You can specify the time zone in the query string. Our goal is to request a URL, such as http://myserver/page.time, and obtain the current time of the server. In addition, you can get the universal coordinated time (UTC) by requesting http://myserver/page.time?utc=true. Listing 3-6 shows the implementation.

Listing 3-6. *Simple Handler Mapped to a New *.time File Extension*

```
public class TimeHandler : IHttpHandler
{
    #region IHttpHandler Members

    public bool IsReusable
    {
        get { return true; }
    }

    public void ProcessRequest(HttpContext context)
    {
        DateTime dt;
        string useUtc = context.Request.QueryString["utc"];
        if (!String.IsNullOrEmpty(useUtc) && useUtc.Equals("true"))
        {
            dt = DateTime.UtcNow;
        }
        else
        {
            dt = DateTime.Now;
        }
        context.Response.Write( ➥
            String.Format("<html><body><h1>{0}</h1></body></html>", ➥
                          dt.ToLongTimeString() ➥
                          ));

    }

    #endregion
}
```

As you assign this handler to a specific extension—time—you'll only receive it when the client uses this specific URL. The response is simple and creates a small HTML page. You could even tailor the response to suit clients that are not browsers.

You use the HttpRequest.QueryString collection to retrieve a query string variable, and write the current time in response using the HttpResponse.Write method. I recommend using the OutputStream if other handlers are processing the request, or if you want to add to the existing response. In the previous example, you write a complete response in the one handler, and thus the Write method is appropriate. Figure 3-5 shows how to add a module using the IIS Manager.

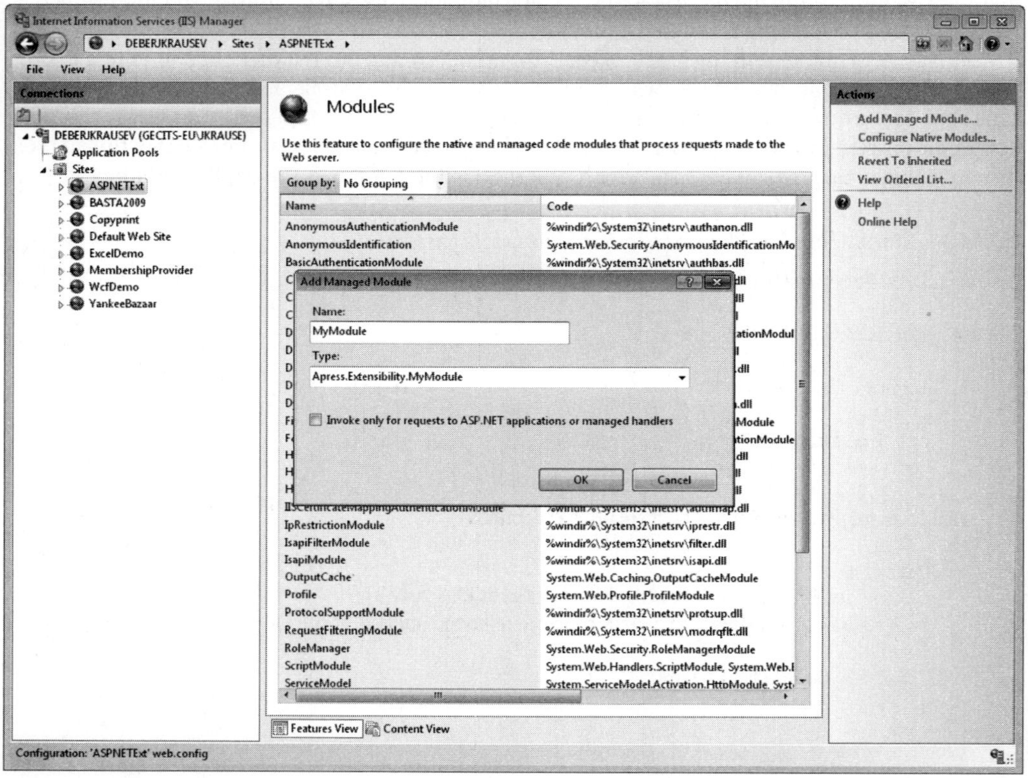

Figure 3-5. *Setting the mapping of a managed handler in IIS7*

IIS7 does not require a restart or any other action in order to activate the handler. A request that uses the mapped extension should work immediately.

Example—Image Handler

A very common scenario for handlers is the manipulation of images. As with any other resource, a browser obtains an image by sending a GET request. Handling large numbers of images at multiple resolutions can be a challenge. Imagine a web shop with thousands of product images stored at one resolution. However, different image sizes are required throughout the site, from catalog thumbnails to large preview panes and icons in the shopping basket. Converting all these images into several different sizes could be expensive, even with a batch script. Images change frequently, and maintaining all current pictures in many different source sizes is an image management headache. Additionally, a watermark is added to the image to protect the intellectual properties of the image's owner.

Writing code and creating images dynamically is a typical task for a handler. Attaching requests to an image could be achieved by using a path filter like *.png. Listing 3-7 shows how easy it is to manipulate content and send it to a client.

Listing 3-7. *Adding a Watermark to an Image and Resizing It Using a Handler*

```
namespace Apress.Extensibility.HttpHandler
{
  public class ImageHandler : IHttpHandler
  {
    #region IHttpHandler Members

    private const float FONTSIZE = 72F;
    private const string FONT = "Verdana";
    private const string TEXT = "Watermark";

    public bool IsReusable
    {
      get { return true; }
    }

    public void ProcessRequest(HttpContext context)
    {
      // determine an image request
      if ((Path.GetDirectoryName( ➥
          context.Request.Url.AbsolutePath)).EndsWith("Images"))
      {
        // load image and add watermark
        Bitmap img = (Bitmap) Bitmap.FromFile( ➥
                      context.Server.MapPath(context.Request.Url.AbsolutePath));
        Graphics g = Graphics.FromImage(img);
        Brush b = new SolidBrush(Color.Silver);
        Font f = new Font(FONT, FONTSIZE);
        SizeF stringMeasure = g.MeasureString(TEXT, f);
        // calculate the string position to center output
        float x, y;
        x = img.Width / 2 - stringMeasure.Width / 2;
        y = img.Height / 2 - stringMeasure.Height / 2;
        g.DrawString(TEXT, new Font(FONT, FONTSIZE), b, x, y);
        // resize to provided data (from QueryString)
        if (context.Request.QueryString["w"] != null &&
            context.Request.QueryString["h"] != null)
        {
          int w, h;
          if (Int32.TryParse(context.Request.QueryString["w"], out w) &&
              Int32.TryParse(context.Request.QueryString["h"], out h))
          {
            img = (Bitmap)img.GetThumbnailImage(w, h, null, IntPtr.Zero);
          }
        }
        // output to the response stream
        img.Save(context.Response.OutputStream, ImageFormat.Jpeg);
        img.Dispose();
      }
    }

    #endregion

  }
}
```

The handler first checks that it is dealing with a file from a particular directory (see Listing 3-8). While the file mapping forces the handler to run for every request for an image with the specified extension, this test restricts the special processing to images in the "Images" folder only. The handler loads the image from disk, resolving the local path via Server.MapPath. Then it applies the watermark to the image. The MeasureString method measures the string size in order to align it with the image so that the text appears centered horizontally and vertically. Streams simplify the output of the image. The Save method sends the output directly into an output stream in JPEG format. Disposing of the image is required, as frequent use of a handler on a system with high workload could prevent the garbage collector from freeing the memory often enough.

Listing 3-8. *The Handler Is As Easy to Use As Any Other Image Resource*

```
<asp:Image runat="server" ID="img1" ImageUrl="~/Images/Img1.png" /><br />
<asp:Image runat="server" ID="Image1" ImageUrl="~/Images/Img1.png?w=100&h=100" />
```

Figure 3-6 shows the output of the watermarked and thumbnail images.

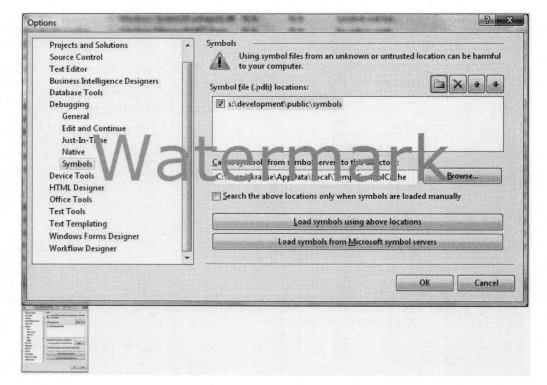

Figure 3-6. *Add a watermark to an image on the fly or create a thumbnail.*

Dynamic image manipulation is powerful and flexible, and there are numerous possibilities for using an image handler in your applications. The final step in creating such a handler is to configure it in *web.config*. Please refer to the section "Configuration and Deployment" to read more about the various settings.

Example—Read Dynamic CSS from Resource

In Listing 3-9, I describe a handler that loads style sheets stored as embedded resources in an assembly. It replaces any call to a style sheet by delivering a specific .css file. The definition in the *web.config* looks like this:

```
<add verb="GET" path="*.css" type="Apress.Extensibility.HttpHandler.CssHandler" />
```

See the section "Configuration and Deployment" for more information about configuring a handler for the IIS7 integrated mode.

To obtain the style files, they must be marked as an embedded resource. There are several ways to handle data from sources other than the file system (see Figure 3-7).

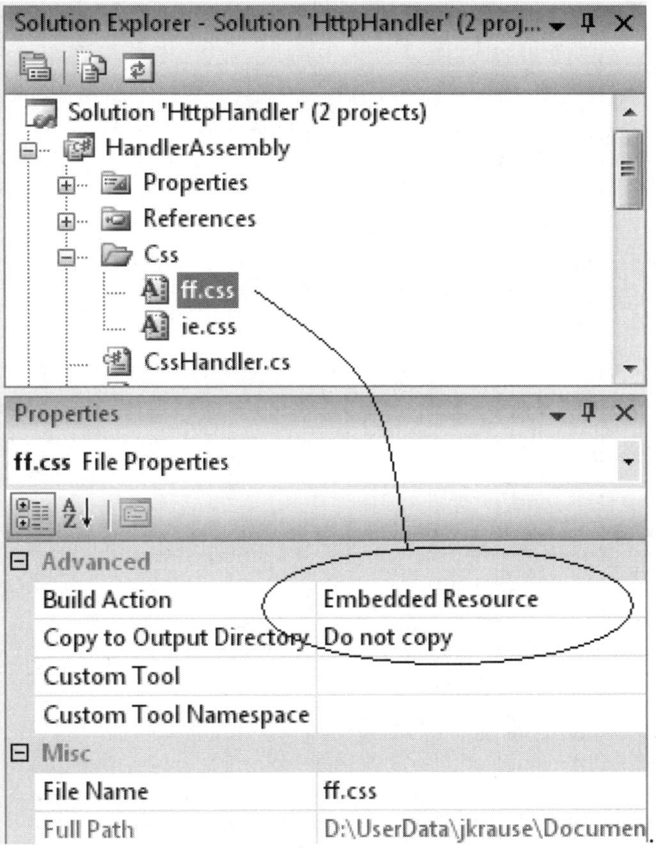

Figure 3-7. *To handle files as embedded resources, use the file's Property box.*

The code itself does not have any quirks. It processes whatever it encounters, and decides how to proceed from the information in HttpContext (see Listing 3-9).

Listing 3-9. *Dynamic Handling of CSS from Embedded Resources*

```
public class CssHandler : IHttpHandler
{
    #region IHttpHandler Members

    public bool IsReusable
    {
        get { return false; }
    }

    public void ProcessRequest(HttpContext context)
    {
        UnmanagedMemoryStream s;
        if (context.Request.UserAgent != null &&
            context.Request.UserAgent.Contains("MSIE"))
        {
            s = (UnmanagedMemoryStream) ➥
                this.GetType().Assembly.GetManifestResourceStream(➥
                            "Apress.HttHandler.HandlerAssembly.Css.ie.css");
        }
        else
        {
            s = (UnmanagedMemoryStream) ➥
                this.GetType().Assembly.GetManifestResourceStream(➥
                            "Apress.HttHandler.HandlerAssembly.Css.ff.css");
        }
        s.Seek(0, SeekOrigin.Begin);
        using (MemoryStream ms = new MemoryStream((int)s.Length))
        {
            byte[] buffer = new byte[s.Length];
            s.Read(buffer, 0, buffer.Length);
            ms.Write(buffer, 0, buffer.Length);
            ms.WriteTo(context.Response.OutputStream);
        }
    }

    #endregion

}
```

First, let's locate the current user agent in this code by using the property UserAgent of the HttpRequest object. If the UserAgent is "MSIE," indicating an Internet Explorer browser, then the resource named "ie.css" is retrieved from the assembly. For any other UserAgents, "ff.css" is loaded instead. The stream is copied to a MemoryStream object. The MemoryStream is helpful, as it is able to copy its own content to another stream by using the WriteTo method. In the case of a handler, this is the output stream provided by the HttpResponse object through the Response property.

This technique can be reused. By looking for specific file extensions and for the "user-agent" header, you can block certain clients from reading the content of these resources or supply them with a replacement resource. Alternatively, reading resources from a database instead of an assembly gives more flexibility without adding code to the pages themselves.

USING WEB RESOURCES

The example shown in this section is just to explain typical scenarios for HTTP handlers. Especially regarding web resource management, the preferred method for storing and retrieving resources is the embedding of web resources. Using an assembly bound attribute, you can add any kind of data to the assembly:

```
[assembly: WebResource("Css.ie.css", "text/css")]
[assembly: WebResource("Css.ff.css", "text/css")]
```

An embedded handler for the designated `.axd` extension retrieves the resources from server. The URL uses two query string values, "d" and "t". "d" takes an encrypted ID of that value and "t" a time stamp. To retrieve such a resource, you can create the URL, using the following code snippet from a page:

```
ClientScriptManager cs = Page.ClientScript;

Type rsType = this.GetType();
HtmlLink hlCss = new HtmlLink();
hlCss.Href = cs.GetWebResourceUrl(rsType, "Css.ie.css");
this.Controls.Add(hlCss);
```

The call of the `GetWebResourceUrl` method assures that the parameters for query string are set properly.

Example—Handler That Does Not Create Content

Handlers usually create content—typically HTML or data that builds an image. However, it's not imperative. Handlers are primarily invoked by the associated file extension. Imagine you define a custom extension named ".counter" and associate it with a handler. Your handler might execute some code, but ignore the Writer and not send anything back to the client. Another idea is to only write data to the client when you run the handler in debug mode and save bandwidth when running on a production server. Whether or not the output is required, you'll still have to invoke the handler by issuing a GET or POST request to the server. Therefore, you'll need an element that can force the browser to create such a request. There are only a few ways to do this:

- Image element
- Form element
- IFrame element
- JavaScript code

I'm using an IFRAME element in the following example, because I want to show the content when in debug mode, and leave the content empty, otherwise. The definition of the IFRAME demonstrates how you invoke the handler, as shown in Listing 3-10.

Listing 3-10. *Invoke a Handler Using a Registered Extension*

```
<iframe src="my.counter" width="100" height="50" scrolling="no"></iframe>
```

Furthermore, the handler itself shows the processing within the `ProcessRequest` method (see Listing 3-11).

Listing 3-11. *Code of the Handler*

```
public class CounterHandler : IHttpHandler
{

    #region IHttpHandler Members

    public bool IsReusable
    {
        get { return true; }
    }

    public void ProcessRequest(HttpContext context)
    {
        string path = context.Request.UrlReferrer.LocalPath;
        string file = context.Server.MapPath("Counter.xml");
        XDocument cntDoc = XDocument.Load(file);
        var cnt = (from e in cntDoc.Root.Elements("page") where ➥
                          e.Attribute("path").Value.Equals(path) ➥
                          select e).FirstOrDefault<XElement>();
        if (Debugger.IsAttached)
        {
            // In debug mode read only and create output
            // reading XML is thread safe
            context.Response.Write(String.Format("Counter = {0}", ➥
                                   cnt.Attribute("count").Value));
        }
        else
        {
            // in production just store values
            ReaderWriterLock rwl = new ReaderWriterLock();
            rwl.AcquireWriterLock(TimeSpan.FromSeconds(2));
            if (cnt == null)
            {
                // page does not exist yet
                XElement newPage = new XElement("page",
                    new XAttribute("count", 1),
                    new XAttribute("path", path));
                cntDoc.Element("Pages").Add(newPage);
            }
            else
            {
                // increase counter, set time stamp
                int i = Int32.Parse(cnt.Attribute("count").Value);
                cnt.Attribute("count").Value = (++i).ToString();
            }
            cntDoc.Save(file);
            rwl.ReleaseWriterLock();
        }
    }

    #endregion
}
```

The handler stores the number of page requests in a single XML document. Other developers can add the IFRAME code to the pages they want included in the counter total. Internally, the file access is shared read mode. The FileStream class used behind the scenes in XDocument.Load supports reading from different threads. However, write access requires an exclusive lock, block-ing other threads. To achieve this, a `ReaderWriterLock` class monitors the threads and blocks other threads from accessing the file during write mode. This isn't a very efficient method. In a real-life scenario, consider replacing the XML access with a database operation. After obtaining access to the XML, LINQ to XML is used to either create elements for the first time or add to the existing counter when the page is requested again.

In the example, you want to distinguish between debug mode and production mode. You can ascertain debug mode by using the `Debugger.IsAttached` property. In debug mode, the content of the IFRAME is filled with the counter for the current page. The LINQ statement prepared at the beginning of the `ProcessRequest` method returns either `null` or the element containing the counter information.

Figure 3-8 shows the output in debug mode. The counter does not increase for requests in debug mode. In production mode, the counter increases but no output displays.

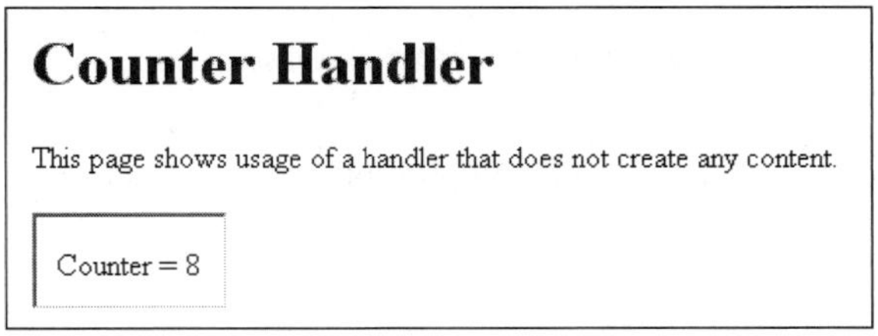

Figure 3-8. *Output of the handler in debug mode*

In this example, I showed a handler that doesn't create content with every use. The concepts behind this are:

- Defining how and where to invoke the handler
- Remembering that concurrent threads access the code
- Recognizing that creating output is not mandatory

Example—Using IHttpHandlerFactory to Perform URL Rewriting

In this example, I'll introduce another interface. For more flexibility with creating handlers on the fly, the `IHttpHandlerFactory` interface is available. A closer look at the default `PageHandlerFactory` shows that it is not derived from `IhttpHandler`, but from `IHttpHandlerFactory`. This class is used to process the regular `.aspx` pages.

You don't have to create a factory, but it gives more control over the creation process. It can be useful in more complex scenarios. First, let's look into the interface definition:

```
public interface IHttpHandlerFactory
{
    IHttpHandler GetHandler(HttpContext context, ➥
                            string requestType, ➥
                            string url, ➥
                            string pathTranslated);
    void ReleaseHandler(IHttpHandler handler);
}
```

■**Note** If you decode this using Reflector, you may see another interface named `IHttpHandlerFactory2`. This provides another overload for the `GetHandler` method. You don't need this at this stage, as you'll only be using the `IHttpHandlerFactory`.

Imagine you have a page with content such as:

`<% = DateTime.Now.ToString("M") %>`

Set the current culture by adding the culture ID to the URL. Typical URLs look like this:

- `http://localhost/Chapter03/UrlRewriteFactoryHandler/Default.aspx`
- `http://localhost/Chapter03/UrlRewriteFactoryHandler/en-us/Default.aspx`
- `http://localhost/Chapter03/UrlRewriteFactoryHandler/de-de/Default.aspx`
- `http://localhost/Chapter03/UrlRewriteFactoryHandler/fr-fr/Default.aspx`

Our goal is to find a way to extract the culture code (such as "de-de" or "en-us") from the URL, set it as the current culture of the thread, and process the page without the culture code, as shown in the first URL. Listing 3-12 shows a factory that creates the required instances.

Listing 3-12. *Using a Factory to Rewrite a URL*

```
public abstract class RewriteFactoryHandler : IHttpHandlerFactory
{
    protected RewriteFactoryHandler()
        : base()
    {
    }

    IHttpHandler IHttpHandlerFactory.GetHandler(HttpContext context, ➥
                                                string requestType, ➥
                                                string url, ➥
                                                string pathTranslated)
    {
        Pair target = GetRemapInfo(context, requestType, url, pathTranslated);
        string filename = context.Server.MapPath(target.First.ToString());
        context.RewritePath(url, url, target.Second.ToString());
        IHttpHandler appHandler = ➥
                PageParser.GetCompiledPageInstance(target.First.ToString(), ➥
                                                    filename, context);
        return appHandler;
    }

    void IHttpHandlerFactory.ReleaseHandler(IHttpHandler handler)
    {
    }

    protected abstract Pair GetRemapInfo(HttpContext context, string requestType, ➥
                                        string url, string pathTranslated);
}

public class CultureRewriteHandler : RewriteFactoryHandler
{
```

```
protected override Pair GetRemapInfo(HttpContext context, ↪
                                    string requestType, ↪
                                    string url, ↪
                                    string pathTranslated)
{
    string originalPath = HttpContext.Current.Request.Path;
    string stemPath = "/"; // Example, replace with virtual directory if any
    string newPath = originalPath.Substring(originalPath.IndexOf(stemPath) + ↪
                                  stemPath.Length);
    string[] segments = newPath.Split('/');
    string queryString = HttpContext.Current.Request.Url.Query;
    try
    {
        string languagePart = segments[0];
        CultureInfo ci = new CultureInfo(languagePart);
        System.Threading.Thread.CurrentThread.CurrentCulture = ci;
        return new Pair("/" + stemPath + string.Join("/", segments, 1, ↪
                        segments.Length - 1), queryString);
    }
    catch (NullReferenceException)
    {
    }
    return new Pair(originalPath, queryString);
}
}
```

The definition in *web.config* or IIS settings is the same as for any other handler. This means that the ASP.NET engine will accept both IHttpHandler and IHttpHandlerFactory in order to obtain access to the handler object.

The code is simplified for clarity. You can extend the error handling by adding code to handle the stem path, even if it's set to a value other than the root path. The core implementation is around the GetHandler method, which returns the used handler. If resources are blocked and need to be freed or disposed of, the required code will appear in the ReleaseHandler method. As shown in the example, this is not always necessary. Keep in mind that the memory consumption of the handler might be an issue if the server has a high workload, in which case releasing resources could help.

Figure 3-9 shows the behavior for several languages. URL rewriting is a flexible, search engine-friendly method of modifying behavior.

Figure 3-9. *Use URL rewriting to set the current culture of a Web application.*

This example demonstrated a very basic handler factory. In the abstract base class, the `GetHandler` method rewrites using `HttpContext.RewritePath`. The default page handler is subsequently retrieved and returned. This is required because otherwise, the processing of all `.aspx` pages is remapped to the new factory. Redefining the internal handler with your own one replaces the mapping, as only one handler can process a specific request. Remapping the default handler requires either a complete implementation of a handler with similar behavior, or creating the original handler and returning it using a factory. From the perspective of extensibility, the latter is the better option.

Advanced Usage of Handlers

The standard handlers cover most, but not all, tasks. Http handlers can go further. In this section, I'll discuss advanced extensibility topics:

- Accessing the session state
- Dynamically dealing with handlers in the pipeline

Handlers and Session State

Handlers are low-level programming constructs. They are critical for overall performance and if badly written or configured, could degrade the server's throughput. While there are ways to deal with long-running threads in the handler code (as you saw in Chapter 2), it's preferable to write handlers that run as fast as possible. To maximize handler speed, Microsoft removed session information from the default handlers. The previous examples show useful tasks accomplished without needing session information.

If you do need to access session state information, it is available by implementing one of the following two interfaces:

- `IRequiredSessionState`
- `IReadOnlySessionState`

It's possible to obtain session information with minimal performance loss. If you only require read access to the session data, the `IReadOnlySessionState` is ideal. `IRequiredSessionState` gives full access to all session data. When adding either interface to your class, you'll notice that Visual Studio does not attempt to implement any method bodies. Both interfaces are simply marker interfaces that modify the internal processing within the base class. Your class declaration should look like this:

```
public class TimeHandlerWithSession : IHttpHandler, IRequiredSessionState
```

The session information is now provided to the `HttpContext` object, and available through the `context` parameter of the entry method. Listing 3-13 passes a value through a session variable to the handler.

Listing 3-13. *The Handler Implementation with Session Support*

```
public class TimeHandlerWithSession : IHttpHandler, IReadOnlySessionState
{
    #region IHttpHandler Members

    public bool IsReusable
    {
        get { return true; }
    }
```

```
public void ProcessRequest(HttpContext context)
{
    DateTime dt;
    string useUtc = context.Request.QueryString["utc"];
    if (!String.IsNullOrEmpty(useUtc) && useUtc.Equals("true"))
    {
        dt = DateTime.UtcNow;
    }
    else
    {
        dt = DateTime.Now;
    }
    context.Response.Write( ➥
        String.Format(context.Session["FormatString"].ToString(),➥
                      dt.ToLongTimeString() ➥
                      ));

}

#endregion
}
```

The only difference from the previous example is the session value named "FormatString" retrieved from context.Session object. In the application, you can set that very value to control the behavior of the handler. For performance purposes, the IReadOnlySessionState interface is used because only read access is required.

Accessing the Pipeline Using the Context

You can use these three properties of the HttpContext object to further modify the behavior of the handler or to retrieve more information about what is taking place:

- context.Handler
- context.PreviousHandler
- context.RemapHandler

Using the Handler property, you have access to the current handler employed in the current context. Since the context is available as a static property, it's easy to access the handler in classes defined elsewhere. This also applies to the PreviousHandler property, a property that is set when the handler is remapped. Remapping a handler might occur in complex scenarios where a default handler processes all requests, but remaps to another handler under certain circumstances. Listing 3-14 demonstrates this technique.

Listing 3-14. *Remapping to Another Handler*

```
public class RemapHandler : IHttpHandler
{
    #region IHttpHandler Members

    public bool IsReusable
    {
        get { return true; }
    }
```

```
    public void ProcessRequest(HttpContext context)
    {
        IHttpHandler remapHandler = null;
        // determine an image request and handle with private handler
        if ((Path.GetExtension(context.Request.Url.AbsolutePath)).Equals(".png"))
        {
            remapHandler = new ImageHandler();
        }
        else
        {
            // process any other request with default handler
            string virtualPath = context.Request.Url.AbsolutePath;
            string filename = HttpContext.Current.Request.Path;
            remapHandler = PageParser.GetCompiledPageInstance(virtualPath, ➥
                                               filename, context);
        }
        context.RemapHandler(remapHandler);
    }

    #endregion
}
```

In this code, the handler searches for `.png` extensions and assigns private handlers to process them. Otherwise, you use the standard page processing; no other custom code is involved. Simply call `context.RemapHandler(remapHandler)` to assign to a different handler. All internal processing is redirected to the new handler from the beginning of the pipeline. As there's no additional overhead, there are no performance issues with the handler remapping.

Asynchronous Pages

The processing of pages relies on just another kind of built-in handler. When processing pages, you have often lengthy operations against databases, Web Services, or external data sources that could block your worker threads. Here you might wonder whether it's possible to process even regular pages asynchronously. Fortunately, the Framework already implements this for us, and there is nothing to do but set a property.

Prepare Pages for Asynchronous Operation

Building asynchronous pages is simple. Begin by including an attribute in the page's @Page directive:

```
<%@ Page Async="true" ... %>
```

Behind the scenes, this tells ASP.NET to implement `IHttpAsyncHandler` in the page instead of `IHttpHandler` used regularly.

Figure 3-10 illustrates the difference between a synchronous page and an asynchronous page. When a synchronous page is requested, ASP.NET assigns the request a thread from the thread pool and executes the page on that thread.

That's enough theory for now. The following examples address a common problem. It calls a Web Service—a current exchange rate service that converts between US$ and Euro. Putting this on a Web Site is a good idea for a shop that has an international audience. However, blocking the server's thread due to unpredictable calls to a foreign service is no solution.

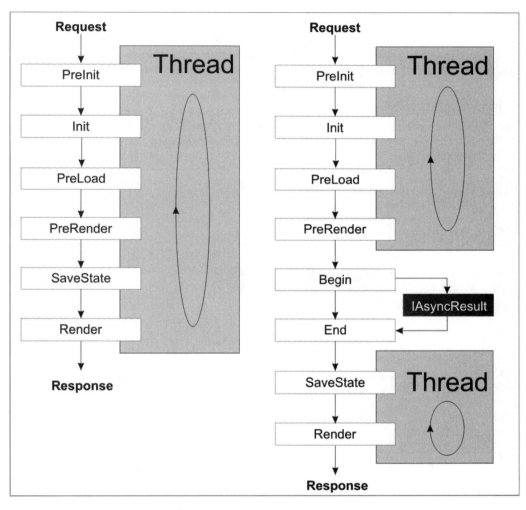

Figure 3-10. *Synchronous vs. asynchronous page processing*

Using a Public Web Service

Using a public Web Service is both convenient and risky. You have a powerful service available and can use it as the terms and conditions permit. However, between the service's host and your server is a long distance and many things could go wrong. Just assume that the service experiences high workload, and either responses are delayed or the service stops working completely. Blocking your application's thread could cause huge performance loss. Just to simplify first steps into the world of asynchronous pages, the following example uses a public service that appears to be almost reliable.

There are several public services available to test such an application. At of the time of publishing, the following works: http://www.webservicex.com/CurrencyConvertor.asmx.

Prepare a Project to Consume a Service

The only step required to consume a service is to reference it. The address previously shown is already the service's endpoint itself. To reference the service, right-click the project and choose "Add Web Reference" (see Figure 3-11).

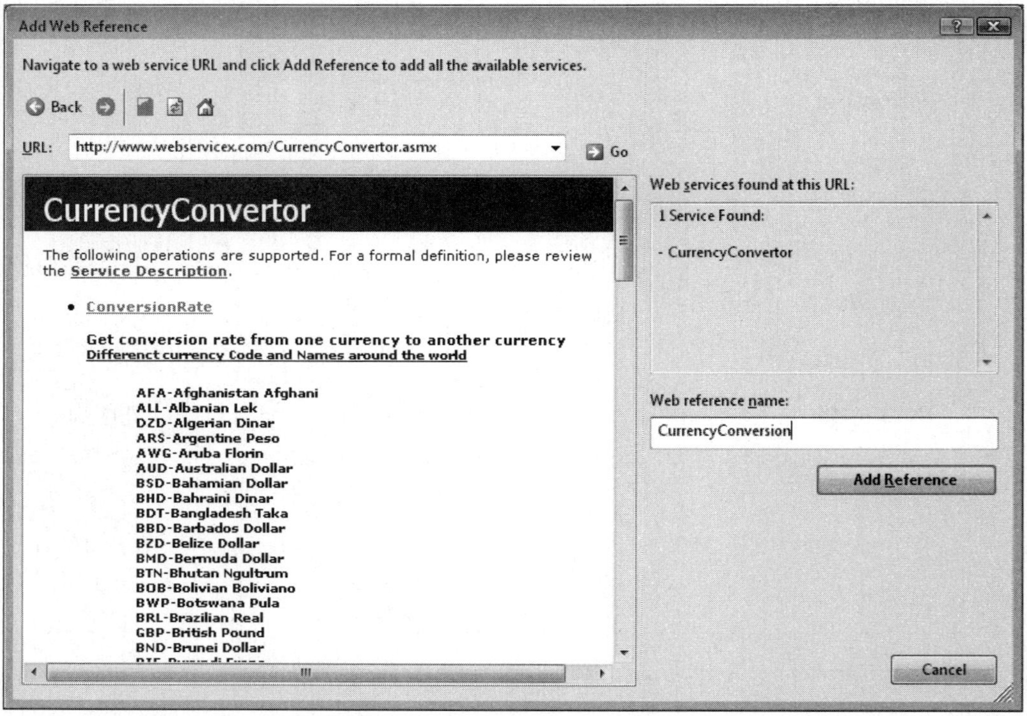

Figure 3-11. *Add a reference to an external Web Service.*

Calling Web Services Asynchronously

If a Web Service has a method named ConversionRate, then the Web Service proxy includes a method named ConversionRateAsync and an event named ConversionRateCompleted. You can call ConversionRate asynchronously by registering a handler for the completed event and calling ConversionRateAsync, as shown in Listing 3-15.

Listing 3-15. *Calling a Web Service from an ASP.NET Page Asynchronously*

```
public partial class _Default : System.Web.UI.Page
{
    CurrencyConvertor cc;

    protected void Page_Load(object sender, EventArgs e)
    {
        cc = new CurrencyConvertor();
    }

    protected void btnSend_Click(object sender, EventArgs e)
    {
        cc.ConversionRateCompleted += new ➥
            ConversionRateCompletedEventHandler(cc_ConversionRateCompleted);
        cc.ConversionRateAsync(Currency.USD, Currency.EUR);
    }

    void cc_ConversionRateCompleted(object sender, ➥
                                ConversionRateCompletedEventArgs e)
    {
        double amount = Double.Parse(txtAmount.Text);
        lblResult.Text = (e.Result * amount).ToString();
    }
}
```

The code in the following sidebar presents a behind class that calls a Web Service's `ConversionRate` method asynchronously using the "MethodAsync" pattern. Functionally, this is identical to the one shown in Listing 3-15. However, internally it is quite different. Again, the `@Page` directive's Async property is set to `true`. Instead of registering the methods that handle the asynchronous callbacks, a direct call and a callback event is used. Behind the scene, it uses an instance of `System.Threading.SynchronizationContext`, a class that receives notifications when the asynchronous calls begin and when they complete.

There are two advantages to using this pattern rather than `AddOnPreRenderCompleteAsync` to implement what is shown in the following sidebar. It supports forwarding impersonation, culture, and `HttpContext.Current` to the complete event handler. Furthermore, imagine a page makes multiple asynchronous calls and delays rendering until all calls have been completed.

Using the `AddOnPreRenderCompleteAsync` method requires you to compose an `IAsyncResult` that remains unsignaled until all the calls are finished. With the "MethodAsync" pattern, the engine is responsible for delaying the rendering until the last callback returns. You may invoke as many asynchronous calls as you need.

The Page class introduces also the `RegisterAsyncTask` method of facilitating asynchronous operations for specific tasks. `RegisterAsyncTask` has several advantages above the `AddOnPreRenderCompleteAsync` method. The support for a timeout would be especially helpful. However, this is still a workaround for the old Begin/End pattern that's indeed required to get the right methods from a proxy.

In case you write your own asynchronous operations and do not use the integrated proxy generator, you can still use the Begin/End pattern. In that case, the `RegisterAsyncTask` method might help by adding the missing timeout support. To use this method, the only thing required is a third callback, which is invoked after the operation timed out.

WHERE THE BEGIN-END PATTERN HAS GONE

You may have read or heard about the classic Begin/End pattern used to call services asynchronously. However, when referencing a Web Service using the new style Web Project as provided in Visual Studio, the BeginMethod and EndMethod proxy methods are hidden as protected methods. Microsoft recommends using the new pattern as described in this section.

However, if you like to use the old pattern, a few more steps are required. First, you can use the old style Web project (use File ➤ New ➤ Web Site instead of File ➤ New ➤ Project ➤ Web Project). Secondly, add the reference to the Web Service. The generated proxy will now expose the BeginMethod and EndMethod methods for all the service's methods.

Next, you have to call the AddOnPreRenderCompleteAsync method early in the page's lifetime. For example, in Load this is early enough. Register a Begin method and an End method, as shown in the following code:

```
AddOnPreRenderCompleteAsync (
    new BeginEventHandler(BeginMethod),
    new EndEventHandler (EndMethod)
);
```

The page runs through its normal processing life cycle until shortly after the PreRender event fires. Then ASP.NET calls the BeginMethod just registered. The method launches an asynchronous operation and returns immediately. This is the lengthy operation previously mentioned that might require more time. At this point, the thread assigned to the request returns to the thread pool. Furthermore, the method returns an IAsyncResult that allows ASP.NET to determine when the asynchronous operation has been completed. ASP.NET then extracts a thread from the thread pool and calls your End method (EndMethod). After this returns, it executes the remaining portion of the page's life cycle. This might sound confusing—getting the thread back from thread pool and blocking the thread again. However, between the time Begin returns and End is called, the request-processing thread is free to serve other requests. Keep in mind that the page processing usually takes only a few milliseconds. The time-consuming operation in the asynchronous handler might run for seconds. The process of freeing the thread pool thread for this time allows ASP.NET to process hundreds, if not thousands, of regular pages on this very same thread. However, until End is called, the rendering of the current asynchronous page is delayed. This is the same as in the previous example. It improves the situation not only for one user, but also for all users. In the sample code, you might look for the IAsyncResult implementation. Instead of implementing our own version, you take one that the Framework implements for us.

The complete code of such an example would look like the following:

```
public partial class _Default : System.Web.UI.Page
{

    CurrencyConvertor cc;

    protected void Page_Load(object sender, EventArgs e)
    {
    }

    IAsyncResult BeginConversion(object sender, EventArgs e,
        AsyncCallback cb, object state)
    {
        cc = new CurrencyConvertor();
        return cc.BeginConversionRate(Currency.USD, Currency.EUR, cb, state);
    }
```

```
    void EndConversion(IAsyncResult ar)
    {
        double result = cc.EndConversionRate(ar);
        double amount = Double.Parse(txtAmount.Text);
        lblResult.Text = (result * amount).ToString();
    }


    protected void btnSend_Click(object sender, EventArgs e)
    {
        AddOnPreRenderCompleteAsync(
            new BeginEventHandler(BeginConversion),
            new EndEventHandler(EndConversion));
    }
}
```

Here the asynchronous methods are registered with the Button's click event. BeginConversionRate and EndConversionRate are the methods used to invoke the service and get the result back.

Configuration and Deployment

To create a handler, you chose "Class Library" as the project template, removed the default class created by the template, and added an object of type "ASP.NET Handler." Now that you have implemented the handler, you can compile it into an assembly loaded by ASP.NET at runtime (see Figure 3-12). As long as the handler remains in the web application, this is simple. No special action is required. You'll probably want to implement several handlers and keep them in different assemblies for easy reuse. Simply reference the assemblies in your web project.

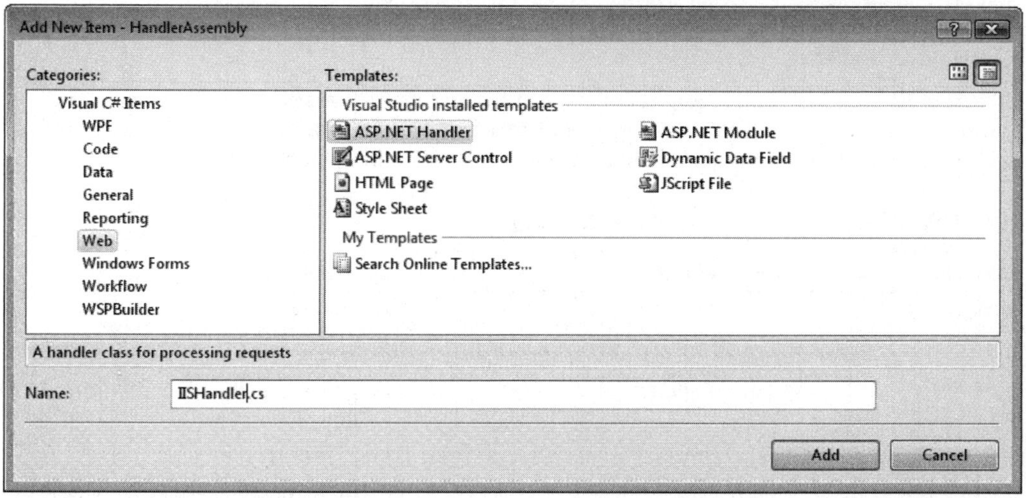

Figure 3-12. *Add a handler to the current project*

Configuring Default Web Server and Development Environment

To test the handler, you'll need to configure the settings in *web.config*. Place the appropriate settings in the `<system.web>` section:

```
<httpHandlers>
  <add verb="GET" path="*.png" type="Apress.HttpHandler.ImageHandler" />
</httpHandlers>
```

In case you have a similar handler definition in the upside configuration path you might consider using either `<remove/>` or `<clear/>` tags to overwrite the values properly.

The settings for the development environment also apply to IIS5, IIS6, and IIS7 in classic mode. There are several advantages—as explained in Chapter 1—to running the IIS7 integrated pipeline, however, which involves the different settings shown in Table 3-12.

Table 3-12. *Options of the httpHandler Settings*

Attribute	Typical Values	Description
verb	GET, POST	The handler responds to the HTTP verbs only.
path	full path or wildcards	The path that defines the requests the handlers responds to.
type	class, assembly	Type information of the handler's definition.

Configuring IIS7 Settings

In the main (web) project, add a reference to this project. If the namespace of the external project is `Apress.HttHandler.ImageHandler`, the following addition to *web.config* will be required:

```
<system.webServer>
  <handlers>
    <add name="ImageHandler" path="*.png" verb="GET"
         type="Apress.HttpHandler.ImageHandler" resourceType="File"
         requireAccess="Read" preCondition="integratedMode" />
  </handlers>
</system.webServer>
```

Compile both the project containing the handler and the web project. Add the mapping in Internet Information Services Manager, as shown before. The mapping will now function perfectly for both the development environment and direct usage from the local IIS7 (see Table 3-13).

Table 3-13. *Handler Settings for IIS7 Integrated Mode*

Attribute	Typical Values	Description
verb	GET, POST	The handler responds to the HTTP verbs only. Other verbs are DEBUG and HEAD.
path	full path or wildcards	The path that defines the requests the handlers respond to.
resourceType	File	Expect that the file exists.
scriptProcessor	a path	Path to the engine (DLL) that handles the request.
requireAccess	Script, Execute, None, Read, Write	Required settings for resource access.

Attribute	Typical Values	Description
resourceType	Directory, Either, File, Unspecified	The type of the resource the handler is mapped to. The default value is Unspecified.
preCondition	See following list	Conditions that must be fulfilled to activate the handler. If the request fails, an HTTP error 412 "precondition failed" is sent to the client.
allowPathInfo	true,false	Specifies whether the handler processes full path information. If set to false, the handler processes the file information part of a path only.
modules	Names	Optional comma separated list of modules the extension is mapped to. By default, handler settings map to ManagedPipelineHandler.
type	class, assembly	The type name of the handler.

Typical values for preCondition are these:

- bitness32, bitness64: Activate 32-bit or 64-bit mode respectively
- runtimeVersion1.1, runtimeVersion2.0: The required runtime on the server
- classicMode, integratedMode: Mode that IIS7 is running in
- managedHandler: Requires the handler to be written in managed code

Configure via IIS Management Console

The settings in *web.config* required by IIS7 integrated mode can be altered via the IIS Management Console. The settings correspond directly. Altering *web.config* will result in an immediate change to the Management Console settings, and vice versa. To configure using the IIS Management Console:

1. Open Internet Information Service Manager.

2. Open the web you want to change.

3. In the IIS section, double-click on the Handler Mappings.

4. Click on Add Managed Handler in the task list to the right.

5. Enter these values in the dialog. Leave the dialog by clicking OK, then:

   a. The Request path: *.time.

   b. Choose the handler from the drop-down list. The handler will appear in the list, as long as you're in the right web and the project compiles.

   c. Give the handler an appropriate name.

   d. Click on Request Restrictions . . .

   e. Open the Verbs tab.

   f. Click on one of the following verbs and enter the value "GET".

6. Leave the main dialog by clicking OK.

Configure Using Generic Handlers

The final option is not a configuration option, but a way of invoking handlers without configuring them in *web.config*. By default, ASP.NET defines handlers using the extension .ashx. Therefore, placing the code for a handler in a file using the following declarative form is sufficient to get it working. There is no further need for *web.config*. An advantage of this is that you won't need to distinguish between the settings for IIS7 integrated mode and other Web Servers, nor will you need to maintain settings in the *web.config* regarding handlers.

Creating such a handler involves two steps:

1. For each handler required, create a file with the extension .ashx.

2. Add the following declaration at the top of the file:

```
<%@ WebHandler Language="C#" Class="Apress.HttpHandler.MyHandler" %>
```

The WebHandler directive is similar to the Page directive. Only a few options are available, however, as shown in Table 3-14.

Table 3-14. *Attributes Supported for WebHandler Directive*

Attribute	Available Values	Usage
Language	C#, VB	Language of the code section.
Class	Name	Name of the class defined in code, including the namespace.
CodeBehind	Name	Name of the file containing the code.
CompilerOptions		Options for on-the-fly compilation.
Debug	True, False	Compile in debug or release mode. In debug mode, the symbol file (.pdb) is created.
WarningLevel	0 to 4	Warning level.
Description		A description for documentation purposes only. The page parser does not recognize this attribute.

Whether you use the configuration file or the .ashx extension is a matter of preference. However, there are some basic guidelines for selecting the best option. Using the .ashx file within an application is better for small projects or handlers that have simple, but specific, tasks. If you plan to reuse the handler several times, or in several projects on the server, you should separate it into its own assembly and register it in the Global Assembly Cache (GAC). Storing handlers in assemblies with signing and deployment capabilities is for larger projects involving handler reuse.

Testing and Debugging Modules and Handlers

Having deployed and configured the module or handler, debugging may be required. In Visual Studio, the normal Debug mode works well for debugging handlers. You're probably already familiar with the debugging capabilities in Visual Studio. Setting breakpoints and viewing variable's values is just as simple for handlers as for any other type of .NET solution.

Debug Using IIS

You may occasionally experience trouble with your application when running on IIS. There are no breakpoints, and adding, logging, and tracing capabilities can be tedious. In large projects there are often coding guidelines that require you to add tracing code and to log pertinent messages (such as exceptions). In smaller projects, it might not be appropriate to write more code for logging and tracing. Setting a simple breakpoint and examining a value or condition during a request would be nice.

It can be done. To do so, you can attach a debugger to a running application. In the case of an ASP.NET application running on IIS7, this is the worker process—w3wp.exe. Let's consider the case where you have not published your project, but simply compiled on the fly, and your sources—the .cs files—are still available beside the .aspx files. (I'll discuss techniques for attaching to a precompiled project later in the section "Problems Debugging the Worker Process".) Here, the Visual Studio debugger attaches automatically to the current process when you hit F5 and start a debug session. This current process is the internal Web Server included in Visual Studio. You can achieve the same thing simply by attaching the debugger to the worker process. If the worker process is not running, force it by requesting the first page and invoking the modules or handlers configured for your application. It doesn't matter whether it is running properly or not.

Here is a brief summary of the pre-conditions so far:

- IIS is configured to run the Web directly from project files.

- Visual Studio is running and has the project loaded (however, there is no debug session so far).

- The Worker process is up and running (see Figure 3-13).

■Tip You can force the worker process to start by invoking a first request to the application. To check whether it is available, open Task Manager, switch to the Processes tab, check the box (Windows Server 2008) or click the button (Windows Vista) Show Processes From All Users, and search for w3wp.exe in the list.

Now open Visual Studio and attach the debugger to the worker process:

1. Open *Debug ➤ Attach to Process . . .*

2. In the subsequent dialog, check these settings:

    - *Transport*: default.

    - *Qualifier*: The name of the server or workstation.

    - In the *Attached to* section, you should at least have the option Managed Code selected. Use the Select button to change settings.

3. In the list of Available Processes, look for the worker process. If it's not there, tick the check-box *Show processes from all users*. This is same option as in the Task Manager.

4. Use the Refresh button to reload the list of processes during the session without closing the dialog.

5. Mark available worker processes and click *Attach,* as shown in Figure 3-14.

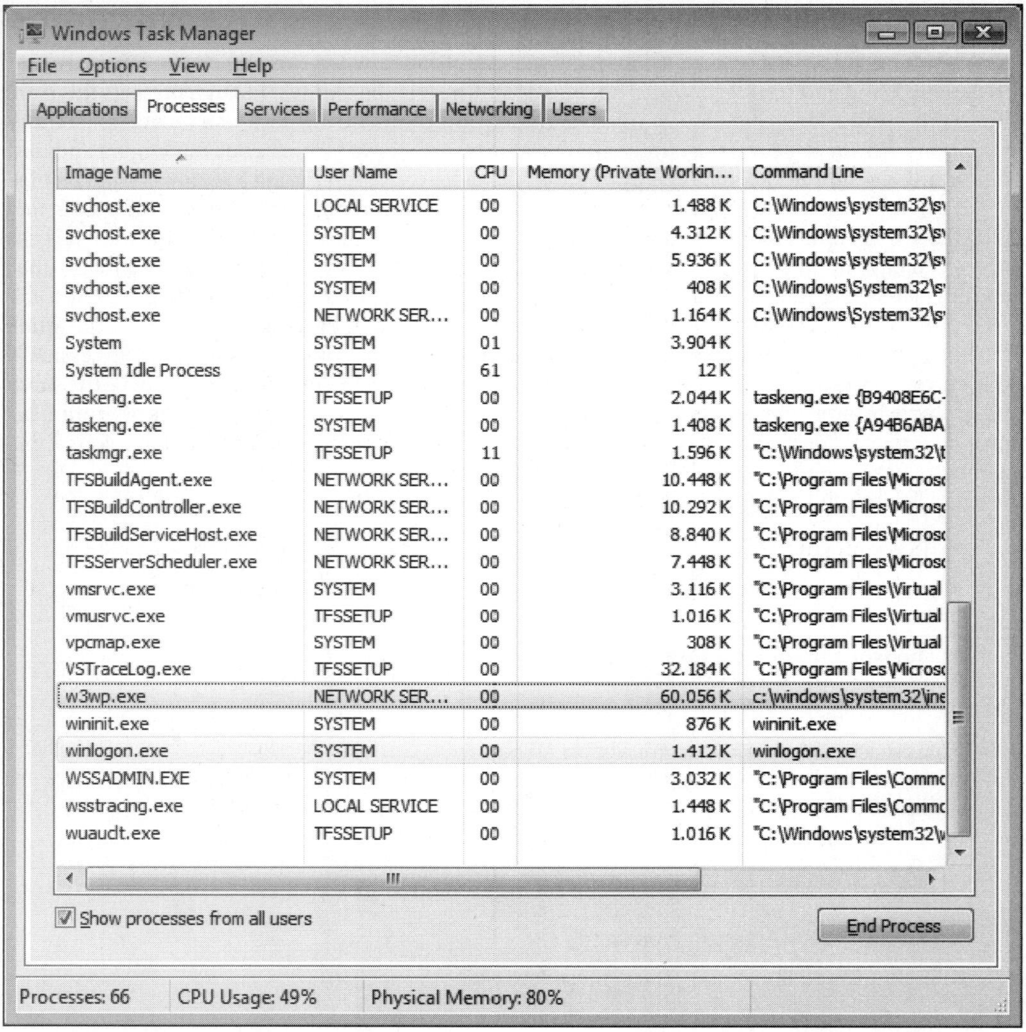

Figure 3-13. *Use the Task Manager to check for the worker process.*

Depending on your server conditions, you may find that several worker processes appear in the list. If you're not sure which process is the one handling the current request, you can attach to all of them. Alternatively, use Task Manager to kill all the worker processes, issue a new request to your application, and refresh the list. If no one else is using the server, one worker process will appear. Of course, the usage of worker processes—as explained in Chapter 2—depends on the threads required. Under rare circumstances, the application needs more power and splits the requests into multiple worker processes. However, attaching several instances of the worker process to the same debugger session is quite easy.

With Visual Studio running in debug mode, as it is when you hit the F5 key, you can set breakpoints within the module or handler code and invoke a request to hit the breakpoint. You can even watch the debug and trace information in the output window.

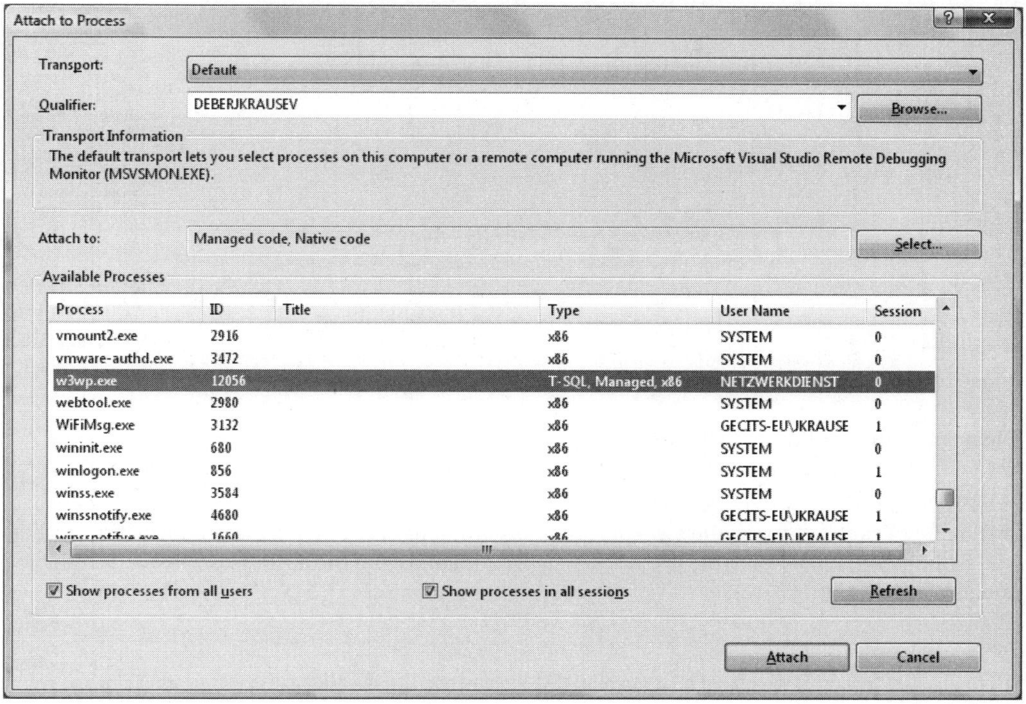

Figure 3-14. *Attaching the debugger to the worker process*

Problems Debugging the Worker Process

Sometimes the behavior of the debugger does not match your expectations. Quite frequently the breakpoints appear inactive, or they can't be "hit," as Visual Studio calls it (see Figure 3-15).

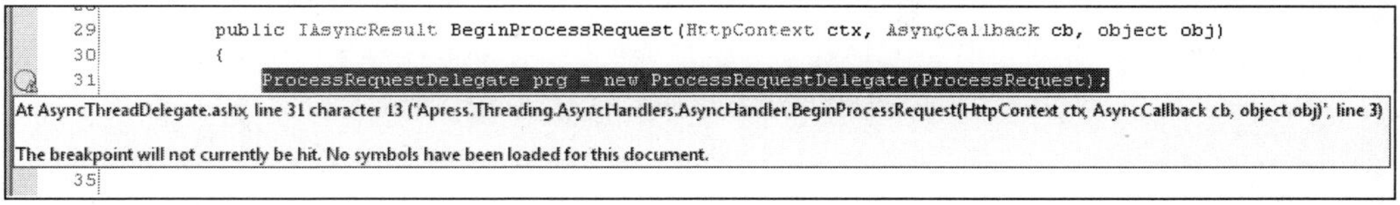

Figure 3-15. *The breakpoint will not currently be hit.*

Usually this is because the page has not yet been loaded. Since you decided to let ASP.NET compile pages on the fly, the current page might not yet be available and therefore the symbols are not built. To check this, use the *Modules* dialog in Visual Studio as shown in Figure 3-16.

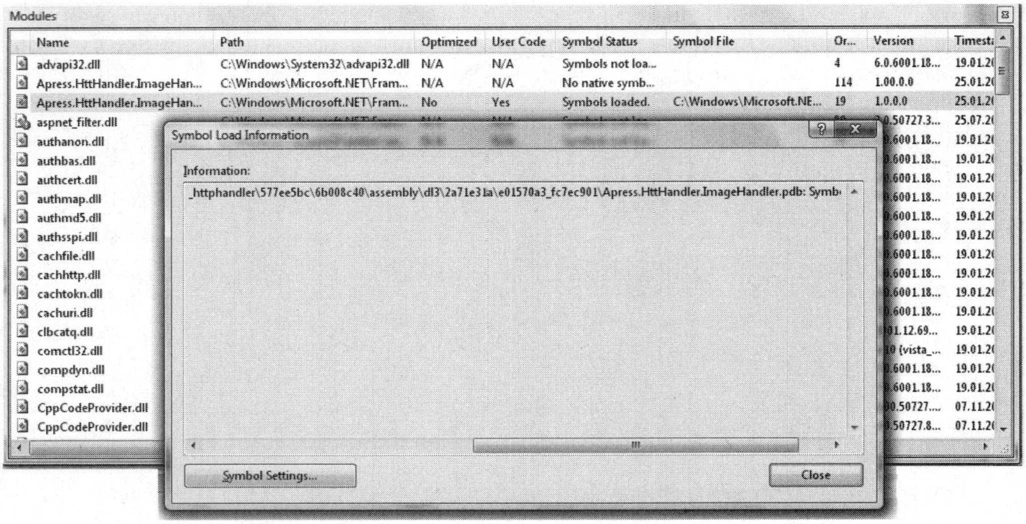

Figure 3-16. *Use the Modules window to retrieve information about loaded symbols.*

In the Modules window, look for the assembly you built for your module or handler. In the context menu of each entry, use the *Symbol load information* item to retrieve more information. Either you'll obtain the full path, or the symbol file (.pdb) is loaded from the list of paths Visual Studio has tried so far (see Figure 3-17).

Tip To debug parts of the operating system or .NET Framework, use the Modules dialog to attach foreign pdb files. Additionally, it can be a good idea to set up a symbol server in your company in order to have common symbol files ready, or, alternatively, attach to Microsoft's public symbol server.

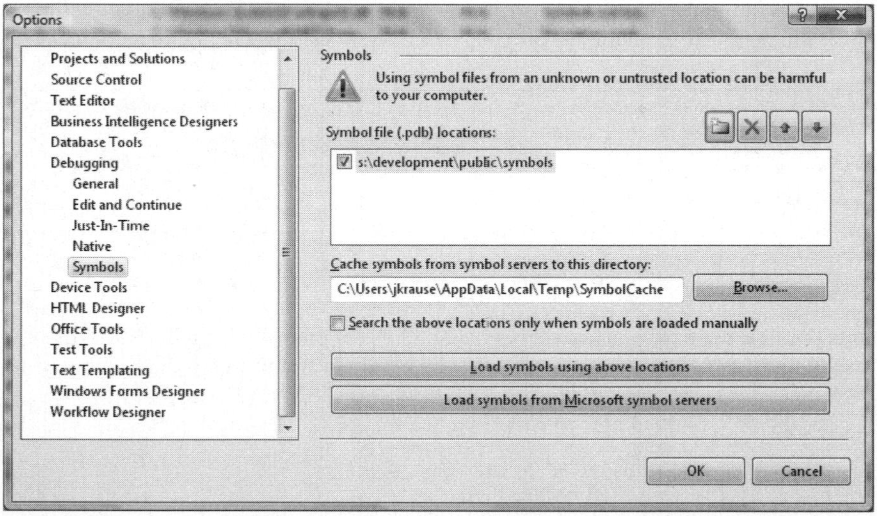

Figure 3-17. *Use the symbols settings in Visual Studio to optimize access to public pdbs.*

Once everything is functioning normally and the attached symbols are available, the breakpoints should function as expected and be "hit" when the code execution reaches them (see Figure 3-18).

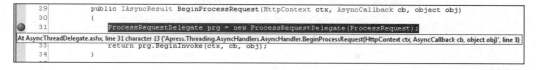

```
29        public IAsyncResult BeginProcessRequest(HttpContext ctx, AsyncCallback cb, object obj)
30        {
31            ProcessRequestDelegate prg = new ProcessRequestDelegate(ProcessRequest);
   At AsyncThreadDelegate.ashx, line 31 character 13 ('Apress.Threading.AsyncHandlers.AsyncHandler.BeginProcessRequest(HttpContext ctx, AsyncCallback cb, object obj)', line 3)
33            return prg.BeginInvoke(ctx, cb, obj);
34        }
```

Figure 3-18. *Everything is ready to go if the breakpoint is active.*

Set Up Tracing for Handlers

Aspx pages have a powerful and popular tracing feature. When you set the following page directive, the page's content will be replaced by a complete analysis of the request:

```
<%@ Page Trace="true" ...
```

However, the @WebHandler directive does not support this. If you write your module or handler in a separate assembly, using plain code, there is no directive at all.

An example of a handler invoked by file extension is the *Trace.axd* file used for debugging. In order to invoke the *Trace.axd* handler, configure the Web site for tracing by adding a trace section to *web.config* like this:

```
<configuration>
    <system.web>
        <trace enabled="true"/>
    </system.web>
</configuration>
```

Call the *trace.axd* file from the root of the Web site: for example, http://localhost/trace.axd. The output starts with information similar to the one in Figure 3-19.

Request Details

Request Details			
Session Id:	0n52wwarimghym550qjr1z45	Request Type:	GET
Time of Request:	19.04.2009 19:33:52	Status Code:	200
Request Encoding:	Unicode (UTF-8)	Response Encoding:	Unicode (UTF-8)

Trace Informationen			
Category	Message	From first(s)	From last(s)
aspx.page	Begin PreInit		
aspx.page	End PreInit	0,0105794870577126	0,010579
aspx.page	Begin Init	0,0106729346886266	0,000093
aspx.page	End Init	0,0107102299314578	0,000037
aspx.page	Begin InitComplete	0,0107256648540527	0,000015
aspx.page	End InitComplete	0,0107411696179263	0,000016
aspx.page	Begin PreLoad	0,0107563251754064	0,000015
aspx.page	End PreLoad	0,0107706426375419	0,000014
aspx.page	Begin Load	0,0107855188299072	0,000015
aspx.page	End Load	0,0109234553553594	0,000138
aspx.page	Begin LoadComplete	0,0109430109133982	0,000020
aspx.page	End LoadComplete	0,0109585855185505	0,000016
aspx.page	Begin PreRender	0,0109733918696371	0,000015
aspx.page	End PreRender	0,0110041918735482	0,000031
aspx.page	Begin PreRenderComplete	0,0110314299722451	0,000027
aspx.page	End PreRenderComplete	0,011047353783791	0,000016
aspx.page	Begin SaveState	0,0133996080507439	0,002352
aspx.page	End SaveState	0,0174463514217589	0,004047
aspx.page	Begin SaveStateComplete	0,0174748466634726	0,000028
aspx.page	End SaveStateComplete	0,0174913292052482	0,000016
aspx.page	Begin Render	0,0175064847627282	0,000015
aspx.page	End Render	0,0182952023232003	0,000789

Figure 3-19. *Part of the trace information output*

Summary

In this chapter, you learned how to extend the pipeline by creating your own modules and handlers. A module provides low-level processing and is invoked twice: when the request bubbles up the pipeline, and again after all internal processing by the designated handler is complete. Using a handler, you can add your own processing code either assigned to your own file extension or using the generic .ashx extension. Handlers process requests and create the output sent to the client.

Asynchronous handlers help to process long-running requests—such as database queries or Web Services—without filling the thread pool with threads. This technique improves the overall performance of a Web application and leads to a consistently smooth user experience.

CHAPTER 4

■ ■ ■

Providers and Configuration

In the previous chapters, you learned how to extend ASP.NET at a low level. For daily tasks, however, you typically work at a higher level. A core concept of the ASP.NET extensibility paradigm is the provider model: a software module that provides a uniform interface to a service. ASP.NET incorporates several common providers that allow developers to replace functionality with their own modules, without breaking compatibility with existing modules.

This chapter includes:

- The provider model concept

- How providers work internally and how to configure them properly

- The built-in providers

- How to develop your own custom provider model to allow others to extend your application

- How to extend the configuration model

- How to use expression syntax and expression generators to access configuration from markup

At the end of this chapter, you'll be able to create and extend your own providers. You'll also know how to integrate them with existing ASP.NET applications so that other developers can extend your application. The extensibility of built-in providers is covered in more detail in Chapters 5 to 8.

The Provider Model

Providers are software modules built on top of interfaces or abstract classes that define the façade for the application. The interfaces constitute a "seam" in the architecture, which allows you to replace providers without affecting other modules. For instance, the data access provider enables access to any kind of storage for data: including databases from different vendors. Hence, the provider model encapsulates the functionality and isolates it from the rest of the application.

Since almost all the major parts of ASP.NET are built on top of providers, there are multiple ways of modifying the internal behavior. Providers are responsible for the extensibility of ASP.NET. Creating your own providers gives you the ability to construct a sophisticated architecture that others might use—and to alter its behavior without disturbing internal processing. Consider an application such as Microsoft Office SharePoint Server 2007 (MOSS), which is an ASP.NET application and a framework that others use as a foundation for their applications. A similar extensibility concept is supplied on this level. Providers build the core technology that all of this is based on.

Goals of the Provider Model

When you work with providers for the first time, you may find that writing or extending a provider can be a complicated task. Due to the constraints of compatibility and transparency towards other modules, there is often no other option but extending internal interfaces. You may still need to decide whether or not to write your own provider model. This chapter gives you the information you need for making that decision.

Recall what the provider model was designed for:

- It makes ASP.NET both flexible and extensible.

- It's robust and well documented.

- It provides a common and modern architecture for your application.

- It's part of a multi-tier architecture.

The provider model does not consist only of simple provider modules. At the top level of the model are services. "Services" in ASP.NET is a generic term for separate modules, such as Membership, site maps, or Profiles. These all are high-level components that make your life as a developer easier. Almost all of these services need some kind of data storage or at least a communication channel. From the perspective of a multi-tier application, the service should be independent of the particulars of data persistence.

The Provider sits between these two layers: the Service and the Data Store (see Figure 4-1). Modifying the Provider allows the Service to use a different Data Store or communication channel without changing the Service functionality. From the perspective of the user, this architecture is transparent.

Additionally, the Provider is a readily configurable module. You can usually change the Provider by editing the *web.config* file or by setting properties in base classes.

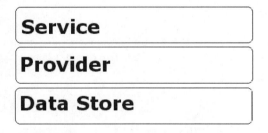

Figure 4-1. *Provider as part of a multi-tier architecture*

Default Provider

ASP.NET comes with several built-in providers. As long as they perform their function for you, they need no modification. However, circumstances change, and at some point you might find it necessary to create your own provider. Before commencing, though, it's illuminating to learn about the existing providers and how they enhance their associated services.

■**Note** In this book, I do not supply a full description of all the built-in providers. Please refer to the documentation on MSDN to learn more about usage and configuration scenarios. Start at `http://msdn.microsoft.com/en-us/library/system.configuration.provider.aspx` to find the official documentation for the underlying types.

Before looking into the provider model, let's differentiate between the two levels, services and providers, as mentioned before. Table 4-1 shows all the services in ASP.NET and the provider associated with each service.

Table 4-1. *ASP.NET Services Using Providers*

Service	Default Provider
Membership	`System.Web.Security.SqlMembershipProvider`
Roles	`System.Web.Security.SqlRoleProvider`
Site Map	`System.Web.XmlSitemapProvider`
Profile	`System.Web.Profile.SqlProfileProvider`
Session State	`System.Web.SessionState.InProcSessionStateStore`
Web Parts	`System.Web.UI.WebControls.Webparts.SqlPersonalizationProvider`

You can deduce the storage location from the naming scheme. Membership, Role Management, Profile, and Web Parts services use SQL Server by default, while the Site Map service defaults to a XML file, the *web.sitemap* file. Session variables are held in memory within the IIS process.

Two services do not include preconfigured built-in providers. In fact, these services do have default providers, but you need to configure them explicitly before you can use them. See Table 4-2 for more information.

Table 4-2. *ASP.NET Services with Unconfigured Default Providers*

Service	Recommended Provider (Not Assigned By Default)
Web Events	`System.Web.Management.EventLogWebEventProvider`
Protected Configuration	`System.Configuration.RsaProtectedConfigurationProvider`

Web events are events that monitor ASP.NET. They are normally off and must be configured in the `<healthMonitoring>` section of *web.config*.

By default, configuration data is saved in plain text. The `RsaProtectedConfigurationProvider` enables encryption of sensitive configuration data—particularly useful if your application is hosted on external servers where unvetted administrators could read the files.

The providers shown in the preceding tables are merely recommendations—there are alternatives. Table 4-3 gives the full list of providers included with ASP.NET.

Built-In Providers

Some of the built-in ASP.NET services have multiple provider options (see Table 4-3):

Table 4-3. *Built-In Providers—The Complete List*

Service	Available Providers
Membership	System.Web.Security.SqlMembershipProvider
	System.Web.Security.ActiveDirectoryMembershipProvider
Roles	System.Web.Security.SqlRoleProvider
	System.Web.Security.AuthorizationStoreRoleProvider
	System.Web.Security.WindowsTokenRoleProvider
Site Map	System.Web.XmlSitemapProvider
Profile	System.Web.Profile.SqlProfileProvider
Session State	System.Web.SessionState.InProcSessionStateStore
	System.Web.SessionState.OutOfProcSessionStateStore
	System.Web.SessionState.SqlSessionStateStore
Web Parts	System.Web.UI.WebControls.Webparts.SqlPersonalizationProvider
Protected Configuration	System.Configuration.RSAProtectedConfigurationProvider
	System.Configuration.DPAPIProtectedConfigurationProvider

If none of the providers available for a specific service fit your needs, you might consider writing your own provider. There are two ways to accomplish this:

- Extend an existing provider in order to change its behavior slightly.
- Write your own provider on top of the provider's base class.

As you can imagine, extending an existing provider is the easier option. Whenever you keep the existing data store but wish to change the behavior, it's better to extend an existing provider. If you want to use a different data store, it is preferable to write your own provider. Third-party developers might also appear as a source of providers for distinct tasks. The next sections of this chapter will provide the necessary information to build your own.

Extending Built-In Providers

Extending the built-in providers is an important feature. Several sections of this book describe extensibility methods based on extending providers. Please refer to related parts in:

- Chapter 5: Extending resource management through resource providers in the section "Programming a Custom Resource Provider"

- Chapter 6: Extending page persistence through session state providers in the sections "Developing a Custom Page State Provider" and "Implementing the Session State Store Provider"

- Chapter 7: Extending the membership and role providers in the section "Extending Membership and Role Providers" and profile provider extensibility features in section "Implementing a Custom Profile Provider"

- Chapter 8: Extending the sitemap provider in the section "Writing a Custom Sitemap Provider"

Extensibility for all the providers is supplied by the same base class, as explained in the next section, while the section "Creating a Custom Provider-Based Service" later in this chapter shows the basic techniques for custom provider implementation. Read these first before proceeding with any of the chapters previously mentioned.

The Anatomy of a Provider

Both custom and built-in providers inherit from the ProviderBase base class. The full definition looks like this:

```
using System;
using System.Collections.Specialized;

namespace System.Configuration.Provider
{
    public abstract class ProviderBase
    {
        protected ProviderBase();

        public virtual string Description { get; }
        public virtual string Name { get; }

        public virtual void Initialize(string name, NameValueCollection config);
    }
}
```

There is nothing specific to providers here so far. The properties Name and Description are for descriptive purposes only. Name is the internal name used in configuration settings, and Description supports graphical tools. If the description is not set, the property returns the name instead. The name is mandatory within the configuration collection.

```
public virtual string Description
{
    get
    {
        if (!string.IsNullOrEmpty(this._Description))
        {
            return this._Description;
        }
        return this.Name;
    }
}
```

The only method to put the provider in operation is Initialize. The config parameter passes the configuration settings. The name parameter is required because you can name the provider in the configuration file, while the call to Initialize transfers this name for further reference.

As you can see from this code snippet, the base class does not do anything useful. This is what makes it hard to develop your own provider from scratch. If you want to modify the behavior, it's much easier to develop one of the existing classes and override the properties or methods that don't fit your needs. However, in this chapter I'll explain how to write a custom provider from scratch.

Making the Provider Available

To make the provider available, you'll need a service that uses the provider. However, there are no one-to-one relationships between services and their providers. The provider model exists to enable the substitution of one provider with another. To create a custom provider, you'll need a custom service and one or more custom providers.

The service itself does not have a base class, but it does hold several references to other types discussed in this section:

- The collection of configured providers
- The particular provider currently associated with the service
- The configuration parameters assigned to the current provider
- The code to instantiate and initialize the provider

Somewhere in your application, there will be a consumer of this service. Consider the service from the perspective of this consumer. The consumer code needs the service in order to obtain data or do something useful. The consumer is not concerned with how the service is configured or how it stores or retrieves data. Even the service itself does not care about this, but handles it using a custom definition of the provider. With both of these abstraction tiers, it's possible to replace the provider without altering anything within either the service or its consumers.

Configuring the Provider

A provider serves as a layer between an upper-level tier and a data tier. It can be simple or complex, but there's nothing specific to providers except for the `Initialize` method. The uniqueness of providers is in the special way you can configure and attach them using the *web.config* file. This makes a provider accessible to those who configure and maintain a Web Server. (Incidentally, the namespace for the provider's base class indicates that providers are all about configuration.)

All provider configurations follow the following pattern:

```
<configuration>
  <system.web>
    <serviceName>
      <providers>
        <clear/>
        <add name="myProvider" />
      </providers>
    </serviceName>
  </system.web>
</configuration>
```

Notice that there is not one provider but a collection of them. Usually there will be only one, but the configuration schema allows you to configure several. The configuration classes, as explained later in the section "Extending the Configuration," manage the typical pattern in the XML file based on the instructions `<clear/>`, `<remove>`, and `<add>`. This is necessary because the *web.config* files form a hierarchy from machine level down to the specific subfolder in the application. As long as you have permission, you can override the inherited settings, remove one or all entries, and add your own.

Since you have to handle a collection of providers even if only one is needed, a collection class is required. As for the provider's base class, there is a base class for collections, too.

```
namespace System.Configuration.Provider
{
    public class ProviderCollection : ICollection, IEnumerable
    {
        public ProviderCollection();
```

```
        public bool IsSynchronized { get; }
        public object SyncRoot { get; }

        public ProviderBase this[string name] { get; }

        public virtual void Add(ProviderBase provider);
        public void CopyTo(ProviderBase[] array, int index);
        public IEnumerator GetEnumerator();
        public void Remove(string name);
        public void SetReadOnly();
    }
}
```

Using the `ProviderBase` type, it's easy to handle the custom provider as well as any of the default built-in ones using this collection. You can also specify one of the providers to be the default provider. This links the service to a provider in the absence of any other selection criteria.

So far, you have a service supplying the consumers, a provider as a late-bound component that hides the details of the data or communication tier, and finally a storage location for a collection of provider definitions. However, the format of the configuration also requires a section definition.

Configuration sections are defined at the beginning of the *web.config* file and extend the configuration by specifying where the actual definitions are stored. Initially, I assumed that provider configurations are stored in the `<configuration><system.web>` hive. This is the default setting for built-in providers but not compulsory for custom providers. In fact, you can use any path within the `<configuration>` top-level element. It's good practice to stay with this model and place custom providers there, too. The configuration sections are defined within the `<configSections>` element. Beneath this element, you'll find a hierarchy of `<sectionGroup>` and `<section>` elements in no particular order. The hierarchy of configuration elements is the exact representation of the sections used below the `<configuration>` part in the *web.config*. However, the default *web.config* has more sections than the `<configSection>` section does. The reason is that your current *web.config* inherits from the global, machine-wide definition. You can find the configuration file that contains all possible section definitions within the following path:

```
%system%\Microsoft.NET\Framework\v2.0.50727\CONFIG\machine.config
```

To add your own configuration section to support a specific location for your custom provider definition, you'll need to add a section definition. First, a custom section definition class has to be implemented. The following base class is the final step in obtaining a complete definition for custom providers:

```
namespace System.Configuration
{
    public abstract class ConfigurationSection : ConfigurationElement
    {
        protected ConfigurationSection();

        public SectionInformation SectionInformation { get; }

        protected internal virtual void DeserializeSection(XmlReader reader);
        protected internal virtual object GetRuntimeObject();
        protected internal override bool IsModified();
        protected internal override void ResetModified();
        protected internal virtual string SerializeSection(
                                        ConfigurationElement parentElement,
                                        string name,
                                        ConfigurationSaveMode saveMode);
    }
}
```

From this declaration, you can see that ConfigurationSection in turn inherits from the ConfigurationElement class. This is the reason why you can mix <sectionGroup> and <section> elements easily. The class contains several implemented methods and others that you must override to obtain the required behavior. The SerializationSection and DeserializationSection methods convert the settings to and from XML.

General Considerations

All providers have certain characteristics in common. The base class, as already explained, forces few typical usage scenarios only. You should know some of the best practices for creating providers that fit well into the framework under all circumstances.

Initialization Procedure of a Provider

All providers derive from ProviderBase. Therefore, they inherit the Initialize method, which is declared virtual. In C#, this indicates a method that you need to override. Doing so transfers a few critical tasks over to you.

Most providers need specific permissions to run. Requesting permissions is the way you let the runtime know what your code needs to be allowed to do. This is required by access to a SQL database or local file system, for instance. The best way to implement permission checks is to add the appropriate attributes from the System.Security.Permissions namespace. Imagine that a provider is a pluggable module that others may reuse, even if it does not operate well. Instead of eventually failing in custom code, the initialization procedure should immediately report an exception indicating what went wrong. This is precisely the purpose of such permission attributes.

Next, the config parameter passed to the Initialize method is important. If it is null, it means that something went wrong within the configuration. In that case, throw an ArgumentNullException, even if there are no configuration parameters required. The error indicates an unexpected condition and must be reported to the calling method.

The base class's Initialize method is not abstract. It contains code and must be called to ensure that basic requirements are met. As shown in the last section, the code validates the name and description settings. Even if you intend to change this, and you replace the name and description values in your code, call the base method. If a future version of the .NET framework adds code here to ensure required functionality, then failing to call the base class could break your provider.

Reading the configuration is an important part. However, textual definitions, even if made in XML, can be error-prone. Use the NameValueCollection class and its indexer to access the configuration values. If a required parameter is missing, throw a ProviderException. Make sure you call Remove each time you read a parameter. That clears the config objects one by one. After all required parameters are processed, nothing should be left in the config object. If config.Count > 0 is still true, throw a ProviderException. This ensures that you have all the required parameters and that the user has no other elements in the configuration that can't be processed. You might wonder why you can't just ignore these values. This is because the user's intention was probably not to add private values to store additional information there. He or she has probably mistyped an attribute. The exception helps to recognize these typos instead of searching for the error in event logs.

There are also best practices regarding provider code. First, the service and the provider are two different things. Even if you develop them together in one project, with nothing else in mind, they should stay independent. Second, never call a method of the service from the provider. This could lead to infinite, recursive loops, or a break in modularity. Exchanging the provider would be impossible because it is tightly bound to the service.

Lifetime

Providers are loaded dynamically the first time the service requires them. This ensures that providers are not held in memory when they are not needed. However, loading a complex provider could be a time-consuming task—clearly not desirable when you're trying to improve the responsiveness of a site. You can force the provider to load by calling certain methods of the services in the `Application_Start` event.

This assumes that the provider has a lifetime equaling the lifetime of the application and that the provider has a global state. A provider should not depend on the current session or the context. However, `HttpContext` and all subsequent classes can be used at any point to retrieve data. This makes it safe to use private fields to store values. It saves memory and speeds up the provider. However, you must remember to write thread-safe code.

Thread Safety

Threads in ASP.NET are explained in depth in Chapter 2. Web applications are multi-user applications—as with mainframe computer software, you can consider web applications as massively parallel applications. Consequently, when dealing with providers, you must handle threads with care. Providers are instantiated only once and shared across all requests. This speeds them up and causes them to consume less memory, which is necessary for basic tasks. Since threads run in parallel—that's what threads are for—one provider might be called at the same time by multiple threads. This means that you must always code a provider to be thread-safe. Otherwise, you risk throwing exceptions or creating garbage on any request. There are subtle differences that might appear under heavy workload only.

The only exception is the `Initialize` method. Since it's only called once, thread safety isn't an issue. As long as the service initializes in `Application_Start`, this is always true. If you cannot be sure of this, the code that calls the method in the service has to be locked, as shown in the following code snippet:

```
if (_provider == null)
{
    lock (_lock)
    {
        if (_provider == null)
        {
```

This ensures that the provider is not loaded twice. The `lock` statement blocks other threads. However, another thread might have passed the lock and already be running inside the method. That's why you must check the existence of the provider again after getting the lock.

For property access, a similar technique is appropriate. Usually, you write your properties like this:

```
private Unit _size;

public Unit Size
{
    get { return _size; }
    set { _size = value; }
}
```

Imagine that two threads access this method. There is only one instance of this class in the memory, and hence one storage (memory place) for the value. If one thread writes the value and the other reads the value at the same time, you'll receive an incorrect value back. The lock statement is again the solution. It's a shortcut to the System.Threading.Monitor class of the framework the compiler creates for us. The code should look like the following snippet:

```
private Unit _size;
private object _synch

public Unit Size
{
   get { lock(_synch) { return _size;  } }
   set { lock(_synch) { _size = value; } }
}
```

The Monitor method is a very basic lock. It blocks all threads, even if they are being accessed for reading only. This could slow down an application under heavy load.

There are several other ways to optimize the behavior. The ReaderWriterLock class improves behavior by allowing shared reads but preventing overlapping write and read access to the property. This improves performance if the values are mostly read rather than written.

Another method uses the System.Runtime.CompilerServices.MethodImplAttribute. See the following code for a usage scenario:

```
private Unit _size;

[MethodImpl(MethodImplOptions.Synchronized)]
public Unit GetSize()
{
   return _size;
}
[MethodImpl(MethodImplOptions.Synchronized)]
public void SetSize(Unit size)
{
   _size = size;
}
```

However, this replaces properties with methods, which isn't the best coding style. The locking experience isn't any better. The compiler also uses the Monitor method. As you can see from the code snippet, there is no object for storing the locking state. The compiler selects an object at the best level, like lock(this). This could be an object on either the type or application level, which is a higher level than within the method. Usually this means that the locking phase is enduring, and this causes the threads to last longer. Unless locking on type level is required, this attribute is not appropriate for providers.

Which method is best will depend on the specific conditions. Generally, you have to ensure thread-safe access to all instance data, including private fields. However, when you write configuration data in the Initialize method (thread-safe because it's only called once) and provide read-only access, no action is required to ensure thread safety. The get statement of the property shown in the last code snippets might omit the lock statement, then.

Calls to access all stack-based data and local variables within a property or method should not be locked.

Creating a Custom Provider-Based Service

Images are an essential part of almost all web applications. Powerful image management makes your life and your users' lives easier. Imagine that your final storage solution isn't clearly defined, so you want to create a flexible and extensible image management solution. Other developers in your organization should be able to adopt your code and replace parts of it to suit their needs without knowing the internal details of the image creation and delivery process. In such a situation, you could consider a custom provider-based service. Again, the multi-tier model points to a solution:

1. You need to create a service that is able to retrieve and send image data.

2. You need a provider interface that makes data storage access replaceable.

3. You need a specific provider to put it into operation.

4. You need a configuration definition to handle the configuration in *web.config*.

Following the model of the provider as previously described in the section "The Anatomy of a Provider," you should create these classes:

- An implementation of a configuration section definition class

- An abstract base class that describes the provider

- An implementation of this base class that creates the provider that serves as a concrete implementation against data storage

- A class that implements the service to do anything useful using the provider

- A provider collection class that stores multiple providers

Additionally, data storage must be provided. Because it's common to use SQL Server, I'll create the image service's default provider using a SQL Server database.

You can build such a solution from the bottom up, beginning with the configuration, followed by the provider and finally the service. This is fine if you have a design and planning phase in your project and clearly defined requirements. However, for learning purposes, you'll create a provider from the top down and start with the last step—the service. This clarifies the purpose of the provider and makes the next steps easier to understand.

Limitations of the Code Samples

Depending on real-life requirements, creating a provider-based solution might require a little more effort. Remember that, for the sake of clarity, all the code snippets here lack error handling, unit testing, and logging features. In addition, no code snippets here feature localization. The best practice is to store resources in resource files and to localize if the application is used in multiple countries. See Chapter 5 for more information about resources.

Certain samples, like in the section "Implementing an Expression Builder with Design-Time Support" in this chapter, access databases. If you are writing more sophisticated providers, you may have multiple database operations for one action. When the database supports transactions, use transactions to ensure the atomicity of updates. Transactions ensure a rollback if one of the database operations fails. If the database does not inherently support transactions, you must ensure the atomicity within your own code. Add `try`/`catch` blocks and check conditions to the code shown here.

Some sample code regarding providers in this and all remaining chapters shows only one part of the provider to explain specific techniques. Any methods or properties that are not implemented have been omitted for the sake of clarity and simplicity. However, for production code you should add a `NotImplementedException` to redundant methods. This verifies that users of the provider only implement the features you intended. If completeness is not required, don't forget to explain this in the documentation as well.

Creating a Service

The purpose of the sample service is to retrieve an image via the `RetrieveImage` method. All the other service properties and methods are required to set up the provider. The provider allows other developers using the service to replace the default provider with their own version. For instance, you could choose to use the file system on a file server to store images instead of the database. No change would be required in the application or the service implementation.

Let's take a look at the class itself, as shown in Listing 4-1.

Listing 4-1. *The Service Itself Is Able to Retrieve an Image*

```
using System.Web.Configuration;
using System.Configuration;
using System.Configuration.Provider;
using System.Drawing;

namespace Apress.Extensibility.CustomProvider
{
  public class ImageService
  {
    private static ImageProvider _provider = null;
    private static ImageProviderCollection _providers = null;
    private static object _lock = new object();

    public ImageProvider Provider
    {
      get { return _provider; }
    }

    public ImageProviderCollection Providers
    {
      get { return _providers; }
    }

    public static Image RetrieveImage(int imageID)
    {
      LoadProviders();
      return _provider.RetrieveImage(imageID);
    }

    private static void LoadProviders()
    {
      if (_provider == null)
      {
        lock (_lock)
        {
          if (_provider == null)
          {
            object[] attributes = ➥
                typeof(ImageProviderSection).GetCustomAttributes(➥
                                            typeof(SectionAttribute), false);
            if (attributes.Length != 1)
                throw new ConfigurationException("SectionAttribute not set");
            SectionAttribute sa = (SectionAttribute)attributes[0];
            ImageProviderSection section = ➥
                    (ImageProviderSection) ➥
                    WebConfigurationManager.GetSection(sa.SectionName);
```

```
                    _providers = new ImageProviderCollection();
                    ProvidersHelper.InstantiateProviders(section.Providers, ➥
                                                _providers, ➥
                                                typeof(ImageProvider));
                    _provider = _providers[section.DefaultProvider];
                    if (_provider == null)
                        throw new ProviderException("Unable to load default ImageProvider");
                }
            }
        }
    }
}
```

The RetrieveImage method is static, because you don't need to handle multiple instances of the service. Although the configuration allows multiple providers, only one can act as the current provider. The other parts of the code interact with this current provider. In this application, the service class is created once and starts working when the LoadProviders method is called.

Each method launches with a call to the LoadProviders method to ensure that a provider is present when retrieving data. Loading the provider is a one-time operation. To avoid claiming the lock if providers are already loaded, the first action is checking the _provider variable. After claiming the lock, this test is made again to ensure the provider is still not loaded. This is required, as parallel running requests might invoke the service and start a duplicate procedure. Changing the _provider variable afterwards could change the conditions, and you're supposed to recheck the state again.

In the next step, the name of the section is retrieved by reading a private attribute. There are several ways to do this. Using an attribute allows a single location definition. The section configuration, which provides the necessary information, is the only class where the definition is used. Using data from the SectionAttribute attribute, it's possible to get a reference to the <imageService> section you use to define the current provider. Then the code loads all the registered providers and points _provider to the default provider to make it the current one. ProviderHelper is a static class in the System.Web.Configuration namespace that simplifies the process.

If anything goes wrong, an exception is raised to inform the calling code. If everything is fine, the ImageService class will be ready to serve images.

Creating the Provider

The provider consists of two classes. One is an abstract base class that extends the ProviderBase class with the required additional methods. The other is the implementation of that class. Again, this provider is just one implementation to bring the whole solution into operation. Other developers could replace this provider with their own creation and extend the behavior of the service at will (Listing 4-2).

Listing 4-2. *Base Class for the Provider*

```
using System.Configuration.Provider;
using System.Drawing;

namespace Apress.Extensibility.CustomProvider
{
    public abstract class ImageProvider : ProviderBase
    {
        public abstract string ApplicationName { get; set; }

        public abstract Image RetrieveImage(int id);
    }
}
```

This class has two characteristics. It must inherit the `ProviderBase` in order to be recognized as a provider in other parts of the application. It must also define the methods that serve the service. In this case, `RetrieveImage` is such a method. The service knows that it can call this method to get an image, and the provider completes the process.

Now the implementation is required. Since you want to pull the images from a database, some preparation are needed. Assuming you have local database, *aspnetdb*, with integrated security, add the table shown in Figure 4-2.

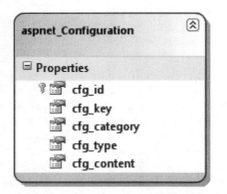

Figure 4-2. *The table that stores the images (see Listing 4-2 for corresponding T-SQL script)*

Internally, you use LINQ to SQL to retrieve the image information from the specified table. The table does not actually contain the images. It contains paths to the image folders and allows further management of the relationship between resources requesting the images. The data storage method leads to the first requirement of the provider: it must store a connection string. It's a good idea to use the predefined `<connectionString>` section in *web.config* and only handle the name that references it.

Next, look into the provider code (see Listing 4-3).

Listing 4-3. *Implementation of the Provider*

```
using System;
using System.Collections.Specialized;
using System.Configuration.Provider;
using System.Data.SqlClient;
using System.Drawing;
using System.Linq;
using System.Security.Permissions;
using System.Web;
using System.Web.Configuration;

namespace Apress.Extensibility.CustomProvider
{
    [SqlClientPermission(SecurityAction.Demand, Unrestricted = true)]
    public class SqlImageProvider : ImageProvider
    {
        public override string ApplicationName
        {
            get;
            set;
        }
        public string ConnectionString
```

```csharp
    {
        get;
        set;
    }

    public override void Initialize(string name, NameValueCollection config)
    {
        if (config == null)
            throw new ArgumentNullException("config");
        if (String.IsNullOrEmpty(name))
            name = "SqlImageProvider";
        if (string.IsNullOrEmpty(config["description"]))
        {
            config.Remove("description");
            config.Add("description",
            "SQL image provider");
        }
        base.Initialize(name, config);
        ApplicationName = config["applicationName"];
        if (string.IsNullOrEmpty(ApplicationName))
            ApplicationName = "/";
        config.Remove("applicationName");
        string connect = config["connectionStringName"];
        if (String.IsNullOrEmpty(connect))
            throw new ProviderException
            ("Empty or missing connectionStringName");
        config.Remove("connectionStringName");
        if (WebConfigurationManager.ConnectionStrings[connect] == null)
            throw new ProviderException("Missing connectionStringName");
        ConnectionString = WebConfigurationManager. ➥
                            ConnectionStrings[connect].ConnectionString;
        if (String.IsNullOrEmpty(ConnectionString))
            throw new ProviderException("Empty connection string");
        if (config.Count > 0)
        {
            string attr = config.AllKeys.First();
            if (!String.IsNullOrEmpty(attr))
                throw new ProviderException
                ("Unrecognized attribute: " + attr);
        }
    }

    public override Image RetrieveImage(int id)
    {
        ImageDataDataContext ctx = new ➥
                                ImageDataDataContext(ConnectionString);
        var qr = from i in ctx.aspnet_Configurations
                 where i.cfg_category == "ImageProvider" ➥
                    && i.cfg_id == id ➥
                    && i.cfg_type == "image"
                 select i.cfg_content;
        string data = qr.FirstOrDefault<string>();
        Image img = Image.FromFile(HttpContext.Current.Server.MapPath(data));
        return img;
    }
    }
}
```

The life of a provider begins with the call to its `Initialize` method. The first step is to verify that `config` is not `null`. If so, an exception is thrown. Remember that configuration is essential for the provider model. As other parts of the configuration might reference the provider, it needs a name. Assign the provider a default name if it doesn't have one. In the example, it's called "SqlImageProvider". It's the same for the description. Even if the description is optional, it should be set properly. Several graphical tools might refer to the description. If the attribute "description" doesn't exist, the code creates one.

Next, the base class's `Initialize` method is called. The provider retrieves the `applicationName` and `connectionStringName` attributes from the configuration file. If the `applicationName` doesn't exist, assume it is the root application "/". The connection string is mandatory, and the lack of it throws an exception. Now, the provider instance should have all the information required to operate. The code checks for the remaining configuration attributes. As explained in the best practice section "General Considerations," the check—if (config.Count > 0)—ensures that unrecognized attributes are reported to the user in order to avoid typos.

Next, the `RetrieveImage` method must be implemented. The `ImageDataDataContext` is a class created with the LINQ to SQL wizard. To create this class, follow these steps:

1. In Visual Studio, choose *Add* ➤ *New Item* in the context menu of the solution.

2. In the section *Data* of the *Add New Item* dialog choose *LINQ to SQL Classes* item.

3. Give the item a common name, such as *ImageData.dbml* (see Figure 4-3).

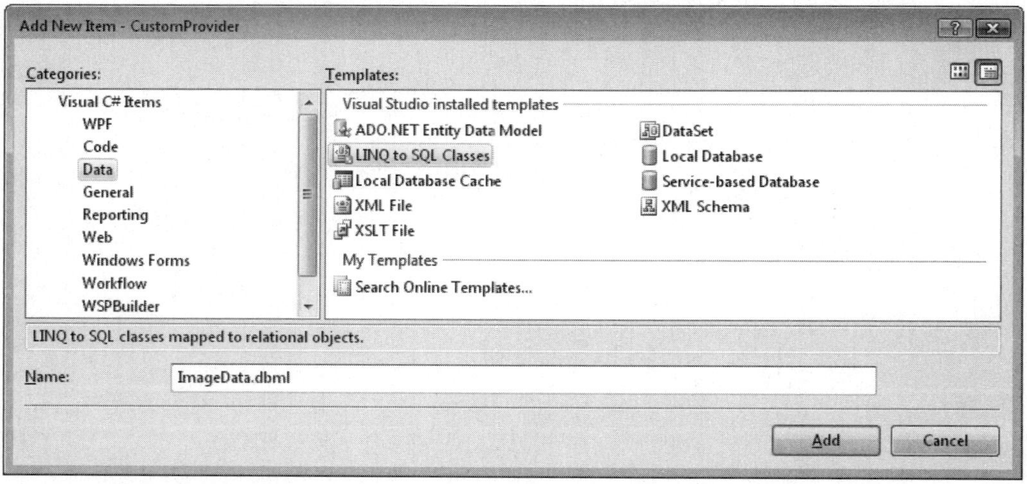

Figure 4-3. *Add a LINQ to SQL item to the provider project.*

Close the dialog and an empty designer surface will appear. Open the Server Explorer (View ➤ Server Explorer, or press Ctrl+Alt+S instead) and add a connection to your database. Either it will already be present or you'll have to add the database and the appropriate tables. The full script for the table is shown in Listing 4-4.

Listing 4-4. *SQL Table Definition for the Provider Project*

```
CREATE TABLE [dbo].[aspnet_Configuration](
    [cfg_id] [int] IDENTITY(1,1) NOT NULL,
    [cfg_key] [varchar](50) NOT NULL,
    [cfg_category] [varchar](50) NOT NULL,
```

```
    [cfg_type] [varchar](10) NOT NULL,
    [cfg_content] [varchar](max) NULL,
CONSTRAINT [PK_aspnet_Configuration] PRIMARY KEY CLUSTERED
(
    [cfg_id] ASC
) WITH (PAD_INDEX   = OFF, ➥
        STATISTICS_NORECOMPUTE  = OFF, ➥
        IGNORE_DUP_KEY = OFF, ➥
        ALLOW_ROW_LOCKS  = ON, ➥
        ALLOW_PAGE_LOCKS  = ON
) ON [PRIMARY]
```

This is just a simple example of a storage method. Real-life projects tend to be more sophisticated. Once the table exists, and the Server Explorer shows the server, you can add a connection. Choose the icon *Data Connections* and *Add Connection* from the context menu; then, in the following dialog, choose the server. If you use a local SQL Express Edition, the name might look like "./ SQLEXPRESS". Select the database where you have created the table. Test the connection and close the dialog to add the connection, as shown in Figure 4-4.

Figure 4-4. *Adding a connection to the current project*

You can now drag and drop the table onto the designer surface of the LINQ to SQL class. The result should look like the image already shown in Figure 4-2. Based on the class's name, the designer will create a context file. If the name is *ImageData,* the data context is called *ImageDataDataContext* (DataContext is the suffix). The context contains a property called aspnet_ Configurations, which represents the table. If you have named the table differently, the property will have that name. Using the context, you can use simple LINQ statements to query the database, as shown in the RetrieveImage method.

In the example, the image is retrieved based on its Id, the category "ImageProvider," and the type "image." This is only a suggestion. Based on the retrieved name, the Server.MapPath method is used to obtain the full path to the image. The Image.FromFile creates the image in memory for further processing.

Imagine another provider that simply takes the image and creates a thumbnail of it. In a derived class, you could override the RetrieveImage method, call the base class, get the image, and manipulate it to create a thumbnail. The configuration is already able to change the provider. This shows once more the power of the provider architecture.

Configuring Providers

The next step is to implement the configuration support. Because many providers can serve a single service, a collection is appropriate. Listing 4-5 shows a simple implementation based on the abstract base class, ProviderCollection.

Listing 4-5. *Provider Collections Represent All Configured Providers*

```
using System;
using System.Configuration.Provider;

namespace Apress.Extensibility.CustomProvider
{
    public class ImageProviderCollection : ProviderCollection
    {

        public ImageProvider this[string name]
        {
            get
            {
                return base[name] as ImageProvider;
            }
        }

        public override void Add(ProviderBase provider)
        {
            if (provider == null)
                throw new ArgumentNullException("provider");
            if (!(provider is ImageProvider))
                throw new ArgumentException
                ("Invalid provider type", "provider");
            base.Add(provider);
        }
    }
}
```

There are only two features. You can add providers of the ImageProvider type and retrieve them using an indexer. The base class handles all the other features. The method and property previously shown ensure the integrity of the base class type. This means that you won't be able to add a provider to the configuration section that does not serve the service.

The last step required in order to operate the service is to define the configuration section, as shown in Listing 4-6.

Listing 4-6. *The Configuration Section and the Supporting Custom Attribute*

```
using System;
using System.Configuration;

namespace Apress.Extensibility.CustomProvider
{

    [AttributeUsage(AttributeTargets.Class)]
    public class SectionAttribute : Attribute
    {

        public SectionAttribute(string sectionName)
            : base()
        {
            SectionName = sectionName;
        }

        public string SectionName
        {
            get;
            set;
        }

    }

    [Section("system.web/imageService")]
    public class ImageProviderSection : ConfigurationSection
    {
        [ConfigurationProperty("providers")]
        public ProviderSettingsCollection Providers
        {
            get { return (ProviderSettingsCollection)base["providers"]; }
        }

        [StringValidator(MinLength = 1)]
        [ConfigurationProperty("defaultProvider", ➥
                        DefaultValue = "SqlImageProvider")]
        public string DefaultProvider
        {
            get { return (string)base["defaultProvider"]; }
            set { base["defaultProvider"] = value; }
        }
    }
}
```

As suggested before, a custom attribute helps to get a single location definition of the configuration path—like "system.web/imageService" in this example. The custom SectionAttribute attribute does not involve anything special. It is used to decorate the ImageProviderSection class, which contains two properties, a collection of providers, and the name of the default provider.

This results in configuration code that could look like this:

```
<system.web>
  <imageService defaultProvider="">
   <providers>
     <clear/>
     <add ... />
   </providers>
  </imageservice>
</system.web>
```

The ConfigurationProperty attribute declares the elements in the *web.config* file. Although it follows the pattern of all provider-based definitions in the configuration, you're free to choose different definitions. However, the best practice is to follow this pattern.

This is all you need to know in order to write your own provider configuration sections.

Using the Service

This service can be used by any code in the application. In Chapter 3, you saw how to use handlers to manage images. Let's create a handler which uses our *ImageService*. Start with a simple .aspx page that uses a handler, as shown in Listing 4-7.

Listing 4-7. *A Simple Page That Calls the Handler*

```
<%@ Page Language="C#" AutoEventWireup="true" ➥
        CodeFile="Default.aspx.cs" Inherits="_Default" %>

<!DOCTYPE html PUBLIC "-//W3C//DTD XHTML 1.0 Transitional//EN" ➥
                    "http://www.w3.org/TR/xhtml1/DTD/xhtml1-transitional.dtd">

<html xmlns="http://www.w3.org/1999/xhtml">
<head runat="server">
    <title></title>
</head>
<body>
    <form id="form1" runat="server">
    <div>
        <asp:Image runat="server" ID="Image2" ImageUrl="~/ImageHandler.ashx?id=4" />
        <br />
        <asp:Image runat="server" ID="Image1" ImageUrl="~/ImageHandler.ashx?id=9" />
    </div>
    </form>
</body>
</html>
```

The *ImageHandler.ashx* file is a generic handler that doesn't need to be assigned in IIS. The parameter id corresponds to the Id column in the image resource table. This is a simplified scenario. In real-life applications, it would be better to use readable strings to define the resources. However, for learning purposes, these code snippets are as short and easy as possible.

The handler calls the service's static method to retrieve the image and adds the Image object to the output stream (see Listing 4-8).

Listing 4-8. *The Image Handler That Uses the Configurable Service*

```
<%@ WebHandler Language="C#" Class="ImageHandler" %>

using System;
using System.Web;
using System.Drawing;
using System.Drawing.Imaging;
using Apress.Extensibility.CustomProvider;

public class ImageHandler : IHttpHandler
{

    public void ProcessRequest(HttpContext context)
    {
        int id;
        if (context.Request.QueryString["id"] != null)
        {
            if (Int32.TryParse(context.Request.QueryString["id"], out id))
            {
                Image img = ImageService.RetrieveImage(id);
                context.Response.ContentType = "image/jpg";
                img.Save(context.Response.OutputStream, ImageFormat.Jpeg);
            }
        }
    }

    public bool IsReusable
    {
        get
        {
            return true;
        }
    }
}
```

Within the `ProcessRequest` method, the handler attempts to retrieve the id from the `QueryString` property. If the id is present and is a number, the service class `ImageService` retrieves the image using the `RetrieveImage` method. Finally, the right content type is set and the image is streamed into the `OutputStream` property using the `Save` method.

The last step—the handler—is our target usage scenario. This is why we've written the configuration, the service, and the provider.

Any developer can use the handler to retrieve images. They only need to know how to use one specific parameter (the image id). They don't need to know how the image is created. This is part of the service. Moreover, they don't need to know how the image is stored. This is the role of the provider. These three parts form a multi-tier model:

- Tier one (the user interface support layer) is created by the handler.

- Tier two (the business logic) is contained in the service.

- Tier three (the data storage) is handled by the provider.

The provider model is a distinct way of creating a multi-tier architecture within your application. It makes the application flexible and extensible, and it simplifies the writing of unit tests, logging, and supervision by splitting a monolithic block of code into smaller chunks.

Extending the Configuration

In the previous sections, you learned how to extend the provider model and configure the provider using the *web.config* file. The extensibility of parts of the *web.config* is not limited to configuring providers. Using the base classes within the System.Configuration namespace, you can create custom sections and handle them directly. If the settings defined in <AppSettings> are too limited for your application's needs, you can extend them.

How to Scaffold a Configuration Section

The first step is to add a reference to the *System.Configuration.dll* assembly and the System.Configuration namespace. Creating a new project of type class library for the new configuration definition is not required, but recommended. This makes the code reusable and easier to test and deploy. Before you start creating a section like this, it's worth examining the anatomy of a configuration section.

Anatomy of a Configuration Section

The configuration section is based on the implementation of two abstract classes, ConfigurationSection and ConfigurationElement. ConfigurationSection is a successor of ConfigurationElement that makes it easy to create hierarchies of sections that contain elements on each level. The concrete ConfigurationSection is defined at the top of the *web.config* file, as shown in Listing 4-9.

Listing 4-9. *Definition of Private Configuration Sections*

```
<configSections>
  <sectionGroup name="system.web.extensions" type="...">
    <sectionGroup name="scripting" type="...">
      <section name="scriptResourceHandler" type="..."
               requirePermission="false" allowDefinition="MachineToApplication"/>
      <sectionGroup name="webServices" type="...">
        <section name="jsonSerialization" type="..." requirePermission="false"
                 allowDefinition="Everywhere" />
        <section name="profileService" type="..." requirePermission="false"
                 allowDefinition="MachineToApplication" />
        <section name="..." requirePermission="false"
                 allowDefinition="MachineToApplication" />
        <section name="roleService" type="..." requirePermission="false"
                 allowDefinition="MachineToApplication" />
      </sectionGroup>
    </sectionGroup>
  </sectionGroup>
</configSections>
```

The type attributes are empty for the sake of clarity. They contain the fully qualified assembly names of the type that holds the configuration definition. The top-level element, <sectionGroup>, defines in which group the new element appears:

```
<sectionGroup name="system.web.extensions">
```

The section <system.web.extensions> is thus defined as the location for all subsequent groups, elements, or any combinations of groups and elements. You can define exactly what appears there simply by implementing the base classes previously mentioned.

The Class Model

Figure 4-5 shows the complete class model behind the configuration classes. To create a private configuration section, you'll need to implement these abstract classes.

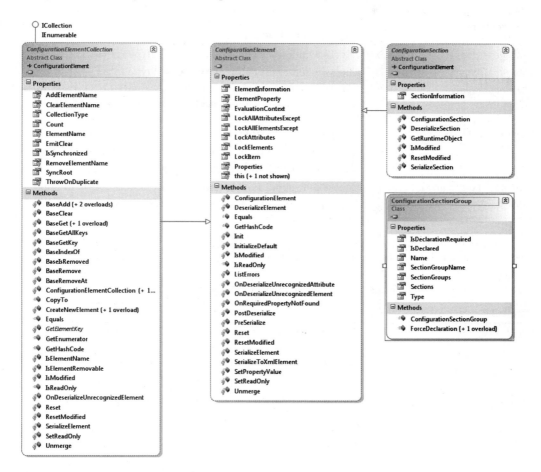

Figure 4-5. *Base classes for a custom configuration*

The ConfigurationSection and ConfigurationElement classes are the most important. Many elements will allow collections. Collections define tags such as <add>, <remove>, and <clear> to handle multiple elements in XML. The corresponding definition in this code is based on the ConfigurationElementCollection class.

These classes form the structure of the configuration elements. You can refine their behavior by adding attributes. Attributes not only decorate the properties that define elements, but also add features in order to:

- Validate scalar data.
- Define custom validation methods.
- Set a default if the value is not set.
- Define a subclass's type to refine the elements hierarchy.

Attributes to Control Elements' Behaviors

Table 4-4 shows all the attributes available to define the behavior of properties.

Table 4-4. *Validator Attributes That Control the Elements' Behaviors*

Validator	Purpose of this Attribute
IntegerValidator	Checks whether the element's value is of type Int32.
LongValidator	Checks whether the element's value is of type Int64.
StringValidator	Checks specific string conditions, such as minimum and maximum Length. It's even possible to define forbidden character (like paths, for instance).
RegexStringValidator	Defines a regular expression the element's value must match.
CallbackValidator	Defines a callback method that is responsible for checking the value.
TimespanValidator	Checks time conditions, declares usually a valid range.
PositiveTimespanValidator	Checks time conditions, usually a positive range (ahead in time).
SubclassTypeValidator	Defines the Type of a class this element must derive from.

The following attributes refine the configuration element properties at a Meta level. They can be used together and with the Validator attributes in any combination (see Table 4-5).

Table 4-5. *Attributes to Refine the Configuration Elements' Behavior*

Attribute	Description
DefaultValue	The default value. If defined, this value is used if no other value is assigned.
IsDefaultCollection	True, if this element represents a collection.
IsRequired	True, if the element is mandatory.
IsKey	True, if this is the key element of a collection. Applies only if it is a collection.
Options	A combination of the IsKey, IsRequired, and IsDefaultCollection elements as a flagged enum.

Definition of a Simple Configuration Section

Now that you have all the parts of the puzzle handy, you can start creating a real-life example that defines a customized configuration section. First, let's take a look at the section definition. Listing 4-10 defines a section with two new elements.

Listing 4-10. *A Section with Two Elements*

```
using System;
using System.Collections;
using System.Text;
using System.Configuration;
using System.Xml;

namespace Apress.Extensibility.Configuration
{
```

```
public class PageAppearanceSection : ConfigurationSection
{
    [ConfigurationProperty("remoteOnly", DefaultValue = "false", ➥
                                        IsRequired = false)]
    public Boolean RemoteOnly
    {
        get
        {
            return (Boolean)this["remoteOnly"];
        }
        set
        {
            this["remoteOnly"] = value;
        }
    }

    [ConfigurationProperty("font")]
    public FontElement Font
    {
        get
        {
            return (FontElement)this["font"];
        }
        set
        { this["font"] = value; }
    }

    [ConfigurationProperty("color")]
    public ColorElement Color
    {
        get
        {
            return (ColorElement)this["color"];
        }
        set
        { this["color"] = value; }
    }
}
}
```

This class defines three allowed properties. The property `RemoteOnly` is of type Boolean and doesn't need any additional definition, beyond declaring it as a `ConfigurationProperty`.

If you have a more complex class and wish to distinguish between private properties and those exposed to the configuration manager, this requires an additional attribute. The two named properties set in the attribute's constructor (`DefaultValue` and `IsRequired`) are explained in Table 4-5. For the other elements (Font and Color), you'll need to create your own structures. This means that an element of type <font> should contain specific attributes, just as for <color>.

The definition of the `FontElement` class demonstrates this, as shown in Listing 4-11.

Listing 4-11. *The FontElement Class Defines a Single Element That Represents a Font*

```
public class FontElement : ConfigurationElement
{
    [ConfigurationProperty("name", DefaultValue = "Arial", IsRequired = true)]
    [StringValidator(InvalidCharacters = "~!@#$%^&*()[]{}/;'\"|\\", ➥
                    MinLength = 1, MaxLength = 60)]
    public String Name
```

```
    {
        get
        {
            return (String)this["name"];
        }
        set
        {
            this["name"] = value;
        }
    }

    [ConfigurationProperty("size", DefaultValue = "12", IsRequired = false)]
    [IntegerValidator(ExcludeRange = false, MaxValue = 24, MinValue = 6)]
    public int Size
    {
        get
        { return (int)this["size"]; }
        set
        { this["size"] = value; }
    }
}
```

For the font's name, a `StringValidator` is used. It limits the length to between 1 and 60.
The name is not allowed to contain several characters. The font's size is limited with an
`IntegerValidator`. `ExcludeRange` defines whether the values provided as `MaxValue` and `MinValue`
are part of the range or not. Here, the range is between 6 and 24, including the values "6" and "24"
respectively.

The access to the underlying configuration element is through an indexer. The code behind this
serializes and deserializes the values to create a link between the element's name and its attribute
in code. This means that the values used as keys for the indexer ("size" and "name" respectively)
are responsible for retrieving the configuration's XML. In the string `<font size="12">`, the name of
the attribute "size" is defined by `this["size"]` and made accessible in the code via the `Size` property. Although it's highly recommended to use the same names, there is no technical restriction on
changing them.

The color element operates similarly, as shown in Listing 4-12.

Listing 4-12. *The ColorElement Class Defines a Single Element That Represents a Color Value*

```
public class ColorElement : ConfigurationElement
{
    [ConfigurationProperty("background", DefaultValue = "FFFFFF", IsRequired = true)]
    [StringValidator( ➥
            InvalidCharacters="~!@#$%^&*()[]{}/;'\"|\\GHIJKLMNOPQRSTUVWXYZ", ➥
            MinLength = 6, MaxLength = 6)]
    public String Background
    {
        get
        {
            return (String)this["background"];
        }
        set
        {
            this["background"] = value;
        }
    }
```

```
[ConfigurationProperty("foreground", DefaultValue = "000000", IsRequired = true)]
[RegexStringValidator(Pattern="[0-9A-Fa-f]{6}")]
public String Foreground
{
    get
    {
        return (String)this["foreground"];
    }
    set
    {
        this["foreground"] = value;
    }
}
}
```

The StringValidator is again used to constrain the Background property. The RegexStringValidator has the same effect by using a regular expression. As you can see, the values have the same constraint. However, the regular expression is shorter, clearer, and easier to read. Using regular expressions is a good style and allows better control when searching, restricting, or replacing strings.

To understand what all this creates, see the following valid *web.config* section. First, the custom configuration itself has to be registered (see Listing 4-13).

Listing 4-13. *The Configuration Definition Must Be Registered Using This Code*

```
<configSections>
    <sectionGroup name="pageAppearanceGroup">
        <section
            name="pageAppearance"
            type="Apress.Extensibility.Configuration.PageAppearanceSection"
            allowLocation="true"
            allowDefinition="Everywhere" />
    </sectionGroup>
...
</configSections>
```

Second, the configuration section can be used (see Listing 4-14).

Listing 4-14. *The Configuration Definition Allows the Following Usage Scenario*

```
<pageAppearanceGroup>
  <pageAppearance remoteOnly="true">
    <font name="TimesNewRoman" size="18"/>
    <color background="000000" foreground="FFFFFF"/>
  </pageAppearance>
</pageAppearanceGroup>
```

However, this does not make sense if the values are not used. Defining values is one issue; using them in custom code is another.

Recall the point of this chapter: providers and their configuration should assist other developers to easily replace parts of your application, simply by defining another provider. On the user interface side, ASP.NET uses powerful server controls as much as possible to construct the HTML markup. On the code side, anything that's configurable in any way should be placed in the *web.config* file, another configuration file, or a database. Custom configuration is a part of the extensibility model.

Usage of a Custom Configuration Section

Assuming the configuration section is defined, present, and filled with data, it's time to access its values at runtime from your own code. Listing 4-15 shows how to achieve this.

Listing 4-15. *Access the Configuration Data*

```
<%@ Page Language="C#" %>

<!DOCTYPE html PUBLIC "-//W3C//DTD XHTML 1.0 Transitional//EN" ➥
                      "http://www.w3.org/TR/xhtml1/DTD/xhtml1-transitional.dtd">

<script runat="server">
  protected void Page_Load(object sender, EventArgs e)
  {
    var config = ➥
        (Apress.Extensibility.Configuration.PageAppearanceSection) ➥
            System.Configuration.ConfigurationManager.GetSection( ➥
            "pageAppearanceGroup/pageAppearance");
    StringBuilder sb = new StringBuilder();
    sb.Append("<h2>Settings in the PageAppearance Section:</h2>");
    sb.Append(String.Format("RemoteOnly: {0}<br>", config.RemoteOnly));
    sb.Append(String.Format("Font name and size: {0} {1}<br>", ➥
                            config.Font.Name, config.Font.Size));
    sb.Append( ➥
        String.Format("Background and foreground color: {0} {1}<br>", ➥
        config.Color.Background, config.Color.Foreground));
    lblConfig.Text = sb.ToString();
  }
</script>

<html >
<head id="Head1" runat="server">
  <title>Custom Configuration Section Example</title>
</head>
<body>
  <form id="form1" runat="server">
  <div>
    <asp:Label runat="server" ID="lblConfig" ></asp:Label>
  </div>
  </form>
</body>
</html>
```

The `ConfigurationManager` class is the entry point into the configuration. You can address any section here by giving the full path or, at least, a distinct part of the leaf path. As shown in the section about providers, "The Provider Model," there are several ways to handle these strings. Consider attributes, constant literals, and helper classes.

Once you have the section, and the section is a private type, you can cast as shown in the listing. The properties will represent the current values in the configuration. This will not only handle private data but also give fully typed access to the elements.

The configuration is based on the serialization and deserialization features that the base class provides. This could make it difficult to read or to modify the values in the *web.config* file. If you understand how the serializer works and can create similar strings by hand, your configuration class should function correctly as is.

Accessing the Configuration Declaratively

You now have an extended configuration model allowing the storage of complex values in a clearly defined way. The programmatic access is easy. However, ASP.NET favors declarative techniques. Making the configuration accessible from markup would be ideal.

Extending the Expression Binding Syntax

Integrated expressions play an important role in accessing data dynamically. You probably work with data binding expressions following the <%# %> pattern. A different declarative syntax is available, with this pattern:

```
<%$ %>
```

This is also an extensible model, allowing the creation of your own syntax in order to access data within the markup:

```
<asp:literal text="<%$ MyConfig:GetData %>" runat="server" />
```

Read this as an enhancement to the configuration extension described in the section "Extending the Configuration." It transfers access to the markup. Developers can access data without writing explicit code. Now page designers working with *.aspx* pages can add specific formatting options without doing any coding tasks.

Introduction to Expression Syntax

Expression builders process expressions. These build code from expressions during the page-processing phase—the parsing procedure. Expressions have this distinct pattern:

```
<%$ [prefix]:[declaration] %>
```

The first part, the prefix, maps to a type that handles the expression. Any string will do for the prefix. The colon is mandatory, but you can enter whatever you like in the declaration part. Anything from the colon to the end of the expression is treated as a String and processed at once. One common usage is the accessing of the AppSettings section in *web.config*. It follows this pattern:

```
<%$ AppSettings:KeyName %>
```

The prefix is "AppSettings". It determines the expression builder via a mapping (explained in the "Declare the Prefix" section) to a built-in class called AppSettingsExpressionBuilder. The expression builder must be able to handle the remaining part, "KeyName" in the example.

For localized resources there is another built-in class:

```
<%$ Resources:ResourceCategory,Name %>
```

The prefix is now "Resources". The expression builder used behind the scenes is the ResourceExpressionBuilder. There is also another, ConnectionStringsExpressionBuilder, which makes connection strings available in markup. All expression builders derive from the abstract base class ExpressionBuilder. The extensibility concept follows the common pattern. By implementing this base class, you can build your own expression builder.

How It Works Internally

Internally, the expression builder creates a code snippet. This code is inserted into the page during the parsing step. The compiler treats this code as part of your custom code and creates the page object. This requires the code snippet to follow specific rules. Essentially, the code is an assignment.

It assigns a value to a property of a control. Where the value comes from might require complex code, but the assignment is simple and limits the usage of such expressions. The most evident limitation is that usage without a control is not allowed. The following code will not function:

```
<div>
  <%$ MyConfig:Value1 %>
</div>
```

Instead, you must use a control:

```
<div>
  <asp:label runat="server" Text="<%$ MyConfig:Value1 %>" />
</div>
```

However, using the prefix is not enough to put it into operation. First, you must map the prefix to a specific type.

Declare the Prefix

The declaration of the prefix takes place in the *web.config* file. The path to the configuration element is `<system.web><compilation><expressionBuilders>`. The `<expressionBuilders>` element is usually absent. Add the following element to define a new mapping between a prefix and a type:

```
<expressionBuilders>
  <add expressionPrefix="prefix" type="type,assembly"/>
</expressionBuilders>
```

The `type` follows the common schema of an assembly reference:

- Namespace.Class, Assembly, Version, Culture, PublicKeyToken
- Namespace.Class, Assembly
- Namespace.Class, __code

The first form defines the fully qualified name of an assembly. The last references the App_Code folder, if the appropriate project type is used in Visual Studio. (Note the two underscores before the word "code" here.) An example could look like this:

- Apress.Extensions.MyBuilder, Apress.Extensions

Now you need to create the type. As mentioned, the abstract base class is where you start.

How the Expression Builder Works

The expression builder has only a few methods. Using these methods, it can parse the expression and generate the required code. Parsing is initiated using the `ParseExpression` method. If this step is successful, the `GetCodeExpression` method generates a code snippet. The only condition is that the compiler must be able to assign the snippet to a property. Therefore, the snippet must form the right-hand side of an assignment:

```
control.Property = <this is the code expression>;
```

While the right-hand side is merely a method call, this method can contain any amount of code (meaning that even the most complex operations are possible).

If the parsing fails, you should throw an exception. Otherwise, the `GetCodeExpression` method is invoked to create the code using the Code Document Object Model (CodeDOM). Although a short explanation follows, this book does not teach CodeDOM in depth. Refer to the MSDN documentation to learn more about source code generation: `http://msdn.microsoft.com/en-us/library/system.codedom.aspx`.

Table 4-6 lists the methods you have to implement to add an expression builder to an operation.

Table 4-6. *Methods of an Expression Builder*

Method	Description
EvaluateExpression	Returns the value for non-compiled pages (see the section "Accessing Settings for Non-Compiled Pages" in this chapter for details)
GetCodeExpression	Creates the code snippet to insert into the page
ParseExpression	Parses the syntax of the expression
SupportsEvaluate	Indicates whether this expression builder supports non-compiled pages

These methods are sufficient for creating our own expression builder.

Creating an Expression Builder

In the first example, you need direct access to values stored in a SQL Server database. You are using the same database and table you created earlier in the section "Creating a Custom Provider-Based Service." Please also refer to Figure 4-2. Specific criteria are used to retrieve the right values. The prefix is called "Cfg" and the syntax of the expressions looks like this:

```
<%$ Cfg:Key FROM category WHERE type %>
```

The syntax is similar to SQL, which makes it more readable. The type refers to the type of data, such as "image" or "label." In the markup portion, this would look like the following:

```
<asp:Label ID="lblHeader" runat="server" ➥
        Text="<%$ Cfg:Header FROM PageData WHERE label %>"></asp:Label>
```

The following code is the same for an image:

```
<asp:Image ID="imgHeader" runat="server" ➥
        ImageUrl="<%$ Cfg:Header FROM PageData WHERE image %>"></asp:Image>
```

The created code for the image example looks like "images/header1.png." Once defined, Visual Studio recognizes the expression syntax, as shown in Figure 4-6.

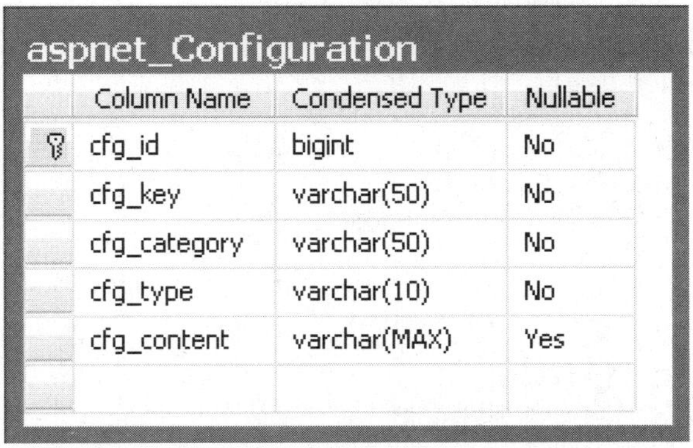

aspnet_Configuration

	Column Name	Condensed Type	Nullable
🔑	cfg_id	bigint	No
	cfg_key	varchar(50)	No
	cfg_category	varchar(50)	No
	cfg_type	varchar(10)	No
	cfg_content	varchar(MAX)	Yes

Figure 4-6. *The private expression builder appears in Visual Studio's expression dialog.*

One solution is shown in Listing 4-16.

Listing 4-16. *Using Expressions for Retrieving Configuration Data from a Database*

```
using System;
using System.Web.Compilation;
using System.CodeDom;

namespace Apress.Extensibility.Expressions
{
  public class CfgExpression : ExpressionBuilder
  {

  private static ConfigDataDataContext ctx;

  private static void EnsureCfgContext()
  {
    ctx = new ConfigDataDataContext();
  }

  public static string GetCfg(string key, string category, string type)
  {
    EnsureCfgContext();
    var res = from row in ctx.aspnet_Configurations ➥
              where row.cfg_key == key ➥
                 && row.cfg_category == category ➥
                 && row.cfg_type == type ➥
              select row.cfg_content;
    return res.FirstOrDefault<string>();
  }

  public override CodeExpression GetCodeExpression( ➥
            System.Web.UI.BoundPropertyEntry entry, ➥
            object parsedData, ➥
            ExpressionBuilderContext context)
  {
    ExpressionValues cfgValues = parsedData as ExpressionValues;
    if (cfgValues == null) throw new ArgumentException("parsedData");
    CodePrimitiveExpression[] cArg = new CodePrimitiveExpression[]
    {
        new CodePrimitiveExpression(cfgValues.Key),
        new CodePrimitiveExpression(cfgValues.Category),
        new CodePrimitiveExpression(cfgValues.Type)
    };
    CodeTypeReferenceExpression t = new CodeTypeReferenceExpression( ➥
                                   typeof(CfgExpression));
    CodeMethodInvokeExpression exp = new CodeMethodInvokeExpression(t, ➥
                                   "GetCfg", cArg);
    return exp;
  }

  public override object ParseExpression(string expression, ➥
                                   Type propertyType, ➥
                                   ExpressionBuilderContext context)
  {
    return TokenParser.Parse(expression);
  }
```

```
public override bool SupportsEvaluate
{
  get
  {
    return false;
  }
}

public override object EvaluateExpression(object target, ➥
                              System.Web.UI.BoundPropertyEntry entry, ➥
                              object parsedData, ➥
                              ExpressionBuilderContext context)
{
  return base.EvaluateExpression(target, entry, parsedData, context);
}

#region ConfigValues

class ExpressionValues
{
  public string Key { get; set; }
  public string Category { get; set; }
  public string Type { get; set; }
}

#endregion

#region SimpleTokenParser

static class TokenParser
{

  static ExpressionValues values;

  static TokenParser()
  {
    values = new ExpressionValues();
  }

  internal static ExpressionValues Parse(string toParse)
  {
    if (String.IsNullOrEmpty(toParse))
      throw new ArgumentNullException(toParse);
    int i = 0;
    string currentToken = String.Empty;
    // value FROM cat WHERE type
    while (true)
    {
      char c = toParse[i];
      switch (c)
      {
      case 'F':
        if (toParse.Substring(i, 5).Equals("FROM "))
        {
          values.Key = currentToken.Trim();
          currentToken = String.Empty;
          i += 4;
```

```
          }
        break;
      case 'W':
        if (toParse.Substring(i, 6).Equals("WHERE "))
        {
          values.Category = currentToken.Trim();
          currentToken = String.Empty;
          i += 5;
        }
      break;
    default:
      currentToken += c;
      break;
    }
    if (++i < toParse.Length) continue;
    values.Type = currentToken;
    break; // end while
  }
  return values;
    }
  }

  #endregion

  }
}
```

The creation of dynamic code is the most important part. However, it doesn't make sense to do everything dynamically. This is why the code for retrieving data is moved to the static method, GetCfg. The dynamic portion calls that method, which leads to generated code, such as the following:

```
lblHeader.Text = GetCfg(...);
```

The method is static because the private expression builder is not instantiated at runtime. It's a design-time tool which supports the page parser and design-time experience in Visual Studio. Only the assignment remains in the page's code after compilation.

The procedure commences with the ParseExpression method. The object created here appears later as the parsedData parameter of the GetCodeExpression method. The TokenParser class in the example demonstrates how to parse custom strings. It analyses the string after the expression's colon and creates three required parameters from it. The private class, ExpressionValues, stores the values, while the GetCodeExpression method builds the necessary code. It must return an object of type System. CodeDom.CodeExpression, which will contain a code fragment assignable to the right-hand side of an assignment statement. Refer to the next table to view the most important CodeDOM functions. In this example, I use a simple call to a static method so that the code generation is as simple as possible. The core element is the method invocation:

```
new CodeMethodInvokeExpression(t, "GetCfg", cArg)
```

The argument *cArg* is the collection of private parameters (see Table 4-7).

Table 4-7. *Important CodeDOM Methods*

Method	Description
CodeExpression	An abstract base class for all CodeDOM types
CodeTypeReferenceExpression	A type reference, such as a type used in code
CodePrimitiveExpression	Any code expression, which does not fit into other categories
CodeMethodInvokeExpression	A method call which requires, as parameters, the type where the method is defined, the name of the method, and an array of code fragments used as parameters for the method

The GetCfg method follows the same pattern used in the configuration example earlier in the section "Extending the Expression Binding Syntax." This draws from the DataContext class and LINQ to SQL to retrieve the values. The name of the context, ConfigDataDataContext, is based on the definition in *ConfigData.dbml*.

Accessing Settings for Non-Compiled Pages

If pages contain mainly static content, the compilation step can be suppressed. Code expressions and expression builders will still function. Moreover, expression builders which support non-compiled pages offer a different way of handling the code creation.

You can suppress the compilation by setting the following attribute in the @Page directive:

```
<%@ Page Language="C#" CompilationMode="Never" %>
```

This can also be set globally in *web.config*.

```
<pages compilationMode="Never" />
```

This might sound strange, but imagine that this is a *web.config* file for a subfolder where all static pages reside. It makes sense to suppress compilation if you have a tool that is modifying the static content directly and frequently, as the compiler causes an additional load on the server when compiling pages over and over, without creating any useful code.

The point of this section is the fact that expression builders are still allowed and assigned. However, they aren't able to create code snippets, as there is no compilation step able to support them. To indicate this usage scenario, the property SupportsEvaluate of the expression builder class must return true. This forces the page parser to call EvaluateExpression. The same will happen at runtime. Even if the page contains no code, and no compiler is invoked, the page handler serving the page will call the expression builder's EvaluateExpression method. As shown in the first example in Listing 4-16, the code invokes the appropriate configuration settings. This is a high-performance technique. It has limitations, but it is not as restricted as HTML pages would be. Beneath the configuration settings, you can also express date specifications or statistical data (see Listing 4-17).

Listing 4-17. *Support for Non-Compiled Pages*

```
using System;
using System.Text;
using System.Web.Compilation;
using System.Data.SqlClient;
using System.CodeDom;
```

```
namespace Apress.Extensibility.Expressions
{
  public class CfgExpression : ExpressionBuilder
  {

  private static ConfigDataDataContext ctx;

  private static void EnsureCfgContext()
  {
    ctx = new ConfigDataDataContext();
  }

  public static string GetCfg(string key, string category, string type)
  {
    EnsureCfgContext();
    var res = from row in ctx.aspnet_Configurations ➥
              where row.cfg_key == key ➥
                 && row.cfg_category == category ➥
                 && row.cfg_type == type ➥
              select row.cfg_content;
    return res.FirstOrDefault<string>();
  }

  public override bool SupportsEvaluate
  {
     get
     {
        return true;
     }
  }

  public override object EvaluateExpression(object target, ➥
                        System.Web.UI.BoundPropertyEntry entry, ➥
                        object parsedData, ExpressionBuilderContext context)
  {
     ExpressionValues cfgValues = parsedData as ExpressionValues;
     return GetCfg(cfgValues.Key, cfgValues.Category, cfgValues.Type);
  }
}
```

Read the EvaluateExpression method as a combination of the ParseExpression and GetCodeExpression methods. The database access is the same as in the last example (see Listing 4-16).

Beyond Simple Expressions

This expression model supports several other features. However, as they are beyond the scope of this book, I'll only give a short overview of them. Please refer to the official documentation for more usage scenarios.

The ParseExpression method has another parameter named context. It's not used in the example, as it's intended for more advanced scenarios. This parameter is of the type ExpressionBuilderContext. Its purpose is to support template-based controls, and it contains the virtual path to the page or user control that contains the control. The expression builder refers to the control and is able to support different code-generation strategies, depending on the requirements of the template-based control.

Another parameter, propertyType, refers to the type of the property. Usually, this is String, but it can be modified to any type that suits your needs. For instance, when using a very limited set of options, an enum would be appropriate. This would create a dropdown element in Visual Studio's expression builder for an advanced design-time experience.

The last parameter named entry is of the BoundPropertyEntry type. This allows access to the control itself, its ControlID property, and the control's type.

Finally, the parameter ExpressionPrefix retrieves the currently used prefix. This assumes that you can assign the same expression builder multiple times and create complex and sophisticated frameworks on top of expression builders.

Design-Time Support

As demonstrated earlier, Visual Studio supports expressions through simple Expression dialogs. These can be invoked using the Expression section of the property browser. Simply select a control on the designer surface, open the property browser (F4), and click on the ellipses in the *Expressions* element in the *Data* section. The dialog contains a mapping tool, which assigns properties to expressions. Here, the property grid uses attributes read by reflection to modify its behavior (Figure 4-7).

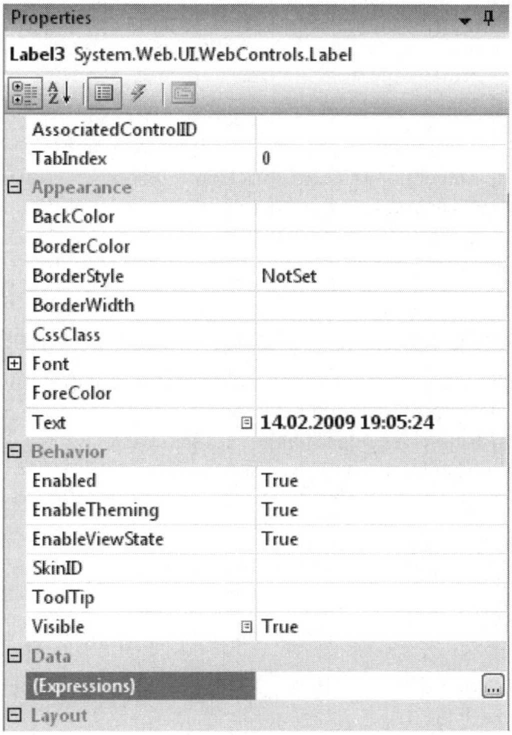

Figure 4-7. *Invoke the Expression dialog using the ellipses button. Bound properties appear with a small icon in the name column.*

To support this, decorate the class of the expression builder with an ExpressionEditorAttribute, defined in the System.Web.UI.Design namespace of the System.Design assembly:

```
[ExpressionEditor(typeof(CfgExpressionEditor))]
```

The type CfgExpressionEditor implements the abstract base class ExpressionEditor. The only required step is to implement the GetExpressionEditorSheet method:

```
public override ExpressionEditorSheet GetExpressionEditorSheet(➡
                                       string expression, ➡
                                       IServiceProvider serviceProvider)
{
  return new CfgExpressionEditorSheet(expression, serviceProvider);
}
```

The CfgExpressionEditorSheet type results from the implementation of the base class ExpressionEditorSheet. This type defines the properties in the property grid of the expression builder dialog that Visual Studio displays. Regarding other types, you can use the classes EditorAttribute and TypeConverterAttribute to change the data the property grid reads via reflection. You can find both types in the System.ComponentModel. In the example, it would be helpful to have three properties, such as "Key," "Category," and "Type." The EditorAttribute defines the editor used in one entry of the property grid. This can be a dropdown list, or another dialog opened by clicking on the ellipses.

■**Note** Dialogs and controls that are used in Visual Studio to extend the design-time experience must be Win-Form controls. You cannot use web controls here. Some familiarity with Windows Forms Control programming is highly recommended before you begin extending Visual Studio's design-time environment.

Implementing an Expression Builder with Design-Time Support

The next example shows the complete implementation of an expression builder with design-time support. The purpose is the output of current data or time including variations like yesterday, tomorrow, and so on. The current value should appear in design-time view. Additionally, it is selectable in the Expressions dialog using a dropdown. The usage in markup could look like this:

```
<asp:Label runat="server" ID="lblHeader" Text='<%$ Time:YesterDay %>' ➡
        Font-Bold="true"></asp:Label>
```

In design-time view, Figure 4-8 shows the current value.

Figure 4-8. *Design-time view with real values*

Listing 4-18 is the basic implementation of the Expression builder itself. In the remaining part of the section, I will show how to extend this to get the full design-time support.

Listing 4-18. *The Complete Definition of the Design-Time Environment*

```
using System;
using System.CodeDom;
using System.Web.Compilation;
using System.Web.UI;
using System.Web.UI.Design;

namespace Apress.Extensibility.Expressions.Time
{
    [ExpressionPrefix("Time")]
    [ExpressionEditor(typeof(TimeExpressionEditor))]
    public class TimeExpression : ExpressionBuilder
    {
        public override CodeExpression GetCodeExpression(BoundPropertyEntry entry, ➥
                                          object parsedData, ➥
                                    ExpressionBuilderContext context)
        {
            TimeOptions to = (TimeOptions)Enum.Parse(typeof(TimeOptions), ➥
                                   entry.Expression, true);
            switch (to)
            {
                case TimeOptions.Today:
                // System.DateTime.Now
                return new CodePropertyReferenceExpression( ➥
                    new CodeTypeReferenceExpression(typeof(DateTime)), "Now");
                case TimeOptions.Yesterday:
                    // System.DateTime.Now.AddDays(-1)
                    return new CodeMethodInvokeExpression( ➥
                        new CodePropertyReferenceExpression( ➥
                        new CodeTypeReferenceExpression(typeof(DateTime)), ➥
                        "Now"), ➥
                        "AddDays", ➥
                        new CodePrimitiveExpression(-1));
                case TimeOptions.Tomorrow:
                        // System.DateTime.Now.AddDays(1)
                        return new CodeMethodInvokeExpression( ➥
                        new CodePropertyReferenceExpression( ➥
                            new CodeTypeReferenceExpression(typeof(DateTime)), ➥
                            "Now"), ➥
                            "AddDays", ➥
                            new CodePrimitiveExpression(1));
                case TimeOptions.NextWeek:
                        // System.DateTime.Now.AddDays(7)
                        return new CodeMethodInvokeExpression(➥
                            new CodePropertyReferenceExpression(➥
                            new CodeTypeReferenceExpression(typeof(DateTime)), ➥
                            "Now"), ➥
                            "AddDays", ➥
                            new CodePrimitiveExpression(7));
                default:
                        throw new InvalidOperationException("The expression ➥
                            value should be one of: ➥
                            Today, Yesterday, Tomorrow, NextWeek.");
            }
        }
    }
}
```

This expression builder takes an enumeration value (see Listing 4-19) and creates code snippets that return a date value based on the current time and date. Note the attribute at the top of the class:

```
[ExpressionEditor(typeof(TimeExpressionEditor))]
```

This assigns the TimeExpressionEditor type to modify the design-time environment.

Listing 4-19. *A Supporting Enumeration*

```
namespace Apress.Extensibility.Expressions.Time
{
    public enum TimeOptions
    {
        Yesterday,
        Today,
        Tomorrow,
        NextWeek
    }
}
```

The TimeExpressionEditor type derives from the ExpressionEditor. Its purpose is twofold. First, it allows the output of values in the designer. If a user opens the designer surface editing a page or user control, the expressions can be used just like any other expression. Instead of showing the expression's code, such as *Time:Today*, it shows the calculated value, *March 20, 2009*. This results in a more realistic design-time experience (see Listing 4-20).

Listing 4-20. *Code That Supports a Custom Editor at Design-Time*

```
using System;
using System.Web.UI.Design;

namespace Apress.Extensibility.Expressions.Time
{
    public class TimeExpressionEditor : ExpressionEditor
    {
        // Evaluates an expression at design-time for preview purposes
        public override object EvaluateExpression(string expression, ➥
                                    object parseTimeData, ➥
                                    Type propertyType, ➥
                                    IServiceProvider serviceProvider)
        {
            TimeOptions to = (TimeOptions) Enum.Parse(typeof(TimeOptions), ➥
                                    expression, true);
            switch (to)
            {
                case TimeOptions.Today:
                    return DateTime.Now.ToString();
                case TimeOptions.Yesterday:
                    return DateTime.Now.AddDays(-1).ToString();
                case TimeOptions.Tomorrow:
                    return DateTime.Now.AddDays(1).ToString();
                case TimeOptions.NextWeek:
                    return DateTime.Now.AddDays(7).ToString();
                default:
                    throw new InvalidOperationException("The expression value➥
                        should be one of: Today, Yesterday, Tomorrow, NextWeek.");
            }
        }
```

```
    }

    public override ExpressionEditorSheet GetExpressionEditorSheet(➥
                    string expression, IServiceProvider serviceProvider)
    {
        return new TimeExpressionEditorSheet(expression, serviceProvider);
    }

    }
}
```

The code demonstrates how to define the editor sheet using the GetExpressionEditorSheet method. The TimeExpressionEditorSheet type used here is shown in Listing 4-21.

Listing 4-21. *Code That Supports the Propertysheet at Design-Time*

```
using System;
using System.ComponentModel;
using System.Web.UI.Design;

namespace Apress.Extensibility.Expressions.Time
{

    public sealed class TimeExpressionEditorSheet : ExpressionEditorSheet
    {
        private string _day;
        public TimeExpressionEditorSheet(string day, ➥
                                         IServiceProvider serviceProvider)
            : base(serviceProvider)
        {
            Day = day;
        }

        [TypeConverter(typeof(TimeConverter))]
        public string Day
        {
            get
            {
                return _day;
            }
            set
            {
                _day = value;
            }
        }

        public override string GetExpression()
        {
            return Day;
        }

        // TypeConverter to provide dropdown of valid values
        private sealed class TimeConverter : StringConverter
        {
            public override bool GetStandardValuesExclusive(➥
                            ITypeDescriptorContext context)
            {
```

```
            return true;
        }

        public override bool GetStandardValuesSupported(➥
                            ITypeDescriptorContext context)
        {
            return true;
        }

        public override TypeConverter.StandardValuesCollection ➥
                        GetStandardValues(ITypeDescriptorContext context)
        {
            string[] standardValues = Enum.GetNames(typeof(TimeOptions));
            return new StandardValuesCollection(standardValues);
        }
    }
  }
}
```

These are the properties shown in the expression builder dialog in Visual Studio. The
[TypeConverter(typeof(TimeConverter))] attribute converts values from the property grid into
the enumeration. This is necessary, as the property grid transforms a type internally into a string
representation, which allows you to select it. In this case, the dropdown will return single strings like
"Today" or "Tomorrow." These values must be converted back and forth by the TimeOptions enumeration.

In the property grid, you handle the enumeration as a dropdown. You can force this by returning
true in the GetStandardValuesSupported method. The GetStandardValues method must return the array
of elements presented in the dropdown. Enum.GetNames performs this function. If the enumeration
values do not fit your needs, you may decorate them with DescriptionAttribute attributes (System.
ComponentModel namespace) and obtain the final strings from this attribute instead of using the enum
values.

```
public enum TimeOptions
{
    [Description("The day before today")]
    Yesterday,
    [Description("Now")]
    Today,
    [Description("The day after today")]
    Tomorrow,
    [Description("Some time in the future")]
    NextWeek
}
```

This is just one of the many options you have in extending the design-time environment.
However, the more code you add, the harder it will be to debug. The next section covers the basic
principles of design-time debugging.

Debugging Design-Time Extensions

Design-time support should be part of any extension model. However, it's difficult to debug these
extensions, and this is probably why developers avoid adding design-time support to their applications. There is no debugger attached to design-time code. This means that you cannot add
breakpoints easily or step into the code to view its internal operations. Using smart exceptions and
try/catch blocks might help, but this is not a good debugging experience.

To debug within the Visual Studio design-time environment, you must launch another instance of Visual Studio and debug the same code there. To accomplish this, open the property pages of the Web project and select the option *Start external program* (see Figure 4-9).

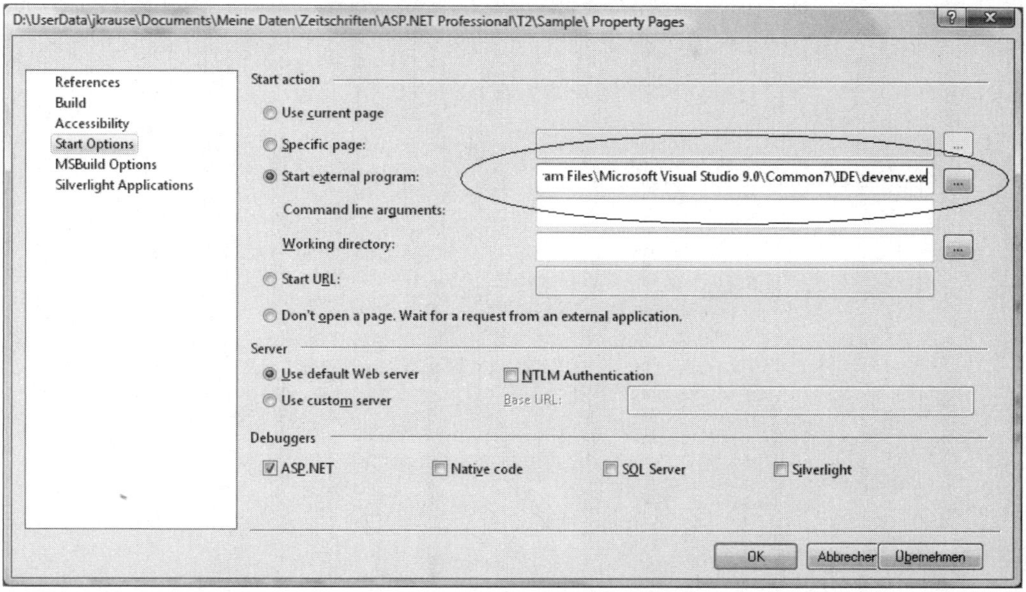

Figure 4-9. *Start another instance of Visual Studio to debug at design-time.*

Choose the Visual Studio executable *devenv.exe* as the external program. When you start debugging the project (by hitting F5), another instance of Visual Studio will appear. In this instance, you load the same project and start using the design-time environment. In the first instance of Visual Studio, you can now set breakpoints and debug as you would do at runtime. To reach specific code sections, just start using the code within the second instance.

Summary

In this chapter, you saw an overview of providers and how they can be used to create modern, multi-tier architecture. Providers result in highly configurable and extensible applications that don't require additional code when changes to basic features are made. The configuration of providers is a major part of this environment. In addition to providers, the whole configuration can be extended through *web.config*. This chapter showed the extensibility of *web.config* in defining private sections and elements. Lastly, the configuration settings were made available in the declarative part of the web pages, the markup, by supporting private expression builders. Expression builders form a final extensibility feature that improves the design-time experience.

■ ■ ■

CHAPTER 5

Extending the Resource Model

Web sites consist of both pure HTML and resources. Resources are everything not directly embedded into the page's source, such as images, JavaScript, ActiveX controls, Flash, and Silverlight code. Resources can also be used more widely. You can structure a page's content by moving parts of it into resources, thus changing its content dynamically based on different resource sources. This technique is primarily used to create localized applications able to display different languages and formats for a global market.

In this chapter, I'll explain how to extend the resource model in ASP.NET. In particular, this chapter includes:

- How the resource model works
- Extending the provider-based resource management
- Creating custom resource providers
- Editing resources online at runtime

Principles of Resource Management

Resource files are usually stored in XML format and located in special folders called either *App_ GlobalResources* for global resources or *App_LocalResources* for page- or control-specific ones. *App_LocalResources* is created on a per folder basis. This means that, within your application, there will normally be several such folders available.

Each resource file has a defined file name format:

```
PageName.Culture.resx
```

However, for fallback reasons, a common base resource is required. The first resource file has the default name *Pagename.resx*. Whenever ASP.NET isn't able to find a particular resource file, it will load the default resource file. It's a good idea to define all your resources there in order to avoid users seeing strange results.

At compile time, the resource compiler takes all these files and compiles them into a binary format. This improves the speed of reading the content and reduces the file size.

The Fallback Strategy

If you think in terms of cultures, you'll see a very straightforward model. A culture is a combination of a language and a country. In many countries around the world, people speak more than one language. You define the country to receive information regarding currency format or calendar, for instance, and you define the language to obtain the correct format of numbers, and names of months and weekdays. Even if several countries only define one such combination, others are much more complex. In some cases, you'll also find information about the script; for example, certain languages can be written in either Cyrillic or Latin letters. Well-globalized pages will support this situation.

For most applications, it may be unwarranted to distinguish between countries—a simple language definition will suffice. A good example is the usage of German in Germany, Austria, and Switzerland. As long as you don't deal with currency, it's almost the same (the differences are subtle). Defining German as the final language will drastically reduce the development effort and still have a great impact on internationalization. In real-life scenarios, browsers will usually transmit preferred culture information, which consists of language and country details. If one sends "German, Austria" and your systems only support German globally, the fallback mechanism must find the appropriate resource information.

Using Global Resources

It's much the same approach for global resources, except that there is no need to bind resources to a specific page. This opens the possibility of holding resources for any situation, with or without adding support for cultures, languages, and fallback behavior. Such resources are called shared resources. It's easy to handle any kind of resource file embedded within an assembly by accessing the resource manager. The access is enabled via implicit definition in the page's markup, using the expression:

```
<%$ Resources:ResourceKey,Tag %>
```

Alternatively, you can call the `Page` class's `GetGlobalResource` method.

Limitations of the Existing Provider

The only drawback is that the internal resource provider has a single method of accessing resources—based on *resx* files. File-based operations are not unusual, but they limit us to just one way of accessing resources at design-time and runtime. Large applications with frequently changing resources might need a different behavior, either with better runtime support or with using a different storage location for the resource information.

Programming a Custom Resource Provider

The system of *.resx* files provided out-of-the-box has some limitations. While it's well supported in Visual Studio at design-time and works at runtime without any coding effort, there is almost no way of parameterizing or configuring the behavior.

Imagine that you have different themes and want to manage different resources for each theme. Even if the resource management fits your needs (apart from wishing to store the data in a database instead of in XML files), you can't use the default resource provider. Developers often discard the whole default resource handling approach and implement their own solution. However, resource management is based on providers and, as shown in the previous chapter, the model is extensible. It is not easy, but it can be done, and this chapter will explain how.

Extending the Provider Model

Whenever you depart from the default resource model, you'll need to manage some specific requirements. Leaving the default resource model and creating an independent solution has serious drawbacks. Not only do you lose the ability to assign a control's property a resource-based value, but you also lose the whole world of design-time support, runtime behavior, and certain optimizations. Therefore, instead of implementing a completely isolated solution, the extension of the provider model is a highly recommended alternative.

To understand the resource model, we'll look first at the classes involved. The classes support three phases:

- The design-time step
- The compilation phase
- The runtime step

Usually we distinguish between runtime and design-time phases only. It might look as though the compilation step has a special meaning.

As you'll see later in the section "Edit Resources at Runtime," this is a quirk of the resource management. The *.resx* files used by default to store resources are compiled into binary resource files. Even if not file-based, the resources must be embedded into each page before being delivered to the browser. The runtime then handles the resources and transforms the pre-compiled data into values read by the controls on the fly.

The design-time stage is mostly for local resources. Visual Studio provides a feature in the Tools menu to create local resources for all the controls on a page. This assigns the *meta:resourcekey* attribute with a key that points to the resource file. This file is a simple key-value list that is able to return the right data. The same approach occurs with any explicit call to the resources, using the <%$ Resource:Key %> expression.

Several *.resx* files co-exist and hold data for each culture supported. Implementing the design-time feature is essential for supplying full support to Visual Studio. At compile time, these expressions are translated into calls to the methods GetLocalResource and GetGlobalResource. At runtime, these methods return values from the compiled resources. The two tiers—the call to resources at the UI level and the access to the data layer—are separate, and the replacement of the data access is quite easy. It's not unusual to change both the behavior and the data source.

The following example extends the default behavior by reading the current theme and managing as many resource file structures as you have themes. It is still using the *.resx* file model. Additionally, you'll see a Web Service–based client application in Figure 5-1 which demonstrates how to handle resources at runtime and allow users to change formerly static content.

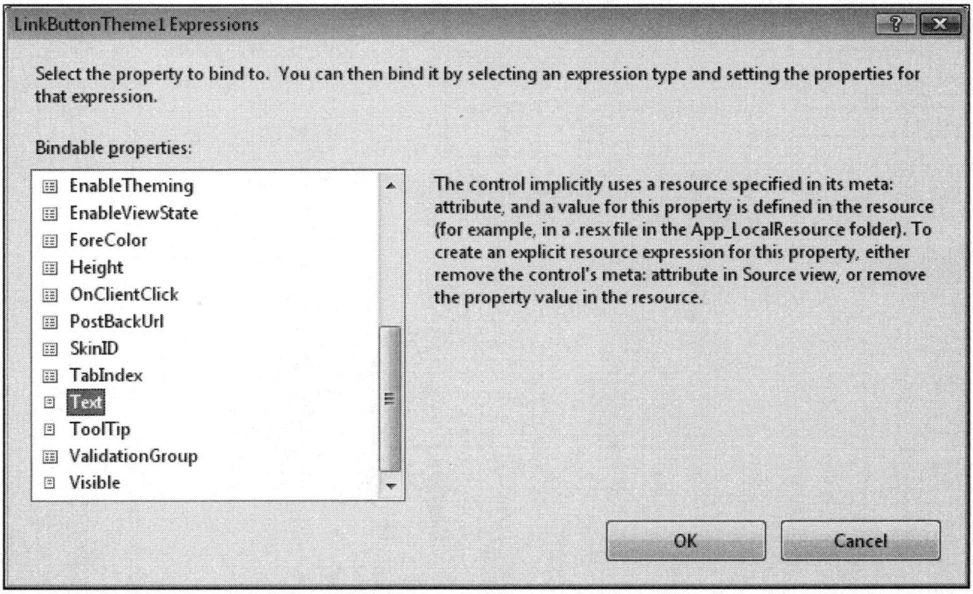

Figure 5-1. *Bindable properties in the Expression editor in Visual Studio*

Prerequisites

There are good examples in the MSDN documentation of how to implement the various interfaces and abstract base classes to create a usable resource provider. The problem is that it doesn't give you the whole picture, or explain how the isolated examples fit together and fill in the gaps. Normally, you'll need the following:

- A factory class that creates the provider at design-time
- A factory class that creates the provider at runtime
- Implementations of both providers

The providers are responsible for using specific reader and writer classes to access the resources. These implementations need:

- A class to read the global resources
- A class to write the global resources
- A class to read the local resources
- A class to write the local resources

You don't have to completely implement all classes. For instance, if your application does not write resources because you manage all resources outside the application, you don't need to implement the writer classes fully.

In Figure 5-2, you can see the base classes and their dependencies.

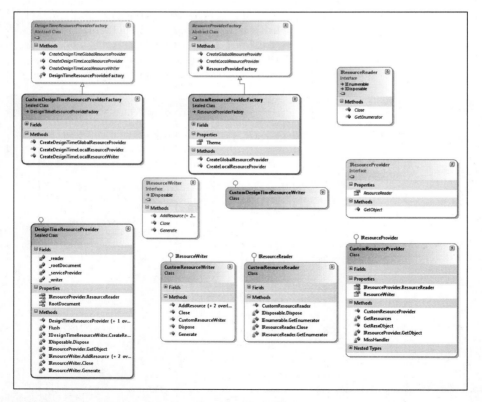

Figure 5-2. *Class diagram of the base classes and interfaces*

Implementing the Custom Provider

The implementation of a custom resource provider starts with the ResourceProviderFactory class. There are two methods required in order to access both global and local resources. Each method returns the configured provider that is responsible for requesting resources from resource storage. Implementing the factory allows some customization features. In the following examples, I customize by adding support for the current theme. Storing the active theme in the factory allows the factory to pass the information to the provider via a parameter. The provider can then modify the storage using this additional information.

In the example shown later in Listing 5-2, the CustomResourceProvider is based on IResource-Provider, and our particular interest is in ResourceReader. This is the class that implements the reader. The main method is GetObject, which returns the resource value based on the conditions obtained from the factory and the current conditions, such as the culture, passed via parameters. CustomResourceReader implements the IResourceReader interface to make the custom implementation available. That means the ResourceReader.GetObject method returns an object of type IResourceReader. The object is of the type that contains the actual implementation.

In a similar manner, to get the resource writer classes, you can use the GetResourceWriter method to return a type that implements IResourceWriter. The implementation in Listing 5-1 is called CustomResourceWriter. As mentioned before, the implementation is only required if you plan to support resource writing at runtime.

The whole schema must be implemented a second time to support the design-time environment. Visual Studio's design-time support creates resource files, and reads and writes resources, if you use the designer view. Visual Studio writes *.resx* files by default. Implementing the design-time support allows your custom resource provider to work inside Visual Studio and still support different storage or schema.

To implement the custom resource provider, begin with the factory class.

Listing 5-1. *The Entry Point Is a Simple Factory Class*

```
using System.Web.Compilation;

public sealed class CustomResourceProviderFactory : ResourceProviderFactory
{
  private string theme;

  public string Theme
  {
    get { return theme; }
    set { theme = value; }
  }


  public override IResourceProvider CreateGlobalResourceProvider(string classKey)
  {
    return new CustomResourceProvider(null, classKey, theme);
  }


  public override IResourceProvider CreateLocalResourceProvider(string virtualPath)
  {
    return new CustomResourceProvider(virtualPath, null, theme);
  }
}
```

This code shows how simple the factory is. It returns a custom resource provider for local and for global resource access. In Listing 5-2, the same provider is used for both, and it distinguishes between access methods by supplying either the virtualPath or classKey parameter.

Listing 5-2. *The Provider with Theme-Based resx Support*

```
public class CustomResourceProvider : IResourceProvider
{

    class ResourceTuple
    {

        public ResourceTuple(IResourceReader reader, IResourceWriter writer)
        {
            this.Reader = reader;
            this.Writer = writer;
            this.Culture = ci;
        }

        public IResourceReader Reader
        {
            get;
            set;
        }
        public IResourceWriter Writer
        {
            get;
            set;
        }
    }

    private string virtualPath;
    private string theme;
    private bool isGlobal;
    private static Dictionary<string, ➥
                        Dictionary<CultureInfo, ResourceTuple>> resourceCache;

    public CustomResourceProvider(string virtualPath, string className, ➥
                                string theme)
    {
        if (theme == null) theme = "Default";
        if (String.IsNullOrEmpty(className))
        {
            this.virtualPath = virtualPath;
            isGlobal = false;
        }
        else
        {
            this.virtualPath = className;
            isGlobal = true;
        }
        this.theme = theme;
        GetResources();
    }


    private CultureInfo GetNativeCulture(CultureInfo culture)
    {
```

```csharp
    if (culture == null)
    {
        culture = System.Threading.Thread.CurrentThread.CurrentUICulture;
    }
    // switch to country neutral parent to handle languages only
    if (culture.Parent != CultureInfo.InvariantCulture)
    {
        culture = culture.Parent;
    }
    return culture;
}

private void GetResources()
{
    try
    {
        if (resourceCache == null)
        {
            resourceCache = new Dictionary<string, ➥
                            Dictionary<CultureInfo, ResourceTuple>>();
        }
        string regPath;
        if (isGlobal)
        {
            // global
            regPath = "";
        }
        else
        {
            // local, XmlResourceHelper is explained in next listing
            regPath = XmlResourceHelper.GetLocalResxBasePath(virtualPath, ➥
                                                    theme);
        }
        // no context means that it's compile time and we don't support this
        if (HttpContext.Current == null) return;
        // read all resources for all cultures for this file
        string filter = Path.GetFileName(virtualPath) + "*.resx";
        if (!resourceCache.ContainsKey(virtualPath))
        {
            resourceCache[virtualPath] = new Dictionary<CultureInfo, ➥
                                            ResourceTuple>();
        }
        foreach (string file in Directory.GetFiles( ➥
                            Path.GetDirectoryName(regPath), filter))
        {
            string[] pathParts = Path.GetFileName(file).Split( ➥
                                            ".".ToCharArray());
            CultureInfo ci = CultureInfo.InvariantCulture;
                if (pathParts.Length == 4)
            {
                // Example: In Default.aspx.de.resx => [2] is "de"
                ci = new CultureInfo(pathParts[2]);
            }
            // per path and per culture we store a reader and a writer
            resourceCache[virtualPath].Add(ci, ➥
                    new ResourceTuple(new CustomResourceReader(file), ➥
                    new CustomResourceWriter(file)));
```

```
            }
        }
        catch (Exception ex)
        {
            throw new ApplicationException(ex.Message, ex);
        }
    }

    object IResourceProvider.GetObject(string resourceKey, CultureInfo culture)
    {
        IResourceReader reader = null;
        if (culture == null)
        {
            // if not explicitly defined take over page's UI culture
            culture = CultureInfo.CurrentUICulture;
        }
        do
        {
            if (resourceCache[virtualPath].ContainsKey(culture))
            {
                // found it
                break;
            }
            else
            {
                // try native culture
                culture = GetNativeCulture(culture);
            }
            // end of fallback path
            if (culture == CultureInfo.InvariantCulture) break;
        } while (reader == null);
        reader = resourceCache[virtualPath][culture].Reader;
        if (reader != null)
        {
            object value = ((CustomResourceReader)reader).GetObject(resourceKey);
            MissHandler(ref value, resourceKey);
            return value;
        }
        return null;
    }

    // get object from key and culture
    public object GetResxObject(string resourceKey, CultureInfo culture)
    {
        culture = GetNativeCulture(culture);
        string uniqueKey = virtualPath;
        ResXResourceReader rr = null;
        object value = null;
        // get the cached object or create it
        if (HttpContext.Current.Cache[uniqueKey] == null)
        {
            uniqueKey = XmlResourceHelper.GetResxPath(uniqueKey, theme, ➥
                                            virtualPath == null, culture);
            if (String.IsNullOrEmpty(uniqueKey)) return "RESX";
            rr = new ResXResourceReader(uniqueKey);
            HttpContext.Current.Cache[uniqueKey] = rr;
        }
```

```csharp
    // Use resource reader to retrieve the value
    rr = (ResXResourceReader)HttpContext.Current.Cache[uniqueKey];
    IDictionaryEnumerator id = rr.GetEnumerator();
    while (id.MoveNext())
    {
        if (String.Compare(id.Key.ToString(), resourceKey, true) == 0)
        {
            value = id.Value;
            break;
        }
    }
    // check whether nothing has been found
    MissHandler(ref value, resourceKey);
    // return
    return value;
}

private void MissHandler(ref object value, string resourceKey)
{
    // Create a generic value if resource object is missing
    if (value == null)
    {
        if (!resourceKey.Contains("."))
        {
            value = String.Format("Missing:{0}", resourceKey);
        }
        else
        {
            switch (resourceKey.Substring(resourceKey.LastIndexOf(".")))
            {
                case ".Visible":
                    value = true;
                    break;
                case ".Tooltip":
                case ".ToolTip":
                    value = "";
                    break;
                default:
                case ".Text":
                    value = String.Format("Missing:{0}", resourceKey);
                    break;
            }
        }
    }
    if (value == null) throw new ArgumentException("Unexpectadly found ➥
                        an unresolvable missing resource: " + resourceKey);
}

IResourceReader IResourceProvider.ResourceReader
{
    get
    {
        if (resourceCache.ContainsKey(virtualPath))
        {
            return resourceCache[virtualPath] ➥
                                [CultureInfo.InvariantCulture].Reader;
        }
```

```
            return null;
        }
    }

    public IResourceWriter ResourceWriter
    {
        get
        {
            if (resourceCache.ContainsKey(virtualPath))
            {
                return resourceCache[virtualPath] ➥
                                [CultureInfo.InvariantCulture].Writer;
            }
            return null;
        }
    }

}
```

The provider itself is not so simple. First, we need to define the storage location and storage handling. The solution used is based on *.resx* files. To improve performance, the provider retains a copy of the resources in an internal cache. This is global and therefore can be defined as static:

```
static Dictionary<string, Dictionary<CultureInfo, ResourceTuple>> resourceCache;
```

This is a nested `Dictionary`. The key to the outer dictionary is the resource key, which is either the `virtualPath` to a local resource or the `className` of a global one. For each resource, we need to handle multiple resource containers. There is one container per culture.

The inner `Dictionary` contains these containers and employs the `CultureInfo` as the index to a particular container. The `Dictionary` value (the container) holds the appropriate reader and writer objects, which are of type `CustomResourceReader` and `CustomResourceWriter`. The `ResourceTuple` class is an inner helper class that stores the reader and writer objects and allows type-safe access to them.

The provider is instantiated on a per file basis. Each local resource (aspx as well as ascx files) creates one provider. The same happens for each global resource. In the `GetResources` method, the provider immediately constructs the cache. The `HttpContext.Current == null` check ensures that the provider is not active at both design and compile time. The provider searches a designated directory from the `GetLocalResxBasePath`. This is a helper method specific to the required behavior. It creates the path to the `.resx` file based on both theme and local resource. In the example, the full path conforms to the pattern:

```
App_Data/Resx/<Theme>/virtualPath/ResourceFile.<Culture>.ResourceType
```

The App_Data folder is defined as the storage location. The Resx subfolder ensures that there is no conflict with other data stored there. The *<Theme>* part is a placeholder for the named theme. At a minimum, the default theme named "Default" must exist. The *virtualPath* is the path to the file that uses the resource within your project. *ResourceFile* is the name of the aspx or ascx file, and these extensions define the *ResourceType*. A full path could look like this:

```
App_Data/Resx/MyTheme/storeFront/Basket.en-us.aspx
App_Data/Resx/Default/storeFront/Basket.en-us.aspx
App_Data/Resx/MyTheme/storeFront/Basket.de.aspx
App_Data/Resx/Default/storeFront/Basket.de.aspx
```

These examples show how to store different resources for one file (`Basket.aspx`) for different themes and cultures. The fallback resource file—the one without any culture information—is handled with the `CultureInfo.InvariantCulture` key.

Once the cache is populated and the provider is loaded, the runtime requests the provider for a specific resource object using the GetObject method. This method is passed a key and the culture. Since each resource store has its own provider (based on the virtualPath member), this is sufficient information to retrieve the correct value. The goal of this method is to implement the fallback strategy. A do-while loop ascends the path of cultures to obtain an existing definition. Either it finds the invariant culture, or, as a final fallback, the default definition is used. You will need to create at least a default resource definition to avoid an exception being thrown if no resource is found.

If the stored resources have been located, the GetObject method of the CustomResourceReader type is called to obtain the resource reader for the current culture. Remember that such an object exists per culture. The resource reader does not know anything about cultures; it only returns the value based on the resource key.

During the process of resource creation, translation, and storing, some values may get lost. In this case, the resource reader would return null. The MissHandler method checks the value to assure valid content. Depending on the property retrieved (".Text," ".Tooltip," etc.), the method adds the prefix "Missing:". This leads to a page that is shown without any exceptions, but with several text portions such as "Missing:Label1Text." Authors can recognize the missing values and the name of the corresponding control, including the property that's not properly set.

So far there is nothing unusual about this code. The final step is to implement the resource reader (see Listing 5-3).

Listing 5-3. *The Resource Reader Used to Retrieve a Specific Resource Object*

```
public class CustomResourceReader : IResourceReader
{
    private Hashtable resources;

    public CustomResourceReader(string fileName)
    {
        using (ResXResourceReader rr = new ResXResourceReader(fileName))
        {
            resources = new Hashtable();
            IEnumerator enu = rr.GetEnumerator();
            enu.Reset();
            // Cache it in a Hashtable
            while (enu.MoveNext())
            {
                resources.Add(((DictionaryEntry)enu.Current).Key.ToString(), ➥
                        ((DictionaryEntry)enu.Current).Value);
            }
        }
    }

    IDictionaryEnumerator IResourceReader.GetEnumerator()
    {
        return resources.GetEnumerator();
    }

    void IResourceReader.Close() {  }

    IEnumerator IEnumerable.GetEnumerator()
    {
        return resources.GetEnumerator();
    }

    void IDisposable.Dispose()
```

```
    {
    }

    internal object GetObject(string resourceKey)
    {
        return resources[resourceKey];
    }
}
```

The resource reader is easy to implement because it still uses *.resx* files. The ResXResourceReader class from the System.Resource namespace provides almost everything we need. The only addition is another internal cache, to provide rapid read-write access to the underlying resources at runtime. This means that the resource reader must have read and write access to the *.resx* files. In the code, the ResXResourceReader loads each XML file, reads all the content, and copies it into the Hashtable. (A Hashtable is appropriate because the values are of type object and a generic List would not have any advantages.) The class returns an enumerator used by the runtime to find keys. It also implements a GetObject method which retrieves the correct resource value using the Hashtable indexer.

At this point, the resource provider could start working if any required resource is present in the appropriate files. The following sections describe the usage scenarios. Refer to the section "Implementing Design-Time Support" for more information about additional tasks, such as:

- Extending the provider by implementing a writer
- Adding support for the design-time experience
- Adding support for handling resources at both design-time and runtime
- Replacing the provider to access a database that stores the resources

However, first we'll put this into operation by starting the configuration step.

Configure the Resource Provider

Since the provider is instantiated and called from a factory, registering the factory is a necessary step. This is a setting in the *web.config* file. In the <system.web> section, the following tag registers the custom factory:

```
<globalization resourceProviderFactoryType="CustomResourceProviderFactory"/>
```

Whether to use just the class name or the fully-qualified assembly name depends on the implementation. If you write the class in a separate Visual Studio project, the fully-qualified name is required.

Using the Custom Resource Provider

Now that everything is implemented and configured, you can start using the resources at runtime. As you can see in the implementation, classes distinguish between local and global resources. For local resources, the key is the name of either the .aspx or .ascx file. Internally, the virtualPath parameter retains this data. For global resources, the classKey parameter is used. To refer to these resources in your web pages, use the following expression format:

```
<%$ classKey:Resource %>
```

Implementing Design-Time Support

Implementing design-time support is required for one feature only. In Visual Studio, you can add a resource's meta attributes through the following:

- Open an aspx page or ascx control in the designer view.

- In the "Tools" menu, click the "Generate Local Resource" item.

This will create a meta:resourcekey attribute for each localizable element. The provider is responsible for creating the corresponding entry in the resource file and writing the current values there. However, our current provider supports runtime operations only, and therefore we need an additional provider for design-time support.

■**Note** If you're sure that the Visual Studio design-time support option will never be used, you should not bother to implement the design-time support classes. But it won't harm your code if you do build it.

Register the Design-Time Support

First, you'll need to register the design-time support. There is no such option in the *web.config* file; instead, an attribute is required. You can register your design-time classes by decorating the factory class like this:

```
[DesignTimeResourceProviderFactory(➥
  typeof(CustomDesignTimeResourceProviderFactory))]
public sealed class CustomResourceProviderFactory : ResourceProviderFactory
```

The CustomDesignTimeResourceProviderFactory type defines another factory used at design-time. This factory is very similar to the one shown earlier, the difference being that the design-time support requires several specific actions:

- You don't have a current theme at design-time; only one predefined theme can be supported (the default theme in the example code).

- You don't have access to HttpContext to resolve paths.

- You don't have a current culture, so anything created at design-time is written into the fallback resource file.

The factory derives from the DesignTimeResourceProviderFactory base class. This abstract base class is defined as:

```
public abstract class DesignTimeResourceProviderFactory
{
    protected DesignTimeResourceProviderFactory();

    public abstract IResourceProvider CreateDesignTimeGlobalResourceProvider( ➥
                    IServiceProvider serviceProvider, string classKey);
    public abstract IResourceProvider CreateDesignTimeLocalResourceProvider( ➥
                    IServiceProvider serviceProvider);
    public abstract IDesignTimeResourceWriter CreateDesignTimeLocalResourceWriter( ➥
                    IServiceProvider serviceProvider);
}
```

As you can see, there are three methods and a constructor only. Two methods are similar to the runtime factory. They create and return the appropriate provider. The third method returns a resource writer. This writer explicitly supports the Visual Studio resource creation option available through the Tools menu.

All these methods obtain the `serviceProvider` parameter. The design-time environment is also highly extensible. Visual Studio doesn't know anything about the various controls handled within the designer. If it were to know, then every new or third-party control would have to be installed and registered in Visual Studio. To avoid such a dependency, the control or the provider itself supplies all features required by Visual Studio to operate well. To determine whether a specific feature is supported, a service provider pattern is used. The `IServiceProvider` interface, implemented by Visual Studio, delivers a collection of services using its `GetService` method. The attached module or plug-in requiring these services requests the `GetService` method for a specific implementation.

Finally, we'll need access to the currently designed document. Visual Studio acts as a Designer Host, represented by the `IDesignerHost` interface. To access it, request the service in this manner:

```
IDesignerHost host;
host = (IDesignerHost) _serviceProvider.GetService(typeof(IDesignerHost));
```

The idea behind this technique is that there is no direct dependency between the provider and the host. If you use another host—not Visual Studio—that is well implemented, your provider should still work. These methods also break the dependency on specific assemblies deployed with Visual Studio. Otherwise, when your code runs on a server, it would require Visual Studio to be installed there—a completely unreasonable prospect.

Once you have the designer host, you can ask for the current root document.

```
WebFormsRootDesigner rootDesigner;
rootDesigner = host.GetDesigner(host.RootComponent) as WebFormsRootDesigner;
```

This type is from `System.Web.UI.Design` and does not depend on Visual Studio. Using the `DocumentUrl` property, you have the full name of the file currently open in the designer view without any direct access to Visual Studio.

With all these techniques in mind, it's time to create the design-time factory, as shown in Listing 5-4.

Listing 5-4. *The Design-Time Factory Implementation*

```
public sealed class CustomDesignTimeResourceProviderFactory : ➥
                DesignTimeResourceProviderFactory
{
    private DesignTimeResourceProvider globalResourceProvider;
    private DesignTimeResourceProvider localResourceProvider;
    private CustomDesignTimeResourceWriter localResourceWriter;
    private string _rootDocument;

    public override IResourceProvider CreateDesignTimeGlobalResourceProvider( ➥
                IServiceProvider serviceProvider, string classKey)
    {
        // Return an IResourceProvider.
        if (globalResourceProvider == null)
        {
            globalResourceProvider = new DesignTimeResourceProvider(classKey, ➥
                                serviceProvider);
        }
        _rootDocument = globalResourceProvider.RootDocument;
        return globalResourceProvider;
    }
```

```csharp
public override IResourceProvider CreateDesignTimeLocalResourceProvider( ➡
                                    IServiceProvider serviceProvider)
{
    // Return an IResourceProvider
    if (localResourceProvider == null)
    {
        localResourceProvider = new DesignTimeResourceProvider(serviceProvider);
    }
    return localResourceProvider;
}

public override IDesignTimeResourceWriter CreateDesignTimeLocalResourceWriter( ➡
                                    IServiceProvider serviceProvider)
{
  if (localResourceWriter == null)
  {
        // Get the host, usually Visual Studio
        IDesignerHost host = (IDesignerHost) ➡
                            serviceProvider.GetService(typeof(IDesignerHost));
        // Get the designer currently represents the design view
        WebFormsRootDesigner rootDesigner = host.GetDesigner(host.RootComponent) ➡
                                    as WebFormsRootDesigner;
        // Retrieve the local URL of the file currently opened in the designer
        _rootDocument = rootDesigner.DocumentUrl;
        if (_rootDocument != null)
        {
            // Create the resource writer for this file
            localResourceWriter = ➡
                    new CustomDesignTimeResourceWriter(_rootDocument);
        }
  }
  return localResourceWriter;
  }
}
```

The factory returns both a global and a local design-time resource provider. Since we can't access global resources in the Visual Studio environment, it's the same provider class in both cases. Future versions or other applications might behave differently, and the class design is ready for this. However, the CreateDesignTimeLocalResourceWriter method is of more interest to us. This method has a serviceProvider parameter containing the current designer host. As shown before, retrieving the URL of the current document is easy with the right services.

If you'd like to extend the behavior, it's a good idea to investigate the options by looking into the provider objects.

System.ComponentModel.Design.DesignerHost provides the following properties out-of-the-box:

- TransactionDescription: This returns the transaction invoked from the user's action, which is usually the "Generate Local Resource" string. That means that you can determine exactly what led to the call.

- RootComponent: The roots for the current transaction, whether it's Page or Control or any derived type currently open in the designer surface. You might modify your action after recognizing the type.

- CurrentCulture: The culture run by the design-time host, which is usually the culture of the operating system. You might decide not to write a default fallback resource but instead write the specified culture. Visual Studio 2008 currently has no option to set the culture, but later versions might support this.

- IsDesignerViewLocked: Returns either true or false depending on if the design-time surface is actually writeable.

- IsLoading: Must return false; otherwise, the control is not completely loaded.

- ReferenceManager: Returns the Microsoft.Web.Design.ReferenceManager type. This type allows access to the @Register directives that the reference user controls. Use this to handle user controls directly instead of on a file-by-file basis.

There are several methods to modify a document file by accessing the controls in it. However, these are beyond the scope of this chapter and left for you to investigate further.

Another access method is more valuable to us. Besides the IServiceProvider interface, the parameter object also implements System.Web.UI.Design.IWebFormsDocumentService:

```
public interface IWebFormsDocumentService
{
    string DocumentUrl { get; }
    bool IsLoading { get; }

    event EventHandler LoadComplete;

    object CreateDiscardableUndoUnit();
    void DiscardUndoUnit(object discardableUndoUnit);
    void EnableUndo(bool enable);
    void UpdateSelection();
}
```

Direct access to the DocumentUrl is the most important feature. In fact, this property does not return the URL but the full local path at design-time. This is exactly what we need. The interface also allows some interaction with undo management.

■**Caution** The IWebFormsDocumentService interface is marked as obsolete. Presumably Microsoft is going to transform the interface into its designated successor WebFormsRootDesigner. Actually, there is no information available as to when and with what consequences this will happen, but keep an eye on it.

The design-time resource provider has support for both reading the current resource at design-time as well as writing from the designer surface using the appropriate command. It therefore implements two interfaces, IResourceProvider and IDesignTimeResourceWriter. Listing 5-5 shows the whole implementation.

Listing 5-5. *The Complete Implementation of the Design-Time Resource Provider*

```
internal sealed class DesignTimeResourceProvider : ➥
                    IResourceProvider, IDesignTimeResourceWriter
{

    private ResXResourceWriter _writer = null;
    private ResXResourceReader _reader = null;
    private string _rootDocument;
```

```csharp
internal string RootDocument
{
    get { return _rootDocument; }
}

public DesignTimeResourceProvider(IServiceProvider serviceProvider) : ➥
        this(null, serviceProvider)
{
}

public DesignTimeResourceProvider(string classKey, ➥
                                  IServiceProvider serviceProvider)
{
    // Get the forms designer provided by Visual Studio
    IWebFormsDocumentService formsDesigner = ➥
        serviceProvider.GetService(typeof(IWebFormsDocumentService)) ➥
        as IWebFormsDocumentService;
    if (formsDesigner == null)
    {
        throw new NullReferenceException("IWebFormsDocumentService is null");
    }
    _rootDocument = formsDesigner.DocumentUrl;
}

object IResourceProvider.GetObject(string resourceKey, CultureInfo culture)
{
    if (_reader == null)
    {
        throw ➥
        new NullReferenceException("IResourceProvider::ResourceReader::NULL");
    }
    object o = null;
    IDictionaryEnumerator ide = _reader.GetEnumerator();
    while (ide.MoveNext())
    {
        if (ide.Key.ToString().ToLowerInvariant().Equals( ➥
            resourceKey.ToLowerInvariant()))
        {
            o = ide.Value;
            break;
        }
    }
    return o;
}

IResourceReader IResourceProvider.ResourceReader
{
    get
    {
        if (_reader == null)
        {
            _reader = new ResXResourceReader(➥
                XmlResourceHelper.GetInvariantResxPathAtDesignTime(➥
                                                _rootDocument));
            // prepare same for writing
            _writer = new ResXResourceWriter(➥
                XmlResourceHelper.GetInvariantResxPathAtDesignTime(➥
                                                _rootDocument));
```

```
            }
            if (_reader != null)
            {
                return _reader;
            }
            else
            {
                throw new Exception("IResourceProvider::ResourceReader::NULL");
            }
        }
    }

    string IDesignTimeResourceWriter.CreateResourceKey(string resourceName, ➡
                                                       object obj)
    {
        ((IResourceWriter)this).AddResource(resourceName, obj);
        return resourceName;
    }

    void IResourceWriter.AddResource(string name, byte[] value)
    {
        _writer.AddResource(name, value);
    }

    void IResourceWriter.AddResource(string name, object value)
    {
        _writer.AddResource(name, value);
    }

    void IResourceWriter.AddResource(string name, string value)
    {
        _writer.AddResource(name, value);
    }

    void IResourceWriter.Generate()
    {
        _writer.Generate();
    }

    void IResourceWriter.Close()
    {
        _writer.Close();
    }

    void IDisposable.Dispose()
    {
        _writer.Close();
        _writer.Dispose();
    }
}
```

This implementation must support both the writing of resources when the user generates the local resource file as well as the reading of current resources when the file is opened for the first time in the designer surface. The full path to the currently loaded file is retrieved in the constructor by obtaining the IWebFormsDocumentService interface:

```
serviceProvider.GetService(typeof(IWebFormsDocumentService))
```

The DocumentUrl property will return what you need. The design-time environment will use the IResourceProvider.ResourceReader property first to retrieve the current values. In previous code, I created the reader as well as the writer because the function's intention is to retrieve and write the values back. The helper class XmlResourceHelper is a private implementation that collects several methods needed in both the design-time and runtime provider. I've called GetInvariantResxPathAtDesignTime to obtain the full path of the *.resx* file. As mentioned, the provider only supports the Default theme. The method points to the paths shown at the beginning of the section in a hard-coded manner. You can find the full implementation of the class in Listing 5-6.

Listing 5-6. *Helper Class to Simplify Developers' Life*

```
internal static class XmlResourceHelper
{

    private const string DESIGNTIME_THEME = "Default";
    private static readonly char[] TRIMCHARS = "/".ToCharArray();

    // The base path according to the example's requirements
    private static string BasePath
    {
        get
        {
            if (HttpContext.Current == null)
            {
                return "/App_Data/Resx/";
            }
            else
            {
                return HttpContext.Current.Server.MapPath("~/App_Data/Resx") + ➥
                                           Path.DirectorySeparatorChar;
            }
        }
    }

    // full path at design-time and runtime
    public static string GetFullPath(string regularPath, string theme, bool global)
    {
        if (String.IsNullOrEmpty(theme)) throw new ArgumentNullException("theme");
        string path = "";
        if (HttpContext.Current == null)
        {
            // assume compile time
            path = GetInvariantResxPathAtDesignTime(regularPath);
        }
        else
        {
            try
            {
                // Trim the path
                regularPath = Regex.Replace(regularPath, ➥
                                            HttpContext.Current.Request. ➥
                                            ApplicationPath.TrimStart(TRIMCHARS), ➥
                                            "", ➥
                                            RegexOptions.IgnoreCase);
                if (global)
                {
```

```csharp
                    path = String.Format("{0}{1}_Global", BasePath, theme, ➥
                                                        regularPath);
                }
                else
                {
                    path = String.Format("{0}{1}{2}", BasePath, theme, regularPath);
                }
            }
            catch (Exception ex)
            {
                throw new Exception(ex.Message + ex.StackTrace);
            }
        }
        return path;
    }


    // Get the local path to file for themed page resources
    public static string GetLocalResxBasePath(string pageId, string theme)
    {
        if (String.IsNullOrEmpty(pageId))
        {
            pageId = "";
        }
        else
        {
            pageId = Regex.Replace(pageId, ➥
                    HttpRuntime.AppDomainAppVirtualPath.TrimStart(TRIMCHARS), "", ➥
                    RegexOptions.IgnoreCase);
        }
        pageId = pageId.Replace("..", ".").TrimStart(TRIMCHARS).Replace('/', ➥
                Path.DirectorySeparatorChar);
        // machine name dependant absolute path
        string file = String.Concat(BasePath, String.Format("{0}{2}{1}", theme, ➥
                            pageId, Path.DirectorySeparatorChar));
        return file;
    }


    // Scaffold file name to resx file from given information
    public static string GetResxPath(string pageId, string theme, bool global)
    {
        pageId = Regex.Replace(pageId, ➥
                HttpRuntime.AppDomainAppVirtualPath.TrimStart(TRIMCHARS), "", ➥
                RegexOptions.IgnoreCase);
        string file = Path.Combine(BasePath, String.Format("{0}{2}{3}{1}.resx", ➥
                            theme, pageId, (global) ? "_Global" : "", ➥
                            Path.DirectorySeparatorChar));
        if (!File.Exists(file))
        {
            throw new FileNotFoundException("The resx file does not ➥
                                    exists [GetInvariantResxPath]", file);
        }
        return file;
    }

    public static string GetResxPath(string pageId, string theme, bool global, ➥
                            CultureInfo ci)
    {
```

```
        pageId = Regex.Replace(pageId, ➡
                HttpRuntime.AppDomainAppVirtualPath.TrimStart(TRIMCHARS), "", ➡
                RegexOptions.IgnoreCase);
        string file = Path.Combine(BasePath, String.Format("{0}{2}{3}{1}.{4}.resx",
            theme, ➡
            pageId, ➡
            (global) ? "_Global" : "", ➡
            Path.DirectorySeparatorChar, ➡
            ci.Name));
        if (!File.Exists(file))
        {
            throw new FileNotFoundException("The resx file does not ➡
                    exists [GetInvariantResxPath]", file);
            //CreateFileIfNotExists(file);
        }
        return file;
    }

    // Scaffold the fallback resource file name locally at design-time
    public static string GetInvariantResxPathAtDesignTime(string pagePath)
    {
        // full path to file, need to get resx to invariant from this
        Uri uri = new Uri(pagePath);
        string path = uri.LocalPath;
        string file = String.Format("{0}{2}{3}{4}{2}{1}.resx",
                Path.GetDirectoryName(path),
                Path.GetFileName(path),
                Path.DirectorySeparatorChar,
                BasePath,
                DESIGNTIME_THEME); // at design-time App_Data/Resx/Default
        if (!File.Exists(file))
        {
            CreateFileIfNotExists(file);
        }
        return file;
    }

    // Create file if one not exists
    private static void CreateFileIfNotExists(string path)
    {
        if (!Directory.Exists(Path.GetDirectoryName(path)))
        {
            Directory.CreateDirectory(Path.GetDirectoryName(path));
        }
        // Use ResXResourcerWriter to create the default resx format
        System.Resources.ResXResourceWriter RwX = ➡
                    new System.Resources.ResXResourceWriter(path);
        RwX.Generate();
        RwX.Close();
    }

    #endregion
}
```

The various path operations are a drawback of the file-based solution. However, a database-driven project might need additional work to support database access at design-time. For the design-time portion, the GetInvariantResxPathAtDesignTime method is required. Because the Uri is built like any web `Uri`, it must be resolved and converted into a local file path. A bit of string concatenation will do the trick. If the file is not present, it will be created on the fly; this is the default behavior of Visual Studio.

The creation of resource files is simple. The `ResXResourceWriter` class provides a `Generate` method that creates a file with unpleasant comments and schema codes. Calling `Close` flushes the content back to disk (see Figure 5-3).

```xml
<root>
  [...]
  <xsd:schema id="root" xmlns="" xmlns:xsd="http://www.w3.org/2001/XMLSchema" xmlns:msdata="urn:schemas-microsoft-com:xml-msdata">
    <xsd:import namespace="http://www.w3.org/XML/1998/namespace" />
    <xsd:element name="root" msdata:IsDataSet="true">
      <xsd:complexType>
        <xsd:choice maxOccurs="unbounded">
          <xsd:element name="metadata">
            <xsd:complexType>
              <xsd:sequence>
                <xsd:element name="value" type="xsd:string" minOccurs="0" />
              </xsd:sequence>
              <xsd:attribute name="name" use="required" type="xsd:string" />
              <xsd:attribute name="type" type="xsd:string" />
              <xsd:attribute name="mimetype" type="xsd:string" />
              <xsd:attribute ref="xml:space" />
            </xsd:complexType>
          </xsd:element>
          <xsd:element name="assembly">
            <xsd:complexType>
              <xsd:attribute name="alias" type="xsd:string" />
              <xsd:attribute name="name" type="xsd:string" />
            </xsd:complexType>
          </xsd:element>
          <xsd:element name="data">
            <xsd:complexType>
              <xsd:sequence>
                <xsd:element name="value" type="xsd:string" minOccurs="0" msdata:Ordinal="1" />
                <xsd:element name="comment" type="xsd:string" minOccurs="0" msdata:Ordinal="2" />
              </xsd:sequence>
              <xsd:attribute name="name" type="xsd:string" use="required" msdata:Ordinal="1" />
              <xsd:attribute name="type" type="xsd:string" msdata:Ordinal="3" />
              <xsd:attribute name="mimetype" type="xsd:string" msdata:Ordinal="4" />
              <xsd:attribute ref="xml:space" />
            </xsd:complexType>
          </xsd:element>
          <xsd:element name="resheader">
            <xsd:complexType>
              <xsd:sequence>
                <xsd:element name="value" type="xsd:string" minOccurs="0" msdata:Ordinal="1" />
              </xsd:sequence>
              <xsd:attribute name="name" type="xsd:string" use="required" />
            </xsd:complexType>
          </xsd:element>
        </xsd:choice>
      </xsd:complexType>
    </xsd:element>
  </xsd:schema>
  <resheader name="resmimetype">
    <value>text/microsoft-resx</value>
  </resheader>
  <resheader name="version">
    <value>2.0</value>
  </resheader>
```

Figure 5-3. *Resx files contain a comment (closed) and a full schema description.*

The `GetResxPath` method is called at compile time. The compiler needs to resolve the implicit expressions that define resources. To determine what values are required to be placed in the page, use the resource provider again. Since neither the `HttpContext` nor the design-time host exist at this point, instead use the `HttpRuntime.AppDomainAppVirtualPath` property. The virtual path is defined at this stage and enables file paths to be resolved. The helper class is used to change the format slightly to meet our needs.

Debugging Design-Time Extensions

Design-time support should be part of any extension model. However, the difficulty of debugging these extensions is probably the reason why developers avoid adding design-time support to their applications. At design-time, there is no debugger attached. Therefore, you cannot easily add break-points or step into the code to see the internal processes. Using smart exceptions and try/catch blocks might help, but this is not a good debugging experience.

To debug within the Visual Studio design-time environment, you must open another instance of Visual Studio and debug the code there. To do this, open the property pages of the Web project and activate the option *Start external program* (see Figure 5-4).

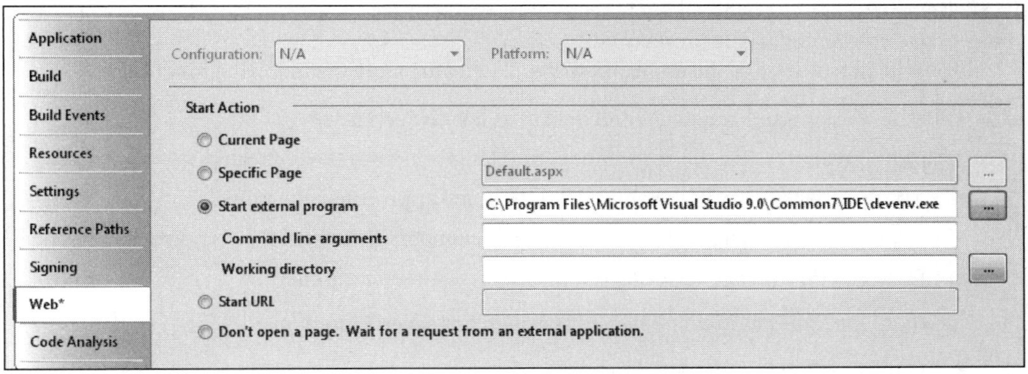

Figure 5-4. *Start another instance of Visual Studio to debug at design-time.*

As the external program, choose the Visual Studio executable, *devenv.exe*. When you start debugging the project by hitting F5, another instance of Visual Studio appears. Load the same proj-ect in this instance and launch the design-time environment. You can now set breakpoints in the first instance and debug as you would do at runtime. To get to specific code sections, just start using the code within the second instance.

Edit Resources at Runtime

Now that we have flexible access to the resources, it is easy to implement additional options. Imag-ine a complex site that contains hundreds or thousands of resources. Several authors add content, change content, and add new languages. Doing so in XML files is very inefficient. Consider also the way translators usually work. Good translators might handle the content well, but dealing with XML is not their area of proficiency. Deploying a separate application to support their translation work introduces additional complications. Text portions often require a different translation depending on the context in which they appear. This context is lost when translating fragments of a sentence or single words.

Editing content online would be a better option. However, handling resources the standard way (in files) and compiling them into binary resources precludes the saving of new content into the resources. In this section, I demonstrate how to use an extended resource provider model to access resource files online—anytime.

How It Works

In the previous sections, we looked at a different storage model. The provider still relays the files, but the file structure and availability is much more flexible. Most importantly, we have total con-trol over it. To have access at runtime, a service must be able to open each *.resx* file, write new or changed content into it, and close the file.

The only disadvantage with the provider reading the data directly from the *.resx* files is: how can we continue to use caching to improve performance?

There are several options. For example, you could recognize the editing mode and suppress caching while editing. Alternatively, you could add a refresh button or link that forces the cache to be destroyed. Both options are easy to implement, but beyond the scope of this chapter.

To access the resources from the client, we must find a way of communicating between the browser and the server. A Web Service and JavaScript could achieve this. As you only need JavaScript when editing pages—not when merely viewing pages—it's a good idea to have a special master page containing all the JavaScript functions.

From the perspective of the application, you'll need to create the following functions:

- Retrieve supported languages and deliver as a Web Service.
- Retrieve resources for the current page and language from the Web Service.
- Write data back to the Web Service to store in the appropriate *.resx* file.
- Extend the page to support the editing of the elements on a control-by-control basis.
- Create an editor to allow editing the control's content on the client.

The client portion is written in JavaScript, which has several functions:

- Create an editor to edit parts of a page.
- Load current resource data from the server.
- Save changed content back to the server.
- Change the currently edited language.

In Listing 5-7, I store the supported languages in another XML file, called *Cultures.xml*.

Listing 5-7. *The Supported Cultures Stored As XML*

```xml
<?xml version="1.0" encoding="utf-8" ?>
<Cultures>
  <CultureInfo name="English" id="en-Us" />
  <CultureInfo name="Deutsch" id="de-De" />
  <CultureInfo name="Italiano" id="it-It" />
</Cultures>
```

The Web Service method exposes this content to the client. To cache this information, I store the data during the application start (see Listing 5-8).

Listing 5-8. *Retrieve Supported Cultures on Application Start*

```csharp
void Application_Start(object sender, EventArgs e)
{
    XDocument xmlDoc = XDocument.Load(Path.Combine(Server.MapPath("~/App_Data"), ➥
                                                   "Cultures.xml"));
    var cultures = from c in xmlDoc.Descendants("CultureInfo") ➥
                   select new CultureInfo(c.Attribute("id").Value);
    Application["cultures"] = cultures.ToList<CultureInfo>();
}
```

The service's method transforms this into a serializable object that is easy to read on the client. First, we need a Web Service class with the following definition (see Listing 5-9).

Listing 5-9. *The Web Service's Class Head*

```
[ScriptService()]
[WebService(Namespace = "http://www.apress.com/ws")]
[GenerateScriptType(typeof(Cultures))]
[WebServiceBinding(ConformsTo = WsiProfiles.BasicProfile1_1)]
public class ResourceService : System.Web.Services.WebService
{
  CustomResourceProviderFactory rf;

  public ResourceService()
  {
    rf = new CustomResourceProviderFactory();
  }
   ...

}
```

This definition makes the code available for JavaScript pages and defines a private data type, Cultures, as shown in Listing 5-10. Additionally, the constructor prepares the factory we created earlier in the section "Implementing the Custom Provider" to obtain access to the resources. This means that the majority of code is in the existing classes, and leaves us with only a few tasks:

Listing 5-10. *The Supported Cultures Exposed Via a Service*

```
[WebMethod()]
public Cultures GetAllLanguages()
{
    List<CultureInfo> cList = (List<CultureInfo>)Application["cultures"];
    Cultures c = new Cultures(cList.Count);
    for (int i = 0; i < cList.Count; i++)
    {
        c.cultureName[i] = cList[i].DisplayName;
        c.cultureID[i] = cList[i].Name;
    }
    return c;
}

[Serializable()]
public class Cultures
{
    public Cultures() : this(2)
    {
    }

    public Cultures(int len)
    {
        this.len = len;
        cultureName = new string[len];
        cultureID = new string[len];
    }

    public string[] cultureName;
    public string[] cultureID;
    public int len;
}
```

The remaining tasks required of the Web Service are coded in two methods—LoadResource and SaveResource. Both receive four parameters:

- pageId: The name of the resource file, which names the aspx or ascx file.

- ctrlId: The Id of the control requesting the resource. This includes the property name, such as *Label1Resource1.Text*.

- culture: The id of the culture, such as "en-us" or "de-de".

- theme: The current theme that the resource is written to or read from. This is the special extension, as explained at the beginning of the chapter in the section "Extending the Provider Model." If themed resources are not a requirement, you can safely remove this parameter.

Listing 5-11 illustrates the methods. The SaveResource method has one additional parameter called content that contains the data to be written into the resource file. The LoadResource method returns exactly that value using the same parameters.

Listing 5-11. *Web Methods to Load and Save Resources Directly from the Client*

```
[WebMethod()]
public string LoadResource(string pageId, string ctrlId, ➥
                           string culture, string theme)
{
    pageId = pageId.Replace("~", "");
    rf.Theme = theme;
    IResourceProvider rp = rf.CreateLocalResourceProvider(pageId);
    object value = ((CustomResourceProvider)rp).GetResxObject( ➥
                                    ctrlId, new CultureInfo(culture));
    return (value == null) ? String.Empty : value.ToString();
}

[WebMethod()]
public void SaveResource(string pageId, string ctrlId, ➥
                         string content, string culture, string theme)
{
    pageId = pageId.Replace("~", "");
    rf.Theme = theme;
    IResourceProvider rp = rf.CreateLocalResourceProvider(pageId);
    CultureInfo ci = new CultureInfo(culture);
    ((CustomResourceProvider)rp).GetResourceWriter(ci).AddResource(ctrlId, ➥
                                    content);
}
```

There are some additional steps required. To display and enable the editor, you'll need to prepare the page. To avoid including all the JavaScript in the page, another master page is used. With two different master pages, you can decide which one to use, depending on whether the page is displayed in edit mode or not. Changing the master page dynamically requires access to the page's PreInit event (see Listing 5-12).

Listing 5-12. *Changing the Master Page and Theme Programmatically*

```
public partial class _Default : BasePage

protected override void OnPreInit(EventArgs e)
{
  base.OnPreInit(e);
  // Set Editor (special handling beyond the domain scope)
```

```
if (Request.QueryString["e"] != null && Request.QueryString["e"] == "on")
{
  Session["Editor"] = true;
}
if (Request.QueryString["e"] != null && Request.QueryString["e"] == "off")
{
  Session["Editor"] = null;
}
string domain = Request.Url.Host;
// Set Dynamic Theming and Master Pages
if (Session["Editor"] != null)
{
  Master.MasterPageFile = "editor.master";
}
else
{
  Master.MasterPageFile = "default.master";
}
if (Session["theme"] != null)
{
  Theme = Session["theme"] as string;
}
}
```

As you can see from the code, a QueryString parameter is used to switch between the master pages with editing capabilities enabled or disabled. Just append ?e=on to the URL, and the editor will appear. Once enabled, a session variable retains the state. To switch the editor off on the fly, add ?e=off. This is only a suggestion—you may find smarter ways of achieving this. Now we need to build the master page to support the necessary features.

Creating an Online Editor

For the online editor to function, the JavaScript on the page must handle all controls and call the Web Service's methods with the right parameters. The first step is preparation. Each control on the page must be tested for the presence of the meta:resourcekey attribute. If this exists, then a connected resource is available, and the editor should handle this control. To achieve this, the ReadControls method loops through all the controls. The Init event is the right place in the pipeline for this method call, as the controls are ready to go at that stage. Later, in the PreRender event, the code uses the data collected here to add the JavaScript calls.

To test for the attribute, a regular expression is used. This may seem strange, since we have an object model which we could access directly. However, although the object model is present, the implicit resource expressions have already been replaced by code snippets at the page parser stage. The meta:resourcekey attributes do not exist in the object model. Your only option is to parse the source code of the page directly and to virtually add another parser cycle after the internal one.

■**Note** The page must exist at runtime with full markup available. Pre-compiled sites with hidden source will not work with this example.

Listing 5-13 shows the methods that parse the page, collect the controls, and add the required JavaScript. Since the scripting is a little tricky, it's explained afterwards in more depth.

Listing 5-13. *The Master Page with the Default Setting for Regular Expression*

```
public partial class EditorMasterPage : System.Web.UI.MasterPage
{
    private static Regex rx;
    private Dictionary<string, Dictionary<string, string>> pages;

    static EditorMasterPage()
    {
        rx = new Regex(@"\<(?<tagName>\w+(:\w+){0,1}) (?<attr>[^>]*) ?>", ➥
                RegexOptions.ExplicitCapture | ➥
                RegexOptions.Multiline | ➥
                RegexOptions.IgnoreCase | ➥
                RegexOptions.IgnorePatternWhitespace);
    }
```

The regular expression simply addresses a tag with several attributes and returns the matching element as a collection of named arrays. This array contains all tags on the page captured with the key <tagName> and the attributes block—the remaining part of the element—with the key <attr>. An element like <asp:button runat="server" meta:resourcekey="ButtonRes1" /> would be divided into the "asp:button" part and the "runat="server" meta:resourcekey="ButtonRes1" part in the first step.

Regular expressions are beyond the scope of this book; please refer to the documentation if you have difficulties reading this expression. For the moment, it's sufficient to know that the string fragments recognized by the expression are collected in named arrays, whereas the names are defined in <angle brackets>. The attributes are split into single ones by using the space as a divider (see Listing 5-14).

Listing 5-14. *Analyzing the Controls Regarding the meta:resourcekey Attribute*

```
protected override void OnInit(EventArgs e)
{
  pages = new Dictionary<string, Dictionary<string, string>>();
  ReadControls(this.Page.AppRelativeVirtualPath);
  base.OnInit(e);
}

privat void ReadControls(string path) {
  if (!pages.ContainsKey(path))
  {
    StreamReader sr = new StreamReader(Server.MapPath(path));
    string s = sr.ReadToEnd();
    sr.Close();
    pages.Add(path, new Dictionary<string, string>());
    MatchCollection mc = rx.Matches(s);
    foreach (Match m in mc)
    {
      Group g = m.Groups["attr"];
      if (g != null)
      {
        string[] attributes = g.Value.Split(" ".ToCharArray(), ➥
                           StringSplitOptions.RemoveEmptyEntries);
        string key = null, id = null;
        foreach (string attr in attributes)
        {
          if (attr.StartsWith("meta:resourcekey"))
          {
```

```
          string param = attr.Split("=".ToCharArray())[1].Trim();
          key = param.Substring(1, param.Length - 2);
        }
        if (attr.StartsWith("id", StringComparison.InvariantCultureIgnoreCase))
        {
          string[] fragments = attr.Split("=".ToCharArray());
          if (fragments.Length == 2) {
            string param = fragments[1].Trim();
            id = param.Substring(1, param.Length - 2);
          }
        }
      }
      if (!String.IsNullOrEmpty(id) && !(String.IsNullOrEmpty(key)))
      {
        // need to support server transfer
        if (!pages[path].ContainsKey(id))
        {
          pages[path].Add(id, key);
        }
      }
    }
  }
}
}
```

The collection pages contain data from all the files scanned so far. Remember that a page can contain several user controls, and that these controls must become available at the same time. For each page, we store the control's id and resource key. This makes it possible to access the control, based on its id, and the resource, based on its key. Once all the data has been collected, the page is processed normally. In PreRender, the information is used to add the JavaScript calls, as shown in Listing 5-15.

Listing 5-15. *Add Editing Capability to the Collected Controls*

```
protected override void OnPreRender(EventArgs e)
{
  foreach (string name in this.ContentPlaceHolders)
  {
    ContentPlaceHolder cph = (ContentPlaceHolder)FindControl(name);
    ControlCollection cc = cph.Controls;
    this.NavigateControls(cc);
  }
  base.OnPreRender(e);
}
```

This is only the first part—the entry point. Assuming we're operating on a page that uses a master page—a prerequisite for this solution—we'll need to handle the ContentPlaceHolders. Each control is processed as its own container. The NavigateControl method works recursively (see Listing 5-16).

Listing 5-16. *Navigating All Controls and Adding the Required Script (the Next Listing)*

```
private void NavigateControls(ControlCollection cc)
{
    string path = String.Empty;
    for (int i = 0; i < cc.Count; i++)
    {
```

```
Control ctl = cc[i];
// updatepanel container might have no id, but children
if (ctl != null && (ctl.ID != null || ctl.HasControls()))
{
    if (ctl.HasControls())
    {
        if (ctl is UserControl && ➥
            !(ctl.GetType().Name.Contains("collapseliteral")) && ➥
            !(ctl.GetType().Name.Contains("pageheader")))
        {
            path = ctl.TemplateCortrol.AppRelativeVirtualPath;
        }
        else
        {
            path = ctl.Page.AppRelativeVirtualPath;
        }
        ReadControls(path);
        this.NavigateControls(ctl.Controls);
        if (!pages.ContainsKey(path)) continue;
        if (ctl.ID == null) continue;
        if (!pages[path].ContainsKey(ctl.ID)) continue;
        string ctlKey = pages[path][ctl.ID];
        if (ctlKey != null)
        {
            if (ctl is UserControl)
            {
                AddEditorControl(ctl, path, ctlKey, i);
            }
        }
    }
    else
    {
        path = ctl.TemplateControl.AppRelativeVirtualPath;
        if (!pages.ContainsKey(path)) continue;
        if (!pages[path].ContainsKey(ctl.ID)) continue;
        string ctlKey = pages[path][ctl.ID];
        if (ctlKey != null)
        {
            switch (ctl.GetType().Name)
            {
                case "ValidationSummary":
                    continue;
                case "WebPartZone":
                    // access the webparts, which are not part
                    // of the control collection
                    foreach (Control part in ((WebPartZone)ctl).WebParts)
                    {
                        path = part.Controls[0].TemplateControl. ➥
                            AppRelativeVirtualPath;
                        AddEditorControl(part, path, ctlKey, i);
                    }
                    break;
                default:
                    AddEditorControl(ctl, path, ctlKey, i);
                    break;
            }
            cc = ctl.Parent.Controls;
```

```
                    }
                }
            }
        }
    }
```

The final step for each valid control located is to call the `AddEditorControl` method. The methods add a small image (8×8 pixel) which appears near the control, allowing the user to click there and open the editor. Different images express different states:

- *validator.gif*: The control is a validator. The control itself might be invisible depending on the page's validation state. However, the editor control is present.

- *webpart.gif*: Webparts do not handle resources, but they have additional content that might contain resources.

- *resx.gif*: Regular control with previously added resources.

- *edit.gif*: Regular control with no attached resources.

Additionally, a tooltip is created in order to inform the user about the control beneath the mouse pointer. This is helpful, as on complex pages it isn't always possible to align the image exactly (see Listing 5-17).

Listing 5-17. *Adding the Script Code*

```
private void AddEditorControl(Control ctl, string path, string ctlKey, int i)
{
    bool HasRes = false;
    string[] attributeList = GetPossibleResourceList(ctl);
    HasRes = this.GetLocalResource(path, ctlKey, attributeList);
    StringBuilder sb = new StringBuilder();
    using (StringWriter sw = new StringWriter(sb))
    {
        HtmlTextWriter ht = new HtmlTextWriter(sw);
        ht.AddStyleAttribute(HtmlTextWriterStyle.Display, "inline");
        ht.AddStyleAttribute(HtmlTextWriterStyle.Cursor, "hand");
        ht.AddStyleAttribute(HtmlTextWriterStyle.Position, "relative");
        ht.AddStyleAttribute(HtmlTextWriterStyle.Left, "-8");
        ht.AddStyleAttribute(HtmlTextWriterStyle.Top, "-8");
        ht.AddStyleAttribute(HtmlTextWriterStyle.ZIndex, "100000");
        if (HasRes)
        {
            if (ctl is IValidator)
            {
                ht.AddAttribute("src", Request.ApplicationPath + ➥
                            "/images/Resxeditor/validator.gif");
            }
            else if (ctl is IWebPart)
            {
                ht.AddAttribute("src", Request.ApplicationPath + ➥
                            "/images/Resxeditor/webpart.gif");
            }
            else
            {
                ht.AddAttribute("src", Request.ApplicationPath + ➥
                            "/images/Resxeditor/resx.gif");
            }
        }
    }
```

```
            else
            {
                ht.AddAttribute("src", Request.ApplicationPath + ➥
                                "/images/Resxeditor/Edit.png");
            }
            ht.AddAttribute("width", Unit.Pixel(8).ToString());
            ht.AddAttribute("height", Unit.Pixel(8).ToString());
            // Add all required data as attributes to let loading them from JScript
            bool allowHtml = (ctl is Literal) || (ctl is LiteralControl) || ➥
                             (ctl is HtmlGenericControl) || ➥
                             (ctl.GetType().Name.Contains("collapseliteral"));
            ht.AddAttribute("allowHtml", (allowHtml) ? "true" : "false");
            ht.AddAttribute("pageID", path);
            ht.AddAttribute("ctrlClientID", ctl.ClientID);
            ht.AddAttribute("ctrlID", ctlKey);
            ht.AddAttribute("attributes", String.Join(",", attributeList));
                ht.AddAttribute("alt", String.Format("Type (What?):{0}\n ➥
                                            Name (Who?):{1}\n➥
                                            Content (Why?):{2}\n➥
                                            Container (Where?):{3}\n➥
                                            State (How?):{4}", ➥
                        ctl.GetType().Name, ➥
                        ctlKey, ➥
                        (allowHtml) ? "HTML" : "Text", ➥
                        path, ➥
                        (ctl.Visible) ? "Visible" : "Hidden by Default"));
            // make the icon clickable
            ht.AddAttribute("onclick", ➥
            String.Format("showEditor({0}, this); return false;", (allowHtml) ? 1 : 0));
            ht.RenderBeginTag(HtmlTextWriterTag.Img);
            ht.RenderEndTag();
            LiteralControl lb = new LiteralControl(sb.ToString());
            ctl.Parent.Controls.AddAt(i + 1, lb);
        }
    }
}

// Check for existence of a local resource to modify icon
private bool GetLocalResource(string path, string ctrlId, string[] reslist)
{
    bool hasRes = false;
    for (int i = 0; i < reslist.Length; i++)
    {
        try
        {
            if (reslist[i] != null)
            {
                string resId = String.Format("{0}.{1}", ctrlId, reslist[i]);
                object oValue = HttpContext.GetLocalResourceObject(path, resId, ➥
                                Thread.CurrentThread.CurrentCulture);
                if (oValue != null)
                {
                    hasRes = true;
                    break;
                }
            }
            else
            {
```

```
                break;
            }

        }
        catch { }

    }
    return hasRes;
}

// Return a list of supported properties by this editor (extend at your will)
private string[] GetPossibleResourceList(Control _Control)
{
    List<string> res = new List<string>();
    switch (_Control.GetType().ToString())
    {
        case "System.Web.UI.WebControls.Literal":
            res.Add("Text");
            break;
        case "System.Web.UI.WebControls.DropDownList":
            res.Add("ToolTip");
            break;
        case "System.Web.UI.WebControls.Menu":
            res.Add("ScrollDownText");
            res.Add("ToolTip");
            res.Add("ScrollUpText");
            res.Add("SkipLinkText");
            break;
        case "System.Web.UI.WebControls.TextBox":
            res.Add("ToolTip");
            res.Add("Text");
            break;
        default:
            if (Control is IWebPart)
            {
                // internally set title
                res.Add("Text");
            }
            else if (_Control is IValidator)
            {
                res.Add("Text");
                res.Add("ToolTip");
                res.Add("ErrorMessage");

            } else {
                res.Add("Text");
                res.Add("ToolTip");
            }
            break;
    }
    return res.ToArray();
}

// Resolve place holders in case of master page driven web site
private Control GetAndFindInPlaceHolder(string controlName)
{
    MasterPage mp = (MasterPage)this.Page.Master;
```

```
PropertyInfo pi = mp.GetType().GetProperty("ContentPlaceHolders", ➥
                          System.Reflection.BindingFlags.Instance | ➥
                          System.Reflection.BindingFlags.NonPublic);
IList names = (IList) pi.GetValue(mp, null);
foreach (string name in names)
{
    ContentPlaceHolder cph = (ContentPlaceHolder)MainContent.FindControl(name);
    if (cph != null)
    {
        Control c = cph.FindControl(controlName);
        if (c != null)
        {
            return c;
        }
    }
}
return null;
}
```

The GetPossibleResourceList method contains a hard-coded sequence of supported attributes. This solution, therefore, does not support all the possible properties of a control. Extending the method is trivial. It takes much more effort to create the JavaScript-based editor to add the content. As long as it's text, simple controls will achieve this. However, editing image paths or colors would require more work.

To understand the entire code, a glance at the result might help (see Listing 5-18).

Listing 5-18. *A Typical JavaScript Sequence Created with the Previous Code*

```
<img src="/DemoApplication/images/Resxeditor/resx.gif"
  width="8px" height="8px"
  allowHtml="false"
  pageID="~/Default.aspx"
  ctrlClientID="ctl00_ctl00_MainContent_MainContent_LinkButtonTheme1"
  ctrlID="LinkButtonTheme1Resource1"
  attributes="Text,ToolTip" alt="Tooltip"
  onclick="showEditor(0, this); return false;"
  style="display:inline;cursor:hand;position:relative;left:-8;top:-8;z-index:100000;" />
```

Before defining the JavaScript editor itself, here is the working editor (see Figure 5-5).

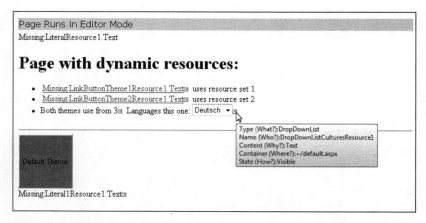

Figure 5-5. *The page in edit mode*

After clicking on one of the small icons, which represents a resource, the editor appears (see Figure 5-6).

Figure 5-6. *The editor in action*

The editor needs access to the Web Service method we defined earlier. To achieve this, a ScriptManager control is helpful. Listing 5-19 references the Web Service definition.

Listing 5-19. *The Supported Cultures Exposed Via a Service*

```
<asp:ScriptManager ID="ScriptManager1" runat="server"
                   EnablePartialRendering="False">
  <services>
    <asp:ServiceReference path="~/ResxEditor/ResourceService.asmx" />
  </services>
</asp:ScriptManager>
```

More code is required for the editor itself. This is accomplished via a user control on the editor master page. The first block of code is sourced from CodeLifter.com—it creates a draggable popup window. As it's helpful to view the resources in the context of the page, let the user move the window around and make hidden parts of the surface accessible (see Listing 5-20).

Listing 5-20. *Part 1: The JavaScript Editor Defined in the edit.ascx control: the Drag Window*

```
<%@ Control Language="C#" AutoEventWireup="false" CodeFile="edit.ascx.cs" Inherits="edit"
%>

<script language="JavaScript1.2" type="text/javascript">
    // Script Source: CodeLifter.com
    // Copyright 2003
    // Do not remove this header
    isIE = document.all;
    isNN = !document.all && document.getElementById;
    isHot = false;

    function ddInit(e) {
        topDog = isIE ? "BODY" : "HTML";
        hotDog = isIE ? event.srcElement : e.target;
        while (hotDog.id != "titleBar" && hotDog.tagName != topDog) {
            hotDog = isIE ? hotDog.parentElement : hotDog.parentNode;
            if (hotDog == null || hotDog.id == null || hotDog.tagName == null)
                return;
        }
        if (hotDog.id == "titleBar") {
            offsetx = isIE ? event.clientX : e.clientX;
            offsety = isIE ? event.clientY : e.clientY;
            nowX = parseInt(whichDog.style.left);
            nowY = parseInt(whichDog.style.top);
            ddEnabled = true;
            document.onmousemove = dd;
        }
    }

    function dd(e) {
        if (!ddEnabled) return;
        whichDog.style.left = isIE ? ➥
                        nowX + event.clientX - offsetx : nowX + e.clientX - offsetx;
        whichDog.style.top = isIE ? ➥
                        nowY + event.clientY - offsety : nowY + e.clientY - offsety;
        return false;
    }

    function hideMe() {
        whichDog.style.visibility = "hidden";
    }

    function showMe() {
        whichDog.style.visibility = "visible";
    }

    document.onmousedown = ddInit;
    document.onmouseup = Function("ddEnabled=false");

</script>
```

This code portion is shown for completeness. It is used to move the editor window around. When editing the page, it's helpful to see the page, which might be partly hidden by the overlaid window (see Listing 5-21).

Listing 5-21. *Part 2: The JavaScript Editor Defined in the edit.ascx Control: the Resource Access*

```
<script language="javascript" type="text/javascript">

    var parentObj;

    function showMessage(msg) {
        var label = document.getElementById('MessageLabel')
        label.innerText = msg;
        label.style.display = (msg.length == 0) ? 'none' : 'block';
        label.style.color = "#00FF33";
    }

    function showError(msg) {
        var label = document.getElementById('MessageLabel')
        label.innerText = msg;
        label.style.display = (msg.length == 0) ? 'none' : 'block';
        label.style.color = "#FF0000";
    }

    // These functions call the Web Service method.

    function initLanguages() {
        showMessage("Calling Server...");
        ResxEditor.ResourceService.GetAllLanguages(initLanguagesCallback, ➥
                                          initLanguagesError);
    }

    function initLanguagesCallback(result) {
        var selLoad = document.getElementById('ResxLanguageSelector');
        var selCopy = document.getElementById('ResxCopySelector');
        selLoad.options.length = 0;
        selCopy.options.length = 0;
        for (i = 0; i < result.len; i++) {
            selLoad.options[i] = new Option(result.cultureName[i], ➥
                                          result.cultureID[i]);
            selCopy.options[i] = new Option(result.cultureName[i], ➥
                                          result.cultureID[i]);
        }
        showMessage("");
        document.getElementById('theContentContainer').setAttribute("disabled", ➥
                                                          false);
    }

    function initLanguagesError(error) {
        showError(error.get_message());
    }

    function saveMe() {
        showMessage("Save the data...");
        var pageId = parentObj.getAttribute("pageID");
        var ctrlId = parentObj.getAttribute("ctrlID");
        var theme = '<% = Theme %>';
        var tb = document.getElementById('<% = EditTextBox.ClientID %>').innerText;
        var sel = document.getElementById('ResxLanguageSelector');
        if (sel.options.length > 0) {
            var culture = sel.options[sel.selectedIndex].value;
```

```
            // Text
            ResxEditor.ResourceService.SaveResource(pageId, ctrlId + ".Text", ➥
                                                tb, culture, theme, ➥
                                                saveMeCallbackText, ➥
                                                saveMeError);
        }
        // close after save is done
        if (document.getElementById('saveMeCloseCheckbox').checked == true) {
            hideEditor();
        }
    }

    // This is the callback function that processes the Web Service return value
    function saveMeCallbackText(result, eventArgs) {
        if (parentObj.getAttribute("attributes").search(/ToolTip/) != -1) {
            showMessage("Save the data....");
            // Tooltip
            var pageId = parentObj.getAttribute("pageID");
            var ctrlId = parentObj.getAttribute("ctrlID");
            var theme = '<% = Theme %>';
            var sel = document.getElementById('ResxLanguageSelector');
            if (sel.options.length > 0) {
                var culture = sel.options[sel.selectedIndex].value;
                var tb = ➥
                document.getElementById('<% = TextBoxTooltip.ClientID %>').value;
                ResxEditor.ResourceService.SaveResource(pageId, ➥
                                                    ctrlId + ".ToolTip", ➥
                                                    tb, culture, theme, ➥
                                                    saveMeCallbackTooltip, ➥
                                                    saveMeError);
            }
        } else {
            saveMeCallbackTooltip(null, null);
        }
    }

    function saveMeCallbackTooltip(result, eventArgs) {
        if (parentObj.getAttribute("attributes").search(/ErrorMessage/) != -1) {
            showMessage("Save the data.....");
            // Tooltip
            var pageId = parentObj.getAttribute("pageID");
            var ctrlId = parentObj.getAttribute("ctrlID");
            var theme = '<% = Theme %>';
            var sel = document.getElementById('ResxLanguageSelector');
            if (sel.options.length > 0) {
                var culture = sel.options[sel.selectedIndex].value;
                var tb = ➥
            document.getElementById('<% = TextBoxErrorMessage.ClientID %>').value;
                ResxEditor.ResourceService.SaveResource(pageId, ➥
                                                    ctrlId + ".ErrorMessage",➥
                                                    tb, culture, theme, ➥
                                                    saveMeCallbackVisibility, ➥
                                                    saveMeError);
            }
        } else {
            saveMeCallbackVisibility(null, null);
        }
```

```
}

function saveMeCallbackVisibility(result, eventArgs) {
    // Properties::Visible
    var pageId = parentObj.getAttribute("pageID");
    var ctrlId = parentObj.getAttribute("ctrlID");
    var theme = '<% = Theme %>';
    var sel = document.getElementById('ResxLanguageSelector');
    if (sel.options.length > 0) {
        var culture = sel.options[sel.selectedIndex].value;
        var cb = document.getElementById('<% = ChkBoxVisible.ClientID %>');
        if (cb.checked == false) {
            ResxEditor.ResourceService.SaveResource(pageId, ➥
                                            ctrlId + ".Visible",➥
                                            "False", culture, theme, ➥
                                            saveMeCallbackErrorMessage,➥
                                            saveMeError);

        } else {
            ResxEditor.ResourceService.SaveResource(pageId, ➥
                                            ctrlId + ".Visible", ➥
                                            "True", culture, theme, ➥
                                            saveMeCallbackErrorMessage,➥
                                            saveMeError);

        }
    }
}

function saveMeCallbackErrorMessage(result, eventArgs) {
    showMessage("");
}

function saveMeError(err) {
    showError(err.get_message());
}

function loadMe() {
    showMessage("Load Resources from Server...");
    var pageId = parentObj.getAttribute("pageID");
    var ctrlId = parentObj.getAttribute("ctrlID");
    var theme = '<% = Theme %>';
    var sel = document.getElementById('ResxLanguageSelector');
    if (sel.options.length > 0) {
        var culture = sel.options[sel.selectedIndex].value;
        document.getElementById('LabelControlId').innerText = ctrlId;
        document.getElementById('LabelPageId').innerText = pageId;
        // Text
        ResxEditor.ResourceService.LoadResource(pageId, ➥
                                            ctrlId + ".Text", ➥
                                            culture, theme, ➥
                                            loadMeCallbackText, ➥
                                            loadMeError);
    }
}

function loadMeCallbackText(result, eventArgs) {
    document.getElementById('<% = EditTextBox.ClientID %>').innerText = result;
    if (parentObj.getAttribute("attributes").search(/ToolTip/) != -1) {
```

```
            showMessage("Load Resources from Server....");
            // Tooltip
            var pageId = parentObj.getAttribute("pageID");
            var ctrlId = parentObj.getAttribute("ctrlID");
            var theme = '<% = Theme %>';
            var sel = document.getElementById('ResxLanguageSelector');
            if (sel.options.length > 0) {
                var culture = sel.options[sel.selectedIndex].value;
                ResxEditor.ResourceService.LoadResource(pageId, ➥
                                        ctrlId + ".Tooltip", ➥
                                        culture, theme, ➥
                                        loadMeCallbackTooltip, ➥
                                        loadMeError);
            document.getElementById('<% = TextBoxTooltip.ClientID %>'). ➥
                                                    disabled = false;
            document.getElementById('<% = TextBoxTooltip.ClientID %>'). ➥
                                    style.backgroundColor = "white";

            }
        } else {
            document.getElementById('<% = TextBoxTooltip.ClientID %>'). ➥
                                                    disabled = true;
            document.getElementById('<% = TextBoxTooltip.ClientID %>'). ➥
                                    style.backgroundColor = "silver";
            getErrorMessage();
        }
    }


    function loadMeCallbackTooltip(result, eventArgs) {
        document.getElementById('<% = TextBoxTooltip.ClientID %>'). ➥
                                                innerText = result;

        getErrorMessage();
    }

    function getErrorMessage() {
        if (parentObj.getAttribute("attributes").search(/ErrorMessage/) != -1) {
            showMessage("Load Resources from Server.....");
            // ErrorMessage
            var pageId = parentObj.getAttribute("pageID");
            var ctrlId = parentObj.getAttribute("ctrlID");
            var theme = '<% = Theme %>';
            var sel = document.getElementById('ResxLanguageSelector');
            if (sel.options.length > 0) {
                var culture = sel.options[sel.selectedIndex].value;
                ResxEditor.ResourceService.LoadResource(pageId, ➥
                                        ctrlId + ".ErrorMessage", ➥
                                        culture, theme, ➥
                                        loadMeCallbackErrorMessage,➥
                                        loadMeError);

            }
        } else {
            // Proceed with next
            getVisibility();
        }
    }

    function loadMeCallbackErrorMessage(result, eventArgs) {
```

```javascript
        // Save result
        document.getElementById('<% = TextBoxErrorMessage.ClientID %>'). ➥
                                            innerText = result;
        // Proceed with next
        getVisibility();
}

function getVisibility() {
    var pageId = parentObj.getAttribute("pageID");
    var ctrlId = parentObj.getAttribute("ctrlID");
    var sel = document.getElementById('ResxLanguageSelector');
    var theme = '<% = Theme %>';
    if (sel.options.length > 0) {
        var culture = sel.options[sel.selectedIndex].value;
        ResxEditor.ResourceService.LoadResource(pageId, ➥
                                            ctrlId + ".Visible", ➥
                                            culture, theme, ➥
                                            loadMeCallbackVisible, ➥
                                            loadMeError);
    }
}

function loadMeCallbackVisible(result, eventArgs) {
    // Save result
    if (result == null || result == true || result == "True") {
        document.getElementById('<% = ChkBoxVisible.ClientID %>').checked = ➥
                                                                    true;
    } else {
        document.getElementById('<% = ChkBoxVisible.ClientID %>').checked = ➥
                                                                    false;
    }
    // Done, clear message
    showMessage("");
}


function loadMeError(err) {
    showError(err.get_message());
}

function copyMe() {
    showMessage("Load Resources from Server...");
    var pageId = parentObj.getAttribute("pageID");
    var ctrlId = parentObj.getAttribute("ctrlID");
    var sel = document.getElementById('ResxCopySelector');
    var theme = '<% = Theme %>';
    if (sel.options.length > 0) {
        var culture = sel.options[sel.selectedIndex].value;
        // Text
        ResxEditor.ResourceService.LoadResource(pageId, ➥
                                            ctrlId + ".Text", ➥
                                            culture, theme, ➥
                                            copyMeCallbackText, ➥
                                            loadMeError);
    }
}
```

```
function copyMeCallbackText(result, eventArgs) {
    document.getElementById('<% = EditTextBox.ClientID %>').innerText = result;
    showMessage("Load Resources from Server....");
    // Tooltip
    var pageId = parentObj.getAttribute("pageID");
    var ctrlId = parentObj.getAttribute("ctrlID");
    var sel = document.getElementById('ResxCopySelector');
    var theme = '<% = Theme %>';
    if (sel.options.length > 0) {
        var culture = sel.options[sel.selectedIndex].value;
        ResxEditor.ResourceService.LoadResource(pageId, ➡
                                   ctrlId + ".Tooltip", ➡
                                   culture, theme, ➡
                                   copyMeCallbackTooltip, ➡
                                   loadMeError);
    }
}

function copyMeCallbackTooltip(result, eventArgs) {
    showMessage("Load Resources from Server.....");
    // Tooltip
    var pageId = parentObj.getAttribute("pageID");
    var ctrlId = parentObj.getAttribute("ctrlID");
    var sel = document.getElementById('ResxCopySelector');
    var theme = '<% = Theme %>';
    if (sel.options.length > 0) {
        var culture = sel.options[sel.selectedIndex].value;
        ResxEditor.ResourceService.LoadResource(pageId, ➡
                                   ctrlId + ".ErrorMessage", ➡
                                   culture, theme, ➡
                                   copyMeCallbackErrorMessage, ➡
                                   loadMeError);
    }
}

function copyMeCallbackErrorMessage(result, eventArgs) {
    document.getElementById('<% = TextBoxErrorMessage.ClientID %>').innerText =➡
                                                              result;
    showMessage("");
}

function showEditor(allowHtml, parent) {
    showMessage("");
    document.getElementById('<% = EditTextBox.ClientID %>').disabled = true;
    document.getElementById('<% = TextBoxTooltip.ClientID %>').disabled = true;
    document.getElementById('<% = EditTextBox.ClientID%>'). ➡
                                      style.backgroundColor= "silver";
    document.getElementById('<% = TextBoxTooltip.ClientID %>'). ➡
                                      style.backgroundColor = "silver";
    document.getElementById('ErrorMessage').style.display = "none";
    parentObj = parent;
    // image with attribute referencing to object data
    var etb = document.getElementById('textBoxContainer');
    // TODO: support more attributes
    var attr = parentObj.getAttribute("attributes");
    var a = attr.split(",");
    for (i = 0; i < a.length; i++) {
```

```
            switch (a[i]) {
                case "Title":
                    break;
                case "Text":
                    document.getElementById('<% = EditTextBox.ClientID %>'). ➥
                                                        disabled = false;
                    document.getElementById('<% = EditTextBox.ClientID %>'). ➥
                                                  style.backgroundColor = "";
                    etb.style.visibility = 'visible';
                    etb.style.display = 'inline';
                    break;
                case "ToolTip":
                    document.getElementById('<% = TextBoxTooltip.ClientID %>'). ➥
                                                  disabled = false;
                    document.getElementById('<% = TextBoxTooltip.ClientID %>'). ➥
                                             style.backgroundColor = "white";
                    break;
                case "ErrorMessage":
                    document.getElementById('ErrorMessage').style.display = "block";
                    break;
            }
        }
        loadMe();
        showMe();
    }

    function hideEditor() {
        var etb = document.getElementById('textBoxContainer');
        etb.style.visibility = 'hidden';
        etb.style.display = 'none';
        hideMe();
    }

    function initEditor() {
        // init
        var sel = document.getElementById('ResxLanguageSelector');
        if (sel.options.length == 0) {
            initLanguages();
        }
        hideEditor();
    }

</script>
```

This longer JavaScript code block invokes the Web Services. The pattern is, according to Ajax convention, asynchronous. One method calls the Web Service, defining callback methods as parameters. Once the Web Service responds, the callback method is invoked. This could be either a success or error path, depending on the outcome. The result is written back into the elements of the editor window. Other methods transfer data from the editor window to the server. Due to the complexity, several methods are required:

- SaveXX: Each Save method saves a particular control's content.
- LoadXX: Each Load method loads the content from the server.
- CopyXX: The copy method copies from one language to another.
- XXCallback: The callback containing the data.

Some callback methods invoke the subsequent step. For the Load procedure, the LoadMe func-tion is the entry point. In the callback, the next control's resource is retrieved from the server and read in its own callback method. This creates a chain of callbacks that are dependent on each other. This is similar for the Save procedure. After defining the access methods to the server, the editor window can be created, as shown in Listing 5-22.

Listing 5-22. *Part 3: The Editor Popup Window Definition*

```
<div id="theLayer" style="background-color: silver; position: absolute; top: 40px; left:
175px; width: 740px; border: solid 2px gray;
 padding: 5px; font-family: Verdana; color: Blue; font-size: 10pt; visibility: visible;
z-index: 10000">
 <table border="0" width="100%" bgcolor="transparent" cellspacing="0" cellpadding="0">
  <tr>
   <td width="100%">
    <table border="0" bgcolor="blue" width="100%" cellspacing="0" cellpadding="3"
          height="32">
     <tr>
      <td id="titleBar" style="cursor: move" width="95%">
       <ilayer width="100%" onselectstart="return false">
        <layer width="100%" onMouseover="isHot=true;if (isN4) ddN4(theLayer)"
                                   onMouseout="isHot=false">
         <span style="font-family:Verdana;font-size:12pt; font-weight:bold;
                  color:Wheat">Online Resource Editor</span>
        </layer>
       </ilayer>
      </td>
      <td style="cursor: hand" valign="top" align="right" width="5%">
       <div onclick="hideEditor();return false" style="padding: 2px; color: #ffffff;
           background-color: Red; width: 8px; height: 12px; font-size: 9px;
           font-family: Verdana; text-decoration: none; text-align: center;
           vertical-align: top">
        x
       </div>
      </td>
     </tr>
     <tr>
      <td width="100%" bgcolor="#FFFFFF" style="padding: 4px" colspan="2"
          disabled="true" id="theContentContainer">
       <table>
        <tr>
         <td>
         Language selection:
         </td>
         <td>
          <select id="ResxLanguageSelector" onchange="loadMe();">
          </select>
         </td>
        </tr>
        <tr>
         <td>
         Copy from language:
         </td>
         <td>
          <select id="ResxCopySelector" onchange="copyMe();">
          </select>
         </td>
```

```
  </tr>
 </table>
 <hr width="100%" size="2" color="gray" />
 Resource: <span style="font-weight: bold;"
     id="LabelControlId"></span> on 
     <span style="font-weight: bold;"
     id="LabelPageId">
     </span>
 <br />
 <hr width="100%" size="2" color="gray" />
 Tooltip:<br />
 <asp:TextBox runat="server" ID="TextBoxTooltip"
     TextMode="SingleLine" Width="720px"
     Visible="true"></asp:TextBox>
 <span style="display: none" id="ErrorMessage">
     ErrorMessage (Message in group, Text = Message text)
 <br />
  <asp:TextBox runat="server" ID="TextBoxErrorMessage"
     TextMode="SingleLine" Width="720px"
     Visible="true"></asp:TextBox>
 </span>
 <hr width="100%" size="2" color="gray" />
 <asp:CheckBox runat="server" ID="ChkBoxVisible"
     Text="Make element visible" />
 <hr width="100%" size="2" color="gray" />
 <div id="textBoxContainer" style="visibility: hidden">
  <asp:TextBox runat="server" ID="EditTextBox"
     TextMode="MultiLine"
     Height="400px" Width="720px"
     Visible="true"></asp:TextBox>
 </div>
 <br />
 <table border="0" width="100%">
  <tr>
   <td align="left" width="80%">
    <label>
     <input id="saveMeCloseCheckbox"
        type="checkbox" value="Close" />
     Close after Save
    </label>
   </td>
   <td align="right" width="20%">
    <input type="button"
        onclick="saveMe();return false;" value="Save" /> 
    <input type="button"
        onclick="hideEditor();return false;" value="Close" />
   </td>
  </tr>
 </table>
 <br />
 <div id="MessageLabel" style="color: Green;
        font-weight: bold">
 </div>
 <br />
 <span style="color: Red"><strong>Hint: </strong> ➡
  Refresh  page by choosing another language!</span>
</td>
```

```
      </tr>
     </table>
    </td>
   </tr>
  </table>
</div>

<script language="javascript" type="text/javascript">
    whichDog = isIE ? document.all.theLayer : document.getElementById("theLayer");
    setTimeout('initEditor()', 100);
    if (typeof (Sys) !== "undefined") Sys.Application.notifyScriptLoaded();
</script>
```

This is simply a fragment of HTML containing the controls and the supporting script that manages the page loading cycle. The control has a few trivial lines of code-behind (Listing 5-23). As written, everything relies on JavaScript in the client. The Web Service on the server acts as an access layer to the underlying resource provider.

Listing 5-23. *The "code-behind" for the Control*

```
using System;
using System.Web.UI;

public partial class edit : System.Web.UI.UserControl
{
    protected override void OnInit(EventArgs e)
    {
        Page.EnableEventValidation = false;
        base.OnInit(e);
    }

    protected override void OnLoad(EventArgs e)
    {
        base.OnLoad(e);
    }

    protected string Theme
    {
        get
        {
            return Session["theme"] as string;
        }
    }
}
```

The only public parameter we need is the currently selected theme. This value is included in the Web Service calls, where it is used to route the resource data into the right resource storage.

Summary

In this chapter, we looked closely at how to handle resource providers. A complete solution is capable of changing internal behavior without losing any default features, and includes a design-time control. Design-time support is an important part of any custom solution, and it would be short-sighted to ignore the option of using designer tools (even if you do not intend to employ them yourself). All code shown in this chapter has full design-time support, including the steps for enabling debugging.

Furthermore, we made the resource provider accessible via a Web Service. We built a JavaScript-based editor on the client to read and save resources at runtime, enabling resource-based pages to be editable online. The examples demonstrate how to implement a highly customized solution, which fits well into the existing ASP.NET framework.

CHAPTER 6

■ ■ ■

Page and Session Management

The Hypertext Transfer Protocol (HTTP) is the reason for the success of the Internet. It is also the source of the drawbacks in the usability of applications. To overcome these limitations, ASP.NET provides several ways of maintaining the state of pages—and the controls between postbacks—throughout the whole session. Whatever the type of data existing within an application, there are two things to consider: the storage of application data on the server, and how to integrate the user's session with the application data.

In this chapter, I'll explain how to customize in both of these areas for your real-life applications. In particular, you'll find information about:

- The page persister technique
- Writing a custom page persister
- The internals of the session state provider
- Writing a custom session state provider

The approach presented here is based on the provider model as explained in Chapter 4. Please refer back for useful information about providers, their purpose, and how they fit into the ASP.NET framework.

The Page State Persister

Handling active content and creating rich internet applications are difficult to integrate. Page persistence is the key to overcoming this challenge, and a good understanding of this feature is the basis of creating complex applications.

A Look Back

The protocol spoken between server and browser is HTTP, and there are many books, articles, blogs, and newsgroup posts complaining about its limitations. However, HTTP has succeeded mainly because of its simplicity. There are three key properties which make HTTP unique:

- It uses text to transport both messages and content.
- It runs on top of TCP.
- It is a stateless protocol.

"Stateless" can be thought of as "fire and forget." The client initiates a request to the server; the server processes the request and responds with the answer. After that, the server forgets all about the procedure. Once the conversation has ended, nothing is left for further processing—at least, this is the case for the protocol.

The Default Page State Persister

The statelessness of HTTP means that there is no formal way of remembering, either on the client or the server, the state of any past actions involving the same user. However, every web development environment provides some means of recognizing session states and storing user data. ASP.NET is no exception, and as for many other parts of the .NET Framework, there are several ways of achieving this.

State Storage in ASP.NET

Since all state management approaches require custom coding by application developers, it's worth looking into them in more detail. Understanding the pros and cons of each method makes it easier to decide which one to use, where to customize it, and how to get the most out of it.

ASP.NET can store information about the page's state in several collections:

- *Cookies*: You can create private cookies and store them on the client's machine in order to obtain information from them. This is not the best method, but it's the default method.

- *View State*: ASP.NET controls, as well as several other parts, use view state to store control-specific information about the previous state. We'll discuss all facets of view state later in the section "Persisting Page State Information."

- *Session*: This is a collection of key-value pairs related to the current user's session. It's a way of adding more information, on the server side, to a session state stored elsewhere (in a cookie, for instance).

The Application collection is another set of key-value pairs that retain application-level data shared among all users. In contrast, the Context collection is limited to the current request-response flow—data in the Context collection does not survive the page cycle.

Cookies, View State and the Session collection give the developer the illusion of stateful page handling. Most commonly, they will use a single cookie, called the session cookie, to store an ID with the shortest lifetime possible in the browser's cookie memory, just until the session ends. When the client makes a new request, the cookie is returned in the request. The server decodes the ID to determine which browser instance (and hence, which user) is sending the request.

As an experienced developer, you might already know how to use the Cookie, Session, and Application collections. Each of them has a different storage mechanism and must be used wisely. You may remember that there are many code snippets scattered throughout the page's code which obtain access to the information whenever it is required. However, this is not ideal, as it detracts from the declarative nature of ASP.NET pages. Not only does it make pages harder to read, but it could lead to bugs if overused.

Persisting Page State Information

The first step in managing state data is to master the techniques for retaining the page state through each postback. The information on the "current" page is generally stored within several controls. Therefore, we'll need a way of storing the controls' state information.

The state storage relies on two similar techniques: the view state and the control state. The internal nature and pitfalls of the view state were described in Chapter 1. Here, I'll show how to change the storage and retrieval mechanism.

View State Explained

Recall the purpose of view state: to store data about the properties of controls that are set programmatically. View state is not responsible for the sticky form behavior that retains the controls' current state according to the user's selection. The control state holding this information is retrieved from the form's data, which is posted back to the server during a normal postback. Additional information is stored in a special hidden field. Internally, view state uses an object of type `StateBag`. It retains data and includes code that serializes the data into text format and stores it in the hidden field.

Consider using a `Label` control, where you set the color to turn red if an error occurs. You'll want to maintain this state until the error has been corrected, without checking and setting the property repeatedly. Once set programmatically, view state stores this value in the `StateBag` and persists it in the page via a hidden field. When the page is initialized after a postback, the value is retrieved and assigned to the property—no custom code required.

Clearly, view state plays a crucial role in page development, and can be used internally to store a control's state.

Control State Explained

View state and control state are related and therefore need to be discussed together. Whereas view state contains programmatically-set property values, control state contains the data required for one control to make it appear after a postback in the same state that it was in beforehand. Frustratingly, the control state is stored as part of the view state data by default. This means that there are two different ways of saving control data during postbacks, but both use the same storage—the hidden view state field. However, control developers may decide to write the control state into private hidden fields to retain the state and decouple view state and control state storage, then.

■**Note** Control state is only for small amounts of critical data that are essential for the control across postbacks. It is not seen as an alternative to view state.

In fact, there is no way to treat both states separately from each other from page-level code. Disabling the view state suppresses the serialization and storage mechanism entirely, so the control state gets lost. Complex controls, such as GridView, store information about paging and sorting, because there are no corresponding HTML fields able to store and send such data as part of a regular form. The GridView has several indices that retain the internal state. Changes to underlying data are tracked and used to fire appropriate events. These are properties such as EditIndex, PageIndex, and SortDirection. Several internal actions might lead to changes that need to be stored during postbacks, but this does not use the same path through the code as the view state would use for public properties.

The view state data stored in the hidden field would expand, and developers using your control might by concerned by the growing page and form data. Control developers should be careful about using the control state because of its dependency on view state. A disabled view state could cause the control state to not function properly.

However, as a control developer, you have several options for managing the way your control stores internal state values. First, the Page.RegisterRequiresControlState method must be called to ensure that the control starts storing the control state. Apart from within view state, there is no StateBag that stores values directly. It's up to you to implement the whole storage level. This is both good and bad, as although you'll have more control of what happens internally, it requires more effort to store a few primitive values.

Listing 6-1 shows a simple control that stores several values in the control state.

Listing 6-1. *A Custom Control Using the Control State*

```
public class MyControl : Control
{
    string stateData;

    protected override void OnInit(EventArgs e)
    {
        Page.RegisterRequiresControlState(this);
        base.OnInit(e);
    }

    protected override void LoadControlState(object savedState)
    {
        object[] ctrlState = (object[]) savedState;
        base.LoadControlState(ctrlState[0]);
        stateData = (string) ctrlState[1];
    }

    protected override object SaveControlState()
    {
        object[] ctrlState = new object[2];
        ctrlState[0] = base.SaveControlState();
        ctrlState[1] = stateData;
        return ctrlState;
    }

}
```

If you plan to write a custom page state persister, you'll have to handle the control state's data as well as the view state's data. The persister's provider must store both; otherwise almost all custom controls will stop functioning properly.

An alternative is to store the values your own way—using private hidden fields, perhaps—in order to remain independent of the provider. However, this is beyond the scope of this chapter. Besides, adding infrastructure logic to custom controls runs counter to the ASP.NET paradigm, in which the base framework contains and exposes a rich infrastructure.

In conclusion, view state and control state are stored in the same place in order to completely and automatically restore a control's properties. Since the storage and management of view state and control state are related, I'll discuss them together in this chapter. When I use the term "view state" consider it as including control state as well.

The Default Providers

ASP.NET uses a provider to manage storage of the view state. The preceding description assumes the usage of one of the two providers' available out-of-the-box. Both providers derive from an abstract base class, `PageStatePersister`:

- `HiddenFieldPageStatePersister`
- `SessionPageStatePersister`

By default, the `HiddenFieldPageStatePersister` is used to store the view state in a hidden field. When you look into a page's source code in the browser, you'll find a field with the name __VIEWSTATE. This is the serialized, encoded, and optionally encrypted collection of properties stored in the `StateBag` (see Figure 6-1).

```
<input type="hidden" name="__VIEWSTATE" id="__VIEWSTATE"
 value="/wEPDwUKLTY4NzM5MDExNg9kFgICAw9kFgICAQ88KwANAgAPFgQeC18hRGFOYUJvdW5kZx4LXyFJdGGVtQ291b
nQCHmQMFCsAARYGHgRUeXB1GSsCHgROYW11BQRJdGVtHglEYXRhRm1lbGQFASEWAmYPZBY+AgEPZBYCZg8PFgIeBFRle
HQFFzAxMjMONTY3ODk6OyZsdDs9Jmd0Oz9AZGQCAg9kFgJmDw8WAh8FBQkwMTIzNDU2NzhkZAIDD2QWAmYPDxYCHwUFB
zAxMjMONTZkZAIED2QWAmYPDxYCHwUFAzAxMmRkAgUPZBYCZg8PFgIfBQUeMDEyMzQ1Njc4OTo7Jmx0OzOmZ3Q7POBBQ
kNERUZHZGQCBg9kFgJmDw8WAh8FBQwwMTIzNDU2Nzg5OjtkZAIHD2QWAmYPDxYCHwUFAjAxZGQCCA9kFgJmDw8WAh8FB
QQwMTIzZGQCCCQ9kFgJmDw8WAh8FBREwMTIzNDU2Nzg9OjsmbHQ7PWRkAgoPZBYCZg8PFgIfBQUcMDEyMzQ1Njc4OTo7J
mx0OzOmZ3Q7POBBQkNERWRkAgsPZBYCZg8PFgIfBQUIMDEyMzQ1NjdkZAIMD2QWAmYPDxYCHwUFGDAxMjMONTY3ODk6O
yZsdDs9Jmd0Oz9AQWRkAgOPZBYCZg8PFgIfBQUWMDEyMzQ1Njc4OTo7Jmx0OzOmZ3Q7P2RkAg4PZBYCZg8PFgIfBQUcM
DEyMzQ1Njc4OTo7Jmx0OzOmZ3Q7POBBQkNERWRkAg8PZBYCZg8PFgIfBQUBMGRkAhAPZBYCZg8PFgIfBQUfMDEyMzQ1N
jc4OTo7Jmx0OzOmZ3Q7POBBQkNERUZHSGRkAhEPZBYCZg8PFgIfBQUKMDEyMzQ1Njc4OWRkAhIPZBYCZg8PFgIfBQUGM
DEyMzQ1ZGQCEw9kFgJmDw8WAh8FBQkwMTIzNDU2NzhkZAIIUD2QWAmYPDxYCHwUFAzAxMmRkAhUPZBYCZg8PFgIfBQUGM
DEyMzQ1ZGQCFg9kFgJmDw8WAh8FBQMwMTJkZAIXD2QWAmYPDxYCHwUFBjAxMjMONWRkAhgPZBYCZg8PFgIfBQURMDEyM
zQ1Njc4OTo7Jmx0Oz1kZAIZD2QWAmYPDxYCHwUFHzAxMjMONTY3ODk6OyZsdDs9Jmd0Oz9AQUJDREVGGROhkZAIaD2QWA
mYPDxYCHwUFGDAxMjMONTY3ODk6OyZsdDs9Jmd0Oz9AQWRkAhsPZBYCZg8PFgIfBQUbMDEyMzQ1Njc4OTo7Jmx0OzOmZ
3Q7POBBQkNEZGQCHA9kFgJmDw8WAh8FBQowMTIzNDU2Nzg5ZGQCHQ9kFgJmDw8WAh8FBQowMTIzNDU2Nzg5ZGQCHg9kF
gJmDw8WAh8FBQQwMTIzZGQCHw9PFgIeB1Zpc21ibGVoZGQYAQUJZ3JkUmFuZG9tDzwrAAoBCAIBZNSvKyIdIpiOuhAYd
OiyXgYs4VpY" />
```

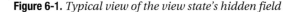

Figure 6-1. *Typical view of the view state's hidden field*

This is what you'll see if the `HiddenFieldPageStatePersister` is used. There are several pros and cons to using this method. Many pages store information, and many users have individual data. The state is associated with the current page, and apart from session data that is independent of the current page, this data is specific to the page and the user. Storing the data on the client computer moves the memory required from the server to the client. This costs bandwidth, but saves server resources.

If you have 1KB of session data and 1,000 users accessing the server simultaneously, you'll need to store 1MB of data. If this happens for 100 pages, you'll need to store 100MB. This isn't usually significant, but growing traffic will increase the resource consumption accordingly. For this reason, using the browser's memory is a better option for scalability, and this is why the default provider uses the `HiddenFieldPageStatePersister` option.

However, sometimes it's not the server's resources that cause the bottleneck, but the bandwidth, particularly on mobile devices. View state is transmitted twice for each request. Accessing a dozen pages with 1KB of session data each would force the device to transfer and process an additional 24KB of data, and this could be even higher for badly-developed pages.

To investigate the contents of the view state, a tool such as Fritz Onion's ViewStateDecoder is invaluable. Knowing what is stored in view state makes it's easier to design a custom page state persister as shown in Figure 6-2. You can find the most recent version of ViewStateDecoder at: http://www.pluralsight.com/community/media/p/51688.aspx.

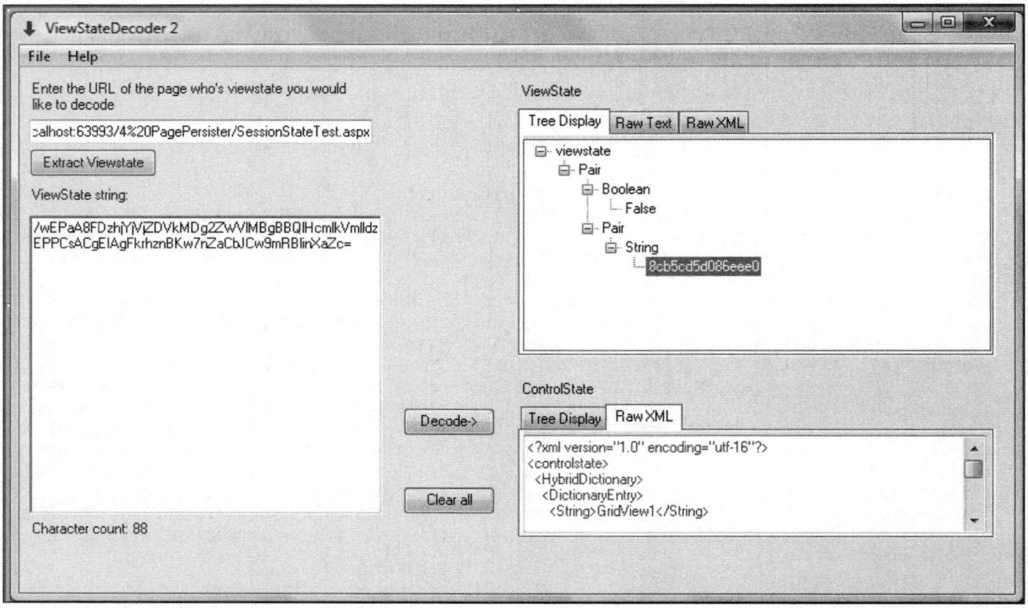

Figure 6-2. *Examine the contents of the view state.*

At this point, the particular contents of the view state aren't important. Decoding the data is merely to understand the internal behavior.

Changing the Default Provider

The alternative provider, `SessionPageStatePersister`, moves the storage strategy from the client to the server. The data is stored in the session, along with other session variables. However, view state data is not session data—merely the state of controls. View state for each page is stored separately in this provider.

To change from the default provider, you must override the `PageStatePersister` property of the Page class:

```
protected override PageStatePersister PageStatePersister
{
    get
    {
        return new SessionPageStatePersister(this);
    }
}
```

It's also possible to set this globally by assigning the following attribute to the `pages` tag in the *web.config* file.

```
<System.web>
    <pages pageBaseType="PersisterBasePage">
    ...
</System.web>
```

This assigns a base page to all pages—*PersisterBasePage*, for example, which derives from the Page class and overrides the `PageStatePersister` property. However, this prevents you from using code-behind.

You could set the base class individually for each page. This is more flexible, but more demanding. The page's definition could look like the following:

```
public partial class _Default : PersisterBasePage
```

As easy as this seems, it always involves a compromise. The workload is either on the client or the server. Fortunately, the extensibility model of ASP.NET allows you to create custom providers to transparently replace the existing ones.

Developing a Custom Page State Provider

As already mentioned, the entry point into a custom provider is the implementation of an abstract base class. Before you start coding, you'll need to answer two questions:

- Where shall I store data during postbacks?
- How do I identify when data is no longer current?

The first answer is easy. Data is typically stored in a file system, a database, or in memory.

The second answer is more complicated. Data is related to a particular page, and when a user leaves the page, the data becomes redundant. This event is difficult to recognize. The user can leave the page by navigating to another page within the same application, by jumping to a different Web site on another server, or even by simply closing the browser. Keeping the data in storage forever is not an option, as this would increase the storage space used and the effort of retrieving the right data. While the default provider is not the ideal solution either, it does answer the second question: if the user moves on to another page, the browser removes the data from the client's memory. Thus, you don't need to worry about obsolete data.

There is no satisfactory answer to this question. It's usually sufficient simply to remove outdated data that has not been refreshed for a specific period of time. This assumes that a user is no longer connected to the server. Selecting a value corresponding to the session timeout will be adequate for most applications.

Choosing the Data Storage

In this example, I'll make the storage as easy as possible to implement. The data is stored on the server in the file system. This could even be a shared drive, if you need to support a web farm. File systems are highly efficient for storing and retrieving data and avoid dependency on a database. However, this is simply an example of how to extend the page state persister. The storage solution you use depends entirely on the characteristics of your application.

You'll notice that the hidden field is still in charge, because it contains some information for identifying unique pages. This is why the hidden field is not empty when using the default provider, even if the view state is disabled. However, the identifier only needs a few bytes, and shouldn't affect bandwidth requirements.

Analyzing a Provider

Before implementing the provider from scratch, let's examine the `SessionPageStatePersister` class for firsthand information about the internal structure of such a provider. This class stores data on the server, just as the custom provider is intended to do. If you investigate the view state value captured from the hidden field, you'll see a simple hexadecimal number, such as 8cb5cd5d086eee0. This is the hexadecimal representation of the procedure. Using the following code sequence, you can decode the value:

```
new DateTime(0x8cb5cd5d086eee0, DateTimeKind.Local).ToString()
```

This value decodes to 14 February 2009, 4:09pm and 57 seconds. The `SessionPageStatePersister` stores not one, but nine of these values internally, to keep the history of page accesses alive. When the user presses the browser's back button, a previous page is pulled from the server. Using the timestamp as a key, the correct data is retrieved from the server's storage. The name of the internal queue is __VIEWSTATEQUEUE. Constraining the number of pages in the history solves the second question raised earlier and limits the storage space used. Since the user's behavior depends on the application's navigation structure, you can alter the queue size using the following entry in the *web.config* file:

```
<sessionPageState historySize="12" />
```

This value allows 12 pages in the history list. The value you choose is always a compromise between convenience and resource usage. If the user exceeds the queue size limit, the view state becomes invalid and an exception is thrown. You can catch the exception, deliver an error page, and end the session, or simply redirect to a default page. However, as this is not an ideal solution, the following example shows an alternative way of dealing with "dead" data.

Implementing the Provider

As we learned from the default implementation, the whole procedure of loading and saving the state consists of two methods, `Load` and `Save`, respectively. Both use the fully implemented serialization and deserialization methods provided by the base class to convert between the `StateBag` object and a text string. The example stores the data in single files in the file system. Each page's data becomes one file. To retrieve the values, two pieces of information must be held in the view state field: the name of the file and the timestamp. The timestamp is needed for private garbage collection to remove expired data. The file name associates the page's view state field with the file itself. After rendering to the browser, the hidden view state looks like the following:

```
<input type="hidden" name="__VIEWSTATEID" id="__VIEWSTATEID" ➥
    value="8cb5cd5d086eee0-2qi0qprzodivhh55uwog3k45.vs" />
```

The first part of the value, before the hyphen, is the timestamp. I have retained the coding schema. The second part is a randomly generated value, plus the extension, .vs.

Listing 6-2 shows the code for the custom provider, as described thus far.

Listing 6-2. *Persisting the View State Using Local File System*

```
public class FilePagePersister : PageStatePersister
{

    private const string ViewStateFormFieldID = "__VIEWSTATEID";
    private const string StateFileFolderPath = "~/StateData/";


    public FilePagePersister(Page p)
        : base(p)
    {
    }

    public override void Load()
    {
        string stateIdentifierValue = ➥
            HttpContext.Current.Request.Form[ViewStateFormFieldID];
        if (stateIdentifierValue.Length > 0)
        {
            string fileName = stateIdentifierValue;
            string filePath = HttpContext.Current.Server.MapPath( ➥
                            StateFileFolderPath + fileName);
            string contents = File.ReadAllText(filePath);

            Pair state = base.StateFormatter.Deserialize(contents) as Pair;
            if (state != null)
            {
                base.ViewState = state.First;
                base.ControlState = state.Second;
            }
        }
    }

    public override void Save()
    {
        if (base.Page.Form != null ➥
            && (base.ControlState != null || base.ViewState != null))
        {
            // Create filename for save
            string fileName = String.Format("{0:x8}-{1}.vs", DateTime.Now.Ticks, ➥
                            HttpContext.Current.Session.SessionID);
            string filePath = HttpContext.Current.Server.MapPath( ➥
                            StateFileFolderPath + fileName);
            Pair p = new Pair(base.ViewState, base.ControlState);
            File.WriteAllText(filePath, base.StateFormatter.Serialize(p));
            var hf = new HiddenField
```

```
            {
                Value = fileName,
                ID = ViewStateFormFieldID
            }
            base.Page.Form.Controls.AddAt(0, hf);
        }
    }
}
```

The base class provides methods of serializing and deserializing the data. You can access these methods by calling base.StateFormatter. The provider saves both the control state and the view state, and creates a Pair from them, to group the values together. The serialized Pair is written directly into the file using File.WriteAllText and retrieved using File.ReadAllText. We are not concerned about threading here, because each storage location is dedicated to one user session and one page. There's a chance that a user could send the same page twice to the server at the same moment, but that's unlikely—and out of our scope. The Load method is the reverse of the Save method, using the same approach. The Save method creates a hidden field using the HiddenField control and adds it to the beginning of the current control collection.

Extending the Provider

Although, from this example, custom implementation seems very simple, this isn't entirely true. Over time, the folder for state files accumulates more and more files. You might consider deleting session state files triggered by the session end event, but that's not reliable. The event is fired only if the session ends by command. If the user closes the browser the session dies "silently," and only the session timeout can be used to remove remaining objects.

One option is to remove old files regularly, but using such a cleanup process for each page request would increase the number of file accesses and thus decrease performance. A better approach is to include a regular folder check independent of any requests. Using this test, you can delete all files over a certain age.

Implementing the tidy-up code in the provider is undesirable. Recall the goals and intended behavior of a provider: it's not a good idea to have them running basic tasks. Rather, the health monitoring system provided by ASP.NET is ideal for managing the "health" of the provider's storage.

Maintaining the Storage by Using the Health Monitor

Since the cleaning-up procedure must be run regularly, the WebHeartbeatEvent is an ideal trigger. This event fires at regular intervals, invoking another provider. The health monitoring system itself is based on a provider model. Therefore, the second part of a custom view state storage solution consists of a "custom cleanup provider."

Before you implement this provider, take a look at the configuration step needed in the *web.config* file in the <system.web> section (see Listing 6-3).

Listing 6-3. *Activating the Health Monitor*

```
<healthMonitoring enabled="true" heartbeatInterval="5">
  <providers>
    <add name="FileCleanupProvider"
        type="Apress.Extensibility.EventProvider.FileCleanupProvider, ➡
            Apress.Extensibility.EventProvider"/>
  </providers>
  <eventMappings>
    <add name="FileCleanupEvent" type="System.Web.Management.WebHeartbeatEvent"
        startEventCode="0" endEventCode="2147483647"></add>
```

```
    </eventMappings>
    <rules>
     <add name="CleanupEvent" eventName="FileCleanupEvent"
          provider="FileCleanupProvider" />
    </rules>
</healthMonitoring>
```

The healthMonitoring element requires three child elements:

- provider: The provider that issues the action
- eventMapping: The event that invokes the action
- rules: A relation between a specific event and a provider

The event is based on the WebHeartbeatEvent class. Enable the monitor using the enabled="true" attribute. The heartbeatInterval="5" attribute sets the heartbeat to five seconds; this is just for testing and debugging purposes. In real-life scenarios, set a value that provides a compromise between memory consumption and cleanup effort in order to monitor the number of files stored in the data folder. A heartbeat interval of one hour is a good starting value.

The example provider configured here is called the FileCleanupProvider. Listing 6-4 demonstrates its implementation. Before beginning, you'll need to know a few things about health monitoring providers. The monitoring system is implemented to observe an ASP.NET application. It must be active before the application starts and after it ends, and it must exist independently of current requests, the current request's state in the pipeline, and IIS. Therefore, the class must be implemented in an assembly that can be loaded separately. Adding the class to App_Code or any place in your current project will fail. Instead, create a simple class library project, reference it from the Web application you wish to monitor, and add the following class to that project.

The code requires the System.Web.Management namespace to be available.

Listing 6-4. *Simple Health Monitor Provider That Tidies Up a Folder*

```
public class FileCleanupProvider : WebEventProvider
{

    private const string StateFileFolderPath = "StateData/";

    public FileCleanupProvider()
        : base()
    {

    }

    public override void Flush()
    {
        // not required
    }

    public override void ProcessEvent(WebBaseEvent raisedEvent)
    {
        DateTime dtRaised = raisedEvent.EventTime;
        // Remove files
        string filePath = Path.Combine(HttpRuntime.AppDomainAppPath, ➥
                                       StateFileFolderPath);
        foreach (string file in Directory.GetFiles(filePath))
        {
            if (dtRaised - File.GetCreationTime(file) > TimeSpan.FromHours(6))
```

```
            {
                File.Delete(file);
            }
        }
    }

    public override void Shutdown()
    {
        // Clean up on shut down
        string filePath = Path.Combine(HttpRuntime.AppDomainAppPath, ➥
                                    StateFileFolderPath);
        foreach (string file in Directory.GetFiles(filePath))
        {
            File.Delete(file);
        }
    }
}
```

Each heartbeat of the monitor invokes the ProcessEvent method. A simple loop locates all the files exceeding the specified age—six hours in the example—and deletes them. The file expiry test can be extended to suit your needs. You could check if the corresponding session is still alive, or if the data in the file matches certain conditions.

The current timestamp is passed to the method with the raisedEvent.EventTime value. The path to the application can be retrieved using the HttpRuntime object. Remember that HttpContext might not be available, because the first heartbeat arrives when the application has not yet begun. Other monitoring events could provide the HttpContext object, but basic events such as the WebHeartbeatEvent don't support this.

Conclusion

In this section, we looked at replacing the default page state persister provider that is responsible for storing view state and embedded control state information. Using the health monitoring system with another custom provider allows us to maintain cleanup routines.

Page states are not the only state persisted during a user's session. Data is also stored in session variables, which are, by default, stored in memory. However, as in several other parts of ASP.NET, the session state is built on the provider model. The next section explains this in detail and shows how to extend the behavior using a custom provider.

Session State Providers

As shown in Chapter 4, providers are responsible for allowing storage access to services. The session state module is one such service relying on several out-of-the-box storage options. For all available options, a dedicated provider exists. You can also add your own provider to implement a fully customized storage strategy.

The Session State Service

The session state service is defined in the System.Web.SessionState.SessionStateModule. Each instance creates a module that in turn creates a space to store data. The data is—as the name implies—associated with the user's session. System.Web.SessionState.SessionStateStoreData is the class that defines the storage space. One instance is created for each user session. The SessionStateStoreData class is responsible for serializing and deserializing the session data.

The serialization uses a highly efficient binary format partly customized with hardcoded transformations for scalar values and the BinaryFormatter type for all other values. This type is defined in the System.Runtime.Serialization.Formatters.Binary namespace. Since the session serializes all objects, the process includes two types of data: static and non-static. Non-static data are held in an Items collection. This collection is defined as an interface of type ISessionStateItemCollection, which is a simple collection based on ICollection and IEnumerable. It's exposed by the Session object through an indexer and the Items property. The StaticObjects property relies on the HttpStaticObjectsCollection type, which in turn is a collection that implements the same interfaces. However, the serialization is implemented slightly differently here. For both Items and StaticObjects, you can call the Serialize and Deserialize methods to translate the data to and from a storable format.

Apart from the two types of data previously mentioned, the data store has its own Timeout property. This is necessary, as the service is implemented as an HTTP module and relies on request events. If the final event is not raised, the store would become an orphan if the timeout did not terminate it. Internally, the session state service class is defined as follows:

```
public sealed class SessionStateModule : IHttpModule
```

The session state module is executed before the handlers in the AcquireRequestState pipeline state. This ensures that session data is already present when the page's handler is loaded. The module attempts to retrieve the session ID from the request and uses this to obtain data from the session store provider. If both function correctly, the session data is rebuilt as a dictionary and exposed to the HttpSession object. The session data is stored at the end of the request processing, within the ReleaseRequestSession stage of the pipeline. If no session ID is present, a new one is created. If the ID is there and some session data is changed, the provider is used to store these data.

The service's providers use the SessionStateStoreProviderBase provider base class, which defines a subset of methods all providers share. As shown in Listing 6-5, this is an embedded class used here as a basis for custom providers.

Listing 6-5. *The SessionStateStoreProviderBase Is the Base for All Session State Providers*

```
[AspNetHostingPermission(SecurityAction.LinkDemand, ➥
                        Level=AspNetHostingPermissionLevel.Minimal),
AspNetHostingPermission(SecurityAction.InheritanceDemand, ➥
                        Level=AspNetHostingPermissionLevel.Minimal)]
public abstract class SessionStateStoreProviderBase : ProviderBase
{
    protected SessionStateStoreProviderBase()
    {
    }

    public abstract SessionStateStoreData CreateNewStoreData(HttpContext context, ➥
                                        int timeout);
    public abstract void CreateUninitializedItem(HttpContext context, ➥
                                        string id, ➥
                                        int timeout);
    public abstract void Dispose();
    public abstract void EndRequest(HttpContext context);
    public abstract SessionStateStoreData GetItem(HttpContext context, ➥
                                        string id, ➥
                                        out bool locked, ➥
                                        out TimeSpan lockAge, ➥
                                        out object lockId, ➥
                                        out SessionStateActions actions);
```

```
        public abstract SessionStateStoreData GetItemExclusive(HttpContext context, ➥
                                            string id, ➥
                                            out bool locked, ➥
                                            out TimeSpan lockAge, ➥
                                            out object lockId, ➥
                                            out SessionStateActions actions);
        internal virtual void Initialize(string name, ➥
                                NameValueCollection config, ➥
                                IPartitionResolver partitionResolver)
        {
        }

        public abstract void InitializeRequest(HttpContext context);
        public abstract void ReleaseItemExclusive(HttpContext context, ➥
                                        string id, ➥
                                        object lockId);
        public abstract void RemoveItem(HttpContext context, ➥
                                    string id, ➥
                                    object lockId, ➥
                                    SessionStateStoreData item);
        public abstract void ResetItemTimeout(HttpContext context, string id);
        public abstract void SetAndReleaseItemExclusive(HttpContext context, ➥
                                            string id, ➥
                                            SessionStateStoreData item, ➥
                                            object lockId, ➥
                                            bool newItem);
        public abstract bool SetItemExpireCallback( ➥
                        SessionStateItemExpireCallback expireCallback);
}
```

Inspecting the GetItem and RemoveItem methods, you'll notice that the provider is responsible for creating (via the out parameter for GetItem) the session-specific SessionStateDataStore. The vital parameter is HttpContext, as it passes all the information required for identifying the session.

However, the base class is abstract. In order to understand the code and learn how to implement a custom provider, we'll need to examine certain implementations. The next sections will cover the nature of sessions and cookies that are tightly coupled with the session provider's behavior.

Identifying the Session

Despite storage management, the session state service needs to retrieve the session ID. The first attempt to overcome this stateless behavior led to the invention of cookies.

Cookies Make HTTP Taste Good . . .

A cookie is a small piece of text-based information stored in the browser's memory or disk space. It's under the browser's control, and it exists to send information about the state back to the server. When the browser requests a new resource, it searches for cookies stored by this specific server and returns this information. The server recognizes the information, reading it back from the headers of the HTTP request, and uses it to obtain the client's state.

. . . and Bad

However, cookies have some serious drawbacks. If a server sends portions of a page only, this very portion would send the information back to this server and not the one serving the main page. An advertising banner is an example of such a section. At the end of the last century, the company

DoubleClick (eventually bought out by Google) invented a business concept based on cookies. Once a banner ad appears, the cookies related to it are placed in the browser's memory. When the user moves to a page drawn from another server, but containing a banner pulled from the original ad server, the ad server's code would receive the same cookie back. The original server knows that the user has been on different pages, and it also recognizes where these pages originated. The cookie makes it possible for the ad server to trace the user and track his or her behavior. By the third page, the banner ad has not been selected at random. Based on the user's behavior, the ad server chooses the banner that best fits the user's interests. This leads to a much higher click rate, which in turn results in more money made. This is the concept invented by DoubleClick—with which Google now generates a lot of revenue. It is as simple as it sounds. However, it has faced criticism in that it compromises the user's privacy. The ad server knows much more of a user's behavior than people would tell strangers voluntarily. Since cookies work silently, the user is never asked to accept or deny them. Even if modern browsers managed cookies well, it's still a complicated task to deal with them, erasing them where appropriate and retaining them if harmless.

Beyond Cookies

Avoiding the usage of cookies or even limiting them to just one—to store the session state—would give your users the opportunity to operate within a restrictive cookie usage policy. It is an advantage for a site avoiding cookies. However, it makes your life as a developer much more difficult because cookies simplify the session handling. Fortunately, ASP.NET provides a number of sophisticated techniques that help you handle the drawbacks of HTTP's statelessness. In terms of the session state, you can decide whether to work with session cookies or without cookies at all.

ASP.NET maintains the cookieless session state by automatically inserting a unique session ID into the URL. This would look like this: `http://www.apress.com/` `(S(lit3jk26t05z64v14vlmo4so9))/default.aspx`.

The following configuration in the *web.config* file is required:

```
<configuration>
  <system.web>
    <sessionState cookieless="true" regenerateExpiredSessionId="true" />
  </system.web>
</configuration>
```

A session ID will eventually expire when the session ends, or has been timed out. In this case, the ID is recycled; a later session could have the same ID. If a URL is stored somewhere on the client—such as within the favorites folder, sent by email, or gathered by a search engine—this could cause a security hole, as the older session ID located in the URL could be the same as that of another current session. The `regenerateExpiredSessionId="true"` attribute reduces that risk by forcing it to create a new ID every time.

If this behavior is not sufficient for your application, you can write your own session ID module. For complete control, consider implementing the `ISessionIDManager` interface. To just control the creation of the ID, inherit from the `SessionIDManager` base class. Both types are defined in the `System.Web.SessionState` namespace.

The next example demonstrates how to replace the session ID with a custom value (see Listing 6-6).

Listing 6-6. *Simple Session ID Manager with Custom ID Creation*

```
namespace Apress.SessionState.Code
{
    public class SimpleSessionIDManager : SessionIDManager
    {
```

```
    public override string CreateSessionID(HttpContext context)
    {
        return Guid.NewGuid().ToString();
    }

    public override bool Validate(string id)
    {
        try
        {
            Guid testGuid = new Guid(id);
            if (id.Equals(testGuid.ToString()))
            {
                return true;
            }
        }
        catch
        {
        }
        return false;
    }

}
}
```

The only methods to override are `CreateSessionID` and `Validate`. However, the basic form of the ID, such as (S(...)), is still used. To obtain completely different behavior, you must implement the interface, which requires several additional methods to be implemented. This is achieved behind the scenes by adding the ID to the URL first and then redirecting to the new URL. The changed URL is then passed to the browser.

However you implement this, you must configure the new session ID manager in the *web.config* file:

```
<sessionState mode="InProc"
              cookieless="true"
              regenerateExpiredSessionId="false"
              timeout="20"
              sessionIDManagerType="Apress.SessionState.Code.MySessionIDManager, ➥
                                    Apress.SessionState"/>
```

The `sessionIDManagerType` attribute contains the class's name and the namespace of the containing assembly. All other options depend on the entire configuration and are not directly associated with the session ID manager.

The Internal State Providers

ASP.NET includes three internal state providers. You should investigate these before planning the development of a custom provider.

- `InProcSessionStateStore`
- `OutOfProcSessionStateStore`
- `SqlSessionStateStore`

This section gives a brief overview of the internal state providers, which have several features in common. You can control their behavior with the EnableSessionState attribute located in the @Page directive (see Figure 6-3).

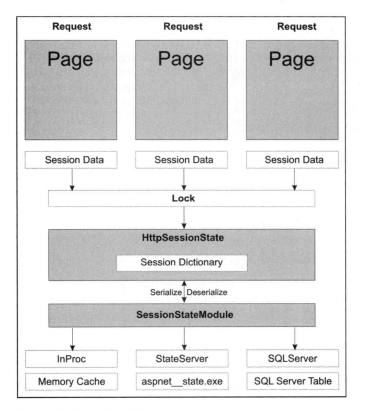

Figure 6-3. *Principles of the session state providers*

InProcSessionStateStore

The InProcSessionStateStore class defines the default session state provider if no other provider is specified. It stores session data within the current process, using the HttpCache module to store data in memory.

This provider is the most efficient. The overhead is limited to the extracting of the session ID and the serializing and deserializing of the data. Everything happens in memory using a cache lookup, which merely retrieves the data and refreshes the cache expiration timestamp.

However, the InProcSessionStateStore has some drawbacks. This provider does not survive an application restart, since the cache objects are rebuilt on restart—meaning all previous sessions would be lost. It also does not function reliably in web farm scenarios, where the next request might reach a different server that doesn't see the session data in the first server's memory.

The following *web.config* file snippet shows the configuration:

```
<sessionState
  mode="InProc"
  cookieless="false"
 />
```

OutOfProcSessionStateStore

This class enables out-of-process storage based on an unmanaged stream that is created when an incoming request is handled by the session state service. The stream is read from and written back to a state server service. This Windows service runs independently of IIS and allows the sharing of memory data through several servers that make up a web farm.

The provider is not as efficient as the in-process version, as it takes time to pass data beyond process boundaries. Internally, the process communicates with a Windows service that passes the data from one server to another using HTTP. This is a very slim and fast implementation of a Web Server handling only a subset of Web Server functions. While the HTTP protocol adds overhead to requests, the `OutOfProcSessionStateStore` will survive an application restart, as the storage is not part of the ASP.NET process.

The following snippet from the *web.config* file shows the configuration:

```
<sessionState
   mode="StateServer"
   stateConnectionString="tcpip=127.0.0.1:42424"
   cookieless="false"
 />
```

The service runs on local machines and on port 42424 by default.

The state service can be found here:

```
%systemroot%\Microsoft.NET\Framework\ <version>\aspnet_state.exe
```

It must be installed and started as a service. By default, it's installed, but set to start manually. To launch the service after the Web Server starts, set the ASP.NET state service's start option to *Automatic.*

SqlSessionStateStore

ASP.NET provides the `SqlSessionStateStore` in order to share state across multiple front-end servers. The provider consists of several pieces you must assemble:

- A data table for the session data

- Stored procedures to write and read the session data from SQL Server

- A connection string defined in *web.config,* which declares the database connection

- The `SqlSessionStateStore` set in the *web.config* as the default provider

To create the data table and add the stored procedures, use the Aspnet_reqsql.exe tool. You can find it at:

```
C:\Windows\Microsoft.NET\Framework\v2.0.50727
```

Details about all the command line options are at:

```
http://msdn.microsoft.com/en-us/library/ms229862.aspx
```

The tool also supports settings required by other SQL Server based modules. For the session state, the following options are important:

- `-S servername`: The name of the database server, such as *localhost\sqlexpress*

- `-d databasename`: The name of the database; requires `-sstype c`

- `-ssadd`: Adds support

- `-ssremove`: Removes support

- `-sstype t`: Installs the data table into the *tempdb* database

- `-sstype p`: Installs the data table into a persistent database, like *aspnetdb*

- `-sstype c`: Installs the data table into a custom database; use `-d databasename` to choose one

---

■Tip If you start the Aspnet_reqsql tool without any parameters, a wizard is launched that leads you through the required steps.

This *web.config* file snippet shows an example of the configuration:

```
<sessionState
   mode="SQLServer"
   cookieless="true"
   sqlConnectionString=" Integrated Security=SSPI;data source=MySqlServer;"
   sqlCommandTimeout="10" />
```

Improving the Session State

The session state service adds a considerable overhead to the performance of your application. Since it's a valuable tool, most developers choose to use session data. However, the serializing and deserializing procedures required for each request take time. If the application comes under pressure, and if you decide to work with a web farm in order to balance the load, things might become worse. The session-related traffic would increase on the local network between the SQL Server or State server and the Web Servers. There are several ways of improving performance, and it's important to think about these before you start creating your own session state providers.

Some optimizations are implemented by default in order to avoid having a bottleneck for standard features. First, the ability to handle the session state can be disabled. You can set this using the @Page directive:

- `EnableSessionState="true"`

- `EnableSessionState="false"`

- `EnableSessionState="ReadOnly"`

Enabling and disabling the session state is trivial; when disabled, no session data is stored. The ReadOnly option is more subtle. Imagine that a user has several browser windows or tabs open and all of them are in the same session using the same session ID. If the user accesses the Web Server multiple times at once, the first request gains exclusive access, locking access for other requests. The second request must wait in order to obtain its exclusive access when the first request ends. This could lead to an unsatisfactory user experience, as the user will probably open several windows to launch simultaneous tasks, such as downloading files. Instead of speeding things up, the windows would be blocked. To avoid this, the ReadOnly option is used to allow concurrent read access to the session data. The lock is still there for write access and it blocks other requests with same session ID. You will only benefit from this setting if you use the session variables carefully.

Implementing the Session State Store Provider

You might wish to create a custom session-state store provider to:

- Store session-state information in a data source other than SQL Server, such as a MySQL database or another third party database.

- Manage session-state information using a database schema that is different from the default database schema.

- Use a totally different storage strategy, such as the file system.

The Session State Module

Session state is managed by the SessionStateModule class, which calls the session-state stored provider to read and write data to the data store during a request. The module uses a SessionStateStoreProviderBase derived class as its data source. The actual implementation provides the members used here. See Table 6-1 for a list of all available members. At the start of a request, the SessionStateModule instance retrieves data from the data source by calling its GetItemExclusive or GetItem method. The exclusive access is the default; the GetItem method also supports the EnableSessionState="ReadOnly" attribute, allowing shared read access, as explained in the previous section. At the end of a request, if the session-state values have been changed, the SessionStateModule instance calls the SetAndReleaseItemExclusive method to write the updated values to the data store.

The SessionStateModule class itself determines the session ID value, rather than relying on the session-state store provider. The session ID manager is responsible for the ID format, which is based on the implementation of the SessionIDManager class. The SessionStateModule class reverts to the ASP.NET process identity in order to access any secured resource, such as a database server. You can specify the SessionStateModule instance to impersonate the process identity by setting the useHostingIdentity attribute of the <sessionState> configuration element to false.

```
<sessionState useHostingIdentity="false" />
```

If the useHostingIdentity attribute is true, ASP.NET will impersonate either the process identity or the user credentials when connecting to the data source. Usually this is a cumbersome process, as you'll have to manage all your users.

Table 6-1. *SessionStateStoreProvider Members*

Member	Description
InitializeRequest	Uses the HttpContext of the current request and performs any initialization required by the provider.
EndRequest	Uses the HttpContext of the current request and performs any cleanup.
Dispose	Frees any resources no longer in use by the provider.
GetItemExclusive	Retrieves session values and information from the session data store for a given Session ID and HttpContext. Locks the session-item data in the store for the duration of the request. Sets several output-parameter values that inform SessionStateModule about the state of the current item.

Member	Description
GetItem	Same as for the GetItemExclusive method, except that it does not attempt to lock the session item in the data store. This method is used when you set the EnableSessionState attribute of @Page directive to ReadOnly.
SetAndReleaseItemExclusive	Updates or releases the lock for the current session-state data. The newItem property forces the creation of a new item. Calls the ResetItemTimeout method internally to extend the expiration period.
ReleaseItemExclusive	This method is called when the GetItem or GetItemExclusive method is called and the item is locked, but the lock duration has exceeded the ExecutionTimeout value. Frees the item and releases the lock.
RemoveItem	This method is called when the Abandon method of the Session object is called. Deletes the session information from the data store.
CreateUninitializedItem	Adds an uninitialized item to the session data store with an actionFlags value set to InitializeItem.
CreateNewStoreData	Returns a new SessionStateStoreData object with empty data collections.
SetItemExpireCallback	Takes a delegate that references the Session_OnEnd event. If this event is supported, the method returns true; otherwise it returns false.

The GetItemExclusive method is the most significant part of the provider. If no session item data is found in the data store, the method sets the locked output parameter to false and returns null. This causes the SessionStateModule to call the CreateNewStoreData method in order to create a new SessionStateStoreData object for the request. If the item is located but the data is locked, the GetItemExclusive method sets the locked output parameter to true, sets the lockAge output parameter to the current age of the item (that is, current timestamp minus creation timestamp), sets the lockId output parameter to the lock identifier retrieved from the data store, and returns null. This causes the SessionStateModule to call the GetItemExclusive method again after a half-second interval in an attempt to retrieve the session-item information and obtain a lock on the data. If the lockAge exceeds the ExecutionTimeout value, SessionStateModule calls the ReleaseItemExclusive method in order to clear the lock on the session-item data and calls the GetItemExclusive method again.

The actionFlags parameter is used with sessions whose Cookieless property is true and whose regenerateExpiredSessionId attribute is set to true. The actionFlags value can be set to either InitializeItem or None. InitializeItem indicates that the entry in the session data store is a new session requiring initialization. Uninitialized entries are created by a call to the CreateUninitializedItem method. If the item from the session data store is already initialized, the actionFlags parameter is set to None.

If your provider supports cookieless sessions, set the actionFlags output parameter to the value returned from the session data store for the current item. If the actionFlags parameter value for the requested session-store item equals InitializeItem, the GetItemExclusive method should set the session data in the data store to zero after setting the actionFlags out parameter.

The CreateUninitializedItem method is used with cookieless sessions when the regenerateExpiredSessionId attribute is set to true. This causes the SessionStateModule to generate a new session ID value when an expired session is encountered. The process of generating a new session ID value requires the browser to be redirected to a URL that contains the newly generated ID. Refer to Listing 6-6 for an example of how to control the session ID generation process. The CreateUninitializedItem method is called during an initial request containing an expired session. After the SessionStateModule acquires a new ID to replace the expired one, it calls the CreateUninitializedItem method. The browser is then redirected to the URL containing the newly generated ID. The existence of the uninitialized entry in the session data store ensures that the redirected request with the newly generated ID is not mistaken for a request for an expired session, and is treated as a new session.

Preface

Before developing a new session state persister, let's briefly investigate what it can be used for. There are three major tasks:

- Handling session locking for concurrent requests to the same data
- Identifying and occasionally removing expired session data
- Allowing more than one application to use the provider

Locking Session-Store Data

ASP.NET applications respond to multiple concurrent requests. Those requests might attempt to access the same session information, as explained previously. When implementing your own provider, you'll need to manage the locking behavior. A lock is set on session-store data at the beginning of the request in the call to the GetItemExclusive method. When the request is completed, the lock is released during the call to the SetAndReleaseItemExclusive method. If the SessionStateModule instance encounters locked session data during the call to either the GetItemExclusive or GetItem method, it will re-request the session data. This occurs at half-second intervals until either the lock is released or the amount of time specified in the ExecutionTimeout property has elapsed. After a timeout occurs, the ReleaseItemExclusive method is called in order to free the session-store data. Additionally, a lock identifier is used to distinguish between concurrent requests accessing the same session data. This is necessary, as these requests run on separate threads. A call to the ReleaseItemExclusive appears before the SetAndReleaseItemExclusive method is called for the current response.

Handling Expired Data

Expiration occurs when a session times out or explicitly ends. A session ends with a user action, when the Abandon method is called. The data for that session is deleted from the data store using the RemoveItem method. The mechanism for deleting expired session data depends on the capabilities of your data source. If the session expires according to the session Timeout property, you can use the SetItemExpireCallback method to handle the Session_OnEnd event.

Set Application Name

To maintain session scope, session-state providers store session information uniquely for each application. This allows multiple ASP.NET applications to use the same data source without conflicting. How you ensure uniqueness depends entirely on the storage mechanism. For a file-based provider, as in the following example, a subfolder named after the application will suffice. In a database scenario, an *ApplicationName* column in the data table would be necessary.

Implementation of a File-Based Session State Persister

There are many steps to a complete implementation. None are difficult, but careful preparation is required. To implement a session store provider, you must create a class that inherits the SessionStateStoreProviderBase abstract class. This class in turn inherits the ProviderBase abstract class, so you must also implement the required members of the ProviderBase class. (Refer to Chapter 4 to read more about the structure of a provider.) The following tables list and describe the properties and methods you must implement from the abstract classes.

The following example shows the basic implementation steps for a file-based store. This is not intended for real-life scenarios, but simply for learning and testing. Files are easy to monitor and you can see where the data goes (see Listing 6-7).

Listing 6-7. *A Simple File-Based Session State Persister*

```
using System;
using System.Collections.Specialized;
using System.IO;
using System.Web;
using System.Web.Configuration;
using System.Web.SessionState;

namespace Apress.Extensibility.SessionState
{
    public sealed class FileSessionStateStore : SessionStateStoreProviderBase
    {
        private SessionStateSection sessconfig = null;
        private string basePath;
        private string applicationName;

        public string ApplicationName
        {
            get
            {
                return applicationName;
            }
        }

        public override void Initialize(string name, NameValueCollection config)
        {
            if (config == null)
            {
                throw new ArgumentNullException("config");
            }
            if (String.IsNullOrEmpty(name))
            {
                name = "FileSessionStateStore";
            }
            if (String.IsNullOrEmpty(config["description"]))
            {
                config.Remove("description");
                config.Add("description", "File Session State Store ➥
                                        provider example");
            }
            base.Initialize(name, config);
            applicationName = System.Web.Hosting.HostingEnvironment➥
                                        .ApplicationVirtualPath;
```

```
        basePath = config["basePath"];
        System.Configuration.Configuration cfg = WebConfigurationManager➥
                                .OpenWebConfiguration(ApplicationName);
        sessconfig = (SessionStateSection)cfg ➥
                            .GetSection("system.web/sessionState");
    }

    public override void Dispose()
    {
    }

    public override bool SetItemExpireCallback(➥
                        SessionStateItemExpireCallback expireCallback)
    {
        return false;
    }

    public override void SetAndReleaseItemExclusive(HttpContext context, ➥
                                            string id, ➥
                                            SessionStateStoreData item, ➥
                                            Object lockId, ➥
                                            bool newItem)
    {
        // Serialize the SessionStateItemCollection as a string.
        string sessItems = Serialize((SessionStateItemCollection)item.Items);
        string path = Path.Combine(basePath, String.Format("{0}.ssd", id));
        FileStream fs = null;
        try
        {
            if (newItem)
            {
                if (File.Exists(path))
                {
                    File.Delete(path);
                }
                fs = new FileStream(path, FileMode.CreateNew, ➥
                                        FileAccess.Write, FileShare.Read);
            }
            else
            {
                // update item
                fs = new FileStream(path, FileMode.Open, ➥
                                        FileAccess.Write, FileShare.Read);
            }
            StreamWriter sw = new StreamWriter(fs);
            sw.Write(sessItems);
            sw.Close();
        }
        catch (IOException exception)
        {
            // add error handling
        }
        finally
        {
            if (fs != null)
            {
                fs.Close();
```

```
                fs.Dispose();
        }
    }
}

public override SessionStateStoreData GetItem(HttpContext context, ➡
                                    string id, ➡
                                    out bool locked, ➡
                                    out TimeSpan lockAge,
                                    out object lockId, ➡
                                out SessionStateActions actionFlags)
{
    return GetSessionStoreItem(false, context, id, out locked, ➡
                        out lockAge, out lockId, out actionFlags);
}

public override SessionStateStoreData GetItemExclusive(HttpContext context,➡
                                    string id, ➡
                                    out bool locked, ➡
                                    out TimeSpan lockAge,
                                    out object lockId, ➡
                                out SessionStateActions actionFlags)
{
    return GetSessionStoreItem(true, context, id, out locked, ➡
                        out lockAge, out lockId, out actionFlags);
}

private SessionStateStoreData GetSessionStoreItem(bool lockRecord,
                                    HttpContext context,➡
                                    string id, ➡
                                    out bool locked, ➡
                                    out TimeSpan lockAge,
                                    out object lockId, ➡
                                out SessionStateActions actionFlags)
{
    // Initial values for Return value and out parameters.
    SessionStateStoreData item = null;
    lockAge = TimeSpan.Zero;
    lockId = null;
    locked = false;
    actionFlags = SessionStateActions.None;
    string serializedItems = String.Empty;
    string path = Path.Combine(basePath, String.Format("{0}.ssd", id));
    FileStream fs = null;
    try
    {
        fs = new FileStream(path, FileMode.Open, FileAccess.Read, ➡
                            FileShare.Read);
        StreamReader sr = new StreamReader(fs);
        serializedItems = sr.ReadToEnd();
        sr.Close();
    }
    catch (IOException)
    {
        // add error handling here
    }
    finally
```

```
        {
            if (fs != null)
            {
                fs.Close();
                fs.Dispose();
            }
        }
        item = Deserialize(context, serializedItems, 1024);
        return item;
    }

    private static string Serialize(SessionStateItemCollection items)
    {
        MemoryStream ms = new MemoryStream();
        BinaryWriter writer = new BinaryWriter(ms);
        if (items != null)
        {
            items.Serialize(writer);
        }
        writer.Close();
        return Convert.ToBase64String(ms.ToArray());
    }

    private static SessionStateStoreData Deserialize(HttpContext context, ➥
                                                     string serializedItems, ➥
                                                     int timeout)
    {
        MemoryStream ms = new MemoryStream( ➥
                              Convert.FromBase64String(serializedItems));
        SessionStateItemCollection sessionItems = ➥
                          new SessionStateItemCollection();
        if (ms.Length > 0)
        {
            BinaryReader reader = new BinaryReader(ms);
            sessionItems = SessionStateItemCollection.Deserialize(reader);
        }
        return new SessionStateStoreData(sessionItems, ➥
              SessionStateUtility.GetSessionStaticObjects(context), timeout);
    }

    public override void ReleaseItemExclusive(HttpContext context, ➥
                                              string id, object lockId)
    {
        // release lock
    }


    public override void RemoveItem(HttpContext context, string id, ➥
                                    object lockId, SessionStateStoreData item)
    {
        string path = Path.Combine(basePath, String.Format("{0}.ssd", id));
        File.Delete(path);
    }

    public override void CreateUninitializedItem(HttpContext context, string id,
                                                 int timeout)
    {
```

```
            string path = Path.Combine(basePath, String.Format("{0}.ssd", id));
            FileStream fs = File.Create(path);
            fs.Close();
        }

        public override SessionStateStoreData CreateNewStoreData(
                                        HttpContext context, int timeout)
        {

            return new SessionStateStoreData(new SessionStateItemCollection(), ➥
                    SessionStateUtility.GetSessionStaticObjects(context), timeout);
        }

        public override void ResetItemTimeout(HttpContext context, string id)
        {
            // refresh item
        }

        public override void InitializeRequest(HttpContext context)
        {
        }

        public override void EndRequest(HttpContext context)
        {

        }

    }
}
```

The implementation lacks error handling and several advanced features. However, the basic parts of the session provider are implemented to demonstrate how you can implement actions appropriate to the provider.

Essentially, the provider obtains session data, serializes it, and stores it in a file. The expiration handling is based on the file's last access timestamp. Concurrent access is also handled on the file level.

Configuring the Provider

Before you start working with the provider, you must configure the sessionState element in the *web.config* file, as shown in Listing 6-8.

Listing 6-8. *Configuring the Provider*

```
<sessionState
    cookieless="true"
    regenerateExpiredSessionId="false"
    timeout="20"
    mode="Custom"
    customProvider="FileSessionProvider"
    sessionIDManagerType="Apress.SessionState.Code.SimpleSessionIDManager,
                        Apress.SessionState">
    <providers>
        <add name="FileSessionProvider"
            type="Apress.Extensibility.SessionState.FileSessionStateStore,
                Apress.Extensibility.SessionState"
```

```
        basePath="c:\temp"/>
    </providers>
</sessionState>
```

There are at least three required settings. Firstly, the mode must be set to "Custom". Secondly, the customProvider attribute must be set to the name of the provider. Finally, the provider itself must be configured as a sub-element of the sessionState element. The additional basePath attribute is a private configuration setting used in the previous code.

With these settings, all session data is written to and retrieved from the file system, using the path *C:\temp* for the default (root) application and *c:\ temp\<appname>* for any other application.

Summary

In this chapter, we examined several persistence techniques, and discovered that both page persisters and session state persisters exist in order to overcome the limitations of HTTP's statelessness.

Page persisters store page or form related data using control state and view state. The default storage location is a hidden field within the form. An alternative method is to store the data in local memory. The provider model is used to customize this storage, and the sample implementation demonstrates how to store data in the file system.

Session state persisters, which are also based on the provider model, store session-related data. The preceding example also shows how to replace the default storage with custom storage, and how to store the data in the file system.

Extending persisters is a great way of improving performance, maintaining data within a web garden or farm, adding special features in order to handle specific environmental conditions, or better serving particular clients, such as mobile devices.

CHAPTER 7

■ ■ ■

Security and User Management

Most business applications include user management. Such applications must therefore handle security and user settings. In ASP.NET, you'll find a comprehensive collection of features, services, classes, and controls to manage users, as well as their roles, settings, and access conditions.

In this chapter, you'll learn about

- The components forming security and user management
- Extending the underlying providers, especially the Membership and Role providers
- Customizing and extending the Profile provider

All of these capabilities are based on the provider model introduced in Chapter 4. (Of course, that is the resource for more about the basic design of providers and how to extend and configure them.)

Built-In Capabilities

Conceptually, ASP.NET employs the principle of "gate keepers." A gate keeper is a module that sits on top of the pipeline observing every incoming request. Like any other module, its implementation is based on the `IHttpModule` interface. There are usually several such modules in a row, each of them handling a specific kind of access security or authorization. As you've learned in Chapters 3 to 6, the provider and module models are highly extensible. This gives you the opportunity to add new modules specific to the needs of your application and your desired security levels.

One of the basic concepts of web security is the statelessness of HTTP. Because the protocol essentially uses a "fire and forget" approach, the security aspects of every request must be checked. Since subsequent actions might require authorization or authentication, the security modules are positioned first in the line invoked by pipeline events, depending on actual configuration as seen in Figure 7-1.

The pipeline fires events in a specific order. First, the user is authenticated via the `AuthenticateRequest` event. After establishing the user's identity, authorization occurs, and the `AuthorizeRequest` event allows the user access to certain resources. The order in which these events are fired is crucial, as the session state becomes available only after both events are handled (see Figure 7-2). This means that no session-related data can be stored to support the authentication and authorization modules.

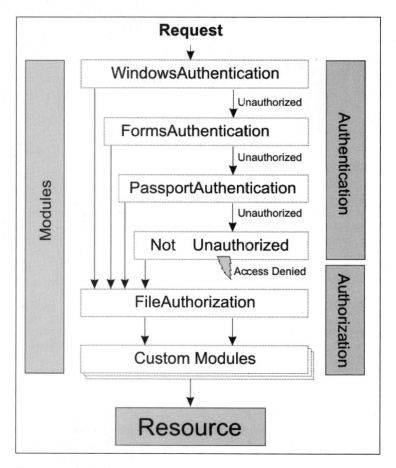

Figure 7-1. *The chain of authentication and authorization providers*

After successful user identification, their credentials are stored as an object containing their information. These credentials consist of a username/password pair and, optionally, additional data such as roles or lifetime. Different authorization techniques, such as Windows authentication or Basic authentication, create different sets of credentials. Information that must be available during the whole processing cycle is bound to the current context, namely the HttpContext object. The user credentials are stored in the User property, and can be accessed in this manner:

```
System.Web.Security.IPrincipal user = Context.User;
```

Context is provided by the Page class. If you're not using the Page class, HttpContext.Current. User retrieves the same object.

The IPrincipal interface is a simple definition for a credential store. It contains the user identity (accessible through the Identity property provided via an object that implements IIdentity) and the IsInRole method, to provide basic authorization support. However, this isn't sufficient for typical applications. Several different implementations of these interfaces are available that fill in the gaps. IIdentity provides additional support properties, while AuthenticationType indicates which method was used to authenticate a user—such as "Forms," "NTLM," or "Custom." IsAuthenticated reveals that one module of the chain of authentication modules has identified the user. Each module can check whether the previous module has identified the user and, if so, create the appropriate identity object and skip the module's own authentication process. Finally, the username is stored in the Name property of the IIdentity object as a unique key. There are several built-in implementations of the IIdentity interface:

- System.Web.Security.FormsIdentity
- System.Security.Principal.WindowsIdentity
- System.Security.Principal.GenericIdentity

The namespaces reveal that the identity model is not limited to Web applications. Instead, the identity model is embedded within the framework's security components, and as with most things in .NET, it is extensible.

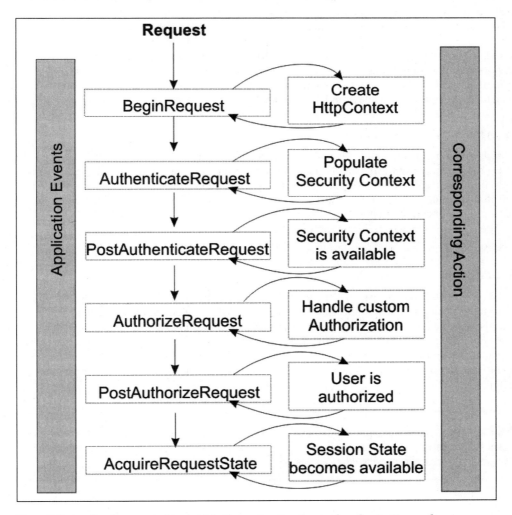

Figure 7-2. *Application events involved in the authentication and authorization cycle*

Authentication Modules

Several authentication modules are available in ASP.NET. Before building your own module, consider modifying an existing one. Identifying a module close to your requirements and customizing it is always a simpler solution than writing a new module from scratch. ASP.NET provides these core modules:

- FormsAuthenticationModule
- WindowsAuthenticationModule

The FormsAuthenticationModule provides a simple form-based technique which is highly compatible with most existing clients, but it is not the most secure. Unless the connection between the client and server uses SSL (secure socket layer), the username and password travel unencrypted at least once through the Internet. For most applications, this isn't acceptable. The WindowsAuthenticationModule, on the other hand, requires specific support from the client. Although most browsers handle it well, keep in mind that some devices (such as mobile gadgets) could fail. The PassportAuthenticationModule is not listed because it isn't a viable alternative and marked as deprecated. Microsoft's Passport concept was discontinued and has now been replaced by Live ID, which has not yet attracted wide-spread client support.

Set Up the Authentication Module

To set up an authentication module, you'll need to make an entry in the *web.config* file. The element `<authentication>` is responsible for defining and configuring the appropriate module. As a module is responsible for handling all incoming requests, you can't define the element in subfolders, and overriding the root settings would create a conflict within the pipeline. (However, this will be possible for the authorization method discussed in the section "Authorization Modules.")

The mode attribute has three commonly used values:

```
<authentication mode="Forms" />
<authentication mode="Windows" />
<authentication mode="None" />
```

As there is no "Custom" value, you'll have to utilize one of the existing techniques when you add your own membership system. (The "Custom" value isn't provided because you'd need to support existing clients, and writing custom clients isn't feasible.) Web applications that deal with private data are usually protected by a form of transport layer security that allows the usage of forms authentication for publicly accessible sites and Windows authentication for intranet applications. For the configuration of forms authentication, the child element `<form>` provides the appropriate settings.

■**Note** IIS7 has several more capabilities to set up both authentication and authorization. Because it's out of scope of this chapter, the security settings provided here are just to get the examples running. The description is in no way complete enough for security-driven applications.

Authorization Modules

After authenticating the user, you need to determine what he or she is permitted to request. This is all about accessing resources. As there are two kinds of resources on a Web Server, files and URLs, there are two built-in authorization modules:

- FileAuthorization

- UrlAuthorization

If you have already set up the membership system and not defined the authorization explicitly, you might wonder how it works as expected. This is because ASP.NET uses the FileAuthorization module if Windows authentication is set. No additional configuration step is required. Thus, if Window authentication is used, the NTFS file access security is employed, based on Windows ACLs (access control lists).

Using Impersonation

In the context of Windows authentication, impersonation occurs when the identity of the logged-in user is changed and the new identity's credentials are used to access resources. This is a common technique, but it's dangerous. If the user base is large, and the roles and access policies grow, management becomes arduous. Furthermore, authentication mistakes create security holes, as parts of the application could run under an account other than that intended by the developer.

Set Up Authorization

The URL authorization controls access to directories and files. It can be configured by setting the appropriate child elements of the current <authorization> element. Restrictions may be set based on both user and role. File authorization does not require any settings here.

To manage the authorization, two elements are crucial: <deny> and <allow>. Both accept a few attributes:

- Users: A list of user accounts

- Roles: A list of roles

- Verbs: A list of HTTP transmission methods

Using these settings, you can explicitly allow or deny access to users, roles, or regarding a HTTP method like GET or POST. The users attribute accepts two special characters. You can specify all users with an asterisk "*" and all anonymous users with a question mark "?". Lists of both roles and users are comma-separated.

The User Management Interfaces

Included with ASP.NET are a number of tools to support user management, the details of which are beyond the scope of this book. However, I'll give a general overview of the extensibility interfaces. There are three parts responsible for handling user management: .

- Membership service

- Role service

- Profile service

Membership is about user identification and management. With the appropriate classes and controls, you can create, edit, and delete user accounts. This includes login and logout facilities based on controls, as well as several features that enhance user experience (such as password recovery or ability to view the current name and login status). ASP.NET includes several built-in management tools to assist administrators with handling users, based on a SQL Server database store.

Role performs authorization tasks. Roles provide access to resources and can be assigned to many users. If the user becomes a member of a role, he or she gains access to the resources the role is permitted to retrieve. The built-in management tools support the role model.

Profile complements the user management by adding a user-specific data store. This allows you to maintain per-user settings between visits. Profiles are not intended to support session-related processes. Instead, they allow a user to customize a site specifically for their own preferences—think of a "MySite" type of functionality. ASP.NET includes many features, services, and object types to support profiles.

Extensibility Issues

The extensibility model is based on providers. The three services previously mentioned use providers to save and retrieve their data. By default, data is stored in a SQL Server database. It's often necessary to use alternative or existing storage, Active Directory, LDAP, or a custom solution. Several built-in providers are included with each service in order to support different stores (see Figure 7-3).

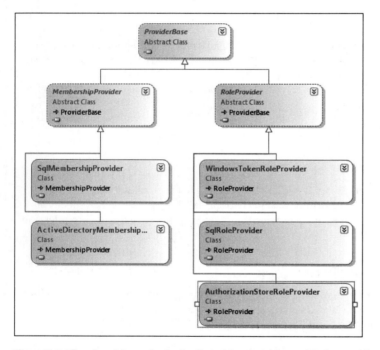

Figure 7-3. *The class hierarchy for built-in Membership and Role providers*

The default providers use a SQL Server database. These are the SqlMembershipProvider and the SqlRoleProvider. ASP.NET also supports Active Directory (AD) out of the box, via the ActiveDirectoryMembershipProvider.

Table 7-1 shows all the basic members of the Membership provider classes.

Table 7-1. *Members of the MembershipProvider Classes**

Name	Description
Methods	
ChangePassword	Changes the password.
ChangePasswordQuestionAndAnswer	Changes the password question and answer.
CreateUser	Creates a new user.
DecryptPassword	Decrypts the password.
DeleteUser	Deletes a user.
EncryptPassword	Encrypts the password.
FindUsersByEmail	Finds a user using his or her email address.
FindUsersByName	Finds a user using his or her name.
GetAllUsers	Retrieves a list of all users.
GetNumberOfUsersOnline	Retrieves a list of all currently logged-in users. The behavior depends on the provider and does not necessarily report the exact value.
GetPassword	Retrieves the password for a given name.
GetUser	Retrieves a System.Web.Security.MembershipUser object based on the name.
GetUserNameByEmail	Retrieves the name using an email address.
Initialize	Initializes the provider. Inherited from ProviderBase.
ResetPassword	Resets the current password with an automatically generated one.
UnlockUser	Unlocks a locked user.
UpdateUser	Updates the user's information in the data store.
ValidateUser	Checks whether the user with the provided password is a legitimate user.
Events	
ValidatingPassword	An event fired while the provider validates the password.
Properties	
ApplicationName	The name of the application. A Membership provider can support several applications and supports different data storage for each application. Inherited from ProviderBase.
EnablePasswordReset	Defines whether or not the user can reset their password.
EnablePasswordRetrieval	Defines whether or not the user can retrieve their password.
MaxInvalidPasswordAttempts	Determines the maximum number of false password attempts allowed before the account is locked.
MinRequiredNonAlphanumericCharacters	Minimum number of non-alphanumeric characters a password must have.
MinRequiredPasswordLength	Minimum password length.
Name	Name of the provider. Inherited from ProviderBase.

Continued

Table 7-1. *Continued*

Name	Description
PasswordAttemptWindow	Prevents "brute force" attempts to guess a password. If the MaxInvalidPasswordAttempts occur within PasswordAttemptWindow (in minutes), that user's account is locked.
PasswordFormat	Format in which the password is saved in the storage. This is a value from the enumeration MembershipPasswordFormat, which provides the values Clear, Hashed, or Encrypted. Hashes are unidirectional encryption methods. The default hash format is SHA1.
PasswordStrengthRegularExpression	A regular expression that is used to check whether or not the password meets the minimum password strength required by your application.
RequiresQuestionAndAnswer	Determines whether the provider supports the password retrieval using the question and answer technique.
RequiresUniqueEmail	Determines whether or not the email address must be unique in the database.

Covers both SqlMembershipProvider and ActiveDirectoryMembershipProvider

For the Role provider, things look a little different. The AuthorizationStoreRoleProvider class supports three kinds of role data storage: the Active Directory itself, an Active Directory Application Mode server (ADAM), or an XML file. For these three modes, a connection string defines the data source. The connection string begins with msxml:// for an XML file, or with msldap:// for Active Directory or ADAM , as shown in the following code:

```
<connectionStrings>
    <add name="AuthorizationServices" ➥
        connectionString="msxml://~\App_Data\MyAdamStore.xml" />
</connectionStrings>
```

The WindowsTokenRoleProvider uses the local Windows user database to retrieve the role information. Don't confuse this with Windows groups. Direct access to Windows group information is not supported by this provider. While you can obtain membership information about a group, you cannot write, delete, or change these memberships even if management tools support this. From the perspective of ASP.NET, the WindowsTokenRoleProvider provides read-only access.

None of these classes are sealed. This means that you can inherit from each class and override methods and properties to change behavior as desired.

Table 7-2 shows all basic members of the Role provider classes.

Table 7-2. *Members of the RoleProvider Classes*

Name	Description	Not Supported In*
Methods		
AddUsersToRoles	Add users to roles. Defined in RoleProvider.	W
CreateRole	Create a new role. Defined in RoleProvider.	W
DeleteRole	Delete a role. Defined in RoleProvider.	W
FindUsersInRole	Find all users within a role. Defined in RoleProvider.	W, A
GetAllRoles	Get a list of all roles. Defined in RoleProvider.	W

Name	Description	Not Supported In*
GetRolesForUser	Get all roles for a user. Defined in `RoleProvider`.	
GetUsersInRole	Get all users in a role. Defined in `RoleProvider`.	W
IsUserInRole	Indicates whether or not a user is in a role. Defined in `RoleProvider`.	
RemoveUsersFromRoles	Remove users from roles. Defined in `RoleProvider`.	W
RoleExists	Indicates whether the role exists. Defined in `RoleProvider`.	
Properties		
ApplicationName	Name of the application. A Role provider can support several applications and different data storage for each application. Defined in `ProviderBase`.	
Description	Description used in `ProviderBase`.	
ScopeName	Scope for the authorization store.	W, S
CacheRefreshInterval	Time (in minutes) the provider caches role information.	W, S

W = WindowsTokenRoleProvider, S = SqlRoleProvider, A = AuthorizationStoreRoleProvider

With this overview of the capabilities of different providers, you can now investigate how to extend them.

Extending Membership and Role Providers

The functionality of the built-in providers suits most common types of applications. Before constructing your own provider, let's take a look at when and why it's more practical to create or extend a built-in one.

Why Create a Membership Provider?

The purpose of a provider is to manage access to data storage. Extending the provider model is necessary if you want to use a different storage for your user database. The `SqlMembershipProvider` supports a SQL Server database, while the `ActiveDirectoryMembershipProvider` supports the Active Directory. Creating a service infrastructure following the principles of service-oriented architectures (SOA) requires another method—Web Services. One reason for creating a custom Membership provider is the ability to use Web Services. As shown in Table 7-1, the `MembershipProvider` base class supports an incredible number of features. Whether you require some or all of these depends on the needs of your application.

In the following example, I'll demonstrate the basic principles of a custom Membership provider in the particular case of authenticating users against a Web Service. The service provides a transparent tier against a data store. This means that the service can run anywhere in your organization as a central point of service, and the users of the service—the provider—knows nothing about the data storage behind the service. Security is enhanced by hiding all data storage implementation details behind the publicly visible Web Service methods. For simplicity and demonstration purposes only, the example service stores user information in a simple XML file. This allows you to observe the file and learn exactly how the provider behaves.

In the following sections, I'll show the sample code and explain the implementation details.

Solution Details

Developing a custom provider first requires a data source. In this example, I'll use an XML file as storage and a WCF (Windows Communication Foundation) service to access the file remotely. This demonstrates that it's possible to transparently access a remote data store using standard framework techniques.

The solution consists of the following:

- A WCF service project with two services, one for membership and the other for roles
- A Web project configured to use the custom provider that has

    - An implementation of a custom Membership provider
    - An implementation of a custom Role provider
    - A service reference to use the WCF service

Developing Membership and Role Providers

Both Membership and Role providers support several features. Whether or not you implement all features, extend additional ones, or simply create a rudimentary service depends on your application and requirements. In this example, I'll implement all the basic features via a simplified approach for the sake of brevity.

Create Web Service–Driven Membership Provider

The Web Service–driven Membership provider consists of the following three parts:

1. The user data store—an XML file
2. The service tier—a Web Service with several useful methods
3. The Membership provider implementation

Create Web Service–Driven Role Provider

The Web service–driven Role provider also consists of the following three parts:

1. The same XML file as used in the user data store, extended with role properties
2. The service tier—a Web Service with several useful methods
3. The Role provider implementation

For both providers, we'll need a simple test environment. Consider creating some pages using various Login controls, such as the CreateUserWizard. This functions well but requires additional work. To begin with, I recommend using the built-in ASP.NET configuration application. Launch it locally in Visual Studio from the *Project* and *ASP.NET configuration* menu items. Using the embedded Web Server, Visual Studio starts a Web application that allows you to manage users and roles with the current provider. Before doing so, you'll need to configure the providers. However, we'll begin by developing the entire application.

Developing the Service Tier

The service tier uses WCF to create two Web Services, one for membership management and one for role management. To create the service:

1. Within Visual Studio, create a new project via *File* ➤ *New* ➤ *Project* ➤ *Web* ➤ *WCF Service Library.*

2. Name the project "Membership."

3. Add two services to the project using *Add* from the context menu. Select *New Item,* and in the following dialog choose *WCF Service* (see Figure 7-4).

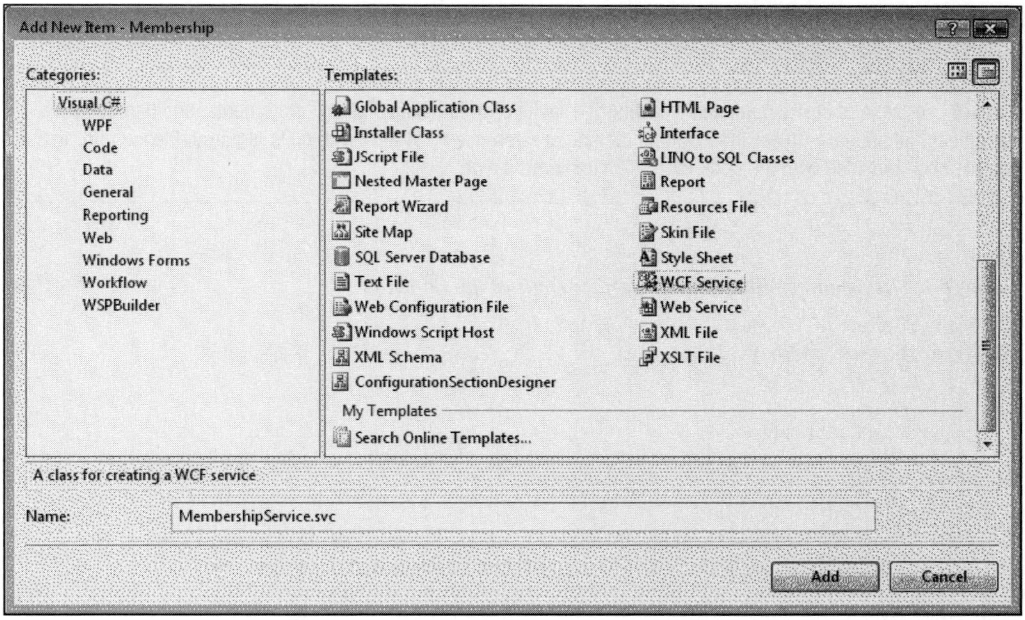

Figure 7-4. *Adding a new WCF service to the service library*

The wizard creates a service interface (the contract for the service), the class with the implementation, and the required entries in *web.config* or *App.config* file to define the service endpoint. The configuration file depends on type of project. The endpoint is a definition used later in the Web application where you can access the service. The contract is usually an interface decorated with the [ServiceContract] attribute. Each method that is exposed as a service call is decorated with the [OperationContract] attribute. Both attributes support several settings for modifying behavior and appearance. However, this is beyond the scope of this book, and default settings can be used for this example as well.

■**Tip** If you want to learn more about professional WCF development, refer to the book *Pro WCF: Practical Microsoft SOA Implementation* by Amit Bahree, Shawn Cicoria, Dennis Mulder, Nishith Pathak, and Chris Peiris (Apress, 2007).

Creating the Membership Service

The Membership service consists of the following interfaces and classes:

- IMembershipService interface
- MembershipService service
- MembershipService class
- UserData class
- User class
- FileManager class

All the code to build the service is shown and explained in the following.

■**Note** For sake of brevity and space, Listing 7-1 lacks error handling, "using" statements, and namespace definitions. Additionally, to get the example running, a reference to System.web.dll is required. Please refer to the sample code provided with the book for the full implementation.

Listing 7-1. *The IMembershipService Interface Defines the Contract*

```
[ServiceContract]
public interface IMembershipService
{

    [OperationContract]
    bool ChangePassword(string username, string oldPassword, string newPassword);

    [OperationContract]
    bool ChangePasswordQuestionAndAnswer(string username, string password, ➥
                                        string newPasswordQuestion, ➥
                                        string newPasswordAnswer);

    [OperationContract]
    User CreateUser(string username, string password, string email, ➥
                    string passwordQuestion, string passwordAnswer, ➥
                    bool isApproved, object providerUserKey, ➥
                    out MembershipCreateStatus status);

    [OperationContract]
    bool DeleteUser(string username, bool deleteAllRelatedData);

    [OperationContract]
    List<User> FindUsersByEmail(string emailToMatch, int pageIndex, ➥
                                int pageSize, out int totalRecords);

    [OperationContract]
    List<User> FindUsersByName(string usernameToMatch, int pageIndex, ➥
                                int pageSize, out int totalRecords);

    [OperationContract]
    List<User> GetAllUsers(int pageIndex, int pageSize, out int totalRecords);
```

```
[OperationContract]
int GetNumberOfUsersOnline();

[OperationContract]
string GetPassword(string username, string answer);

[OperationContract(Name = "GetUserbyName")]
User GetUser(string username, bool userIsOnline);

[OperationContract]
string GetUserNameByEmail(string email);

[OperationContract]
string ResetPassword(string username, string answer);

[OperationContract]
bool UnlockUser(string userName);

[OperationContract]
void UpdateUser(User user);

[OperationContract]
bool ValidateUser(string username, string password);

}
```

The interface is not unusual. Each method decorated with the OperationContract attribute is exposed by the service. As shown in the listing for the GetUser method, the method's name can be modified. This is necessary if you wish to use overloaded methods (methods that have the same name, but a different parameter list signature). The service lacks this capability and requires unique names. The OperationContract attribute's Name property separates internal logic from the external service façade.

Once the interface is completed, it must be implemented. Begin with a service file that links to a code-behind file (see Listings 7-2).

Listing 7-2. *The MembershipService.svc File Is Required in Order to Publish the Service*

```
<%@ ServiceHost Language="C#" Debug="true" ➥
    Service="Apress.Extensibility.Membership.MembershipService" ➥
    CodeBehind="MembershipService.svc.cs" %>
```

The logic of the service is coded in the code-behind file, shown in Listing 7-3.

Listing 7-3. *The MembershipService Class Is the Implementation*

```
[FileIOPermission(SecurityAction.LinkDemand)]
public class MembershipService : IMembershipService
{

    public bool ChangePassword(string username, string oldPassword, ➥
                               string newPassword)
    {
        throw new NotImplementedException();
    }

    public bool ChangePasswordQuestionAndAnswer(string username, string password, ➥
                                        string newPasswordQuestion, ➥
```

```
                                                  string newPasswordAnswer)
    {
        throw new NotImplementedException();
    }

    public User CreateUser(string username, string password, string email, ➥
                           string passwordQuestion, string passwordAnswer, ➥
                           bool isApproved, object providerUserKey, ➥
                           out System.Web.Security.MembershipCreateStatus status)
    {
        User user = null;
        UserData ud = FileManager.Load();
        // check users, consider adding more data here
        var hasUser = from u in ud.Users where u.UserName.Equals(username) select u;
        if (hasUser.Count() > 0)
        {
            status = MembershipCreateStatus.DuplicateUserName;
            return null;
        }
        var hasEmail = from u in ud.Users where u.Email.Equals(email) select u;
        if (hasEmail.Count() > 0)
        {
            status = MembershipCreateStatus.DuplicateEmail;
            return null;
        }
        try
        {
            user = new User(
                username,
                email,
                passwordQuestion,
                "",
                isApproved,
                false,
                DateTime.Now,
                DateTime.MinValue,
                DateTime.MinValue,
                DateTime.Now,
                DateTime.MinValue);
            // Store Hash Only
            user.Password = FileManager.CalculateSHA1(password);
            ud.Users.Add(user);
            FileManager.Save(ud);
            status = MembershipCreateStatus.Success;
        }
        catch
        {
            status = MembershipCreateStatus.ProviderError;
        }
        return user;
    }

    public bool DeleteUser(string username, bool deleteAllRelatedData)
    {
        UserData ud = FileManager.Load();
        var user = (from u in ud.Users
                    where u.UserName.Equals(username)
```

```
                        select u).FirstOrDefault<User>();
        if (user != null)
        {
            ud.Users.Remove(user);
            FileManager.Save(ud);
            return true;
        }
        return false;
    }

    public List<User> FindUsersByEmail(string emailToMatch, int pageIndex, ➥
                                 int pageSize, out int totalRecords)
    {
        UserData ud = FileManager.Load();
        var users = (from u in ud.Users
                     where u.Email.Equals(emailToMatch)
                     select u).ToList<User>();
        totalRecords = users.Count();
        return GetPaged(users, pageIndex, pageSize);
    }

    public List<User> FindUsersByName(string usernameToMatch, int pageIndex, ➥
                                 int pageSize, out int totalRecords)
    {
        UserData ud = FileManager.Load();
        var users = (from u in ud.Users
                     where u.UserName.Equals(usernameToMatch)
                     select u).ToList<User>();
        totalRecords = users.Count();
        return GetPaged(users, pageIndex, pageSize);
    }

    public List<User> GetAllUsers(int pageIndex, int pageSize, out int totalRecords)
    {
        UserData ud = FileManager.Load();
        totalRecords = ud.Users.Count;
        return GetPaged(ud.Users, pageIndex, pageSize);
    }

    private List<User> GetPaged(List<User> ud, int pageIndex, int pageSize)
    {
        pageSize = Math.Min(ud.Count, pageSize);
        return ud.GetRange(pageIndex * pageSize, pageSize);
    }

    public int GetNumberOfUsersOnline()
    {
        // Users who logged in within the last 15 mins
        UserData ud = FileManager.Load();
        var users = (from u in ud.Users
                     where u.LastActivityDate.AddMinutes(15) > DateTime.Now
                     select u);
        return users.Count();
    }

    public string GetPassword(string username, string answer)
    {
```

```csharp
        UserData ud = FileManager.Load();
        var user = (from u in ud.Users
                    where u.UserName.Equals(username) &&  ➥
                        u.PasswordAnswer.Equals(answer)
                    select u).First<User>();
        if (user != null)
        {
            return user.Password;
        }
        return null;
    }

    public User GetUser(string username, bool userIsOnline)
    {
        UserData ud = FileManager.Load();
        var user = (from u in ud.Users
                    where u.UserName.Equals(username) &&
                    (userIsOnline) ?
                        u.LastActivityDate.AddMinutes(15) > DateTime.Now :
                        true // all users
                    select u).FirstOrDefault<User>();
        return user;
    }

    public string GetUserNameByEmail(string email)
    {
        UserData ud = FileManager.Load();
        var user = (from u in ud.Users
                    where u.Email.Equals(email)
                    select u).FirstOrDefault<User>();
        if (user != null)
        {
            return user.UserName;
        }
        return null;
    }

    public string ResetPassword(string username, string answer)
    {
        UserData ud = FileManager.Load();
        var user = (from u in ud.Users
                    where u.UserName.Equals(username) &&  ➥
                        u.PasswordAnswer.Equals(answer)
                    select u).FirstOrDefault<User>();
        if (user != null)
        {
            return user.Password;
        }
        return null;
    }

    public bool UnlockUser(string userName)
    {
        throw new NotImplementedException();
    }

    public void UpdateUser(User user)
```

```
    {
        UserData ud = FileManager.Load();
        var userToUpdate = (from u in ud.Users
                            where u.UserName.Equals(user.UserName)
                            select u).FirstOrDefault<User>();
        foreach (PropertyInfo pi in user.GetType().GetProperties(➥
                 BindingFlags.Public | BindingFlags.Instance))
        {
            PropertyInfo piTarget = typeof(User).GetProperty(pi.Name);
            if (piTarget != null)
            {
                piTarget.SetValue(userToUpdate, pi.GetValue(user, null), null);
            }
        }
        FileManager.Save(ud);
    }

    public bool ValidateUser(string username, string password)
    {
        UserData ud = FileManager.Load();
        string hash = FileManager.CalculateSHA1(password);
        var user = (from u in ud.Users
                    where u.UserName.Equals(username) &&
                          u.Password.Equals(hash)
                    select u).FirstOrDefault<User>();
        user.LastActivityDate = DateTime.Now;
        FileManager.Save(ud);
        return (user != null);
    }
}
```

Most of these methods follow the same code pattern. The current content of the membership data store—an XML file—is loaded by calling `FileManager.Load` (see Listing 7-6, later in this chapter). This ensures that changes made by parallel calls are handled properly. Each method uses a LINQ query to obtain the required data. If the method needs to persist changes, the updated `UserData` object is saved back to the storage file.

■**Tip** If you want to learn more about LINQ, I recommend *LINQ for Visual C# 2008* by Fabio Claudio Ferracchiati (Apress, 2008).

Passwords require special treatment. They aren't usually stored in an unencrypted format, so you'll need to choose to either encrypt the password or store a hash of the password.

Hashes are a one-way encryption technique. To validate a user logging in, you simply hash their supplied password and compare the result with the stored hash value. Storing a hash is good practice, because the hash algorithm was designed to make it almost impossible to derive the original text from the hash value. On the other hand, the hash doesn't support password retrieval. Instead, the user receives a new password when he or she requests a lost one. This requires more effort, as the provider must create generic passwords, and the application must support password change forms, and so forth. In the example, the password is stored as a hash, despite there being no password generator. The password is hashed using the SHA1 hash algorithm. This is safe and easy to use. Listing 7-6 shows the `FileManager.CalculateSHA1` method. If you plan to implement the provider in an application, consider using an encrypted password that you can decrypt on request.

The code also has a hard-coded setting for the calculation of the number of users online (the GetNumberOfUsersOnline method). Based on the time of last activity, all users that have logged in within the last 15 minutes are counted as being online. The LastActivityDate property is set in the ValidateUser method. This is an extremely simplified algorithm, but it demonstrates one possible approach.

One significant method is CreateUser. It checks several conditions in order to avoid duplicate usernames, email addresses, or other unwanted data. The example checks just two of a wide range of possible conditions. First, it tests for duplicate user names. If this occurs, the method sets the property status to MembershipCreateStatus.DuplicateUserName. Second, it checks for duplicate email addresses and sets the status to MembershipCreateStatus.DuplicateEmail, if required. You can refer to the MembershipCreateStatus enumeration to find more return values and conditions to test. If everything checks out, the MembershipCreateStatus.Success value is set. The MembershipCreateStatus.ProviderError condition is used if unexpected errors are caught by the try-catch statement.

The class uses the UserData class heavily. This class is straightforward, containing a serializable collection of User and Role objects, as shown in Listing 7-4.

Listing 7-4. *The UserData Class Is the Container for Serializing Users and Roles*

```
public class UserData
{

    public UserData()
    {
    }

    [XmlElement]
    public List<User> Users
    {
        get;
        set;
    }

    [XmlElement]
    public List<string> Roles
    {
        get;
        set;
    }

}
```

Because the serialization uses the XmlSerializer, all elements requiring serialization are tagged with the XmlElement attribute. The User object contains all data pertaining to a specific account. This class is shown next in Listing 7-5.

Listing 7-5. *The User Class Serializes a Single User*

```
[Serializable]
[DataContract]
public class User
{
    public User()
    {
    }
```

```
public User(string name, string email, string passwordQuestion, ➡
        string comment, bool isApproved, bool isLockedOut, ➡
        DateTime creationDate, DateTime lastLoginDate, ➡
        DateTime lastActivityDate, DateTime lastPasswordChangedDate, ➡
        DateTime lastLockoutDate)
{
    this.UserName = name;
    this.Email = email;
    this.Comment = comment;
    this.IsApproved = isApproved;
    this.IsLockedOut = isLockedOut;
    this.CreationDate = creationDate;
    this.LastLoginDate = lastLoginDate;
    this.PasswordQuestion = passwordQuestion;
    this.LastActivityDate = lastActivityDate;
    this.LastPasswordChangedDate = lastPasswordChangedDate;
    this.LastLockoutDate = lastLockoutDate;
}

[DataMember]
[XmlElement]
public string Comment { get; set; }
[DataMember]
[XmlElement]
public DateTime CreationDate { get; set; }
[DataMember]
[XmlElement]
public string Email { get; set; }
[DataMember]
[XmlAttribute]
public bool IsApproved { get; set; }
[DataMember]
[XmlAttribute]
public bool IsLockedOut { get; set; }
[DataMember]
[XmlElement]
public DateTime LastActivityDate { get; set; }
[DataMember]
[XmlElement]
public DateTime LastLockoutDate { get; set; }
[DataMember]
[XmlElement]
public DateTime LastLoginDate { get; set; }
[DataMember]
[XmlElement]
public DateTime LastPasswordChangedDate { get; set; }
[DataMember]
[XmlElement]
public string PasswordQuestion { get; set; }
[DataMember]
[XmlElement]
public string PasswordAnswer { get; set; }
[DataMember]
[XmlElement]
public string UserName { get; set; }
[DataMember]
[XmlElement]
```

```csharp
        public string Password { get; set; }

        [DataMember]
        [XmlArray(ElementName="Roles"), XmlArrayItem(ElementName="Role")]
        public List<string> Roles
        {
            get;
            set;
        }

        public bool ChangePassword(string oldPassword, string newPassword)
        {
            if (Password.Equals(oldPassword))
            {
                Password = newPassword;
                return true;
            }
            return false;
        }
        public bool ChangePasswordQuestionAndAnswer(string password, ➥
                string newPasswordQuestion, string newPasswordAnswer)
        {
            if (Password.Equals(password))
            {
                PasswordQuestion = newPasswordQuestion;
                PasswordAnswer = newPasswordAnswer;
                return true;
            }
            return false;
        }
        public string GetPassword(string passwordAnswer)
        {
            return Password;
        }
        public string ResetPassword()
        {
            return Password;
        }
        public string ResetPassword(string passwordAnswer)
        {
            return Password;
        }
        public bool UnlockUser()
        {
            return IsLockedOut = false;
        }
}
```

This class supports two features. It must be transferred via the service and it is part of the data contract. A data contract in WCF defines the structure of complex data. Applying the DataContract attribute to a class makes that class into a data contract. Each serializable member in the data contract class is tagged with the DataMemberAttribute. In the example, the same class is used internally to serialize the user objects to the XML file. The XmlElement attributes mark the elements to be serialized.

Each user can be the member of none, one, or many roles. The roles are simple strings stored in another collection. To reference the roles in the user object, a copy of the role's name is stored. A List<string> object is used internally. However, in XML, the format should be more readable. The XmlArray and XmlArrayItem attributes ensure that the element names are correct. Refer to Listing 7-7, later in this chapter, to view the created XML.

In Listing 7-6, the helper class is shown to complete the code needed to build the service.

Listing 7-6. *A Helper Class That Is Used to Access the Data File*

```
internal static class FileManager
{
    private const string DATAPATH = "App_Data\\UserData.xml";
    private static readonly string dataPath;
    private static object locker = new object();

    static FileManager()
    {
        Uri codeUri = new Uri(typeof(UserData).Assembly.CodeBase);
        dataPath = Path.Combine(Directory.GetParent( ➥
                    Path.GetDirectoryName(codeUri.LocalPath)).FullName, DATAPATH);
        // check file permissions
        FileIOPermission permission = new FileIOPermission( ➥
                    FileIOPermissionAccess.AllAccess, dataPath);
        permission.Demand();
    }

    internal static UserData Load()
    {
        lock (locker)
        {
            XmlSerializer xs = new XmlSerializer(typeof(UserData));
            UserData ud = null;
            try
            {
                using (FileStream fs = new FileStream(dataPath, FileMode.Open))
                {
                    ud = xs.Deserialize(fs) as UserData;
                }
            }
            catch
            {
                // save rudimentary format
                ud = new UserData();
                Save(ud);
            }
            return ud;
        }
    }

    internal static void Save(UserData ud)
    {
        lock (locker)
        {
            XmlSerializer xs = new XmlSerializer(typeof(UserData));
            using (FileStream fs = new FileStream(dataPath, FileMode.Create))
            {
```

```
                xs.Serialize(fs, ud);
            }
        }
    }

    internal static string CalculateSHA1(string text)
    {
        byte[] buffer = Encoding.ASCII.GetBytes(text);
        SHA1CryptoServiceProvider cryptoTransformSHA1 = ➥
                            new SHA1CryptoServiceProvider();
        string hash = BitConverter.ToString( ➥
                    cryptoTransformSHA1.ComputeHash(buffer));
        return hash;
    }
}
```

The class is static and provides three methods. With Load, the caller can retrieve the current contents of the stored data. In Save, the data is written back to disk. Both methods block concurrent threads because this is a multi-threaded environment. The thread handling is in neither way optimized but gives you the idea what you should be aware of.

The CalculateSHA1 method creates the SHA1 hash of a given string. It's used internally to hash the password.

If everything works as intended, the service creates a XML file similar to the one shown in Listing 7-7.

Listing 7-7. *The Data File Filled with Some Users and Roles*

```xml
<?xml version="1.0"?>
<UserData xmlns:xsi="http://www.w3.org/2001/XMLSchema-instance" xmlns:xsd="http://www.
w3.org/2001/XMLSchema">
  <Users IsApproved="false" IsLockedOut="false">
    <Comment>Test</Comment>
    <CreationDate>2009-04-30T13:12:23.6008895+02:00</CreationDate>
    <Email>krause@comzept.de</Email>
    <LastActivityDate>0001-01-01T01:00:00+01:00</LastActivityDate>
    <LastLockoutDate>0001-01-01T01:00:00+01:00</LastLockoutDate>
    <LastLoginDate>0001-01-01T01:00:00+01:00</LastLoginDate>
    <LastPasswordChangedDate>0001-01-01T01:00:00+01:00</LastPasswordChangedDate>
    <UserName>JoergKrause</UserName>
    <Roles />
  </Users>
  <Users IsApproved="true" IsLockedOut="false">
    <Comment />
    <CreationDate>2009-04-30T19:06:42.3928895+02:00</CreationDate>
    <Email>nissan@comzept.de</Email>
    <LastActivityDate>0001-01-01T00:00:00</LastActivityDate>
    <LastLockoutDate>0001-01-01T00:00:00</LastLockoutDate>
    <LastLoginDate>0001-01-01T00:00:00</LastLoginDate>
    <LastPasswordChangedDate>0001-01-01T00:00:00</LastPasswordChangedDate>
    <UserName>BerndAlbrecht</UserName>
    <Password>56-5E-E9-0F-A9-60-2C-0C-16-49-1A-7A-0F-3F-6C-70-D9-17-A3-2B</Password>
    <Roles>
      <Role>User</Role>
      <Role>Contributor</Role>
    </Roles>
  </Users>
```

```
  <Users IsApproved="true" IsLockedOut="false">
    <Comment />
    <CreationDate>2009-04-30T19:39:44.1528895+02:00</CreationDate>
    <Email>joerg@krause.net</Email>
    <LastActivityDate>0001-01-01T00:00:00</LastActivityDate>
    <LastLockoutDate>0001-01-01T00:00:00</LastLockoutDate>
    <LastLoginDate>0001-01-01T00:00:00</LastLoginDate>
    <LastPasswordChangedDate>0001-01-01T00:00:00</LastPasswordChangedDate>
    <UserName>Joerg</UserName>
    <Password>4E-B8-C5-DE-4C-76-60-80-C5-91-C6-94-D5-47-5D-B8-E3-53-B0-F3</Password>
    <Roles>
      <Role>Editor</Role>
    </Roles>
  </Users>
  <Roles>Admin</Roles>
  <Roles>User</Roles>
  <Roles>Contributor</Roles>
  <Roles>Editor</Roles>
</UserData>
```

The collection of Roles elements at the end contains the list of roles used in the provider. In the Users element, the Roles element contains the assigned roles for that user. The other elements contain the properties. IsApproved and IsLockedOut are stored as attributes because they only contain scalar values. The Password element displays the hash in plain text format.

In this section, we've looked at the basic operations of the membership service and its storage classes. The roles are already in this schema, and the User object accepts setting the assigned roles. All available roles are stored in separate Roles items at the end of the file—see the bold elements in Listing 7-7. From where do the roles originate? In the next section, we'll look at a Role service. It requires less code, as it reuses portions of the Membership service.

Creating the Role Service

The role service is much simpler than the Membership service. Instead of dealing with a "Role" object, we'll simply store roles as strings. The functions of the role service are to assign users to existing roles, create or remove roles, and search for users that are members of specific roles. The data storage is the same as for the membership service. Refer to the Membership classes to see how both parts operate together.

The Role service requires three components:

- IRoleService interface

- RoleService service

- RoleService class

As before, the interface defines the service contract, while the class implements the service. The service file is the service exposed by WCF as the endpoint, and it refers to the class's implementation in a code-behind file (see Listing 7-8).

Listing 7-8. *The Contract Defined by an Interface*

```
[ServiceContract]
public interface IRoleService
{
    [OperationContract]
    void AddUsersToRoles(string[] usernames, string[] roleNames);

    [OperationContract]
    void CreateRole(string roleName);

    [OperationContract]
    bool DeleteRole(string roleName, bool throwOnPopulatedRole);

    [OperationContract]
    string[] FindUsersInRole(string roleName, string usernameToMatch);

    [OperationContract]
    string[] GetAllRoles();

    [OperationContract]
    string[] GetRolesForUser(string username);

    [OperationContract]
    string[] GetUsersInRole(string roleName);

    [OperationContract]
    bool IsUserInRole(string username, string roleName);

    [OperationContract]
    void RemoveUsersFromRoles(string[] usernames, string[] roleNames);

    [OperationContract]
    bool RoleExists(string roleName);
}
```

The service defines a direct mirror of the `RoleProvider` class. This makes it easier to call the service's methods from the provider shown later. So far, this is very straightforward, as shown in Listing 7-9.

Listing 7-9. *The Service Class*

```
<%@ ServiceHost Language="C#" Debug="true" ➥
    Service="Apress.Extensibility.Membership.RoleService" ➥
    CodeBehind="RoleService.svc.cs" %>
```

The service class (`.svc` file) points to the code-behind file containing the implementation (see Listing 7-10).

Listing 7-10. *The Implementation of the Service*

```
public class RoleService : IRoleService
{
    public void AddUsersToRoles(string[] usernames, string[] roleNames)
    {
        UserData ud = FileManager.Load();
        var users = (from u in ud.Users
```

```
                    where usernames.Contains(u.UserName)
                    select u);
    foreach (User user in users)
    {
        user.Roles.RemoveAll(role => roleNames.Contains(role));
        user.Roles.AddRange(roleNames);
    }
    FileManager.Save(ud);
}

public void CreateRole(string roleName)
{
    UserData ud = FileManager.Load();
    if (!ud.Roles.Contains(roleName))
    {
      ud.Roles.Add(roleName);
      FileManager.Save(ud);
    }
}

public bool DeleteRole(string roleName, bool throwOnPopulatedRole)
{
    UserData ud = FileManager.Load();
    var userInRole = from u in ud.Users
                    where u.Roles.Contains(roleName)
                    select u;
    if (userInRole.Count() > 0 && throwOnPopulatedRole)
    {
        return false;
    }
    ud.Roles.Remove(roleName);
    FileManager.Save(ud);
    return true;
}

public string[] FindUsersInRole(string roleName, string usernameToMatch)
{
    UserData ud = FileManager.Load();
    var userInRole = from u in ud.Users
                    where u.UserName.Contains(usernameToMatch) && ➥
                        u.Roles.Contains(roleName)
                    select u.UserName;
    return userInRole.ToArray<string>();
}

public string[] GetAllRoles()
{
    UserData ud = FileManager.Load();
    var roles = from r in ud.Roles select r;
    return roles.ToArray<string>();
}

public string[] GetRolesForUser(string username)
{
    UserData ud = FileManager.Load();
    var roles = (from u in ud.Users
                where u.UserName.Equals(username)
                select u.Roles).First();
```

```
            return roles.ToArray();
        }

        public string[] GetUsersInRole(string roleName)
        {
            UserData ud = FileManager.Load();
            var roles = (from u in ud.Users
                         where u.Roles.Contains(roleName)
                         select u.UserName);
            return roles.ToArray();
        }

        public bool IsUserInRole(string username, string roleName)
        {
            UserData ud = FileManager.Load();
            var roles = (from u in ud.Users
                         where u.UserName.Equals(username) && u.Roles.Contains(roleName)
                         select u.UserName);
            return roles.Count() > 0;
        }

        public void RemoveUsersFromRoles(string[] usernames, string[] roleNames)
        {
            UserData ud = FileManager.Load();
            var roles = (from u in ud.Users
                         where usernames.Contains(u.UserName) && ➥
                               roleNames.Intersect(u.Roles).Count() > 0
                         select u.UserName);
            FileManager.Save(ud);
        }

        public bool RoleExists(string roleName)
        {
            UserData ud = FileManager.Load();
            var roles = (from r in ud.Roles
                         where r.Equals(roleName)
                         select r);
            return roles.Count() > 0;
        }
    }
}
```

Again, LINQ is used to access the data store. As the UserData class already covers the roles by providing the Roles element, the whole RoleService class doesn't require its own data access. The FileManager.Save method is called for methods that create roles data.

Configuring the Services

Once the services have been defined, they must be configured. WCF has its own definition language which extends the *web.config* file. The definition has three parts, but some settings can be omitted if the default values are suitable. WCF is based on the ABC mnemonic, which stands for Address, Binding, and Contract. Contract is defined by adding specific attributes to a class or interface definition, as shown earlier. The binding and address are defined in the configuration. The address defines where a client can reach the service. The binding defines the protocol used between client and service. A complete description consisting of address and binding is also called an endpoint. A sample XML configuration is shown in Listing 7-11.

Listing 7-11. *The Configuration of the Service*

```
<system.serviceModel>
    <services>
        <service behaviorConfiguration="MembershipServiceBehavior" ➥
                name="Apress.Extensibility.Membership.MembershipService">
            <endpoint address="" binding="wsHttpBinding" ➥
                    contract="Apress.Extensibility.Membership.IMembershipService">
                <identity>
                    <dns value="localhost" />
                </identity>
            </endpoint>
            <endpoint address="mex" binding="mexHttpBinding" ➥
                    contract="IMetadataExchange" />
            <host>
                <baseAddresses>
                    <add baseAddress="http://localhost/service" />
                </baseAddresses>
            </host>
        </service>
        <service behaviorConfiguration="RoleServiceBehavior" ➥
                name="Apress.Extensibility.Membership.RoleService">
            <endpoint address="" binding="wsHttpBinding" ➥
                    contract="Apress.Extensibility.Membership.IRoleService">
                <identity>
                    <dns value="localhost" />
                </identity>
            </endpoint>
            <endpoint address="mex" binding="mexHttpBinding" ➥
                    contract="IMetadataExchange" />
        </service>
    </services>
    <behaviors>
        <serviceBehaviors>
            <behavior name="MembershipServiceBehavior">
                <serviceMetadata httpGetEnabled="true" />
                <serviceDebug includeExceptionDetailInFaults="true" />
            </behavior>
            <behavior name="RoleServiceBehavior">
                <serviceMetadata httpGetEnabled="true" />
                <serviceDebug includeExceptionDetailInFaults="false" />
            </behavior>
        </serviceBehaviors>
    </behaviors>
</system.serviceModel>
```

The system.serviceModel section contains all the settings required by the WCF services. Its definition consists of two services and two corresponding behaviors. Because a regular Web Service is required, the wsHttpBinding is used. An additional endpoint is defined for meta data exchange, using the mexHttpBinding. This allows the client to create a proxy that talks to the service. (The client is technically created when you reference the service in Visual Studio.) When this occurs, the meta data endpoint is called to retrieve the service's description. This includes all methods, signatures, and data objects used by the service, as well as the endpoint configuration.

If you use and debug the whole solution, you might encounter an exception. For security reasons, the details of an exception are not transferred to the client, as intruders could try to provoke an error by attacking the service. If the internally thrown exception exposes details, the hackers will receive information with which they can refine their attack. During the development cycle, however, you'll need as much information as possible in order to troubleshoot errors. Set the includeExceptionDetailInFaults attribute to "true" while debugging and change it to "false" before publishing the service.

Now the service is up and running. You can check this by launching the .svc endpoints in the browser. Just right-click the service and choose *View in browser*. You should see a service description similar to that shown in Figure 7-5.

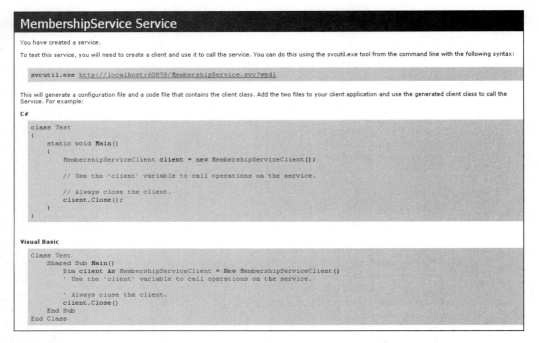

Figure 7-5. *The service is up and running.*

Use the same procedure to check the RoleService.

Implementing the Provider

The provider requires a few more steps:

1. Referencing the services

2. Implementing the Membership provider

3. Implementing the Role provider

4. Configuring the Web project so that it accepts the providers

The reference is easy. Simply choose *Add service reference* from the context menu of your project. Then click on *Discover* and *Services in Solution* (see Figure 7-6).

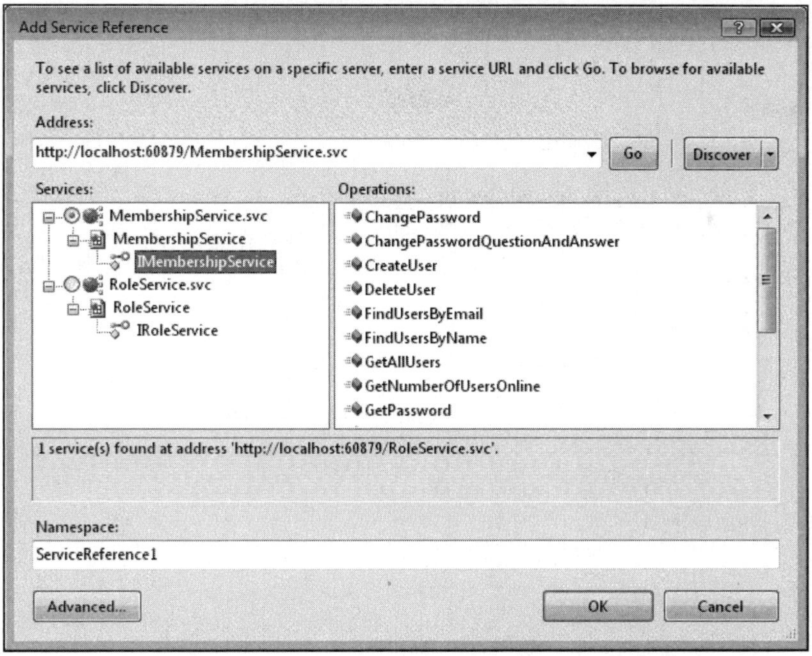

Figure 7-6. *Adding the service references*

Open the service in the tree view to the left and choose the contract. Give the service a suitable name. In the example, I've used MembershipService and RoleService, respectively. Repeat the steps for the other service. You now have two service references in your project.

Provider-Specific Configuration

The provider can be combined with its own configuration to support specific settings. Refer to Chapter 4 for more information about the basic steps of provider implementation. For the sake of brevity, I have removed from the example any code not required for basic tasks.

Create the Membership Provider

The Membership provider implements the MembershipProvider base class. To avoid confusion I named the class WSMembershipProvider, where the WS prefix reminds us that it's based on a Web Service (see Listing 7-12).

Listing 7-12. *The WSMembershipProvider*

```
public class WSMembershipProvider : MembershipProvider
{

    private MembershipServiceClient client;
    private bool _enablePasswordReset;

    public override void Initialize(string name, ➥
            System.Collections.Specialized.NameValueCollection config)
    {
        if (config == null)
```

```csharp
            throw new ArgumentNullException("config");
        if (String.IsNullOrEmpty(name))
        {
            name = this.GetType().Name;
        }
        if (String.IsNullOrEmpty(config["description"]))
        {
            config.Remove("description");
            config.Add("description", "WS Based Membership Provider");
        }
        base.Initialize(name, config);
        client = new MembershipServiceClient();
        // optional parameters
        if (!String.IsNullOrEmpty(config["EnablePasswordReset"]))
        {
            _enablePasswordReset = Boolean.Parse(config["EnablePasswordReset"]);
            config.Remove("EnablePasswordReset");
        }

        // mandatory parameters
        ApplicationName = config["ApplicationName"];

    }

    public override string ApplicationName
    {
        get;
        set;
    }

    public override bool ChangePassword(string username, string oldPassword, ➥
                                   string newPassword)
    {
        return client.ChangePassword(username, oldPassword, newPassword);
    }

    public override bool ChangePasswordQuestionAndAnswer(string username, ➥
                                               string password, ➥
                                               string newPasswordQuestion,
                                               string newPasswordAnswer)
    {
        return client.ChangePasswordQuestionAndAnswer(username, password, ➥
                                               newPasswordQuestion, ➥
                                               newPasswordAnswer);
    }

    public override MembershipUser CreateUser(string username, ➥
                                           string password, ➥
                                           string email, ➥
                                           string passwordQuestion, ➥
                                           string passwordAnswer, ➥
                                           bool isApproved, ➥
                                           object providerUserKey, ➥
                                           out MembershipCreateStatus status)
    {
        User user = client.CreateUser(out status, username, password, email, ➥
                                passwordQuestion, passwordAnswer, ➥
```

```
                                    isApproved, providerUserKey);
    if (user == null) return null;
    MembershipUser mu = new MembershipUser(this.GetType().Name,
        user.UserName,
        providerUserKey,
        user.Email,
        user.PasswordQuestion,
        "",
        user.IsApproved,
        user.IsLockedOut,
        user.CreationDate,
        user.LastLoginDate,
        user.LastActivityDate,
        user.LastPasswordChangedDate,
        user.LastLockoutDate
        );
    return mu;
}

public override bool DeleteUser(string username, bool deleteAllRelatedData)
{
    return client.DeleteUser(username, deleteAllRelatedData);
}

public override bool EnablePasswordReset
{
    get { return _enablePasswordReset; }
}

public override bool EnablePasswordRetrieval
{
    get { throw new NotImplementedException(); }
}

public override MembershipUserCollection FindUsersByEmail(string emailToMatch, ➥
                        int pageIndex, int pageSize, out int totalRecords)
{
    return CopyToMembershipCollection(client.FindUsersByEmail(out totalRecords,➥
                            emailToMatch, pageIndex, pageSize));
}

public override MembershipUserCollection FindUsersByName(string usernameToMatch,
                        int pageIndex, int pageSize, out int totalRecords)
{
    return CopyToMembershipCollection(client.FindUsersByName(out totalRecords,
                            usernameToMatch, pageIndex, pageSize));
}

public override MembershipUserCollection GetAllUsers(int pageIndex, ➥
                                    int pageSize, out int totalRecords)
{
    return CopyToMembershipCollection(client.GetAllUsers(out totalRecords, ➥
                                        pageIndex, pageSize));
}

private MembershipUserCollection CopyToMembershipCollection(User[] users)
{
```

```
        MembershipUserCollection muc = new MembershipUserCollection();
        foreach (User user in users)
        {
            muc.Add(CopyToMembershipUser(user));
        }
        return muc;
    }

    private MembershipUser CopyToMembershipUser(User user)
    {
        MembershipUser mu = new MembershipUser(this.GetType().Name,
                user.UserName,
                "",
                user.Email,
                user.PasswordQuestion,
                user.Comment,
                user.IsApproved,
                user.IsLockedOut,
                user.CreationDate,
                user.LastLoginDate,
                user.LastActivityDate,
                user.LastPasswordChangedDate,
                user.LastLockoutDate);
        return mu;
    }

    public override int GetNumberOfUsersOnline()
    {
        return client.GetNumberOfUsersOnline();
    }

    public override string GetPassword(string username, string answer)
    {
        return client.GetPassword(username, answer);
    }

    public override MembershipUser GetUser(string username, bool userIsOnline)
    {
        return CopyToMembershipUser(client.GetUserbyName(username, userIsOnline));
    }

    public override MembershipUser GetUser(object providerUserKey, ➥
                                        bool userIsOnline)
    {
        throw new NotImplementedException();
    }

    public override string GetUserNameByEmail(string email)
    {
        return client.GetUserNameByEmail(email);
    }

    public override int MaxInvalidPasswordAttempts
    {
        get { return 5; }
    }
```

```
public override int MinRequiredNonAlphanumericCharacters
{
    get { return 1; }
}

public override int MinRequiredPasswordLength
{
    get { return 6; }
}

public override int PasswordAttemptWindow
{
    get { return 10; }
}

public override MembershipPasswordFormat PasswordFormat
{
    get { return MembershipPasswordFormat.Clear; }
}

public override string PasswordStrengthRegularExpression
{
    get { return ""; }
}

public override bool RequiresQuestionAndAnswer
{
    get { return false; }
}

public override bool RequiresUniqueEmail
{
    get { return false; }
}

public override string ResetPassword(string username, string answer)
{
    return client.ResetPassword(username, answer);
}

public override bool UnlockUser(string userName)
{
    throw new NotImplementedException();
}

public override void UpdateUser(MembershipUser user)
{
    User u = new User();
    foreach (PropertyInfo pi in u.GetType().GetProperties())
    {
        PropertyInfo piTarget = user.GetType().GetProperty(pi.Name);
        if (piTarget != null)
        {
            pi.SetValue(u, piTarget.GetValue(user, null), null);
        }
    }
```

```
        client.UpdateUser(u);
    }

    public override bool ValidateUser(string username, string password)
    {
        return client.ValidateUser(username, password);
    }
}
```

The client is instantiated in the Initialize method. The provider's methods subsequently use the client to call the appropriate functions remotely. The only issue requiring more work is the fact that the MembershipUser class cannot be used directly by the service. The internally employed User class has a similar structure but no dependencies on the underlying provider. Later, in Listing 7-13, I use reflection to iterate over the properties and, where a property is both public and available in the target class, copy the value from the MembershipUser class to the User class. This is in the UpdateUser method. The provider also has several hard-coded settings. In a full-fledged application, these would be obtained from *web.config*. Additionally, in a real-world example, I would suggest separating the data layer into another assembly to get a multi-tier architecture.

Create the Role Provider

The Role provider implements the RoleProvider base class. Again, to avoid confusion, our new class is named WSRoleProvider, where the WS reminds us that it's based on a Web Service. See Listing 7-13.

Listing 7-13. *The WSRoleProvider*

```
public class WSRoleProvider : RoleProvider
{

    private RoleServiceClient client;

    public override void Initialize(string name, ➥
            System.Collections.Specialized.NameValueCollection config)
    {
        if (config == null)
            throw new ArgumentNullException("config");
        if (String.IsNullOrEmpty(name))
        {
            name = this.GetType().Name;
        }
        if (String.IsNullOrEmpty(config["description"]))
        {
            config.Remove("description");
            config.Add("description", "WS Based Membership Provider");
        }
        base.Initialize(name, config);
        client = new RoleServiceClient();
        // mandatory parameters
        ApplicationName = config["ApplicationName"];
    }

    public override void AddUsersToRoles(string[] usernames, string[] roleNames)
    {
        client.AddUsersToRoles(usernames, roleNames);
    }
```

```
    public override string ApplicationName
    {
        get;
        set;
    }

    public override void CreateRole(string roleName)
    {
        client.CreateRole(roleName);
    }

    public override bool DeleteRole(string roleName, bool throwOnPopulatedRole)
    {
        return client.DeleteRole(roleName, throwOnPopulatedRole);
    }

    public override string[] FindUsersInRole(string roleName, ➥
                                    string usernameToMatch)
    {
        return client.FindUsersInRole(roleName, usernameToMatch);
    }

    public override string[] GetAllRoles()
    {
        return client.GetAllRoles();
    }

    public override string[] GetRolesForUser(string username)
    {
        return client.GetRolesForUser(username);
    }

    public override string[] GetUsersInRole(string roleName)
    {
        return client.GetUsersInRole(roleName);
    }

    public override bool IsUserInRole(string username, string roleName)
    {
        return client.IsUserInRole(username, roleName);
    }

    public override void RemoveUsersFromRoles(string[] usernames, ➥
                                    string[] roleNames)
    {
        client.RemoveUsersFromRoles(usernames, roleNames);
    }

    public override bool RoleExists(string roleName)
    {
        return client.RoleExists(roleName);
    }
}
```

Configuring the Provider

After the provider is implemented, it must be configured. As for any other provider, this is achieved within the *web.config* file. As you can see in Listing 7-14, the WSRoleProvider class is simpler than the provider shown before. The methods predominantly call the corresponding service methods and do not add additional logic. Again, the Initialize method contains the instantiation of the RoleServiceClient class.

Listing 7-14. *Configuring the Providers*

```
<system.web>
<membership defaultProvider="WSMembershipProvider">
    <providers>
       <add name="WSMembershipProvider"
            type="Apress.Extensibility.Membership.WSMembershipProvider,
                  Apress.Extensibility.Membership"
            EnablePasswordReset="True"
        />
    </providers>
</membership>
<roleManager defaultProvider="WSRoleProvider" enabled="true" >
    <providers>
        <clear/>
        <add name="WSRoleProvider"
            type="Apress.Extensibility.Membership.WSRoleProvider,
                  Apress.Extensibility.Membership" />
    </providers>
</roleManager>
```

The provider's add element requires the name, the type and optionally the parameters defined in the configuration. The type is the full class name, including the assembly name. In this case, I've used a regular Visual Studio 2008 project, which compiles into a DLL. The name and namespace of the DLL are specified here.

Testing the Providers

You can now use the providers. However, you'll need several additional pages in order to add users or roles, retrieve data, check users, assign roles, etc. Fortunately, Visual Studio contains an embedded tool that allows you to manage users and roles.

This tool is available from the *Project* menu and is called *ASP.NET configuration*. You can add and change users, add and assign roles, and test all common settings of the new providers without writing a single line of code. On the start page, choose the Security tab to view the current state of the providers. If you have already defined some users and roles, their quantities are displayed, as shown in Figure 7-7.

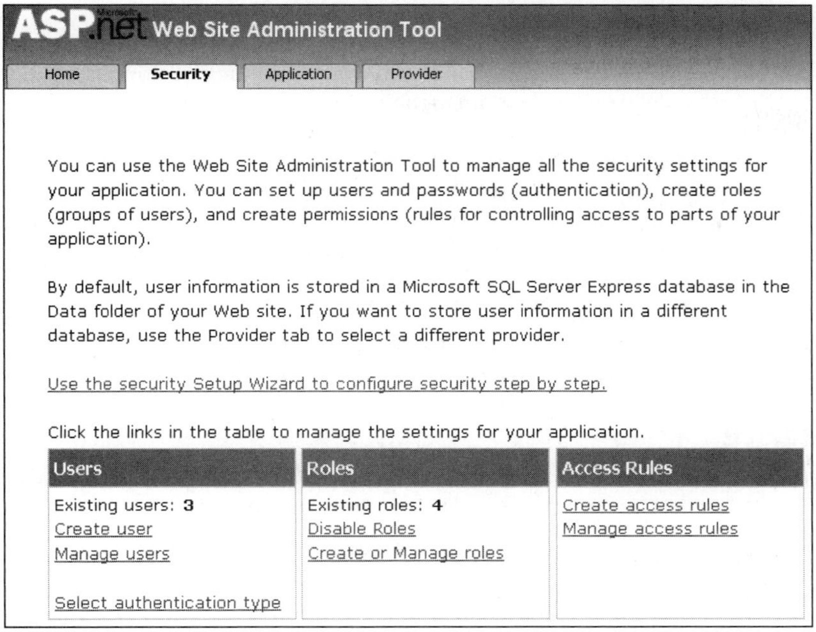

Figure 7-7. *The security tab uses the custom provider if properly configured.*

You can use the tool to create or modify users and add or assign roles. If the tool does not work as expected, check whether or not the custom providers are properly registered. Open the Provider tab and click on *Select a different provider for each feature (advanced)*. Your custom providers (WSMembershipProvider and WSRoleProvider) should be selected, as shown in Figure 7-8.

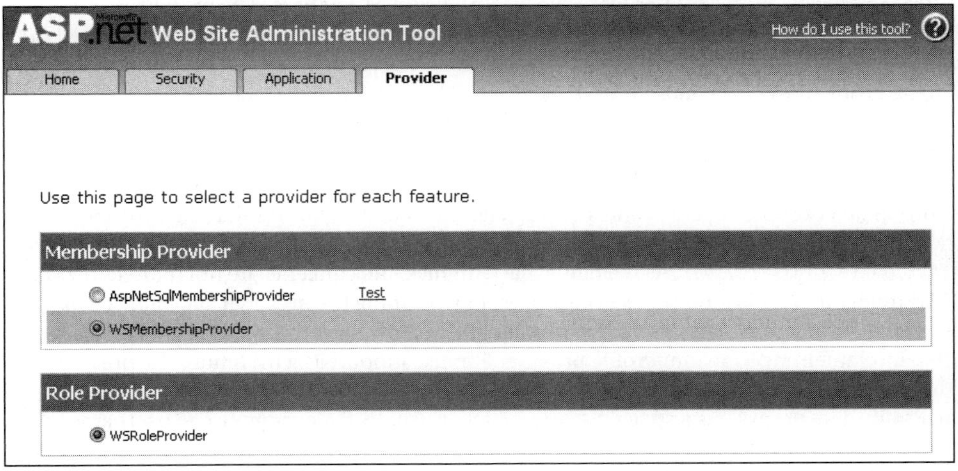

Figure 7-8. *The provider tab shows the custom provider if properly configured.*

Extending Profile Providers

The Profile service is an integrated module for storing and retrieving user settings. Settings are not limited to ASP.NET, but are widely used in distributed multi-user environments; even for Win Forms application, a similar concept exists. The Profile service employs a Profile provider to read data from, and save data to, a storage device. By default, the data store is a SQL Server or SQL Server Express instance, and the provider class is `System.Web.Profile.SqlProfileProvider`. This provider is also responsible for allowing users to update their settings. Common management functions, such as deleting a Profile after a period of inactivity, are located here as well.

■**Note** Profile providers are part of the provider model. It is described in detail in Chapter 4.

The Profile Service

The purpose of the Profile service is to store and retrieve user settings. With these settings, users can personalize their web pages. Typical information stored here includes the following:

- User information, such as city and phone number
- Preferences for accessibility, colors, and font size
- Data related to the current session, such as the contents of a shopping basket
- Individual selections of services, such as news feeds or newsletter topic

The personalization possibilities are limitless. Instead of building custom database modules from scratch to store the users' settings, this is where the Profile service excels.

The services' definition consists of two parts—Profile properties and related user. The Profile service retrieves properties for the current user from the underlying provider. In order to use Profiles, you must first activate this feature by defining the Provider in the *web.config* file. By default, the `SqlProfileProvider` stores properties in the local SQL Server database. The properties are defined in the *web.config* file, too. Unlike application settings, where key/value pairs are stored in *web.config*, the Profile property definition consists of the property definition only. Actual values are stored in the Profile provider's data store.

Understanding the Profile Provider

Before you consider extending the Profile provider, let's look at the features that the provider supports. The `ProfileProvider` class implements the `ProviderBase` base class and the `System.Configuration.SettingsProvider`. As the namespace implies, the concepts are not limited to ASP.NET. The Profile provider extends the settings concept with some features that allow for the management of user Profiles, such as deleting of Profiles and activity monitoring (see Table 7-3).

When implementing a custom Profile provider, it must support as a minimum the preceding methods in order to be used transparently in applications.

The Profile data always has a specific scope, which is usually the current user's username. However, the Profile provider also supports anonymous users. This means that a user not currently logged in gets a Profile as a non-authenticated user.

Consider a visitor who selects several items to purchase at a Web site, but they have not yet logged in. Their Profile contains several items in their shopping basket. It is therefore important to keep their Profile (containing their selections) separate from the Profiles of other non-authenticated users. To accomplish this, the Profile provider assigns each anonymous user an ID that is used as a key in the absence of a username.

Table 7-3. *Methods and Properties Defined by the ProfileProvider Class*

Method	Description
Initialize	Derived from ProviderBase. Contains the code for setting up the provider and reading the settings.
ApplicationName	Derived from SettingsProvider. Name of the current application. The data store can use this to handle multiple applications that use the same database.
GetPropertyValues	Derived from SettingsProvider. Retrieves a list of properties using a SettingsContext object containing information about the user. You could use this to retrieve Profile information for a user. The context provides information about authenticated or anonymous users. The method returns an object of type SettingsPropertyCollection, which is a collection of SettingsProperty objects, each containing the name and type of a property, as well as additional information such as default settings and read-only state. Using this method updates the LastActivityDate value that is used to track activity (and thus monitor logged-on or inactive users).
SetPropertyValues	Derived from SettingsProvider. Uses a SettingsContext object and a SettingsPropertyValueCollection object to write property values back to the data store. Using this method also updates the LastActivityDate.
DeleteProfiles	Using an array of usernames, this method deletes the related Profiles. An overloaded version of the same method accepts ProfileInfo objects.
DeleteInactiveProfiles	Accepts a ProfileAuthenticationOption value and a DateTime object in order to delete inactive Profiles. The Profiles should be deleted if the supplied date and time value is equal to or less than the Profile's LastActivityDate.
GetAllProfiles	Retrieves all available Profile objects using a ProfileAuthenticationOption value and an integer value for the page and the maximum number of Profiles. The page index allows a paged retrieval. The method returns a ProfileInfoCollection with ProfileInfo objects.
GetAllInactiveProfiles	Using the same conditions as GetAllProfiles, this method returns only Profiles that have not been used for a given time.
FindProfilesByUserName	Retrieves Profiles via their usernames. In derived classes, this method might accept wildcards, regular expressions, or any other kind of search pattern in order to retrieve multiple values matching the search string. This method behaves similarly to GetAllProfiles.
FindInactiveProfilesByUserName	Retrieves inactive Profiles via their usernames. In derived classes, this method might accept wildcards, regular expressions, or any other kind of search pattern in order to retrieve multiple values matching the search string. This method behaves similarly to GetAllProfiles.
GetNumberOfInactiveProfiles	Retrieves the number of inactive Profiles.

When the user leaves the session, the Profile becomes obsolete. This is why the last activity date is important. If you specify a minimum inactivity time period, the provider is able to delete expired Profiles. The ProfileAuthenticationOption parameter determines which of the anonymous or authenticated Profiles are to be deleted. You can use a different time span for each type.

The data store itself is data agnostic—any properties can be stored there. The definition of acceptable values is set in the *web.config* file for all users.

Serializing and Deserializing

Values for custom settings can support several data types. Most storage systems require serialized values instead of .NET objects. Fortunately, the base class provides the code for serializing and deserializing objects. However, when retrieving values, this code is not called automatically. Consider the case where you have several settings, and deserializing them takes some time. If the calling party requires only one or two of these values, deserializing all of them will waste resources. To improve performance, you can call the base methods to deserialize the desired properties and ignore all the others. This method is known as "lazy deserialization" (see Listing 7-15).

Listing 7-15. *Typical Strategy for Retrieving and Deserializing Values*

```
SettingsPropertyValueCollection settings = new SettingsPropertyValueCollection ();
foreach (SettingsProperty property in properties)
{
  SettingsPropertyValue pp = new SettingsPropertyValue (property);
  object val = GetPropertyValueFromDataSource (property.Name);
  if (val == null)
  {
    pp.PropertyValue = null;
    pp.Deserialized = true;
    pp.IsDirty = false;
  }
  else
  {
    pp.PropertyValue = Deserialize(val);
    pp.Deserialized = true;
    pp.IsDirty = false;
  }
  settings.Add (pp);
}
return settings;
```

Defining Profile Settings

A typical setting definition looks like the code in Listing 7-16.

Listing 7-16. *Define Available Properties*

```
<profile>
  <properties>
    <add name="Greeting" type="String" />
    <add name="Count" type="Int32" defaultValue="0" />
  </properties>
</profile>
```

The name of the property and the type are required. A default value can also be specified, which the provider will use if the data store does not retrieve one.

The serialization can be refined by adding the `serializeAs` attribute to the Profile property definition shown in the next section. This attribute allows the pre-selection of a predefined serializer:

- String
- Binary
- Xml
- ProviderSpecific

The provider can also be selected on a per-property basis. This allows for different data stores for different types of data.

Each property can be limited to authenticated users only by setting the attribute `allowAnonymous` to `false`.

For more complex scenarios, you can group settings with the `<group>` tag. If you plan on supporting hundreds of settings, groups can help you to manage your settings.

Using the Profile Data

There are two ways of reaching Profile data from within your code. In a Web application project (as opposed to a Web site project), the `Profile` class is not auto-generated from the current configuration. You will need to use the following two techniques to manage your Profile settings. To retrieve values, use the following pattern:

```
string myValue = (string) Context.Profile.GetPropertyValue("MyValue");
```

Setting values is similarly straightforward:

```
if (Context.Profile.UserName != null) {
  Context.Profile.SetPropertyValue("MyValue", "something");
  Context.Profile.Save();
}
```

In a Web site project, Visual Studio generates a `Profile` class from the configuration settings, which exposes the Profile properties as typed properties:

```
string myValue = Profile.MyValue;
```

Several free tools are available for overcoming the limitation of Web application projects that doesn't support Profile creation. The Web Profile Builder found at `http://code.msdn.microsoft.com/WebProfileBuilder` is a good starting point. However, digging deeper into the build techniques used in Visual Studio is beyond the scope of this book.

■Note To overcome the limitations of Web application projects, in this chapter I use the Web site project template. This is the opposite of what I recommend in other parts of the book. As long as you're not using Profiles, you should stay with Web application projects. If you do use Profiles, it depends on whether strongly typed access is important.

Configuring Custom Profile Providers

The Profile settings use the embedded provider if no other is specified. The settings follow the schema for providers explained in Chapter 4. Listing 7-17 shows how to define settings and how to configure the provider typically.

Listing 7-17. *Define Available Properties*

```
<profile defaultProvider="MyProfileProvider">
    <properties>
        <add name="FirstName" type="System.String" />
        <add name="LastName" type="System.String" />
        <add name="EmailAddress" type="System.String" />
        <add name="MakeNamePublic" type="System.Boolean" />
        <add name="NewsFeed" type="System.String" />
    </properties>
    <providers>
        <add name="MyProfileProvider"
            type="Apress.Extensibility.XmlProfileProvider" />
    </providers>
</profile>
```

To implement the custom Profile provider, select the preferred data access method.

Implementing a Custom Profile Provider

The custom Profile provider shown in the following example uses an XML file to store all users' data. It does not implement usage functions such as checking inactivity or deleting Profiles. However, it does implement the save and load functions as well as the underlying serialization and deserialization methods.

A Profile provider requires several steps to run properly. Even if only one provider class is necessary for retrieving the code, you need several users and authentication capabilities in order to check the provider.

Preparation Steps

To test a custom provider, which requires the ability to log in and log out of different user accounts, I set up Forms Authentication in *web.config*. Furthermore, I defined the users' credentials directly in *web.config* and force the Membership provider to use data from that file instead of from the default SQL Server. This is accomplished by handling the authentication event manually. The *web.config* section defining the users looks like the code in Listing 7-18.

Listing 7-18. *Define Several Users to Test the Application*

```
<authorization>
    <deny users="?"/>
</authorization>
<authentication mode="Forms">
    <forms>
        <credentials passwordFormat="Clear">
            <user name="User1" password="User1"/>
            <user name="User2" password="User2"/>
            <user name="User3" password="User3"/>
        </credentials>
    </forms>
</authentication>
```

■**Caution** Storing user credentials in clear text format in *web.config* is not intended to run in a production environment. It is here only in order to rapidly set up a test environment.

Next, the application requires at least one page for changing and using Profile settings, plus a login page. The login page consists of a single `Login` control and an event handler, as shown in Listings 7-19 and 7-20.

Listing 7-19. *The "Core" Component of the Login Page*

```
<body>
    <form id="form1" runat="server">
    <div>
        <asp:Login ID="Login1" runat="server" onauthenticate="Login1_Authenticate">
        </asp:Login>
        <br />
        Not yet registered? Create new account <asp:HyperLink ID="HyperLink1"
        runat="server" NavigateUrl="~/CreateUser.aspx">here</asp:HyperLink>.
    </div>
    </form>
</body>
```

Listing 7-20. *An Event Handler Forces the Login Control to Use the Configured User Names*

```
public partial class Login : System.Web.UI.Page
{
    protected void Page_Load(object sender, EventArgs e)
    {
    }

    protected void Login1_Authenticate(object sender, AuthenticateEventArgs e)
    {
        e.Authenticated = FormsAuthentication.Authenticate(Login1.UserName, ➥
                                                Login1.Password);
    }
}
```

The next page is also for testing purposes. It contains a simple form to save new Profile settings, display current settings, and change accounts (see Listing 7-21).

Listing 7-21. *ASPX Page Used to Test the Profile Provider*

```
<body>
    <form id="form1" runat="server">
    <br />Set your Profile data,
        <asp:LoginName ID="LoginName1" runat="server" />
        :<br />
    <br />E-mail:
        <asp:TextBox runat="server" ID="txtEmail"></asp:TextBox>
    <br />Fore Color:
        <asp:DropDownList ID="drpForeColor" runat="server">
            <asp:ListItem>Red</asp:ListItem>
            <asp:ListItem>Green</asp:ListItem>
            <asp:ListItem>Blue</asp:ListItem>
            <asp:ListItem></asp:ListItem>
```

```
    </asp:DropDownList>
    <br />Back Color:<asp:DropDownList ID="drpBackColor" runat="server">
        <asp:ListItem>White</asp:ListItem>
        <asp:ListItem>Beige</asp:ListItem>
        <asp:ListItem>Yellow</asp:ListItem>
    </asp:DropDownList>
    <br />
    <br />
    <asp:Button ID="btnSend" runat="server" onclick="btnSend_Click"
            Text="Set Profile Data" />
    <br />
    <br />
    Logout to use anonymous mode, login as different user to test different
    settings:
    <asp:LoginStatus ID="LoginStatus1" runat="server" />
 (Predefined: <i>User1</i>, <i>User2</i>, <i>User3</i>, in each case use the
    name as password, too)<br />
    <br />Result of your current settings:<br />
    <div>
        <asp:Panel ID="PanelSettings" runat="server">
            This panel&#39;s design is read from current user&#39;s Profile.
        </asp:Panel>
    </div>
    </form>
</body>
```

The page allows you to set an email address and a color. The color type is used here to demonstrate serialization of non-scalar values (see Figure 7-9).

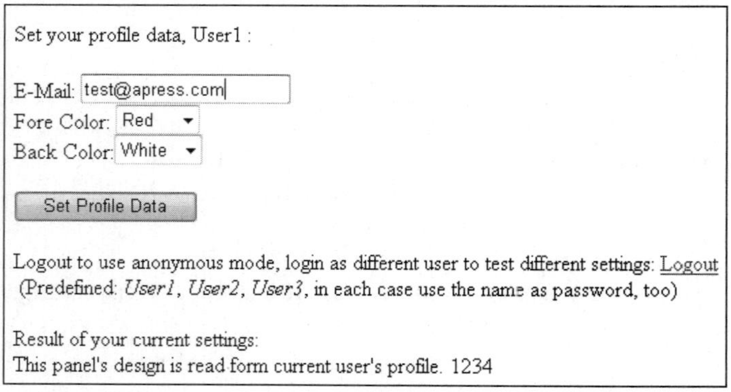

Figure 7-9. *A simple form to set and retrieve Profile data*

The page shows the currently logged-in user and the settings that format a Panel control (see Listing 7-22). The code-behind section shows how the Profile provider is invoked.

Listing 7-22. *Direct Calls to the Profile Provider and Typed Access*

```
public partial class _Default : System.Web.UI.Page
{
    protected void Page_Load(object sender, EventArgs e)
    {
        SetProfileData();
    }
```

```csharp
protected void btnSend_Click(object sender, EventArgs e)
{
    Profile.ForeColor = Color.FromName(drpForeColor.SelectedValue);
    Profile.BackColor = Color.FromName(drpBackColor.SelectedValue);
    Profile.User.Email = txtEmail.Text;
    SetProfileData();
}

private void SetProfileData()
{
    PanelSettings.BackColor = Profile.BackColor;
    PanelSettings.ForeColor = Profile.ForeColor;
    Label l = new Label();
    l.Text = Profile.User.Email;
    PanelSettings.Controls.Add(l);
}
}
```

The Profile class shown in Listing 7-23 is auto-generated and derives from the ProfileBase. It provides typed access to properties. The Profile provider returns settings of type object and the access layer casts these types to the final values.

Listing 7-23. *An Auto-Generated Profile Class*

```csharp
//------------------------------------------------------------------------------
// <auto-generated>
//     This code was generated by a tool.
//     Runtime Version:2.0.50727.3074
//
//     Changes to this file may cause incorrect behavior and will be lost if
//     the code is regenerated.
// </auto-generated>
//------------------------------------------------------------------------------
using System;
using System.Web;
using System.Web.Profile;

public class ProfileGroupUser : System.Web.Profile.ProfileGroupBase {

    public virtual string Name {
        get {
            return ((string)(this.GetPropertyValue("Name")));
        }
        set {
            this.SetPropertyValue("Name", value);
        }
    }

    public virtual string Email {
        get {
            return ((string)(this.GetPropertyValue("Email")));
        }
        set {
            this.SetPropertyValue("Email", value);
        }
    }
```

```
}

public class ProfileCommon : System.Web.Profile.ProfileBase {

    public virtual int Size {
        get {
            return ((int)(this.GetPropertyValue("Size")));
        }
        set {
            this.SetPropertyValue("Size", value);
        }
    }

    public virtual System.Drawing.Color ForeColor {
        get {
            return ((System.Drawing.Color)(this.GetPropertyValue("ForeColor")));
        }
        set {
            this.SetPropertyValue("ForeColor", value);
        }
    }

    public virtual System.Drawing.Color BackColor {
        get {
            return ((System.Drawing.Color)(this.GetPropertyValue("BackColor")));
        }
        set {
            this.SetPropertyValue("BackColor", value);
        }
    }

    public virtual ProfileGroupUser User {
        get {
            return ((ProfileGroupUser)(this.GetProfileGroup("User")));
        }
    }

    public virtual ProfileCommon GetProfile(string username) {
        return ((ProfileCommon)(ProfileBase.Create(username)));
    }
}
```

To understand these settings, take a look at the *web.config* file where the properties are defined, as shown in Listing 7-24.

Listing 7-24. *Definition of Profile Properties*

```
<profile automaticSaveEnabled="true" defaultProvider="XmlProfileProvider">
 <properties>
  <group name="User">
   <add name="Name" type="System.String" />
   <add name="Email" type="System.String" />
  </group>
  <add name="Size" type="System.Int32"/>
  <add name="ForeColor" type="System.Drawing.Color"/>
  <add name="BackColor" type="System.Drawing.Color"/>
 </properties>
```

```
<providers>
  <clear/>
  <add name="XmlProfileProvider"
       type="Apress.Extensibility.ProfileProvider.XmlProfileProvider"/>
</providers>
</profile>
```

The settings for username and email are grouped by the "User" group element. This is merely for organizational purposes, and has no direct influence on the behavior of the provider. The <providers> section contains the definition of the provider's type. The name is used to set this provider as the default one.

Implementing the Provider

You now have the requisite components. The last step is to construct the custom Profile provider itself, as shown in Listing 7-25. An explanation follows the code.

Listing 7-25. *A Custom Profile Provider That Can Save and Retrieve Settings*

```csharp
using System;
using System.Collections.Generic;
using System.ComponentModel;
using System.Configuration;
using System.Configuration.Provider;
using System.IO;
using System.Linq;
using System.Security.Permissions;
using System.Text;
using System.Web;
using System.Web.Profile;
using System.Xml.Linq;

namespace Apress.Extensibility.ProfileProvider
{
  [SecurityPermission(SecurityAction.Assert,
  Flags = SecurityPermissionFlag.SerializationFormatter)]
  public class XmlProfileProvider : System.Web.Profile.ProfileProvider
  {

    private const string DATAPATH = "~/App_Data/Profile_Data";

    public override string ApplicationName
    {
      get { throw new NotSupportedException(); }
      set { throw new NotSupportedException(); }
    }

    public override void Initialize(string name, ➥
        System.Collections.Specialized.NameValueCollection config)
    {
      base.Initialize(name, config);

      if (config.Count > 0)
        throw new ProviderException("Unrecognized attribute: " + ➥
                    config.GetKey(0));
    }
```

```csharp
public override System.Configuration.SettingsPropertyValueCollection ➡
  GetPropertyValues(System.Configuration.SettingsContext context, ➡
        System.Configuration.SettingsPropertyCollection collection)
{
  SettingsPropertyValueCollection settings = ➡
        new SettingsPropertyValueCollection();

  // Make sure you have an entry for this username in the XML data
  string username = context["UserName"] as string;
  if (!string.IsNullOrEmpty(username))
  {
    // Get the profile values for the user
    Dictionary<string, object> usersProperties = GetUserProfile(username);
    foreach (SettingsProperty property in collection)
    {
        if (property.PropertyType.IsPrimitive || ➡
            property.PropertyType == typeof(String))
          property.SerializeAs = SettingsSerializeAs.String;
        else
          property.SerializeAs = SettingsSerializeAs.Xml;

      SettingsPropertyValue setting = new SettingsPropertyValue(property);

      if (usersProperties != null)
      {
        setting.IsDirty = false;

        if (usersProperties.ContainsKey(property.Name))
        {
          setting.SerializedValue = usersProperties[property.Name];
          setting.Deserialized = false;
        }
      }

      settings.Add(setting);    // Add the settings value to the collection
    }

  }

  return settings;  // Return the settings collection
}

protected virtual Dictionary<string, object> GetUserProfile(string username)
{
  Dictionary<string, object> propertyValues = new Dictionary<string, object>();

  XDocument xProfiles = XDocument.Load(ProfileFilePath);
  var xProf = (from p in xProfiles.Root.Elements() ➡
              where p.Attribute("UserName").Value.Equals(username) ➡
              select p);

  foreach (XElement xmlProperty in xProf.Elements())
  {
    SettingsSerializeAs ss = (SettingsSerializeAs)➡
                        Enum.Parse(typeof(SettingsSerializeAs), ➡
                        xmlProperty.Attribute("serializedAs").Value);
    switch (ss)
```

```csharp
    {
      case SettingsSerializeAs.Binary:
        propertyValues.Add(
          xmlProperty.Name.LocalName,
          Encoding.ASCII.GetString(➥
            Convert.FromBase64String((((XCData) xmlProperty.FirstNode).Value))));
        break;
      case SettingsSerializeAs.String:
        propertyValues.Add(
          xmlProperty.Name.LocalName,
          xmlProperty.Value);
        break;
      case SettingsSerializeAs.Xml:
        if (xmlProperty.Attribute("typeConverter") != null)
        {
          TypeConverter converter = (TypeConverter) ➥
                  Activator.CreateInstance(➥
                  Type.GetType(xmlProperty.Attribute("typeConverter").Value));
          propertyValues.Add( ➥
            xmlProperty.Name.LocalName, ➥
            converter.ConvertFromString(xmlProperty.Value));
        }
        break;
      case SettingsSerializeAs.ProviderSpecific:
        throw new NotSupportedException();
    }
  }

  return propertyValues;
}


public override void SetPropertyValues(➥
      System.Configuration.SettingsContext context, ➥
      System.Configuration.SettingsPropertyValueCollection collection)
{
  string username = context["UserName"] as string;
  bool userIsAuthenticated = (bool)context["IsAuthenticated"];
  // If no username is specified, or if no properties are to be saved, exit
  if (string.IsNullOrEmpty(username) || collection.Count == 0)
    return;

  if (!ExistsDirtyProperty(collection))
    return;

  XDocument xProfiles = XDocument.Load(ProfileFilePath);
  // check elements
  var xProf = (from p in xProfiles.Root.Elements() ➥
              where p.Attribute("UserName").Value.Equals(username) ➥
              select p).FirstOrDefault();
  if (xProf == null)
  {
    // Add a default empty profile
    xProf = new XElement("Profile", new XAttribute("UserName", username));
    xProfiles.Root.Add(xProf);
    xProfiles.Save(ProfileFilePath);
  }
```

```
// assure empty element as write everything back
xProf.RemoveNodes();
foreach (SettingsPropertyValue setting in collection)
{
  // If the user is not authenticated and the property does
  // not allow anonymous access, skip serializing it
  if (!userIsAuthenticated && ➡
      !(bool)setting.Property.Attributes["AllowAnonymous"])
    continue;

  // Skip the current property if it's not dirty and is currently
  // assigned its default value
  if (!setting.IsDirty && setting.UsingDefaultValue)
    continue;

  // Serialize data based on property's SerializeAs type
  switch (setting.Property.SerializeAs)
  {
    case SettingsSerializeAs.String:
      xProf.Add(new XElement(➡
        setting.Name, ➡
        Convert.ToString(setting.SerializedValue), ➡
        new XAttribute("serializedAs", setting.Property.SerializeAs)));
      break;
    case SettingsSerializeAs.Xml:
      // instead of XML we ask the default converter
      TypeConverter converter = TypeDescriptor.GetConverter(➡
                                setting.Property.PropertyType);
      string data = converter.ConvertToString(setting.PropertyValue);
      xProf.Add(new XElement(➡
        setting.Name, ➡
        data, ➡
        new XAttribute("serializedAs", setting.Property.SerializeAs), ➡
        new XAttribute("typeConverter", , ➡
            converter.GetType().AssemblyQualifiedName)));
      break;
    case SettingsSerializeAs.Binary:
      // encode the binary data using base64 encoding
      string encodedBinaryData = Convert.ToBase64String(, ➡
                           setting.SerializedValue as byte[]);
      xProf.Add(new XElement(➡
        setting.Name, ➡
        new XCData(encodedBinaryData), ➡
        new XAttribute("serializedAs", setting.Property.SerializeAs)));
      break;
    default:
      // unknown serialize type!
      throw new ProviderException(string.Format(, ➡
      "Invalid value for SerializeAs; expected String, Xml, or Binary, , ➡
       received {0}", , ➡
         System.Enum.GetName(setting.Property.SerializeAs.GetType(),, ➡
         setting.Property.SerializeAs)));
  }
}
xProfiles.Save(ProfileFilePath);
}
```

```csharp
protected virtual string ProfileFilePath
{
  get
  {
    return Path.Combine(HttpContext.Current.Server.MapPath(DATAPATH), ➥
                        "Profiles.xml");
  }
}

protected virtual bool ExistsDirtyProperty(➥
      System.Configuration.SettingsPropertyValueCollection collection)
{
  foreach (SettingsPropertyValue setting in collection)
    if (setting.IsDirty)
      return true;

  // If we reach here, none are dirty
  return false;
}

public override int DeleteInactiveProfiles(➥
        ProfileAuthenticationOption authenticationOption, ➥
        DateTime userInactiveSinceDate)
{
  throw new Exception("The method or operation is not implemented.");
}

public override int DeleteProfiles(string[] usernames)
{
  throw new Exception("The method or operation is not implemented.");
}

public override int DeleteProfiles(ProfileInfoCollection profiles)
{
  throw new Exception("The method or operation is not implemented.");
}

public override ProfileInfoCollection FindInactiveProfilesByUserName(➥
      ProfileAuthenticationOption authenticationOption, ➥
      string usernameToMatch, ➥
      DateTime userInactiveSinceDate, ➥
      int pageIndex, int pageSize, out int totalRecords)
{
  throw new Exception("The method or operation is not implemented.");
}

public override ProfileInfoCollection FindProfilesByUserName(➥
      ProfileAuthenticationOption authenticationOption, ➥
      string usernameToMatch, int pageIndex, int pageSize, out int totalRecords)
{
  throw new Exception("The method or operation is not implemented.");
}

public override ProfileInfoCollection GetAllInactiveProfiles(➥
      ProfileAuthenticationOption authenticationOption, ➥
      DateTime userInactiveSinceDate, int pageIndex, ➥
      int pageSize, out int totalRecords)
```

```
    {
      throw new Exception("The method or operation is not implemented.");
    }

    public override ProfileInfoCollection GetAllProfiles(➥
        ProfileAuthenticationOption authenticationOption, ➥
        int pageIndex, int pageSize, out int totalRecords)
    {
      throw new Exception("The method or operation is not implemented.");
    }

    public override int GetNumberOfInactiveProfiles(➥
        ProfileAuthenticationOption authenticationOption, ➥
        DateTime userInactiveSinceDate)
    {
      throw new Exception("The method or operation is not implemented.");
    }

  }
}
```

The class has two principal methods, GetPropertyValues and SetPropertyValues, for retrieving and saving Profile settings. The GetPropertyValues method is called to obtain data from the Profile class. It then calls GetUserProfile to read the specific Profile from the XML file. Within the GetUserProfile method, a LINQ query retrieves the Profile. A loop reads each value and deserializes it depending on its settings. Binary data is saved in Base64 encoded format and protected within the <!CDATA> section. The content node is cast to Xcdata and string values are read directly. More complex types are treated as ProviderSpecific, which means that the provider is responsible for finding the right serialization. To support typical .NET types like System.Drawing.Color, without writing type specific code, the internal use type converter is used. This type converter usually supports the design-time experience. For instance, to show colors within the PropertyGrid control, a type converter is used. In this example, the type converter's type is saved into the document and retrieved from the typeConverter attribute. In the XML file, the fully qualified name is stored and used to create an instance of the converter. The converter provides a ConvertFromString method, which converts from string format to the specified object.

The SetPropertyValues method reverses the whole process. First, the same LINQ statement is used to retrieve the specific user's section. If it doesn't exist, an empty section is added. The collection of settings defined in the *web.config* file is used to assemble the current user's Profile. Each setting's "type" (as defined in the *web.config*) is used to obtain the associated TypeConverter object, whose ConvertToString method serializes the setting's value. If everything goes correctly, the XML fragment is saved in the XML file.

■**Note** This is a simplified scenario lacking error handling and multiuser support. It is only intended to show the construction of a custom provider and how to change the way the data is persisted.

The XML written using this code looks very simple, as shown in Listing 7-26.

Listing 7-26. *XML That Stores User Profile Settings*

```
<?xml version="1.0" encoding="utf-8"?>
<Profiles>
  <Profile UserName="User1">
    <BackColor serializedAs="ProviderSpecific"
```

```
                    typeConverter="System.Drawing.ColorConverter, System.Drawing,
                                   Version=2.0.0.0, Culture=neutral,
                                   PublicKeyToken=b03f5f7f11d50a3a">Red/BackColor>
    <User.Email serializedAs="String">joerg@krause.net</User.Email>
    <ForeColor serializedAs="ProviderSpecific"
                    typeConverter="System.Drawing.ColorConverter, System.Drawing,
                                   Version=2.0.0.0, Culture=neutral,
                                   PublicKeyToken=b03f5f7f11d50a3a">White</ForeColor>
  </Profile>
  <Profile UserName="User2">
    <BackColor serializedAs="ProviderSpecific"
                    typeConverter="System.Drawing.ColorConverter, System.Drawing,
                                   Version=2.0.0.0, Culture=neutral,
                                   PublicKeyToken=b03f5f7f11d50a3a">Blue</BackColor>
    <User.Email serializedAs="String">User3@user.de</User.Email>
    <ForeColor serializedAs="ProviderSpecific"
                    typeConverter="System.Drawing.ColorConverter, System.Drawing,
                                   Version=2.0.0.0, Culture=neutral,
                                   PublicKeyToken=b03f5f7f11d50a3a">Red</ForeColor>
  </Profile>
</Profiles>
```

Each Profile consists of a `<Profile>` element. This element has a `UserName` attribute which associates the settings with a particular user. The content depends on the property definition, as previously shown in Listing 7-10. Each element has the `serializedAs` attribute to indicate the serializer used. In the case of "ProviderSpecific" serializers, the `typeConverter` attribute defines how a value is converted into a string and back.

A Client Side–Driven Profile Provider

With AJAX (Asynchronous JavaScript and XML), you can also work with the custom Profile technology directly from your client-side script. This section is slightly different, as most of the code is JavaScript, instead of C#. The code extends the profile usage to the client and empowers script developers predominantly.

Exposing Profile Settings to AJAX Using Web.config

There's a minor addition required to the *web.config* file to enable AJAX to manage Profiles (Listing 7-12). You need to specify which properties in the Profile can be read from and which ones can be changed. The Profiles settings you saw in Listing 7-10 are unchanged. The required settings are shown in Listing 7-27.

Listing 7-27. *Web.config Settings to Configure AJAX Access to User Profile Properties*

```
<system.web.extensions>
    <scripting>
        <webServices>
            <profileService enabled="true"
                readAccessProperties="User.Name, User.Email,Size,ForeColor,BackColor"
                writeAccessProperties="User.Email,ForeColor,BackColor" />
        </webServices>
    </scripting>
</system.web.extensions>
```

All you need to do now is write the appropriate client code.

Creating the User Interface

Because we'll use pure AJAX to communicate with the server, you don't need server-side controls. The following form uses basic HTML to build the UI. There are a few HTML input controls, with an ID attribute assigned to each one (see Listing 7-28).

Listing 7-28. *Client Side Part of the Solution—the HTML Form*

```
<form runat="server">
<asp:ScriptManager ID="ScriptManager" runat="server" />
<fieldset id="ContactFieldset">
    <label>
        E-mail
        <input type="text" id="eMail" /></label><br />
    <label>
        User Name
        <input type="text" id="userName" disabled="disabled" /></label>
    <label>
        <br />
        Fore Color:
        <br />
        Red
        <input type="radio" name="ForeColor" id="fc1" value="Red" />
        Blue
        <input type="radio" name="ForeColor" id="fc2" value="Blue" />
        Green
        <input type="radio" name="ForeColor" id="fc3" value="Green" />
    </label>
    <br />
    <label>
        Back Color:
        <br />
        White
        <input type="radio" name="BackColor" id="bc1" value="White" />
        Beige
        <input type="radio" name="BackColor" id="bc2" value="Beige" />
        Yellow
        <input type="radio" name="BackColor" id="bc3" value="Yellow" />
    </label>
    <br />
    <button onclick="SaveProperties();">
        Save</button>
</fieldset>
<hr />
<p id="Status">
</p>
</form>
```

Figure 7-10 shows the form that appears.

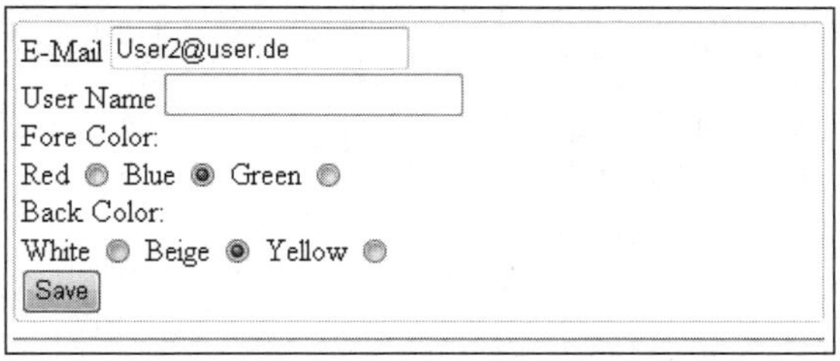

Figure 7-10. *The form with simple HTML form controls*

The JavaScript to Tie It Together

The final step is to add the JavaScript code which will communicate between the client and the server. First, we'll bring up the Profile for the current user and populate the form when the page loads. Then we'll expose a "Save" button so that the user can update their Profile. The final step is to inform the user that their Profile has been saved. We'll accomplish this with a status label that will hide itself after 5 seconds.

Breaking this down into steps, we'll first load the Profile for the authenticated user by calling the Load method of the Sys.Services.ProfileService object. If this call is successful, we'll populate the form. If there was an error, we'll alert the user. The callback methods are used to check success and error conditions. If successful, the values are read directly from the generic JavaScript class, using the same syntax for properties as the server. See Listing 7-29.

Listing 7-29. *JavaScript That Stores User Profile Settings*

```
window.onload = function() {
    Sys.Services.ProfileService.load(null, onLoadSuccess, onError);
}

function onLoadSuccess(obj) {
    $get("eMail").value = Sys.Services.ProfileService.properties.User.Email;
    $get("userName").value = Sys.Services.ProfileService.properties.User.Name;
    var fc = Sys.Services.ProfileService.properties.ForeColor.Name;
    $get("fc1").checked = (fc == 'Red');
    $get("fc2").checked = (fc == 'Blue');
    $get("fc3").checked = (fc == 'Green');
    var bc = Sys.Services.ProfileService.properties.BackColor.Name;
    $get("bc1").checked = (bc == 'White');
    $get("bc2").checked = (bc == 'Beige');
    $get("cc3").checked = (bc == 'Yellow');
}

function onError(error) {
    $get("Status").innerHTML = error.get_message();
}
```

The preceding code will attempt to load the Profile for the current user when the page loads. If this is successful, the onLoadSuccess function will fire and you can populate the form. If there was an error, the onError function will fire and an error message will be displayed to the user.

The final step is to build the "Save Profile" function. This is similar to the Load method that was previously called. Assign the new values to the Profile object in JavaScript and then call Save on the Sys.Services.ProfileService object. Again, the callback methods are used to check for success (and errors), as shown in Listing 7-30.

Listing 7-30. *Script Code That Stores User Profile Settings*

```
function SaveProperties() {
    Sys.Services.ProfileService.properties.User.Email = $get("eMail").value;
    Sys.Services.ProfileService.properties.User.Name = $get("username").value;
    var fc = '';
    fc += ($get("fc1").checked) ? 'Red' : '';
    fc += ($get("fc2").checked) ? 'Blue' : '';
    fc += ($get("fc3").checked) ? 'Green' : '';
    Sys.Services.ProfileService.properties.ForeColor = fc;
    var bc = '';
    bc += ($get("fc1").checked) ? 'White' : '';
    bc += ($get("fc2").checked) ? 'Beige' : '';
    bc += ($get("fc3").checked) ? 'Yellow' : '';
    Sys.Services.ProfileService.properties.BackColor = bc;
    Sys.Services.ProfileService.save(null, onSaveSuccess, onError);
}

function onSaveSuccess() {
    clearTimeout();
    // Display the success message to the user.
    $get("Status").innerHTML = "Your profile has been saved.";

    // Reset the display after 5 seconds have passed.
    setTimeout(function() { $get("Status").innerHTML = ""; }, 5000);
}
```

If all goes well, when you click the Save button you should see a message like the one in Figure 7-11.

Figure 7-11. *The form response when the Profile access was successful*

This is a very simple example which demonstrates how to access the Profile using the AJAX library. Its power comes from the library and its close relation to basic ASP.NET features. If you're not confident using the ASP.NET AJAX libraries because of their size or performance, keep in mind that they support larger parts of ASP.NET out of the box. This is very useful for smaller projects, as well as for constructing complex features quickly. However, in large projects with heavy access you might consider different ways, like other third-party libraries that support the specific parts required for Profiles only.

Extending Web Parts Personalization Providers

Web Parts are specialized user controls that have extensive client support. Web Parts make up portions of a web page, and allow users to change the page design. For example, users can move Web Parts around, hide or close them, and change their behavior. Web Parts are typically used to create portal pages that users can personalize. ASP.NET comes with all the pieces needed to construct a completely personalizable page. The framework includes components which perform the following tasks:

- Define and handle customizable sections through zones.

- Pull Web Parts from a catalogue.

- Export and import Web Parts so that users can share them like gadgets.

- Save the user's preferences to a permanent data store.

By now, it should be clear that a provider plays a role in this. Web Parts' settings, locations, and properties must be stored and retrieved when the user revisits the site. This implies that the user must be authenticated. There is an indirect relationship between the Membership and Role providers, and the Web Part personalization provider. There is no dependency on the Profile provider, as explained in the previous section.

Understanding the Web Parts Personalization Provider

Before you start working with the personalization provider and planning a custom implementation, you should understand the default provider and how it behaves. The default provider is `System.Web.UI.WebControls.WebParts.SqlPersonalizationProvider`, and it accesses the same SQL Server database used to support membership, roles, and profiles internally. The prime job of the personalization provider is to store the state of Web Parts, which consists of Web Parts content and the layout of Web Parts pages. The state is held in a container of type `System.Web.UI.WebControls.WebParts.PersonalizationState`. The personalization service using the provider serializes the data and sends it to the provider as a stream of bytes to store. Conversely, it retrieves and deserializes data to restore the state of Web Parts.

Because the `SqlPersonalizationProvider` is a final implementation, there exists an abstract base class for such personalization providers—the `PersonalizationProvider` class.

```
public abstract class PersonalizationProvider : ProviderBase
{
    protected PersonalizationProvider();
    public abstract string ApplicationName { get; set; }
    protected virtual IList CreateSupportedUserCapabilities();
    public virtual PersonalizationScope DetermineInitialScope( ➥
            WebPartManager webPartManager, PersonalizationState loadedState);
    public virtual IDictionary DetermineUserCapabilities( ➥
            WebPartManager webPartManager);
    public abstract PersonalizationStateInfoCollection FindState( ➥
            PersonalizationScope scope, PersonalizationStateQuery query, ➥
            int pageIndex, int pageSize, out int totalRecords);
    public abstract int GetCountOfState(PersonalizationScope scope, ➥
                                    PersonalizationStateQuery query);
    protected abstract void LoadPersonalizationBlobs(WebPartManager webPartManager,➥
            string path, string userName, ➥
            ref byte[] sharedDataBlob, ref byte[] userDataBlob);
    public virtual PersonalizationState LoadPersonalizationState( ➥
                WebPartManager webPartManager, bool ignoreCurrentUser);
```

```
        protected abstract void ResetPersonalizationBlob(➥
                    WebPartManager webPartManager, string path, string userName);
        public virtual void ResetPersonalizationState(WebPartManager webPartManager);
        public abstract int ResetState(PersonalizationScope scope, ➥
                                string[] paths, ➥
                                string[] usernames);
        public abstract int ResetUserState(string path, DateTime userInactiveSinceDate);
        protected abstract void SavePersonalizationBlob(WebPartManager webPartManager, ➥
                        string path, string userName, byte[] dataBlob);
        public virtual void SavePersonalizationState(PersonalizationState state);
}
```

The following table explains the methods and properties. The various `abstract` and `virtual` keywords indicate that only a few methods need to be implemented—the other methods are optional. As a result, this base class is a better starting point for a custom implementation than the `ProviderBase` base class (see Table 7-4).

Table 7-4. *Members of the PersonalizationProvider Base Class*

Member	Description
ApplicationName	Gets or sets the name of the application.
Name	Name of the provider.
Description	Friendly name or description.
CreateSupportedUserCapabilities	Returns a list of System.Web.UI.WebControls.WebParts. WebPartUserCapability objects that represent the set of known capabilities.
DetermineInitialScope	Determines whether the initial personalization scope should be Shared or User (from PersonalizationScope enum). Takes a WebPartManager object that manages the personalization information and the personalization state information. The method returns a PersonalizationScope enum value.
DetermineUserCapabilities	Returns a dictionary containing WebPartUserCapability instances that represent the personalization-related capabilities of the currently executing user account.
FindState	Returns a collection containing zero or more PersonalizationStateInfo objects based on scope and specific query parameters. Depends on scope, query, and paging information.
GetCountOfState	Returns the number of rows in the underlying data store that exist within the specified scope. Depends on query and scope.
LoadPersonalizationBlobs	Loads raw personalization data from the underlying data store. Takes a reference to the WebPartManager object managing the personalization data, a path as key, the user's name, and the blob data for shared and user part.
LoadPersonalizationState	Loads the raw data from the underlying data store and converts it into a PersonalizationState object.
ResetPersonalizationBlob	Deletes raw personalization data from the underlying data store.
ResetPersonalizationState	Resets personalization data to the underlying data store.
ResetState	Deletes personalization state from the underlying data store based on the specified parameters. Returns the number of rows deleted.

Member	Description
ResetUserState	Deletes Web Parts personalization data from the underlying data store based on the specified parameters.
SavePersonalizationBlob	Saves raw personalization data to the underlying data store.
SavePersonalizationState	Saves personalization data to a data store.

Implementing this is not difficult. The Load, Save, and Reset methods are the core parts of this class.

One crucial aspect is the scope of the personalization data. Web Parts personalization has two scopes: by user and by path. This allows you to personalize the behavior either for each individual user or by each page's path. Scoping by request path is called "shared" in the method names used by the provider. In these cases, the user name is set to null and all settings apply to all users. The provider must take care of such data and store it separately from the users' storage.

The provider support is optional for multiple applications based on the ApplicationName property, but recommended. If you use a local store, such as an XML file (as shown in the following example), the application name can be ignored.

Implementing a Custom Personalization Provider

A custom personalization provider has several prerequisites:

- A portal page must exist that handles several Web Parts.
- The site must support Authentication and user membership.
- The custom Web Part personalization provider and its store must exist.
- The *web.config* file must be properly configured to support Web Part personalization.

The next sections explain the required steps one-by-one.

Creating a Portal Page

Our Portal page to test the solution is a simple Web Part page, as shown in Listing 7-31.

Listing 7-31. *The "Portal" Page to Test the Solution*

```
<form id="form1" runat="server">
<div>
    <asp:WebPartManager ID="WebPartManager1" runat="server">
        <Personalization Enabled="true" ProviderName="XmlPersonalizationProvider" />
    </asp:WebPartManager>
    <table style="width: 100%">
        <tr valign="middle" style="background: #dddddd">
            <td colspan="2">
                <h2>
                    Welcome to our Portal,
                    <asp:LoginName ID="LoginName1" runat="server" />
                </h2>
            </td>
            <td>
                <asp:Menu ID="Menu1" runat="server" ➥
                        OnMenuItemClick="Menu1_MenuItemClick">
                </asp:Menu>
```

```
                </td>
            </tr>
            <tr valign="top">
                <td style="width: 20%">
                    <asp:CatalogZone ID="CatalogZone1" runat="server">
                        <ZoneTemplate>
                            <asp:PageCatalogPart ID="PageCatalogPart1" runat="server" />
                        </ZoneTemplate>
                    </asp:CatalogZone>
                            <asp:EditorZone ID="EditorZone1" runat="server">
                            </asp:EditorZone>
                </td>
                <td style="width: 60%">
                    <asp:WebPartZone ID="WebPartZone1" runat="server">
                    </asp:WebPartZone>
                </td>
                <td style="width: 20%">
                    <asp:WebPartZone ID="WebPartZone2" runat="server">
                    <TitleBarVerbStyle BackColor="ActiveBorder" />
                        <ZoneTemplate>
                            <asp:Calendar ID="Calendar1" runat="server"></asp:Calendar>
                            <asp:FileUpload ID="FileUpload1" runat="server" />
                        </ZoneTemplate>
                    </asp:WebPartZone>
                </td>
            </tr>
            <tr>
                <td colspan="3">
                    <asp:LoginStatus ID="LoginStatus1" runat="server" />
                </td>
            </tr>
        </table>
    </div>
</form>
```

The only dependency on other code parts is the selection of the current provider:

```
<Personalization Enabled="true" ProviderName="XmlPersonalizationProvider" />
```

As shown, the personalization must be turned on in order to activate the provider using the Enabled attribute. The name of the provider is defined in *web.config*. (See the section "Configure the Provider" for more details.)

To force the page to change the settings and invoke the provider, the user must enter the Edit mode of the Web Part page. To do this easily, the following code-behind code is used:

```
public partial class _Default : System.Web.UI.Page
{
    protected void Page_Load(object sender, EventArgs e)
    {
        if (!IsPostBack)
        {
            // Create a menu of web part modes
            MenuItem rootItem = new MenuItem("Select Web Part Mode");
            foreach (WebPartDisplayMode mode in WebPartManager1.DisplayModes)
            {
                rootItem.ChildItems.Add(new MenuItem(mode.Name));
            }
            Menu1.Items.Add(rootItem);
```

```
        }
    }

    protected void Menu1_MenuItemClick(object sender, MenuEventArgs e)
    {
        WebPartManager1.DisplayMode = WebPartManager1.DisplayModes[e.Item.Text];
    }
}
```

The menu is filled with items from the collection of acceptable modes. In the `MenuItemClick` event handler, the same value is used to set the current mode (see Figure 7-12).

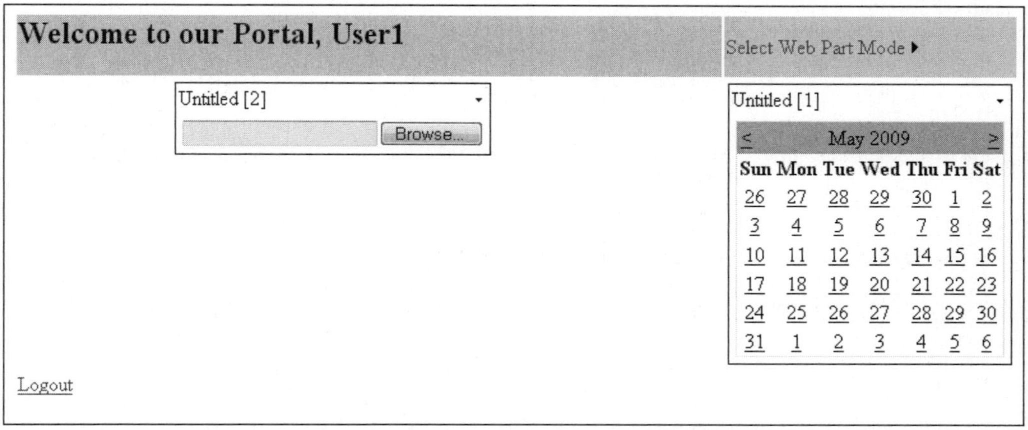

Figure 7-12. *The Web Part page*

Prepare Authentication

For a simple scenario to login and logout users, I set up Forms authentication in *web.config*. Furthermore, I store the users' credentials directly in *web.config* and configure the `Membership` provider to use that data instead of data from the default provider (SQL Server). This can be accomplished by handling the authentication event manually. The *web.config* section that defines the users looks like Listing 7-32.

Listing 7-32. *Define Some Users Quickly to Test the Application*

```
<authorization>
    <deny users="?"/>
</authorization>
<authentication mode="Forms">
    <forms>
        <credentials passwordFormat="Clear">
            <user name="User1" password="User1"/>
            <user name="User2" password="User2"/>
            <user name="User3" password="User3"/>
        </credentials>
    </forms>
</authentication>
```

The application then requires at least one page in order to change and use the profile settings, as well as a login page. The login page consists of a single `Login` control and an event handler (see Listings 7-33 and 7-34).

Listing 7-33. *The Login Page in Its Simplest Form*

```
<body>
    <form id="form1" runat="server">
    <div>
        <asp:Login ID="Login1" runat="server" onauthenticate="Login1_Authenticate">
        </asp:Login>
        <br />
    </div>
    </form>
</body>
</html>
```

Listing 7-34. *An Event Handler Forces the Login Control to Use the Configured User Names*

```
public partial class Login : System.Web.UI.Page
{
    protected void Page_Load(object sender, EventArgs e)
    {
    }

    protected void Login1_Authenticate(object sender, AuthenticateEventArgs e)
    {
        e.Authenticated = FormsAuthentication.Authenticate(Login1.UserName, ↦
                                                           Login1.Password);
    }
}
```

The next page is also for testing purposes. It contains a simple form to save new profile settings, show current settings, and change accounts.

Create the Provider

The following implementation uses XML to store data. It renders the application independent of a SQL Server database. The implementation is as simple as possible—only the basic methods for loading and saving data are fully implemented (see Listing 7-35).

Listing 7-35. *A Web Part Personalization Provider Using XML*

```
using System;
using System.Collections.Generic;
using System.Linq;
using System.Web;
using System.Web.UI.WebControls.WebParts;
using System.IO;
using System.Web.Hosting;
using System.Data;
using System.Xml.Linq;
using System.Xml.XPath;

namespace Apress.Extensibility.WebPartProvider
{
    public class XmlPersonalizationProvider : PersonalizationProvider
    {
        private const string SETTINGSNAME = "WPSettings.xml";
        private const string SETTINGSTAG = "WPSettings";
        private string configFile;
```

```csharp
public override void Initialize(string name, , ➥
          System.Collections.Specialized.NameValueCollection config)
{
    base.Initialize(name, config);
    configFile = HttpContext.Current.Request.MapPath(, ➥
              Path.Combine("~/App_Data/", SETTINGSNAME));
    // XML
    if (!File.Exists(configFile))
    {
        XDocument cfgDoc = new XDocument(
            new XElement("WebPartData", new XAttribute("Created", , ➥
                          DateTime.Now.ToShortDateString()),
                new XElement("UserScope"),
                new XElement("SharedScope")));
        cfgDoc.Declaration = new XDeclaration("1.0", "utf-8", "true");
        cfgDoc.Save(configFile);
    }
}

// NOTE: only Shared-scope personalization is loaded
protected override void LoadPersonalizationBlobs(
  WebPartManager webPartManager,
  string path,
  string userName,
  ref byte[] sharedDataBlob,
  ref byte[] userDataBlob)
{
    XDocument cfgDoc = XDocument.Load(configFile);
    var root = cfgDoc.Element("WebPartData");
    if (userName == null)
    {
        object cachedPageSettings = HttpContext.Current.Cache[ ➥
                                    SETTINGSTAG + ":" + path];
        if (cachedPageSettings != null)
        {
            sharedDataBlob = (byte[])cachedPageSettings;
        }
        else
        {
            var shared = root.Element("SharedScope")
                        .Elements("Page")
                        .Single(n => ➥
                          n.Attribute("name").Value.Equals(userName));
            if (shared == null)
            {
                sharedDataBlob = null;
            }
            else
            {
                sharedDataBlob = Convert.FromBase64String(shared.Value);
                // cache shared settings
                webPartManager.Page.Cache.Insert(SETTINGSTAG + ":" + path,➥
                                        sharedDataBlob, ➥
                      new System.Web.Caching.CacheDependency(configFile));
            }
        }
```

```csharp
        }
        else
        {
            var pageElement = root.XPathSelectElement(
                String.Format("//UserScope/User[@name='{0}']/Page[@name='{1}']",
                userName,
                path));
            if (pageElement != null)
            {
                userDataBlob = Convert.FromBase64String(pageElement.Value);
            }
        }
    }
}

protected override void ResetPersonalizationBlob(
  WebPartManager webPartManager,
  string path,
  string userName)
{
}

protected override void SavePersonalizationBlob(
  WebPartManager webPartManager,
  string path,
  string userName,
  byte[] dataBlob)
{
    string sBlob = Convert.ToBase64String(dataBlob);
    lock (this)
    {
        XDocument cfgDoc = XDocument.Load(configFile);
        var root = cfgDoc.Element("WebPartData");
        if (!String.IsNullOrEmpty(userName))
        {
            // Scope: user
            var userElement = root.XPathSelectElement(
                    String.Format("//UserScope/User[@name='{0}']",
                    userName));
            if (userElement == null)
            {
                userElement = root.Element("UserScope");
                // no user, add complete tree
                userElement.Add(
                    new XElement("User", new XAttribute("name", userName),
                        new XElement("Page", new XAttribute("name", path),
                            sBlob)));
            }
            else
            {
                // with user, check page
                var pageElement = userElement.Elements("Page")
                            .Single(n => ➥
                            n.Attribute("name").Value.Equals(path));
                if (pageElement == null)
                {
                    // no page
                    userElement.Add(new XElement("Page",
```

```
                    new XAttribute("name", path),
                        sBlob));
            }
            else
            {
                // new data for page
                pageElement.Value = sBlob;
            }
        }
    }
    else
    {
        // Scope: Shared
        var sharedElement = root.Elements("SharedScope")
                                .Elements("Page")
                                .Single(p => ➥
                                    p.Attribute("Name").Value.Equals(path));
        if (sharedElement == null)
        {
            sharedElement.Add(new XElement("Page",
                new XAttribute("name", path),
                sBlob));
        }
        else
        {
            sharedElement.Value = sBlob;
        }
    }
    cfgDoc.Save(configFile);
    }
}

public override string ApplicationName
{
    get;
    set;
}

public override int GetCountOfState(
  PersonalizationScope scope,
  PersonalizationStateQuery query)
{
    return 0;
}

public override PersonalizationStateInfoCollection FindState(
  PersonalizationScope scope,
  PersonalizationStateQuery query,
  int pageIndex,
  int pageSize,
  out int totalRecords)
{
    totalRecords = 0;
    return null;
}

public override int ResetState(
```

```
        PersonalizationScope scope,
        string[] paths,
        string[] usernames)
    {
        return 0;
    }

    public override int ResetUserState(
        string path,
        DateTime userInactiveSinceDate)
    {
        return 0;
    }
}

}
```

During the call to Initialize, a data store in the form of an XML file will be created, if there isn't one already. When the user changes properties of Web Parts, the SavePersonalizationBlob method is called. The approach used is to search for the userName, and if it is null, meaning the user is not authenticated, assume that it's a shared scope setting. Otherwise, it's a personal setting, and the user element is retrieved. I also assume that data for this user does not already exist. (This is why XPath expressions are used instead of XLinq expression chains.) If the <User> element does not exist, it's created using the current data. The data is passed to the provider as a byte array, and stored as a Base64 encoded string in the XML element. If the <User> element exists, the <Page> element is retrieved. Each personalized page has its own XML element. If this element does not exist, it's created and the encoded string is used as its value. If it does exist, the current contents are replaced with the Value property.

A similar technique is used to retrieve the data. Every time the page refreshes, the provider is called to return the data as a byte array. If there is no data, you can safely return null. While the shared data is stored in a cache, the data for each user is retrieved directly from the XML file. There is plenty of scope for improving the file handling and caching, but that's beyond the scope of this chapter. To locate the data again, an XPath expression is used. If a value is present, the FromBase64String method converts the string into a byte array.

This code produces an XML file in the App_Data folder in this manner:

```
<?xml version="1.0" encoding="utf-8"?>
<WebPartData Created="5/16/2009">
  <UserScope>
    <User name="User1">
      <Page name="~/Default.aspx">/wEUKwAKAgICARkqMVN5c3RlbS5XZWIuVUkuV2ViQ29udHJvbHMuV-
2ViUGFydHMuV2ViUGFydE1hbmFnZXIFBV9fd3BtZgIBHhBXZWJQYXJ0U3RhdGVVc2VyFCsACAUMZ3dwQ2FsZW5kYX-
IxBQxXZWJQYXJ0OWm9uZTJmaAUOZ3dwRmlsZVVwbG9hZDEFDFdlYlBhcnRab25lMWZoaGg=</Page>
    </User>
    <User name="User2">
      <Page name="~/Default.aspx">/wEUKwAKAgICARkqMVN5c3RlbS5XZWIuVUkuV2ViQ29udHJvbHMuV-
2ViUGFydHMuV2ViUGFydE1hbmFnZXIFBV9fd3BtZgIBHhBXZWJQYXJ0U3RhdGVVc2VyFCsACAUMZ3dwQ2FsZW5kYX-
IxBQxXZWJQYXJ0OWm9uZTFmaAUOZ3dwRmlsZVVwbG9hZDEFDFdlYlBhcnRab25lMmZoaGg=</Page>
    </User>
  </UserScope>
  <SharedScope />
</WebPartData>
```

Although its format is not impressive, this has everything you need in order to store data for any number of users and any number of personalized pages. The number of pages is usually low—for a customizable portal page it's one—and the number of active users depends on your application. For an intranet with up to several hundred users, the XML file storage solution is easy to implement and sufficiently fast.

Configure the Provider

Having built the provider, it needs to be configured for use. I use Forms Authentication in the example and store the users' data in *web.config*, as shown in the following. This is not meant to be used as production code, but it simplifies development by making user management very easy.

```
<system.web>
   <webParts>
     <personalization defaultProvider="XmlPersonalizationProvider">
        <providers>
          <add name="XmlPersonalizationProvider"
      type="Apress.Extensibility.WebPartProvider.XmlPersonalizationProvider"/>
        </providers>
     </personalization>
   </webParts>
   <authentication mode="Forms">
    <forms>
     <credentials passwordFormat="Clear">
        <user name="User1" password="user1"/>
        <user name="User2" password="user2"/>
        <user name="User3" password="user3"/>
     </credentials>
    </forms>
   </authentication>
   <authorization>
    <deny users="?"/>
   </authorization>
```

Testing the Custom Web Part Personalization Provider

You can use the three prepared user accounts to test the provider. Simply launch the application and log on using one of the previous credentials. Switch to "Edit" mode with the menu. Move the Web Parts around and rearrange the page. The data is saved immediately. Logout and log back in as a different user. Create another page layout. Log out again and log in with the account you used first. The page layout for the first user should reappear. Other than the provider, there is no other custom code enabling this feature. The Web Part Personalization infrastructure is already available in ASP.NET, and Web Parts used here are oblivious to the custom provider.

■**Caution** The sample provider lacks error handling and testing, and does not fully implement all the features of Web Parts providers. Before using it as production code, more development is required.

Summary

In this chapter, you looked at security and Profile features. The user-driven security model is covered by the Membership and Role services, both of which use providers to access a data store. Creating customized providers significantly extends the built-in role and membership models.

Once a user is authenticated, you can associate data with his or her Profile. The Profile service uses a provider that can be extended—or rewritten using a completely customized version. A Profile provider can also be reached by a client using pure AJAX, enabling you to save values to and retrieve values from the server without invoking server-side code.

Both extension models provide a transparent and simple way of extending and customizing behavior, while allowing the existing controls to function as they would with default providers. The Web Part Personalization Provider is an integrated technique which stores settings of Web Part pages for an authenticated user in a custom data store. In this chapter, you learned which base class to implement in order to change the default behavior and storage medium.

CHAPTER 8

■ ■ ■

Site Management

In this chapter, I'll look at site-specific extensibility features such as the Site Map provider, which is based on the extensible provider model that we've already learned about. A site map defines the navigation structure of a Web site. By default, the data store is the *web.sitemap* XML file. Although it's easy to change the default setting, you'll need a custom site map provider in order to store data anywhere other than in an XML file.

The navigation depends usually on the web pages on disc. If you wish to hide the internal physical structure of your site or to serve pages that do not originate from disk files, the VirtualPathProvider can accomplish this. Using this you can create a virtual site structure.

In this chapter, you'll learn how to implement and modify the behavior of the SiteMapProvider and VirtualPathProvider.

Site Map Providers

ASP.NET features a data-driven navigation system that uses hierarchical data sources and associated controls. It's much easier to create a site navigational system and track the current position of the user if you use the Menu control, TreeView control, or SiteMapPath control.

As is common in ASP.NET, these controls use a provider to obtain data from a specific data source.

Internal Site Map Provider

Before you start writing your own provider, let's look at how the internal one is implemented and how it works. The XmlSiteMapProvider provider reads an XML file containing the site structure as a hierarchy of SiteMapNode elements. The file itself looks like this:

```
<siteMap>
  <siteMapNode title="Home" description="Home" url="~/default.aspx" >
    <siteMapNode title="Services" description="Services we offer" ➥
                 url="~/Services.aspx">
    <siteMapNode title="Training" description="Training classes" ➥
                 url="~/Training.aspx" />
    <siteMapNode title="Consulting" description="Consulting services" ➥
                 url="~/Consulting.aspx" />
    </siteMapNode>
  </siteMapNode>
</siteMap>
```

The file is named *web.sitemap* by default. However, you can configure the provider to accept any filename. The best way is to use the SiteMapDataSource control. A page using these controls could look like this:

```
<body>
  <form id="form1" runat="server">
  <div>
  <h2>Using SiteMapPath</h2>
  <asp:SiteMapPath ID="SiteMapPath1" Runat="server"></asp:SiteMapPath>

  <asp:SiteMapDataSource ID="SiteMapDataSource1" Runat="server" />

  <h2>Using TreeView</h2>
  <asp:TreeView ID="TreeView1" Runat="Server" DataSourceID="SiteMapDataSource1">
  </asp:TreeView>

  <h2>Using Menu</h2>
  <asp:Menu ID="Menu2" Runat="server" DataSourceID="SiteMapDataSource1">
  </asp:Menu>

  <h2>Using a Horizontal Menu</h2>
  <asp:Menu ID="Menu1" Runat="server" DataSourceID="SiteMapDataSource1"
    Orientation="Horizontal"
    StaticDisplayLevels="2" >
  </asp:Menu>

  </div>
  </form>
</body>
```

This web page already has a complete navigation structure. The SiteMapPath control indicates your current position in the site structure via a "breadcrumb" style display. The TreeView and Menu controls create a tree of all pages. The Menu control provides additionally a JavaScript-driven drop-down menu. Both include plenty of features and assistance for creating sophisticated menus. As shown in the example, the controls can appear several times to create top level, side level, or other kinds of menu. You can even use several SiteMapDataSource controls to define different entry points in the site structure or prepare submenus and partial menus.

■**Tip** If you have not yet used these controls intensively, the following web address is one entry point into the documentation: http://msdn.microsoft.com/en-us/library/ms227558.aspx.

This model has several advantages—as well as disadvantages. On the positive side, it's easy and fast to use, and the structure of the content relates directly to the navigation. Navigation is usually structured hierarchically, and XML represents this perfectly.

There are also some negatives. First, the URL is used internally as a key, which means that you cannot use the same URL twice to point to a page from different locations in the hierarchy. It's possible to work around this—you could add a dummy querystring parameter, or use the UrlMappings defined in the *web.config*, but this isn't ideal. Furthermore, the default provider reads the definition file once the application starts, and holds the whole content in memory. Large structures operating on several levels for submenus consume a lot of memory.

The internal provider is defined in the *web.config* file like any other:

```
<system.web>
  <siteMap defaultProvider="XmlSiteMapProvider" enabled="true">
    <providers>
      <add name="XmlSiteMapProvider"
        description="Default SiteMap provider."
        type="System.Web.XmlSiteMapProvider"
```

```
        siteMapFile="Web.sitemap" />
    </providers>
  </siteMap>
</system.web>
```

The configuration, the Site Map file, and the appropriate controls are everything you need for complete site navigation.

Localization

The embedded Site Map provider supports full localization. The resource provider (demonstrated in Chapter 4) is aware of the encoded resource keys and can obtain the content from a resource file. When providing different resource files for languages or cultures, you only need one Site Map definition for each different language. It is, however, not possible to have different site structures for each culture.

Security Issues

The Site Map provider model does support a security concept. If you define the roles for each node, the provider will display only those nodes the user is permitted to view. Security trimming can be switched on and off. Microsoft states that using more than 150 nodes will have a serious performance impact. When using the Site Map programmatically, the provider will return null if the current user has no access rights, and an exception will occur if the user is not permitted to read the root node.

Reasons to Write a Custom Site Map Provider

There are several reasons why you might consider creating a custom provider:

- You support localization and need a different site structure for each culture without using several files.
- You have hundreds of nodes and need security trimming.
- You have limited memory but a large structure.
- You want to support the same nodes several times in the hierarchy.
- You want to allow users to add/remove nodes.
- You want to persist the structure in an alternative data store.

There are two ways of customizing the provider's behavior: either extending the default provider, or writing your own. Extending the default provider lets you keep the XML file, but allows different behavior when retrieving nodes or adding security features. Using your own provider gives you the ability to use a different data source.

■Tip You can use XmlDocument or XDocument classes to retrieve and change nodes directly in the *web.sitemap* file in order to edit the site structure on the fly. This does not require a new provider, but extends the behavior of the site navigation universe. Consider this before writing a lot of code just to get read-write access.

Writing a Custom Site Map Provider

The purpose of the provider shown here is to access another data source. For web farm or web garden scenarios, or flexible access to the site structure definition, a SQL Server database is the best choice. The amount of data is relatively small, and SQL Server retains it in memory, resulting in fast access.

Prerequisites

A custom provider inherits from a base class (as we've seen many times). For the Site Map provider, you have a choice between the System.Web.StaticSiteMapProvider class and its abstract base class, System.Web.SiteMapProvider. These greatly simplify things, because they come with several basic methods already implemented.

You can use the StaticSiteMapProvider if

- You read nodes either once or rarely.

- All information is cached through the lifetime of the provider.

The lifetime of the provider is usually the lifetime of the application. Changing the Site Map requires a restart.

If any one of the following conditions is met, the SiteMapProvider type is a better choice:

- The data is stored in a database.

- The data changes frequently throughout the application's lifetime.

- The user can change the structure and personalize the menu.

Learning About the Base Classes

Before you start implementing, you'll need to know which methods you'll be dealing with. First, take a look at the SiteMapProvider class:

```
public abstract class SiteMapProvider : ProviderBase
{
    protected SiteMapProvider();

    public virtual SiteMapNode CurrentNode { get; }
    public bool EnableLocalization { get; set; }
    public virtual SiteMapProvider ParentProvider { get; set; }
    public string ResourceKey { get; set; }
    public virtual SiteMapNode RootNode { get; }
    public virtual SiteMapProvider RootProvider { get; }
    public bool SecurityTrimmingEnabled { get; }

    public event SiteMapResolveEventHandler SiteMapResolve;

    protected virtual void AddNode(SiteMapNode node);
    protected internal virtual void AddNode(SiteMapNode node, ➥
                                    SiteMapNode parentNode);
    public virtual SiteMapNode FindSiteMapNode(HttpContext context);
    public abstract SiteMapNode FindSiteMapNode(string rawUrl);
    public virtual SiteMapNode FindSiteMapNodeFromKey(string key);
    public abstract SiteMapNodeCollection GetChildNodes(SiteMapNode node);
    public virtual SiteMapNode GetCurrentNodeAndHintAncestorNodes(int upLevel);
```

```
    public virtual SiteMapNode GetCurrentNodeAndHintNeighborhoodNodes(int upLevel, ➥
                                                        int downLevel);
    public abstract SiteMapNode GetParentNode(SiteMapNode node);
    public virtual SiteMapNode ➥
            GetParentNodeRelativeToCurrentNodeAndHintDownFromParent(➥
                                            int walkupLevels, ➥
                                            int relativeDepthFromWalkup);
    public virtual SiteMapNode GetParentNodeRelativeToNodeAndHintDownFromParent(➥
                SiteMapNode node, int walkupLevels, int relativeDepthFromWalkup);
    protected internal abstract SiteMapNode GetRootNodeCore();
    protected static SiteMapNode GetRootNodeCoreFromProvider(➥
                SiteMapProvider provider);
    public virtual void HintAncestorNodes(SiteMapNode node, int upLevel);
    public virtual void HintNeighborhoodNodes(SiteMapNode node, int upLevel, ➥
                                        int downLevel);
    public override void Initialize(string name, NameValueCollection attributes);
    public virtual bool IsAccessibleToUser(HttpContext context, SiteMapNode node);
    protected internal virtual void RemoveNode(SiteMapNode node);
    protected SiteMapNode ResolveSiteMapNode(HttpContext context);
}
```

Tables 8-1, 8-2, and 8-3 explain the methods, events, and properties, as we need to know what to implement and the intended behavior. The only unusual thing is the length of some method names, but these names clarify the methods usage.

Because the provider is transparent, controls such as Menu or TreeView using the abstract base class to get their data work with a custom implementation, too. First, the properties defined by the provider are shown in Table 8-1.

Table 8-1. *Properties Defined in SiteMapProvider*

Property	Description
Name	The name of the provider as configured in *web.config* (inherited from ProviderBase).
Description	A friendly description (inherited from ProviderBase).
CurrentNode	Reference to the current node (and therefore the related page).
EnableLocalization	Indicates whether the provider supports localization using resources.
ParentProvider	The parent provider, if the provider supports a hierarchy of providers.
ResourceKey	The root name of the resources used to localize content.
RootNode	The root node.
RootProvider	The root provider, if a hierarchy of providers is used.
SecurityTrimmingEnabled	Indicates whether or not the provider supports security settings. If supported, the provider doesn't return nodes that don't match the security level.

Second, an event that the provider should support is shown in Table 8-2.

Table 8-2. *Events Defined in SiteMapProvider*

Event	Description
SiteMapResolve	Event raised when data requested from data sources is ready. In the original implementation, this is the case when the CurrentNode property is called.

Third, the methods that build most features are shown in Table 8-3.

Table 8-3. *Methods Defined in SiteMapProvider*

Method	Description
AddNode	Adds either the root node or another node
FindSiteMapNode	Finds a node
FindSiteMapNodeFromKey	Finds a node using a key
GetChildNodes	Gets all child nodes of the specified node
GetCurrentNodeAndHintAncestorNodes	Gets the current node and pre-loads the ancestors
GetCurrentNodeAndHintNeighborhoodNodes	Gets the current node and pre-loads the neighbors
GetParentNode	Gets the parent node
GetParentNodeRelativeToCurrentNodeAndHintDownFromParent	Gets the current node's parent node and pre-loads all ancestors for the provided number of levels
GetParentNodeRelativeToNodeAndHintDownFromParent	Gets the given node's parent and pre-loads all ancestors for the provided number of levels
GetRootNodeCore	Gets the parent regardless of the provider if a hierarchy of providers is used
GetRootNodeCoreFromProvider	Gets the parent of the specified provider if a hierarchy of providers is used
HintNeighborhoodNodes	Pre-loads a number of levels down or up the hierarchy from the given node
HintAncestorNodes	Returns ancestor nodes for the given number of levels above the current node
IsAccessibleToUser	Checks whether the given node is accessible to the user
Initialize	Initializes the provider (inherited from base class)
RemoveNode	Removes a node
ResolveSiteMapNode	Fires the SiteMapResolved event

Several methods include "Hint" in their name. Use these methods to handle data in huge hierarchies, as they allow you to deal with large amounts of data and they avoid holding the whole tree in memory. Consider implementations such as SharePoint, which could create deep hierarchies of site collections, sites, pages, and subpages that might have their own navigation systems. Using the "Hint" methods, you can define the depth that is populated from the tree. This limits the data handled by the provider to an amount that makes sense for the specific action taken by the user. It also assumes that nobody wants to see the whole hierarchy at once.

Sitemap Nodes in Code

The provider transforms the data from the data source into a hierarchy of SiteMapNode objects. The base class implements three interfaces, ICloneable, IHierarchyData, and INavigateUIData. This indicates the true nature of the object hierarchy, as well as how to deal with the nodes (see Table 8-4).

Table 8-4. *Members Defined in SiteMapNode*

Member	Description
GetAllNodes	Gets a read-only list of all nodes beginning from the current node.
GetDataSourceView	Gets the SiteMapDataSourceView object that represents the underlying data source.
GetHierarchicalDataSourceView	Gets the SiteMapHierarchicalDataSourceView object that represents the underlying hierarchical data source.
IsAccessibleToUser	Determines whether the node is accessible according to current security context.
IsDescendantOf	Determines whether the current node is a descendant of the given node.
GetExplicitResourceString	Gets the localized string to retrieve the explicit resource definition. Accessible in derived classes only.
GetImplicitResourceString	Gets the localized string to retrieve the implicit resource definition.
ChildNodes	Gets all child nodes.
ParentNode	Gets the parent node.
HasChildNodes	Indicates whether a node has children.
Item	Gets the current node.
Path	Gets the path that describes the node.
Type	Gets the node's type.
Description	Gets the node's description.
Name	Gets the node's name.
NavigateUrl	Gets the node's URL.
Value	Gets the node's title.
Attributes	Additional attributes of the node as NameValueCollection.
Key	Key the node uses internally to get identified.
NextSibling	The next sibling node.
PreviousSibling	The previous sibling node.
ReadOnly	Indicates whether the node is read only.
ResourceKey	The resource key used to localize the parameters.
Roles	The assigned roles that indicate who can access the nodes.
RootNode	The root node.
Title	The title of the node.
Url	The URL the node leads to.

Implementing Security

The SecurityTrimmingEnabled property indicates if the nodes are limited for the current user. It can be set in *web.config* as shown next. The authorization settings added show role definitions that correspond to the roles attribute of the associated *web.sitemap* file.

```
<siteMap defaultProvider="XmlSiteMapProvider" enabled="true">
    <providers>
      <add name="XmlSiteMapProvider"
        description="Default SiteMap provider."
        type="System.Web.XmlSiteMapProvider "
        siteMapFile="Web.sitemap"
        securityTrimmingEnabled="true" />
    </providers>
</siteMap>
<location path="~/admin.aspx">
    <system.web>
      <authorization>
        <allow roles="Admin"/>
        <deny users="*"/>
      </authorization>
    </system.web>
</location>
```

The default implementation used in XmlSiteMapProvider resolves the roles attributes defined in the siteMapNode elements in the *web.sitemap* file. If the current user is in the role, and the RoleProvider is activated, the XmlSiteMapProvider limits visibility to the correct nodes. If used programmatically, the IsAccessibleToUser property possessed by each SiteMapNode instance indicates the same thing. The list of available roles is also available in the Roles property. A query can use either the IList type directly or "*" for all. The programmatic access uses a simple fallback strategy:

- If the role was found or the query consists of "*", return the node.
- If the role was not found, attempt to authenticate the URL defined by the node.
- If Windows authentication is used, attempt to authenticate again using the credentials of the current user and the ACL (access control list) of the target file for the URL.

If everything fails, the provider does not return the node and assumes that the user does not have sufficient authority. Note that this is not an inheritance strategy. If a user has the right to read a specific node, it does not follow that he or she has the right to read any subsequent node. This allows different security settings for each level. However, if the right to access a specific node is denied, the strategy stops and all child nodes are blocked. This ensures that there are no isolated child nodes accessible from any places other than the sitemap hierarchy.

Implementing a SQL Server–Based Navigation

SQL Server 2008 includes a new data type, HierarchyId. This can be used to implement a custom database-driven Site Map provider.

Preparing the Database

First, a database is required. In this example, I use the common *aspnetdb.mdf* database created for the role and membership provider, if default providers are used. Listing 8-1 defines an additional table named *aspnet_Navigation*.

Listing 8-1. *The Table Definition Using the HierarchyId Data Type*

```
CREATE TABLE aspnet_Navigation
(
    SiteMapNode    hierarchyid     NOT NULL,
    Title          varchar(100)    NOT NULL,
    Description    varchar(200)    NULL,
    Url            varchar(200)    NULL,
    Roles          varchar(200)    NULL
)
```

Let's proceed by filling in some data, as shown in Figure 8-1.

	SiteMapNode	Title	Description	Url	Roles
	/	Navi	Navigation	default.aspx	*NULL*
	/1/	Menu	Menu Page	menu.aspx	*NULL*
	/2/	Tree	Treeview Page	tree.aspx	*NULL*
	/3/	Pfad	Path Page	path.aspx	*NULL*
	/1/1/	Untermenu	Submenu Page	menu1.aspx	*NULL*
►*	*NULL*	*NULL*	*NULL*	*NULL*	*NULL*

Figure 8-1. *Table with some test values in Visual Studio Professional*

The HierarchyId column contains the node definition as a path beginning with a slash. The internal format is binary and must be transformed using the ToString method SQL provides for this type. This is what Visual Studio does when presenting the table data in edit mode.

Creating the Provider

Now that we have everything, we can create the custom provider. Listing 8-2 shows the final result. You can create it in the current Web project or in a separate project. Using it in a Web project will change the configuration slightly. The big advantage of building a custom Site Map provider in its own project is to be able to reuse it with other web applications.

Listing 8-2. *The SqlSiteMapProvider Using the HierarchyId Data Type*

```
using System;
using System.Collections.Generic;
using System.Collections.Specialized;
using System.Configuration.Provider;
using System.Data;
using System.Data.Common;
using System.Data.SqlClient;
using System.Linq;
using System.Security.Permissions;
using System.Web;
using System.Web.Configuration;

namespace Apress.Extensibility.SqlSiteMap
{

    [SqlClientPermission(SecurityAction.Demand, Unrestricted = true)]
    public class SqlSiteMapProvider : StaticSiteMapProvider
    {
        private string _connect;
        private int _indexNode;
        private int _indexTitle;
```

```
        private int _indexUrl;
        private int _indexDesc;
        private int _indexRoles;
        private int _indexParent;
        private int _indexRoot;

        private SiteMapNode _root;
        private Dictionary<string, SiteMapNode> _nodes = ➡
            new Dictionary<string, SiteMapNode>(16);

        public override void Initialize(string name, NameValueCollection config)
        {
            if (config == null)
                throw new ArgumentNullException("config");
            if (String.IsNullOrEmpty(name))
                name = "SqlSiteMapProvider";

            base.Initialize(name, config);
            string connect = "siteMap";
            if (WebConfigurationManager.ConnectionStrings[connect] == null)
                throw new ProviderException("No connection");
            _connect = WebConfigurationManager.ConnectionStrings[connect]. ➡
                    ConnectionString;
            if (String.IsNullOrEmpty(_connect))
                throw new ProviderException("no connection string");
        }

        public override SiteMapNode BuildSiteMap()
        {
            lock (this)
            {
                if (_root != null)
                    return _root;
                SqlConnection connection = new SqlConnection(_connect);
                try
                {
                    connection.Open();
                    SqlCommand command;
                    command = new SqlCommand(
                        @"SELECT *, SiteMapNode.ToString() AS SiteMapNodeString,
                    SiteMapNode.GetAncestor(1).ToString() AS Parent,
                    hierarchyid::GetRoot().ToString() AS Root
                    FROM aspnet_Navigation", connection);
                    command.CommandType = CommandType.Text;
                    SqlDataReader reader = command.ExecuteReader();
                    _indexNode = reader.GetOrdinal("SiteMapNodeString");
                    _indexUrl = reader.GetOrdinal("Url");
                    _indexTitle = reader.GetOrdinal("Title");
                    _indexDesc = reader.GetOrdinal("Description");
                    _indexRoles = reader.GetOrdinal("Roles");
                    _indexParent = reader.GetOrdinal("Parent");
                    _indexRoot = reader.GetOrdinal("Root");
                    string parentKey;
                    if (reader.Read())
                    {
                        _root = CreateSiteMapNode(reader, true, out parentKey);
                        AddNode(_root, null);
                        while (reader.Read())
```

```csharp
                    {
                        SiteMapNode node = CreateSiteMapNode(reader, false, ➥
                                                    out parentKey);
                        SiteMapNode parent = GetParentSiteMapNode(parentKey);
                        AddNode(node, parent);
                    }
                }
            }
            finally
            {
                connection.Close();
            }
            return _root;
        }
    }

    protected override SiteMapNode GetRootNodeCore()
    {
        BuildSiteMap();
        return _root;
    }

    private SiteMapNode CreateSiteMapNode(DbDataReader reader, bool forRoot, ➥
                                    out string parentKey)
    {
        string nodeString = reader.GetString(forRoot ? _indexRoot : _indexNode);
        string title = reader.IsDBNull(_indexTitle) ? null : ➥
                    reader.GetString(_indexTitle).Trim();
        string url = reader.IsDBNull(_indexUrl) ? null : ➥
                    reader.GetString(_indexUrl).Trim();
        string description = reader.IsDBNull(_indexDesc) ? null : ➥
                    reader.GetString(_indexDesc).Trim();
        string roles = reader.IsDBNull(_indexRoles) ? null : ➥
                     reader.GetString(_indexRoles).Trim();
        string[] rolelist = null;
        if (!String.IsNullOrEmpty(roles))
            rolelist = roles.Split(new char[] { ',', ';' }, 512);
        SiteMapNode node = new SiteMapNode(this, nodeString,
                                    url,
                                    title,
                                    description,
                                    rolelist, null, null, null);
        parentKey = reader.IsDBNull(_indexParent) ? null : ➥
                reader.GetString(_indexParent);
        _nodes.Add(nodeString, node);
        return node;
    }

    private SiteMapNode GetParentSiteMapNode(string parentKey)
    {
        var parent = from n in _nodes ➥
                    where n.Key.Equals(parentKey) ➥
                    select n.Value;
        return parent.FirstOrDefault<SiteMapNode>();
    }

    }
}
```

The implementation is intentionally brief. The HierarchyId datatype makes it much easier to fetch a hierarchy. The heart is this SQL query, which retrieves all the needed data in one query:

```
SELECT *, SiteMapNode.ToString() AS SiteMapNodeString,
        SiteMapNode.GetAncestor(1).ToString() AS Parent,
        hierarchyid::GetRoot().ToString() AS Root
FROM aspnet_Navigation
```

A great attribute of SQL Server is the ability to provide additional methods for data types. Here I use the GetAncestor and GetRoot methods. GetAncestor(1) fetches the parent element, while GetRoot() obtains the hierarchy's root. Bear in mind that some methods of these T-SQL functions are members, such as GetAncestor, while other methods are static, like GetRoot. The double colon, "::" indicates access to static methods in SQL Server syntax.

A DataReader object provides fast forward-only access to the SQL query results, from which we assemble SiteMapNode objects. The node type is provided so that the same method can be reused. The value is retrieved using reader.GetString(<index>). The index is the number of the column returned by the SQL query. The member fields' _indexRoot, _indexNode, or _indexParent contain the ordinal number for the column. In the SQL statement, the result is cast using ToString. This requires the GetString method when returning results.

The AddNode method from the StaticSiteMapProvider base class is responsible for building the hierarchy. To obtain the necessary information, provide a parent for each node. In the example, I assume that the parent is already defined as a node. This requires the table data to be ordered so that parents appear before their children. The GetParentSiteMapNode method is used to retrieve the parent from the private _nodes collection when building the map. This collection exists for that purpose and is no longer used when the nodes are retrieved from the sitemap controls. The parentKey used here is simply the value returned from SQL with the GetAncestor method, as mentioned before.

Configuring the Custom Provider

The configuration consists of two parts. The first step is to define the connection string in order to access the data source.

```
<connectionStrings>
  <add connectionString="Data Source=.\SQLEXPRESS;Initial ➡
                          Catalog=aspnetdb;Integrated Security=True" ➡
                          name="siteMap"/>
</connectionStrings>
```

The provider itself needs the basic format, as shown before:

```
<system.web>
  <siteMap enabled="true" defaultProvider="MySqlSiteMapProvider">
    <providers>
      <add name="MySqlSiteMapProvider"
            type="Apress.Extensibility.SqlSiteMap.SqlSiteMapProvider"
            description="My SqlSiteMapProvider"
            securityTrimmingEnabled="false"
            connectionStringName="siteMap"
      />
    </providers>
  </siteMap>
</system.web>
```

Finally, the data source used on the web pages needs to point to the provider. If you have several providers, each data source can use its own provider.

```
<asp:SiteMapDataSource ID="SiteMapDataSource1" runat="server" ➥
                   SiteMapProvider="MySqlSiteMapProvider" />
```

Although there are no changes to the various controls using this data source, some features, such as security trimming, are not yet implemented. However, you've learned how to extend the default provider model regarding site maps, and how to benefit from the new features SQL Server 2008 provides.

Testing the Provider

To test the provider, write a simple page that contains at least a Menu and a SiteMapPath control bound to the modified SiteMapDataSource control. A page such as this one will suffice:

```
<form id="form1" runat="server">
    <div>

        <asp:SiteMapPath ID="SiteMapPath1" runat="server"
            SiteMapProvider="MySqlSiteMapProvider">
        </asp:SiteMapPath>
        <br />
        <br />
        Menu:<br />
        <asp:Menu ID="Menu1" runat="server" ➥
                StaticDisplayLevels="1" DataSourceID="SiteMapDataSource1" >
        </asp:Menu>
        <br />
        <br />

    </div>
    <asp:SiteMapDataSource ID="SiteMapDataSource1" runat="server"
                       SiteMapProvider="MySqlSiteMapProvider" />
</form>
```

The data source is only required for the Menu control. Breadcrumbs are displayed using a SiteMapPath control, which can connect directly to the custom provider using its name. Figure 8-2 shows the output.

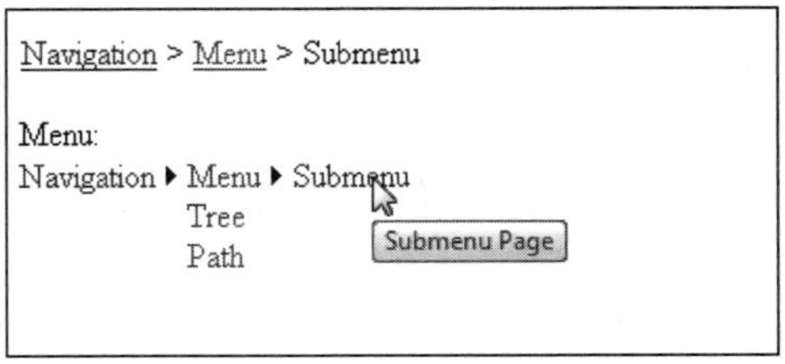

Figure 8-2. *Menu and SiteMapPath controls with data from SQL Server*

Remember that you need to add the page names to the table data. Otherwise, you'll encounter page load errors when you choose the menu items.

Suggestions for Extending the Example

The example is as simple as possible, containing nothing more than the code required to get it working. It lacks error checking and proper exception handling. Consider making the following changes before using the code in a production environment:

- Allow duplicate nodes.
- Dispose of the dictionary that stores the parents.
- Order the SQL query to accept unordered node definitions.
- Add a primary key to the table in order to improve speed for large node sets.

There are further ways of extending the behavior.

Extending the VirtualPathProvider

Complex sites with hundreds of pages are difficult to maintain. For some sections, a file structure with static data seems to be more productive, whereas other sections are composed dynamically from databases. This difference should be indiscernible to regular users and search engines alike. Search engines follow each link on a page and find the navigation paths through a site, indexing the content of each page on the way. Users bookmark pages and return directly to them later. However, neither of these behaviors are what developers are looking for in creating pages.

The VirtualPathProvider is designed to separate the internal and external structures. Like any other provider, it works transparently, using a pluggable approach. The difference is that the virtual path provider does not access a database and internally is different from all providers described so far. However, to implement a virtual path provider, you'll have to inherit and implement an abstract base class—VirtualPathProvider.

Using the VirtualPathProvider

In Chapters 4 to 7, I started with a brief overview of the default provider before looking at a custom implementation. Here it's a bit different. There is no default provider, which means that each page is handled at its physical location and dynamically-generated content appears as is, within the one and only page possessing that functionality.

Implementing a virtual path provider is all about changing the default behavior of the path resolution for any regular Web site. Some examples of what it can accomplish might help you decide if it's worth the effort:

- Storing all content in a database
- Intercepting the parsing of pages in scenarios where pages come from different sources
- Customizing the path resolution for the root of the application using "~"
- Modifying the compilation process

The parsing aspect especially is not one that you'll be using on a daily basis. You might have heard about large ASP.NET-based projects such as SharePoint. SharePoint is an application providing a content management system, among several other features. Users can create content and add active parts—called webparts—to these pages. The content is stored in a database and pages are built dynamically. ASP.NET does not support this out-of-the-box, as the compiler would not be able to locate any pages to compile. A powerful virtual path provider is used to resolve pages found in the database, mix them with those still stored as files, and create a final structure.

While SharePoint is a technically admirable example of a virtual path provider, in our example we'll consider a more modest scenario. Given a Web site with a "MySite" section, let's expose it with a structure like this:

```
Site
  MySiteJoerg
    Controls
  MySiteJohn
    Controls
  MySiteKathryn
    Controls
```

Users will think that they have a private site. They can upload and modify pages there, and you could even allow them to store files. However, if users follow convention and use paths such as *~/controls/mycontrol.ascx* to link their web pages to user controls, it will fail. Consider this example:

```
<%@ Register Src="~/Controls/my.ascx" TagName="my" TagPrefix="john" %>
```

User John is allowed to upload active content to his private space under the path *MySiteJohn*. He assumes—wrongly—that this is the root for his private space. John expects it to resolve to */MySiteJohn/Controls/my.ascx*. It actually resolves to */Site/Controls/my.ascx*. Of course, this causes a compilation exception.

Register the VirtualPathProvider

In the previous description, I noted that the virtual path provider is unlike other providers. In fact, "provider" is probably not the best word to describe it, as it's different from other providers in the way it works, the way it accesses the data, and the way it's configured. To correctly resolve paths, even during compilation, the provider must be initialized earlier in the ASP.NET framework. Thus, the *web.config* file is not the correct place for defining it. Instead, it has to be defined using a special static method, AppInitialize, or in the *global.asax* file.

THE NATURE OF APPINITIALIZE

You can use any class in either the code path of your Web site or in the App_Code folder of your web application project to define a public, static method called AppInitialize:

```
public class SomeInitClass
{
    public static void AppInitialize()
    {
        // Action required to initialize the application
    }
}
```

The method is called during the initialization cycle of the application. This is exactly the same as if you'd put the code in the Application_Start event handler defined in *global.asax*. There is little information available about why two ways exist to achieve the same thing. Perhaps it's because some applications lack a *global.asax* file, and creating and maintaining one for a single event would be overkill or—if a non-HTTP environment is used—not an option at all. In this case, the AppInitialize method is a better option, as it moves the code portion to one location. You can use any class to define this method—even the one we created here to define a VirtualPathProvider. This puts the two parts—configuration and definition—tightly together.

With either method of registering the provider, the following code is required:

```
namespace Apress.Extensibility.PathProvider
{
  public static class AppStart
  {
    public static void AppInitialize()
    {
      ThemesPathProvider customProvider = new ThemesPathProvider ();
      HostingEnvironment.RegisterVirtualPathProvider(customProvider);
    }
  }
}
```

This code assumes that the custom provider is named ThemesPathProvider, as shown in the following example. The code also uses other types, and those that are useful regarding virtual path providers are explained.

Prerequisites for a VirtualPathProvider

A custom VirtualPathProvider requires specific permissions, according to MSDN. If you look into the code using Reflector, you'll find the following:

```
[AspNetHostingPermission(SecurityAction.Demand, ➥
                         Level=AspNetHostingPermissionLevel.High)]
public static void RegisterVirtualPathProvider( ➥
                   VirtualPathProvider virtualPathProvider)
{
    if (_theHostingEnvironment == null)
    {
        throw new InvalidOperationException();
    }
    if (!BuildManager.IsPrecompiledApp)
    {
        RegisterVirtualPathProviderInternal(virtualPathProvider);
    }
}
```

The AspNetHostingPermission attribute means that you'll need to run in full trust in order to register a provider. If you don't have permission, a SecurityException is thrown. This is the same reason for the check regarding pre-compilation. Both tests ensure that a VirtualPathProvider cannot be used without permissions or within a running environment. The third check searches for an existing hosting environment. Without this, a path provider cannot function.

While the missing hosting environment throws an exception, the pre-compilation check allows the method to fail silently. To understand why, let's examine the Initialize method in RegisterVirtualPathProviderInternal. It's not the public method, but the internal one that looks like this:

```
internal virtual void Initialize(VirtualPathProvider previous)
{
    this._previous = previous;
    this.Initialize();
}
```

If a VirtualPathProvider supports a fallback scenario, this setting ensures that the "fallback provider" is available. The overridden Initialize method that you may have changed is called after this.

Helpful Classes for Path and File Operations

HostingEnvironment is a class defined in System.Web.Hosting that defines the very basic types used to support the ASP.NET hosting environment. The same namespace contains the VirtualPathProvider base class. The HostingEnvironment class contains several static methods. Some are useful when dealing with paths and path resolving issues.

The HostingEnvironment Class

Let's take a look at the path handling capabilities provided by ASP.NET before we start writing a path provider. Table 8-5 shows a selection of methods in the class, which explicitly support path operations.

Table 8-5. *Members of the HostingEnvironment Class Pertaining to Path Operations*

Method or Property	Description
MapPath	Maps a virtual path to its physical counterpart on the server
RegisterVirtualPathProvider	Registers a virtual path provider
ApplicationPhysicalPath	Gets the physical path of the application
ApplicationVirtualPath	Gets the virtual path of the application
VirtualPathProvider	Gets the currently registered path provider
SiteName	The name of the site

All properties and methods mentioned here are static and don't require an instance of the class. The other methods and properties concern application domains, object registering, caching, and impersonation. However, that's beyond the scope of this chapter. If you'd like to learn more, take a look at the following MSDN page:

http://msdn.microsoft.com/en-us/library/system.web.hosting.hostingenvironment.aspx

VirtualFile and VirtualDirectory

VirtualFile allows direct access to virtual files and reads the file contents as a stream:

```
public abstract class VirtualFile : VirtualFileBase
{
    protected VirtualFile(string virtualPath);
    public override bool IsDirectory { get; }
    public abstract Stream Open();
}
```

IsDirectory always returns false. The Open method must be overridden and return a read-only stream to the virtual resource.

The VirtualDirectory class is similar and manages a directory:

```
public abstract class VirtualDirectory : VirtualFileBase
{
    protected VirtualDirectory(string virtualPath);
    public abstract IEnumerable Children { get; }
    public abstract IEnumerable Directories { get; }
    public abstract IEnumerable Files { get; }
    public override bool IsDirectory { get; }
}
```

Directories lists the subdirectories in this virtual directory. Files returns the files only. Children returns both the files and the folders. IsDirectory always returns true.

VirtualPathUtility

This class is defined in the System.Web namespace and provides further useful methods (see Table 8-6).

Table 8-6. *Members of the VirtualPathUtility Class*

Method or Property	Description
AppendTrailingSlash	Adds a slash at the end of the path if there isn't one
Combine	Concatenates a base path and a relative path
GetDirectory	Gets the directory path of a virtual path
GetExtension	Gets the extension of a file with a virtual path
GetFileName	Gets the file name of a file with a virtual path
IsAbsolute	Indicates whether a path is absolute
IsAppRelative	Indicates whether a virtual path is relative against the application
MakeRelative	Transforms an application relative path with stem operator "~" into a relative virtual path
RemoveTrailingSlash	Removes a trailing slash from the end; does nothing if there is no slash present
ToAbsolute	Converts a virtual path into an absolute one
ToAppRelative	Converts an absolute path into a relative one

All of these methods are static, and thus don't require an instance of the class to be created.

Creating a Virtual Path Provider to Get Themes from Database

Now that we have all the prerequisites, let's write a provider. In this example, I want to change the behavior of the App_Themes folder. A theme is usually a static conglomeration of skins, style sheet files, and images. You can specify a theme either in *web.config* or within each web page. Let's define individual themes in another folder and relate them to pages. This is possible using a custom VirtualPathProvider. Its path is defined in *web.config*, and you can either set it dynamically or manipulate it. The provider shown in this section gives you the basic framework for handling file access and file resolving.

Prepare the Project

The themes are still in a folder in your project. The database only defines a reference to the theme's name. To avoid confusing Visual Studio with a regular theme, all themes are kept in a different folder named *Path_Themes*. You can use any valid name except for App_Themes, which is reserved.

Create the VirtualPathProvider

The path provider should function as a transparent layer for ASP.NET. Implementing it completely requires more steps than other providers. For the sake of brevity, I've created a simplified but functional path provider that consists of three classes:

- VirtualThemeFile
- VirtualThemeDirectory
- ThemePathProvider

This provider lacks caching, which causes it to work slowly, but it's fully functional. However, the cache implementation is not particularly difficult and can be added easily. I've excluded it, as it's out of this section's scope.

The VirtualThemeFile class holds a reference to a specific file from the *Path_Themes* folder. This is usually a skin file, a style sheet, or a resource (such as an image) used with a theme. The file's complete location is stored in the AbsolutePath property and used in the Open method. (The Open method is called to read the file's contents.) The Parent property points to the containing directory (see Listing 8-3).

Listing 8-3. *Handling Virtual Files*

```
public class VirtualThemeFile : System.Web.Hosting.VirtualFile
{
    private string _themeAbsolutePath = String.Empty;
    private string _globalAbsolutePath = String.Empty;
    private VirtualThemeDirectory _parent = null;

    public VirtualThemeFile(String virtualPath,
        string themeAbsolutePath,
        string globalAbsolutePath,
        VirtualThemeDirectory parent)
        : base(virtualPath)
    {
        _themeAbsolutePath = themeAbsolutePath;
        _globalAbsolutePath = globalAbsolutePath;
        _parent = parent;
    }

    public override Stream Open()
    {
        return File.Open(AbsolutePath, FileMode.Open);
    }

    public VirtualThemeDirectory Parent
    {
        get
        {
            return _parent;
        }
    }

    private String AbsolutePath
    {
        get
        {
            // Get the current set value
            String currentSet = ThemePathProvider.Current.CurrentSet;

            if ((!String.IsNullOrEmpty(_themeAbsolutePath))
                && (Parent.FileIsIncluded(Name, currentSet, true)))
                return _themeAbsolutePath;
```

```
            else if ((!String.IsNullOrEmpty(_globalAbsolutePath))
                && (Parent.FileIsIncluded(Name, currentSet, false)))
                return _globalAbsolutePath;

            return String.Empty;
        }
    }

    internal Boolean ExistsInThemeDirectory
    {
        get
        {
            return (!String.IsNullOrEmpty(_themeAbsolutePath));
        }
    }

    internal Boolean ExistsInGlobalDirectory
    {
        get
        {
            return (!String.IsNullOrEmpty(_globalAbsolutePath));
        }
    }
}
```

The main focus of the implementation is the directory handling. Hence, the VirtualThemeDirectory class contains much more code (see Listing 8-4).

Listing 8-4. *Handling Virtual Directories*

```
public class VirtualThemeDirectory : VirtualDirectory
{
    struct ItemSearchInfo
    {
        public String Name;
        public String VirtualPath;
        public String ThemeAbsolutePath;
        public String GlobalAbsolutePath;
    }

    private VirtualThemeDirectory _parent = null;
    private String _themeAbsolutePath = String.Empty;
    private String _globalAbsolutePath = String.Empty;
    private Dictionary<String, VirtualThemeDirectory> _directories = null;
    private Dictionary<String, VirtualThemeFile> _files = null;
    private Dictionary<String, VirtualFileBase> _children = null;

    public VirtualThemeDirectory(String virtualPath)
        : this(virtualPath, String.Empty, String.Empty, null)
    {
    }

    public VirtualThemeDirectory(String virtualPath,
        String themeAbsolutePath,
        String globalAbsolutePath)
        : this(virtualPath, themeAbsolutePath, globalAbsolutePath, null)
    {
```

```
}

public VirtualThemeDirectory(String virtualPath,
    String themeAbsolutePath,
    String globalAbsolutePath,
    VirtualThemeDirectory parent)
    : base(virtualPath)
{
    if (String.IsNullOrEmpty(themeAbsolutePath))
    {
        String sThemeRelativePath = ➥
          ThemePathProvider.Current.ConvertToThemeRelativePath(virtualPath);
        themeAbsolutePath = ➥
          HttpContext.Current.Server.MapPath(sThemeRelativePath);
    }

    if (!Directory.Exists(themeAbsolutePath))
    {
        themeAbsolutePath = String.Empty;
    }
    if (String.IsNullOrEmpty(globalAbsolutePath))
    {
        String sGlobalRelativePath = ➥
          ThemePathProvider.Current.ConvertToGlobalRelativePath(VirtualPath);
        globalAbsolutePath = ➥
          HttpContext.Current.Server.MapPath(sGlobalRelativePath);
    }

    if (!Directory.Exists(globalAbsolutePath))
        globalAbsolutePath = String.Empty;

    _themeAbsolutePath = themeAbsolutePath;
    _globalAbsolutePath = globalAbsolutePath;

    _parent = parent;

    // Create the collections to hold the virtual items
    _files = new Dictionary<string, VirtualThemeFile>();
    _directories = new Dictionary<string, VirtualThemeDirectory>();
    _children = new Dictionary<string, VirtualFileBase>();

    FindFiles();
    FindSubDirectories();
    FindChildren();
}

private void FindFiles()
{
    Dictionary<String, ItemSearchInfo> fileList = ➥
        new Dictionary<string, ItemSearchInfo>();
    if (Directory.Exists(ThemeAbsolutePath))
    {
        var files = from f in Directory.GetFiles(ThemeAbsolutePath)
                    select new ItemSearchInfo
                    {
                        Name = Path.GetFileName(f),
                        VirtualPath = VirtualPathUtility.Combine(VirtualPath, ➥
```

```
                                                    Path.GetFileName(f)),
                    ThemeAbsolutePath = f
                };
        foreach (ItemSearchInfo fileInfo in files)
        {
            fileList.Add(fileInfo.Name, fileInfo);
        }
    }

    if (Directory.Exists(GlobalAbsolutePath))
    {
        var files = from f in Directory.GetFiles(GlobalAbsolutePath)
                    select new ItemSearchInfo
                    {
                        Name = Path.GetFileName(f),
                        VirtualPath = VirtualPathUtility.Combine(VirtualPath, ➥
                                        Path.GetFileName(f)),
                        GlobalAbsolutePath = f
                    };

        foreach (ItemSearchInfo fileInfo in files)
        {
            if (fileList.ContainsKey(fileInfo.Name))
            {
                ItemSearchInfo themeFileInfo = fileList[fileInfo.Name];
                fileList.Remove(themeFileInfo.Name);
                fileList.Add(themeFileInfo.Name, themeFileInfo);
            }
            else
            {
                fileList.Add(fileInfo.Name, fileInfo);
            }
        }
    }

    // Loop through each file found
    foreach (ItemSearchInfo fileInfo in fileList.Values)
    {
        // Add each file to the files dictionary using the
        // information stored for the file
        _files.Add(fileInfo.Name, new VirtualThemeFile(fileInfo.VirtualPath, ➥
                                        fileInfo.ThemeAbsolutePath, ➥
                                        fileInfo.GlobalAbsolutePath, ➥
                                                        this));
    }
}

private void FindSubDirectories()
{
    Dictionary<String, ItemSearchInfo> directoryList = ➥
            new Dictionary<string, ItemSearchInfo>();
    Func<string, string, string> MakePath = delegate(string b, string v)
    {
        return VirtualPathUtility.AppendTrailingSlash(➥
                            VirtualPathUtility.Combine(b, v));
    };
    if (Directory.Exists(ThemeAbsolutePath))
```

```
        {
            var themeDirectories = ➡
                        from t in Directory.GetDirectories(ThemeAbsolutePath)
                        select new ItemSearchInfo
                        {
                            Name = Path.GetFileName(t),
                            VirtualPath = MakePath(VirtualPath, ➡
                                        Path.GetFileName(t)),
                            ThemeAbsolutePath = t
                        };

            foreach (ItemSearchInfo directoryInfo in themeDirectories)
            {
                directoryList.Add(directoryInfo.Name, directoryInfo);
            }
        }
        if (Directory.Exists(GlobalAbsolutePath))
        {
            var themeDirectories = ➡
                        from t in Directory.GetDirectories(GlobalAbsolutePath)
                        select new ItemSearchInfo
                        {
                            Name = Path.GetFileName(t),
                            VirtualPath = MakePath(VirtualPath, ➡
                                        Path.GetFileName(t)),
                            GlobalAbsolutePath = t
                        };

            foreach (ItemSearchInfo directoryInfo in themeDirectories)
            {
                if (directoryList.ContainsKey(directoryInfo.Name))
                {
                    ItemSearchInfo themeDirectoryInfo = ➡
                                directoryList[directoryInfo.Name];
                    directoryList.Remove(themeDirectoryInfo.Name);
                    directoryList.Add(themeDirectoryInfo.Name, themeDirectoryInfo);
                }
                else
                {
                    directoryList.Add(directoryInfo.Name, directoryInfo);
                }
            }
        }
        foreach (ItemSearchInfo directoryInfo in directoryList.Values)
        {
            VirtualThemeDirectory directory = new VirtualThemeDirectory(➡
                                    directoryInfo.VirtualPath, ➡
                                    directoryInfo.ThemeAbsolutePath, ➡
                                    directoryInfo.GlobalAbsolutePath, ➡
                                    this);
            _directories.Add(directory.Name, directory);
        }
    }

    private void FindChildren()
    {
        foreach (VirtualThemeDirectory directory in Directories)
```

```
        {
            _children.Add(directory.Name, directory);
        }
        foreach (VirtualThemeFile file in Files)
        {
            _children.Add(file.Name, file);
        }
    }

    public Boolean GetFileIsIncluded(String fileName)
    {
        String currentSet = ThemePathProvider.Current.CurrentSet;
        if (FileIsIncluded(fileName, currentSet, true))
        {
            return true;
        }
        else
        {
            return FileIsIncluded(fileName, currentSet, false);
        }
    }

    public Boolean GetDirectoryIsIncluded(String directoryName)
    {
        String currentSet = ThemePathProvider.Current.CurrentSet;
        if (DirectoryIsIncluded(directoryName, currentSet, true))
        {
            return true;
        }
        else
        {
            return DirectoryIsIncluded(directoryName, currentSet, false);
        }
    }

    internal Boolean FileIsIncluded(string fileName, string currentSet, ➥
                                    bool checkAgainstTheme)
    {
        if (!_files.ContainsKey(fileName))
            return false;
        VirtualThemeFile file = _files[fileName];
        if ((checkAgainstTheme)
            && (!file.ExistsInThemeDirectory))
        {
            return false;
        }
        else if ((!checkAgainstTheme)
            && (!file.ExistsInGlobalDirectory))
        {
            return false;
        }
        if (String.IsNullOrEmpty(currentSet))
            return true;
        String fileExtension = Path.GetExtension(fileName);
        if (fileExtension.ToUpper() == ".SKIN"
            ||
            fileExtension.ToUpper() == ".CSS")
```

```
                ||
                fileExtension.ToUpper() == ".JPG")
        {
            return true;
        }
        return false;
}

internal Boolean DirectoryIsIncluded(string directoryName, ➥
                                     string currentSet, ➥
                                     bool checkAgainstTheme)
{
        if (!_directories.ContainsKey(directoryName))
            return false;
        VirtualThemeDirectory directory = _directories[directoryName];
        if (checkAgainstTheme
            && !directory.ExistsInThemeDirectory)
        {
            return false;
        }
        else if (!checkAgainstTheme
            && !directory.ExistsInGlobalDirectory)
        {
            return false;
        }
        return true;
}

internal VirtualThemeFile GetFile(String fileName)
{
        return _files[fileName];
}

internal VirtualThemeDirectory GetDirectory(String virtualDir)
{
        if (_directories.Count == 0)
            return null;
        if (!virtualDir.StartsWith(VirtualPath, ➥
            StringComparison.InvariantCultureIgnoreCase))
            return null;
        String relativeVirtualPath = virtualDir.Substring(VirtualPath.Length);
        String directoryName = relativeVirtualPath.Substring(0, ➥
                            relativeVirtualPath.IndexOf("/"));
        VirtualThemeDirectory childDirectory = _directories[directoryName];
        if (childDirectory.VirtualPath == virtualDir)
            return childDirectory;
        else
            return childDirectory.GetDirectory(virtualDir);
}

public VirtualThemeDirectory Parent
{
        get
        {
            return _parent;
        }
}
```

```
public Boolean Exists
{
    get
    {
        return ((Directory.Exists(_themeAbsolutePath))
            || (Directory.Exists(_globalAbsolutePath)));
    }
}

private Boolean ExistsInThemeDirectory
{
    get
    {
        return (!String.IsNullOrEmpty(_themeAbsolutePath));
    }
}

private Boolean ExistsInGlobalDirectory
{
    get
    {
        return (String.IsNullOrEmpty(_globalAbsolutePath));
    }
}

public override IEnumerable Directories
{
    get
    {
        return _directories.Values;
    }
}

public override IEnumerable Files
{
    get
    {
        return _files.Values;
    }
}

public override IEnumerable Children
{
    get
    {
        return _children.Values;
    }
}

private String ThemeAbsolutePath
{
    get
    {
        return _themeAbsolutePath;
    }
}
```

```
    private String GlobalAbsolutePath
    {
        get
        {
            return _globalAbsolutePath;
        }
    }

}
```

The main purpose of this class is to build a copy of the directory and file structure found in the physical theme folder (*Path_Themes*) and to store references to the files. When the provider retrieves the files, it accesses this virtual structure.

Three internal methods are called in the constructor: FindFiles, FindSubDirectories, and FindChildren. The Findfiles method reads files in the current base folder. FindSubDirectories loads directories recursively. In each directory located, the FindFiles method is called to load the files for that folder. The FindChildren method creates a single combined list of both directories and files.

The provider calls the GetDirectory method to retrieve a specific directory. A simple filter, FileIsIncluded, limits the allowed file types. This is exclusive to the handling of themes; other VirtualPathProvider implementations might require different types. The example ignores all files except for *.skin, *.css, and *.jpg, but you can extend the list to support any file type used in your themes.

The GetFile method allows access to a file once it has been located in a directory. The resolving of files and their paths occurs in the compiler module. A simple file list handles all files in all directories. The key contains the full path, so files with the same filename but located in different folders still have a unique full name (see Listing 8-5).

Listing 8-5. *Implementation of a Custom VirtualPathProvider*

```
public sealed class ThemePathProvider : VirtualPathProvider
{
    private static ThemePathProvider _currentProvider = null;
    private const string ASPNetThemeBasePath = "/App_Themes/";
    private string _themeRelativePath = String.Empty;
    private string _currentThemeSet = String.Empty;
    private string _globalThemeName = String.Empty;

    private ThemePathProvider()
    {
        _themeRelativePath = ➥
                WebConfigurationManager.AppSettings["CustomThemeBasePath"];
    }

    public override System.Web.Caching.CacheDependency GetCacheDependency(➥
            string virtualPath, ➥
            System.Collections.IEnumerable virtualPathDependencies, ➥
            DateTime utcStart)
    {
        return null;
    }

    public override bool DirectoryExists(string virtualDir)
    {
        if (virtualDir.IndexOf(ASPNetThemeBasePath) == -1)
            return base.DirectoryExists(virtualDir);
```

```
                VirtualThemeDirectory directory = GetDirectory(virtualDir) as ➥
                                            VirtualThemeDirectory;
            return directory.Exists;
        }

        public override bool FileExists(string virtualPath)
        {
            if (virtualPath.IndexOf(ASPNetThemeBasePath) == -1)
                return base.FileExists(virtualPath);
            string fileName = System.Web.VirtualPathUtility.GetFileName(virtualPath);
            string virtualDirectoryPath = ➥
                        System.Web.VirtualPathUtility.GetDirectory(virtualPath);
            VirtualThemeDirectory directory = ➥
                        GetDirectory(virtualDirectoryPath) as VirtualThemeDirectory;
            return directory.GetFileIsIncluded(fileName);
        }

        public override VirtualDirectory GetDirectory(string virtualDir)
        {
            if (virtualDir.IndexOf(ASPNetThemeBasePath) == -1)
                return base.GetDirectory(virtualDir);
            if (IsThemeDirectoryVirtualPath(virtualDir))
            {
                return new VirtualThemeDirectory(virtualDir);
            }
            else
            {
                String themeVirtualPath = GetThemeDirectoryVirtualPath(virtualDir);
                VirtualThemeDirectory directory = new VirtualThemeDirectory(virtualDir);
                return directory.GetDirectory(virtualDir);
            }
        }

        public override VirtualFile GetFile(string virtualPath)
        {
            if (virtualPath.IndexOf(ASPNetThemeBasePath) == -1)
                return base.GetFile(virtualPath);
            String virtualDirectoryPath = ➥
                        System.Web.VirtualPathUtility.GetDirectory(virtualPath);
            VirtualThemeDirectory directory = ➥
                        GetDirectory(virtualDirectoryPath) as VirtualThemeDirectory;
            String fileName = System.Web.VirtualPathUtility.GetFileName(virtualPath);
            return directory.GetFile(fileName);
        }

        private StringCollection GetDependentDirectories(
            String parentDirectoryPath,
            StringCollection dependentPaths)
        {
            String[] directories = Directory.GetDirectories(parentDirectoryPath);
            for (int loopIndex = 0; loopIndex < directories.Length; loopIndex++)
            {
                dependentPaths.Add(directories[loopIndex]);
                GetDependentDirectories(directories[loopIndex], dependentPaths);
            }
            return dependentPaths;
        }
```

```
private Boolean IsThemeDirectoryVirtualPath(String virtualPath)
{
    String parentVirtualPath = ➥
            System.Web.VirtualPathUtility.GetDirectory(virtualPath);
    return parentVirtualPath.EndsWith(ASPNetThemeBasePath, ➥
            StringComparison.InvariantCultureIgnoreCase);
}

private String GetThemeDirectoryVirtualPath(String virtualPath)
{
    String parentVirtualPath = ➥
            VirtualPathUtility.GetDirectory(virtualPath);
    while (!IsThemeDirectoryVirtualPath(parentVirtualPath))
    {
        parentVirtualPath = ➥
            System.Web.VirtualPathUtility.GetDirectory(parentVirtualPath);
    }
    return parentVirtualPath;
}

internal String ConvertToThemeRelativePath(String relativePath)
{
    return ConvertToThemeNameRelativePath(relativePath, false);
}

internal String ConvertToGlobalRelativePath(String relativePath)
{
    return ConvertToThemeNameRelativePath(relativePath, true);
}

private String ConvertToThemeNameRelativePath(String relativePath, ➥
                          Boolean replaceThemeNameWithGlobal)
{
    String themeNameRelativePath = String.Empty;
    if ((!relativePath.StartsWith(ASPNetThemeBasePath))
        && (!_themeRelativePath.StartsWith("/")))
    {
        themeNameRelativePath = relativePath.Substring(0, ➥
                        relativePath.IndexOf(ASPNetThemeBasePath));
    }

    if ((!themeNameRelativePath.EndsWith("/"))
        && (!_themeRelativePath.StartsWith("/")))
    {
        themeNameRelativePath = ➥
                    System.Web.VirtualPathUtility. ➥
                    AppendTrailingSlash(themeNameRelativePath);
    }

    themeNameRelativePath += _themeRelativePath;

    String remainderPath = relativePath.Substring(➥
                        relativePath.IndexOf(ASPNetThemeBasePath) + ➥
                        ASPNetThemeBasePath.Length);

    if (replaceThemeNameWithGlobal)
```

```
        {
            remainderPath = remainderPath.Substring(remainderPath.IndexOf("/"));
        }
        themeNameRelativePath += remainderPath;

        return themeNameRelativePath;
    }

    public static ThemePathProvider Current
    {
        get
        {
            if (_currentProvider != null)
                return _currentProvider;

            _currentProvider = new ThemePathProvider();
            return _currentProvider;
        }
    }

    public String CurrentSet
    {
        get
        {
            return _currentThemeSet;
        }
        set
        {
            _currentThemeSet = value;
        }
    }
}
```

The GetCacheDependency returns null in order to suppress any internal caching. You must either return null or fully implement the caching. Otherwise, the compiler will try to resolve the default path (*App_Themes*) from the cache and this will fail.

Two methods are called when the compiler tries to resolve an internal path: GetDirectory and GetFile. If a file is referenced in a page that points to a theme, the compiler asks the provider to retrieve the same. Using the GetFile method, we first check whether the theme's folder is being used. This is the folder for which the provider in the example is responsible. From the file's name, the containing directory is built. The directory is used to obtain the VirtualThemeDirectory implementation, which in turn returns the file held there.

At the core of this implementation is a path manipulation algorithm. It could be far more sophisticated than the simple code in the example.

Before a folder or file is retrieved, the DirectoryExists and FileExists methods are called. This allows the provider to programmatically "hide" parts of the structure or to check for the physical presence of the requested resource.

The basic approach is always the same. The calling instance "asks" the provider for a physical file. The provider returns a VirtualFile instance, which allows direct access to the file's contents via a Stream object. The remarkable thing is that the file might not necessarily exist anywhere on the file system. If, for example, the stream is obtained from a database call, the VirtualPathProvider is simulating a physical file system. The "Exists" methods could always return true in order to simulate a system where the page developers can use any value, and the system returns a set of globally predefined resources.

Configuring the Path Provider

The provider requires two final configuration steps. First, it must have a setting in *web.config* to show that it's configurable. Second, the provider must be registered, which follows the pattern previously explained. To demonstrate, I've used the `Application_Start` event handler defined in the *global.asax* file, as shown in Listing 8-6.

Listing 8-6. *Configuration Settings in web.config*

```
<appSettings>
    <add key="CustomThemeBasePath" value="/Path_Themes/"/>
</appSettings>
```

In Listing 8-7, the key is used to configure the physical path.

Listing 8-7. *Registering the Path Provider Using the Application_Start event*

```
protected void Application_Start(object sender, EventArgs e)
{
    HostingEnvironment.RegisterVirtualPathProvider(ThemePathProvider.Current);
}
```

The registration uses a singleton instance of the provider instead of the constructor. This results in slightly shorter code. A singleton instance works well because the provider works globally and exists only once in the application.

Limitations of the VirtualPathProvider Approach

The `VirtualPathProvider` is deeply integrated in the ASP.NET engine. Although it's very powerful, certain tasks can be problematic. In this section, I explain two typical issues found when working with custom path providers.

Working with LoadControl

The `VirtualPathProvider` allows you to override the way in which tilde-based paths are resolved in page directives:

```
<%@ Register TagPrefix="Test" TagName="MyControl" Src="~/userctrl.ascx" %>
```

However, the `VirtualPathProvider` cannot affect the way in which tilde-based paths are resolved for dynamically loaded user controls:

```
MyPlaceHolder.Controls.Add(LoadControl("~/userctrl.ascx"));
```

For the `LoadControl` method to resolve tilde-based paths in the same way as `Register` directives, the page code-behind needs to override this method:

```
public new Control LoadControl(string relativePath)
{
    string newPath = relativePath;
    string site = this.Request.QueryString["site"];
    if (!String.IsNullOrEmpty(site))
    {
        newPath = VirtualPathUtility.ToAppRelative(newPath);
        newPath = newPath.Substring(1);
        newPath = "~/MySites/" + site + newPath;
    }
    return base.LoadControl(newPath);
}
```

This workaround will function as long as `LoadControl` is called directly on your derived class, since it's not `virtual`. A similar override in a `UserControl` base class might be also required, since `LoadControl` lives on `TemplateControl`.

Working with Precompiled Sites

Unfortunately, `VirtualPathProvider` is not supported in precompiled Web sites at the moment. As shown in the section "Prerequisites for a VirtualPathProvider," the precompiled state is explicitly detected. Consequently, MSDN notes that, "if a Web site is precompiled for deployment, content provided by a `VirtualPathProvider` instance is not compiled, and no `VirtualPathProvider` instances are used by the precompiled site."

One way to avoid deploying source code is to use the Web Application Project model, in which all classes and code-behind files are compiled. Although pre-compilation will give our site a performance boost, the difference in speed will only be noticeable during the first request to each folder. A more significant benefit is the new deployment option made available by pre-compilation—the option to deploy a site without copying any of the original source code to the server. This includes the code and markup in *aspx*, *ascx*, and *master* files.

HACK MODE

There is also a hack available to force the path provider to work with pre-compiled pages. This is not intended for production code, but if you're under pressure to solve a similar issue, this tip might help. The solution is DynamicMethod. Just call a Microsoft internal method to register `VirtualPathProvider` directly. This method is internal and therefore only reflection can obtain it. The definition in `HostingEnvironment` looks like this:

```
internal static void RegisterVirtualPathProviderInternal( ➡
                 VirtualPathProvider virtualPathProvider)
{
    VirtualPathProvider previous = _theHostingEnvironment._virtualPathProvider;
    _theHostingEnvironment._virtualPathProvider = virtualPathProvider;
    virtualPathProvider.Initialize(previous);
}
```

This is, again, a simple hack that may fail in future versions due to changes to the internal code by Microsoft.

Summary

In this chapter, we looked at site management. Providing an existing structure to the navigation is the primary task of the `SiteMapProvider`. This provider allows the management of larger sites based on any data store you decide to implement. It's transparent to the controls used to create navigational elements.

The `VirtualPathProvider` gives you more control over internal (physical) and external (virtual) paths for directories and files. Replacing the provider allows you to "fake" the paths and set them to virtual ones, which makes it easy to manage complex file structures. The `VirtualPathProvider` is not as straightforward as the other ones, but it makes sense to use it if your embedded features, such as themes that can be extended or customized, are based on special folders.

CHAPTER 9

■ ■ ■

Control Extensibility

Web Server controls are the essence of ASP.NET, as most ASPX pages contain both static HTML and dynamic Web Server controls. Although ASP.NET includes a comprehensive collection of controls, third-party developers have also built up an impressive array of controls, both free and commercial, for almost any task you can imagine. Furthermore, you can create your own controls by implementing both design-time and runtime behavior.

Purchasing controls may not be the best solution if embedded ones will fit your needs with minor modification. A third-party control is usually a sophisticated component designed for a specific purpose. For basic functionality in a lightweight package, it's probably not optimal.

Another option is to extend a standard ASP.NET control and modify the way it renders. ASP.NET's extensibility concepts are not limited to providers; controls are extensible and customizable if you use adapters. In this chapter, I'll cover adapter techniques and explain:

- How to implement and activate a control adapter
- How to make the adapter work depending on the current browser
- How to create adapters at a page level

After reading this chapter, you'll be able to "adapt" an existing control so that it renders according to your needs. This could include different ways of creating HTML, adding JavaScript, or using cascading style sheets to format the output.

Adaptive Control Behavior

Adaptive control behavior is architecture that changes the way controls render in order to suit the needs of specific clients. Adapters intercept states of the life cycle to alter rendering behavior. By default, each control has a designated adapter in a one-to-one relationship. It's possible to change this relationship under certain circumstances—when, for example, you encounter a browser that requires a different kind of markup.

To control the adaptive behavior, choose from the following techniques:

- Configure the application to support different markups.
- Choose the `XhtmlTextWriter` or `ChtmlTextWriter` class to create specific markup.
- Create a `TextWriter` class that writes the markup to the output stream.
- Use a filter to recognize a client device and decide what kind of markup you need.
- Create an adapter and assign the adapter to a control.

The markup is not the only aspect you may want to change. Depending on the capabilities of the target device, you may need to think about:

- How to work with postback data
- Managing the view state
- Preventing changes to the control

The Default Behavior

The render process of a page uses the HtmlTextWriter class by default. The RenderControl method is called recursively with an instance of the HtmlTextWriter. Each control adds its markup to the writer. By the end of the process, the writer holds the complete markup of the page and writes it to the output stream.

ASP.NET includes several writer types compatible with specific output devices. For HTML 3.2, the Html32TextWriter is used. Which writer to use depends on the TagWriter of the System. Web.HttpRequest.Browser. If a browser supports HTML 4.0, the page framework should compose XHTML. Using *web.config*, you can configure this behavior and replace the Html32TextWriter with an XHtmlTextWriter. The Browser property of the HttpRequest class returns an HttpBrowserCapabilities object.

The underlying code is relatively straightforward. If a custom TextWriter is defined, the CreateHtmlTextWriterFromType is used. If not, the default Html32TextWriter is used. The following code snippets are decompiled from the System.Web.HttpRequest class and the System.Web.UI.Page class, respectively.

```
internal HtmlTextWriter CreateHtmlTextWriterInternal(TextWriter tw)
{
    Type tagWriter = this.TagWriter;
    if (tagWriter != null)
    {
        return Page.CreateHtmlTextWriterFromType(tw, tagWriter);
    }
    return new Html32TextWriter(tw);
}

public Type TagWriter
{
    get
    {
        try
        {
            if (!this._havetagwriter)
            {
                string str = this["tagwriter"];
                if (string.IsNullOrEmpty(str))
                {
                    this._tagwriter = null;
                }
                else if (string.Compare(str, typeof(HtmlTextWriter).FullName, ➥
                        StringComparison.Ordinal) == 0)
                {
```

```
                this._tagwriter = typeof(HtmlTextWriter);
            }
            else
            {
                this._tagwriter = BuildManager.GetType(str, true);
            }
            this._havetagwriter = true;
        }
    }
    catch (Exception exception)
    {
        throw this.BuildParseError(exception, "tagwriter");
    }
    return this._tagwriter;
    }
}

public static HtmlTextWriter CreateHtmlTextWriterFromType(TextWriter tw, ➡
                                                Type writerType)
{
    HtmlTextWriter writer;
    if (writerType == typeof(HtmlTextWriter))
    {
        return new HtmlTextWriter(tw);
    }
    if (writerType == typeof(Html32TextWriter))
    {
        return new Html32TextWriter(tw);
    }
    try
    {
        Util.CheckAssignableType(typeof(HtmlTextWriter), writerType);
        writer = (HtmlTextWriter) HttpRuntime.CreateNonPublicInstance(➡
                            writerType, new object[] { tw });
    }
    catch
    {
        throw new HttpException(SR.GetString("Invalid_HtmlTextWriter", ➡
                            new object[] { writerType.FullName }));
    }
    return writer;
}
```

As you can see, the instance of the abstract TextWriter class is responsible for the rendering process. Because ASP.NET produces HTML, the HtmlTextWriter class is the optimum point for beginning to implement a custom writer class. The XhtmlTextWriter and ChtmlTextWriter types mentioned earlier derive from the HtmlTextWriter and Html32TextWriter respectively. They are concrete implementations for specific rendering behavior. See Figure 9-1.

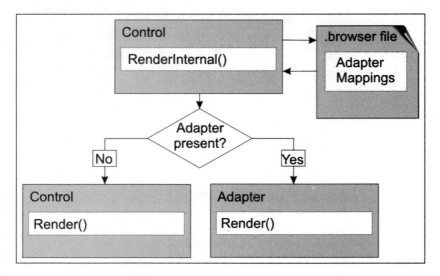

Figure 9-1. *The control adapter architecture*

Using Control Adapters

To modify the behavior described earlier, you'll need an implementation of the System.Web.
UI.Adapters.ControlAdapter base class. In each phase of the life cycle, the control checks whether
or not an adapter is available. If there is one present, the adapter provides an alternative method
that replaces the default method that would otherwise be called in that step in the life cycle. If the
adapter only modifies portions of the behavior, it can call the control's default method instead.
Adapters that modify the state persistence behavior differ in that they don't modify, but completely
replace, the default behavior. When the adapter intercepts the life cycle, the following actions (at
a minimum) must occur:

- Override the OnInit method of the control adapter to modify the initializing phase.
- Override the Render or RenderChildren method to add custom markup.

The abstract base class has the following structure:

```
public abstract class ControlAdapter
{
    protected ControlAdapter();
    protected HttpBrowserCapabilities Browser { get; }
    protected Control Control { get; }
    protected Page Page { get; }
    protected PageAdapter PageAdapter { get; }
    protected internal virtual void BeginRender(HtmlTextWriter writer);
    protected internal virtual void EndRender(HtmlTextWriter writer);
    protected internal virtual void LoadAdapterControlState(object state);
    protected internal virtual void LoadAdapterViewState(object state);
    protected internal virtual void OnInit(EventArgs e);
    protected internal virtual void OnLoad(EventArgs e);
    protected internal virtual void OnPreRender(EventArgs e);
    protected internal virtual void OnUnload(EventArgs e);
    protected internal virtual void Render(HtmlTextWriter writer);
    protected virtual void RenderChildren(HtmlTextWriter writer);
    protected internal virtual object SaveAdapterControlState();
```

```
protected internal virtual object SaveAdapterViewState();
}
```

Before you start implementing adapters to change a control's behavior, you'll need to learn the purpose for each property and method (see Table 9-1).

Table 9-1. *The ControlAdapter Base Class*

Class Member	Description
Browser	The browser capabilities (HttpBrowserCapabilities) of the client making the current HTTP request.
Control	The control to which this control adapter is attached.
Page	The page containing the control associated with this adapter.
PageAdapter	The page adapter (System.Web.UI.Adapters.PageAdapter) for the page defined by Page.
BeginRender	Called prior to the rendering of a control. The method generates opening tags required by a specific target. It takes a System.Web.UI.HtmlTextWriter object to render the target-specific output.
EndRender	Called after the rendering of a control. The method generates closing tags that are required by a specific target. It takes a System.Web.UI.HtmlTextWriter object to render the target-specific output.
CreateChildControls	Creates the target-specific child controls for a composite control.
LoadAdapterControlState	Loads adapter control state information saved by the System.Web.UI.Adapters.ControlAdapter.SaveAdapterControlState method during a previous request to the Page. Receives the state as a StateBag object.
LoadAdapterViewState	Loads adapter view state information saved by the System.Web.UI.Adapters.ControlAdapter.SaveAdapterViewState method during a previous request to the Page. Receives the state as a StateBag object.
OnInit	Overrides the System.Web.UI.Control.OnInit method for the associated control in order to hook into the initializing phase.
OnLoad	Overrides the System.Web.UI.Control.OnLoad method for the associated control in order to hook into the load phase.
OnPreRender	Overrides the System.Web.UI.Control.OnPreRender method for the associated control.
OnUnload	Overrides the System.Web.UI.Control.OnUnload method for the associated control.
Render	Generates target-specific markup for the control to which the adapter is attached. Takes a System.Web.UI.HtmlTextWriter object to render the target-specific output.
RenderChildren	Generates the target-specific markup for the child controls in a composite control to which the adapter is attached. Takes a System.Web.UI.HtmlTextWriter object to render the target-specific output.
SaveAdapterControlState	Saves control state information for the control adapter into a StateBag object.
SaveAdapterViewState	Saves view state information for the control adapter into a StateBag object.

You now have all the information you need in order to implement a custom control adapter. However, before the adapter can be used, it must be configured. Configuration depends on a device filter.

The `System.Web.UI.WebControls.Adapters.WebControlAdapter` base class is the preferred way to change the behavior of built-in web controls. This class adds virtual methods `RenderBeginTag`, `RenderEndTag`, and `RenderContents`, to more closely mirror the render behavior of web controls.

```
public class WebControlAdapter : ControlAdapter
{
    protected WebControl Control { get; }
    protected bool IsEnabled { get; }
    protected virtual void RenderBeginTag(HtmlTextWriter writer);
    protected virtual void RenderContents(HtmlTextWriter writer);
    protected virtual void RenderEndTag(HtmlTextWriter writer);
}
```

Table 9-2 explains its properties and methods.

Table 9-2. *WebControlAdapter*

Member	Description
Control	The web control to which this adapter is attached
IsEnabled	Indicates whether the web control and all its parent controls are enabled
Render	Generates the target-specific markup for the control to which the adapter is attached
RenderBeginTag	Creates the beginning tag in the markup for the web control
RenderContents	Generates the target-specific inner markup for the web control to which the adapter is attached
RenderEndTag	Creates the closing tag in the markup for the web control

Note that the `WebControlAdapter` is not an abstract class, but the basic class in the hierarchy of adapters responsible for regular web controls. It's in the `System.Web.UI.WebControls.Adapters` namespace. The `WebControlAdapter` class is the base class for the following implementations:

- `HierarchicalDataBoundControlAdapter`
- `DataBoundControlAdapter`
- `HideDisabledControlAdapter`
- `MenuAdapter`

The `MenuAdapter` is a concrete implementation used to render `Menu` controls. The `HierarchicalDataBoundControlAdapter` provides a virtual method, `PerformDataBinding`, which calls `Control.PerformDataBinding`. Overriding this method in a derived class allows you to change the binding behavior. (This is also the case for the `DataBoundControlAdapter` class.) The `HideDisabledControlAdapter` can be applied to any control. Using this adapter removes the control from pages in which the control is disabled. It overrides the adapter's `Render` method and, if its `Enabled` property is false, the control's `Render` method is not called, as shown in Figure 9-2.

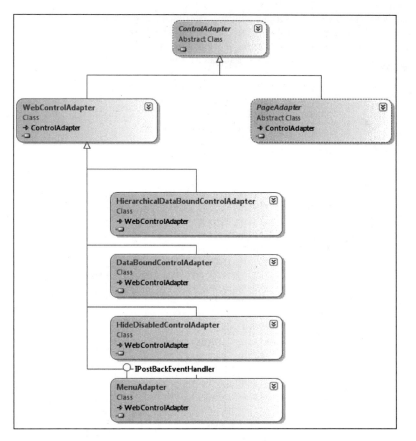

Figure 9-2. *The class diagram for control adapter classes*

The base classes can be used to perform basic tasks without you having to implement your own adapter. With them you can also vary a single behavior, such as data binding, while benefiting from all the other default adapter functionality.

In the class diagram, you'll also find a PageAdapter class that derives from ControlAdapter. Thus, pages can have adapters, too.

Using Page Adapters

As a Page is essentially a specialized Control, the control adapter also supports pages. The PageAdapter base class exists to make writing a custom page adapter easy. This base class inherits from the ControlAdapter described earlier and extends the adapter with page-specific features.

```
public abstract class PageAdapter : ControlAdapter
{
    public virtual StringCollection CacheVaryByHeaders { get; }
    public virtual StringCollection CacheVaryByParams { get; }
    protected string ClientState { get; }
    public virtual NameValueCollection DeterminePostBackMode();
    protected internal virtual string GetPostBackFormReference(string formId);
    public virtual ICollection GetRadioButtonsByGroup(string groupName);
    public virtual PageStatePersister GetStatePersister();
```

```
        public virtual void RegisterRadioButton(RadioButton radioButton);
        public virtual void RenderBeginHyperlink(HtmlTextWriter writer, ➡
                                    string targetUrl, ➡
                                    bool encodeUrl, ➡
                                    string softkeyLabel);
        public virtual void RenderBeginHyperlink(HtmlTextWriter writer, ➡
                                    string targetUrl, ➡
                                    bool encodeUrl, ➡
                                    string softkeyLabel, ➡
                                    string accessKey);
        public virtual void RenderEndHyperlink(HtmlTextWriter writer);
        public virtual void RenderPostBackEvent(HtmlTextWriter writer, ➡
                                    string target, ➡
                                    string argument, ➡
                                    string softkeyLabel, ➡
                                    string text);
        public virtual void RenderPostBackEvent(HtmlTextWriter writer, ➡
                                    string target, ➡
                                    string argument, ➡
                                    string softkeyLabel, ➡
                                    string text, ➡
                                    string postUrl, ➡
                                    string accessKey);
        protected void RenderPostBackEvent(HtmlTextWriter writer, ➡
                                    string target, ➡
                                    string argument, ➡
                                    string softkeyLabel, ➡
                                    string text, ➡
                                    string postUrl, ➡
                                    string accessKey, ➡
                                    bool encode);
        public virtual string TransformText(string text);
}
```

Table 9-3 explains the properties and methods provided by the PageAdapter. (The PageAdapter attaches to a web page. This is the "page" referred to in the table descriptions.)

The PageAdapter supports the persistence layer and the render behavior of controls that group multiple tags. RadioButtons need special treatment when handling groups. You can define a group of radio buttons in HTML by giving them the same name. However, ASP.NET requires different IDs for each radio button, and by default the name and ID are the same. The PageAdapter will thus render each radio button group appropriately to keep the groups separate.

The GetStatePersister property can be overloaded in order to change the view state persister globally. Using the abstract base class, you can write a custom page adapter to change the behavior of all pages.

Why does the rendering of a page depend on the client device? Remember that the view state has a strong influence on the client. The view state could grow and consume a significant portion of the page's rendered content. (Refer to Chapter 1 for a refresher about view state.) The user experience on mobile devices and smart phones generally deteriorates with large pages. To mitigate this, you could write a page adapter that creates a regular view state for PC-based browsers and server-side view state for mobile devices.

The implication is that, as for ControlAdapter implementations, the PageAdapter must be configured and associated with a set of clients.

Table 9-3. *Properties and Methods in the PageAdapter, Additional to Those Provided by the ControlAdapter*

Member	Description
CacheVaryByHeaders	A list (of type IList) of additional HTTP headers by which caching is varied for the web page.
CacheVaryByParams	A list (of type IList) of additional parameters from HTTP GET and POST requests by which caching is varied for the web page.
ClientState	An encoded string containing the view and control state data of the web page.
DeterminePostBackMode	Evaluates whether the web page is in postback mode and returns a name/value collection of type System.Collections.Specialized.NameValueCollection of the postback variables.
GetPostBackFormReference	Returns a DHTML code fragment that the client browser can use to reference the form on the page that was posted.
GetRadioButtonsByGroup	Retrieves a collection of radio button controls specified by groupName. Takes the name of a System.Web.UI.WebControls.RadioButton group and returns an ICollection object with RadioButton instances.
GetStatePersister	Returns a PageStatePersister object used by the web page to maintain the control and view states.
RegisterRadioButton	Adds a radio button control to the collection for a specified radio button group.
RenderBeginHyperlink	Renders an opening hyperlink tag, including the target URL, to the response stream. It takes the current TextWriter instance to write the data. This method is overloaded in order to support different sets of parameters.
RenderEndHyperlink	Renders a closing hyperlink tag to the response stream.
RenderPostBackEvent	Renders a postback event to the response stream as a hyperlink, including the encoded and possibly encrypted view state, and the event target and argument. This method is overloaded to support different sets of parameters.
TransformText	Transforms text for the target browser.

Device-Specific Filter for Adaptive Behavior

A device filter recognizes a client device and assigns a device-specific adapter to its controls. The filter can also identify control properties, user defined attributes and templates, and can be controlled with @Page and @Control directives. Recall that each control has a one-to-one relationship with an adapter, so if the filter returns several adapters, the most specific one is used.

Device filters are based on browser definition files. You can find the default definition files in the folder:

```
%SystemRoot%\Microsoft.NET\Framework\v2.0.50727\CONFIG\Browsers
```

Browser files are used to create the HttpBrowserCapabilities object that exposes the device's properties. The definitions form a hierarchy, preventing the files from redefining basic definitions. For instance, the *ie.browser* file contains several IE-related definitions. The following snippet shows settings specific to Internet Explorer:

```
<browsers>
    <browser id="IE" parentID="Mozilla">
        <identification>
            <userAgent match="^Mozilla[^(]*\([C|c]ompatible;\s*MSIE
```

```
                    (?'version'(?'major'\d+)(?'minor'\.\d+)(?'letters'\w*))(?'extra'[^)]*)" />
                <userAgent nonMatch="Opera|Go\.Web|Windows CE|EudoraWeb" />
        </identification>

        <capture>
        </capture>

        <capabilities>
            <capability name="browser"            value="IE" />
            <capability name="extra"              value="${extra}" />
            <capability name="isColor"            value="true" />
            <capability name="letters"            value="${letters}" />
            <capability name="majorversion"       value="${major}" />
            <capability name="minorversion"       value="${minor}" />
            <capability name="screenBitDepth"     value="8" />
            <capability name="type"               value="IE${major}" />
            <capability name="version"            value="${version}" />
        </capabilities>
    </browser>

    <browser id="IE5to9" parentID="IE">
        <identification>
            <capability name="majorversion" match="^[5-9]" />
        </identification>

        <capture>
        </capture>

        <capabilities>
            <capability name="activexcontrols"    value="true" />
            <capability name="backgroundsounds"   value="true" />
            <capability name="cookies"            value="true" />
            <capability name="css1"               value="true" />
            <capability name="css2"               value="true" />
            <capability name="ecmascriptversion"  value="1.2" />
            <capability name="frames"             value="true" />
            <capability name="javaapplets"        value="true" />
            <capability name="javascript"         value="true" />
            <capability name="jscriptversion"     value="5.0" />
            <capability name="msdomversion"       ➥
                                value="${majorversion}${minorversion}" />
            <capability name="supportsCallback"   value="true" />
            <capability name="supportsFileUpload" value="true" />
            <capability name="supportsMultilineTextBoxDisplay" value="true" />
            <capability name="supportsMaintainScrollPositionOnPostback" ➥
                                value="true" />
            <capability name="supportsVCard"      value="true" />
            <capability name="supportsXmlHttp"    value="true" />
            <capability name="tables"             value="true" />
            <capability name="tagwriter"          ➥
                                value="System.Web.UI.HtmlTextWriter" />
            <capability name="vbscript"           value="true" />
            <capability name="w3cdomversion"      value="1.0" />
            <capability name="xml"                value="true" />
        </capabilities>
    </browser>
    ...
</browsers>
```

The filter consists of two parts. First, the `userAgent` tag provides a `match` attribute which contains a regular expression. This expression is matched against the user-agent HTTP header sent by each client device.

The capabilities section contains a setting for the preferred `tagwriter`, which you can use to assign a particular behavior when creating tags. This is much less common than using a full-blown adapter, but is expedient if you simply want to write XHTML instead of HTML (see Figure 9-3).

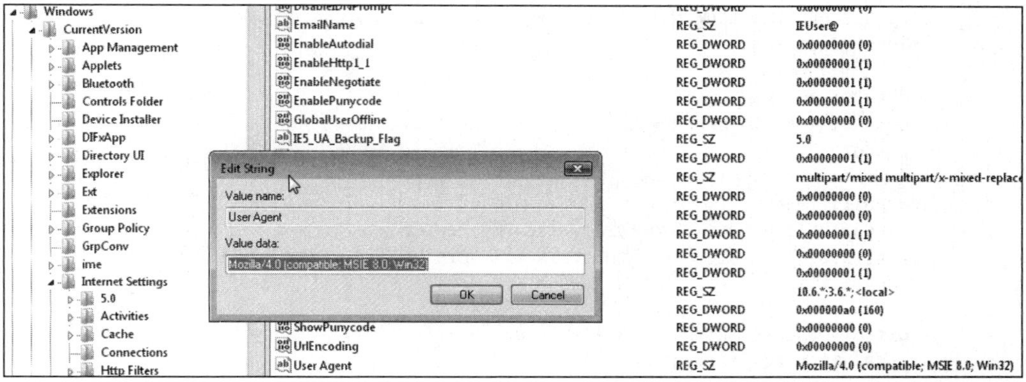

Figure 9-3. *User Agent settings for Internet Explorer*

■Caution As the User Agent string can be fake, don't trust the settings for security-related activities.

Adding client device filters can be accomplished on a per-application basis using the *App_Browsers* folder (see Figure 9-4). This is a special folder which can be added to any Web application project. Place a custom browser file into this folder and define device-specific settings there.

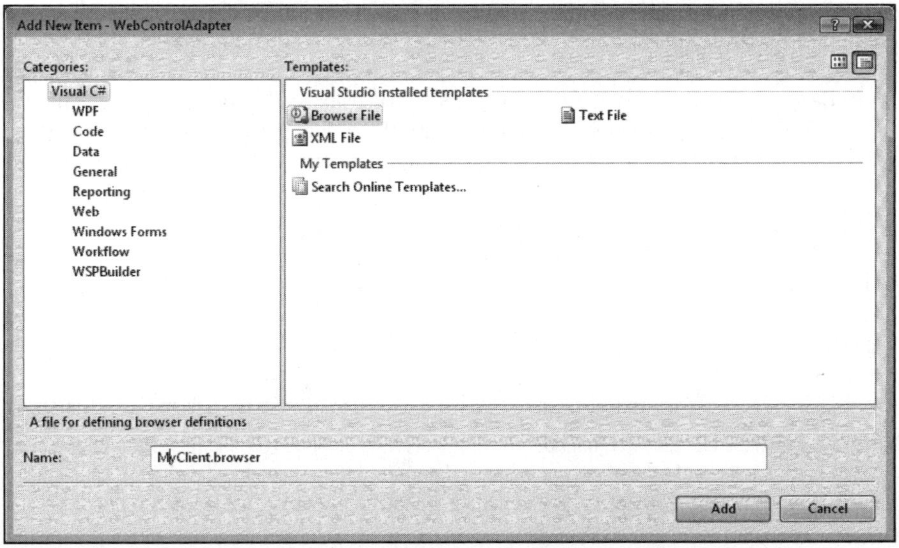

Figure 9-4. *Adding a *.browser file to the current project's App_Browsers folder*

The browser file has a similar structure to the default ones. The inheritance behavior is crucial. By using the right parentID attribute, you can inherit all common settings from an existing device and add or change a few values to match your current device.

A typical file contains the following tags, at a minimum:

```
<browsers>
    <browser id="NewBrowser" parentID="Mozilla">
        <identification>
            <userAgent match="Unique User Agent Regular Expression" />
        </identification>

        <capture>
            <userAgent match="NewBrowser (?'version'\d+\.\d+)" />
        </capture>

        <capabilities>
            <capability name="browser" value="My New Browser" />
            <capability name="version" value="${version}" />
        </capabilities>

        <controlAdapters markupTextWriterType="">
            <adapter adapterType=""
                     controlType="" />
        </controlAdapters>

    </browser>

    <browser refID="Mozilla">
        <capabilities>
            <capability name="xml" value="true" />
        </capabilities>
    </browser>
</browsers>
```

The types defined in the controlAdapters tag build the relationship between controls and adapters. They are specific to the current device. However, by using a common matching pattern, you can assign the filter to any device.

While the adapterType is a type derived from the System.Web.UI.Adapters.ControlAdapter, the controlType must derive from System.Web.UI.Control. The markupTextWriterType attribute defines the writer to render the content. This type is instantiated and the object passed to the Render and RenderChildren methods of the control adapter. For an embedded control, this looks like the following:

```
<controlAdapters markupTextWriterType="System.Web.UI.XhtmlTextWriter" >
    <adapter controlType="System.Web.UI.WebControls.Menu"
             adapterType="System.Web.UI.WebControls.Adapters.MenuAdapter">
    </adapter>
</controlAdapters>
```

■**Note** The browser capabilities file does not function for certain browser settings. The file matches the user agent string against a predefined set of properties. For instance, Internet Explorer supports JavaScript, hence the HttpBrowserCapabilities object returns true for that setting. If, however, a user disables JavaScript, this action does not change the property. You should read the object's name literally—as a capability rather than as actual behavior.

Using Control Adapters

There are several usage scenarios for adapters. In fact, adapters are one of the most powerful tools for extending control behavior.

Device-Friendly Adapters

The main purpose of control adapters is to support specific client devices that do not function well with the standard HTML created by built-in controls. The intended behavior is defined within the .browser configuration file.

CSS-Friendly Adapters

When you read about adapters, you'll often see the term "CSS-friendly control adapters." This wrongly implies that the adapter supports CSS (cascading style sheets). An adapter is simply an extensibility technique that allows page developers to alter the render behavior for all or particular client devices. Replacing pure HTML with CSS support is a common scenario, but it is not the only one supported by adapters. The reason for the name is the lack of CSS support in ASP.NET, and the development of adapters to overcome this limitation. For a sophisticated example of the usage of adapters to support CSS, refer to the Web site www.asp.net/CSSAdapters. This site offers a complete set of adapters using specific style definitions to format controls. The MenuAdapter shows how the replacement of <table> tags with nested <ul> tags and CSS styles, saves a lot of space and results in a freely configurable menu control. Other examples in the package support complex controls such as FormView and TreeView.

Other Adapter Ideas

An adapter can output any kind of markup. It's not limited to HTML or XHTML, and you can even create XAML to support WPF applications or Silverlight. (As this does sound strange, I'll reiterate it so that you know it's not a mistake.) It is possible to write a regular ASP.NET page consisting entirely of ASP.NET controls and render them in XAML—or anything else. The TextWriter class, used to add content to the output stream, writes text, whether or not it consists of markup. You can also use adapters to expose the source of a page by replacing the tags with < and > entities.

Writing a Custom Control Adapter

The following example shows how a custom control derived from a built-in control can be modified with an adapter.

Steps for Creating the Example

The example consists of the following parts:

- A custom control that adds two properties to the built-in CheckBoxList
- An adapter that changes the render behavior using these properties
- A page that uses the custom control
- A .browser file that assigns the adapter to the control

The Example Code

Listing 9-1 shows the custom control. The two properties store the names of the image resources. The purpose of the control is to display an image list. The control takes ListItem members, and instead of rendering CheckBox elements, two images are used—an OnImage if the item is selected (checked) and an OffImage otherwise.

The control behaves as any standard CheckBoxList would. You can add ListItems and fill in the appropriate data. However, the adapter changes the render behavior to just display images. There is no treatment of content because the list is read-only, and the user can't change anything or post back the data.

Imagine that the adapter is used to render the control for devices that don't allow interaction, such as a kiosk application. In that situation, a disabled CheckBox would look unprofessional.

Listing 9-1. *A Custom Control That Modifies a Built-In One*

```
public class MyCheckBoxList : CheckBoxList
{

    [Browsable(true)]
    public string OffImage
    {
        get
        {
            if (ViewState["OffImage"] == null)
            {
                OffImage = "";
            }
            return (string)ViewState["OffImage"];
        }
        set
        {
            ViewState["OffImage"] = value;
        }
    }

    [Browsable(true)]
    public string OnImage
    {
        get
        {
            if (ViewState["OnImage"] == null)
            {
                OnImage = "";
            }
            return (string)ViewState["OnImage"];
        }
        set
        {
            ViewState["OnImage"] = value;
        }
    }
}
```

This control has two additional properties. The images the properties refer to can be defined as embedded resources. To achieve this, use the WebResourceAttribute as follows:

```
[assembly: WebResourceAttribute( ➥
        "Apress.Extensibility.Adapters.Resources.OnImage.png", "image/jpg")]
```

```
[assembly: WebResourceAttribute( ➥
            "Apress.Extensibility.Adapters.Resources.OffImage.png", "image/jpg")]
```

Furthermore, we'll need a simple test scenario in order to get the control working. The following code is a snippet from an ASPX page. The attribute goes anywhere but inside a class. Specifically, the *AssemblyInfo.cs* file is a great place, as shown in Listing 9-2.

Listing 9-2. *A Simple Usage Scenario*

```
<form id="form1" runat="server">
<div>
    <cc1:MyCheckBoxList ID="MyCheckBoxList1" runat="server"
ControlOrientation="Horizontal" BackColor="Red" ForeColor="Blue">
    </cc1:MyCheckBoxList>
</div>
</form>
```

The code-behind file contains only the data source. To see the control in action, add a few ListItems, and choose images via the Selected property. If Selected equals true, OnImage is shown—otherwise, it's OffImage (see Listing 9-3).

Listing 9-3. *The Code-Behind File Adds a Few Items for Testing Purposes*

```
public partial class _Default : System.Web.UI.Page
{
    protected void Page_Load(object sender, EventArgs e)
    {
        if (!IsPostBack)
        {
            var lic = new List<ListItem>();
            lic.Add(new ListItem("Value 1", "1") { Selected = true });
            lic.Add(new ListItem("Value 2", "2") { Selected = false });
            lic.Add(new ListItem("V-alue 3", "3") { Selected = true });
            lic.Add(new ListItem("Value 4", "4") { Selected = false });
            MyCheckBoxList1.Items.AddRange(lic.ToArray());
        }
    }
}
```

Last, but not least, the adapter is required. This renders the control through a reference to the control, using the appropriate Render methods, as shown in Listing 9-4.

Listing 9-4. *The Adapter Creates Images and Labels Instead of Checkbox Controls*

```
public class MyCheckBoxListAdapter : ➥
System.Web.UI.WebControls.Adapters.WebControlAdapter
{

    private MyCheckBoxList CheckBoxListControl
    {
        get
        {
            return ((MyCheckBoxList)Control);
        }
    }

    protected override void RenderBeginTag(System.Web.UI.HtmlTextWriter writer)
```

```
{
    writer.WriteLine();
    writer.WriteBeginTag("table");
    writer.Write(HtmlTextWriter.TagRightChar);
    writer.Indent++;
}

protected override void RenderEndTag(System.Web.UI.HtmlTextWriter writer)
{
    writer.WriteEndTag("table");
    writer.WriteLine();
    writer.Indent--;
}

protected override void RenderContents(System.Web.UI.HtmlTextWriter writer)
{
    switch (CheckBoxListControl.RepeatDirection)
    {
        case RepeatDirection.Horizontal:
            writer.WriteBeginTag("tr");
            writer.Indent++;
            writer.Write(HtmlTextWriter.TagRightChar);
            for (int i = 0; i < CheckBoxListControl.Items.Count; i++)
            {
                writer.WriteBeginTag("td");
                writer.Write(HtmlTextWriter.TagRightChar);
                RenderCheckbox(writer, i);
                writer.WriteEndTag("td");
            }
            writer.WriteEndTag("tr");
            writer.Indent--;
            break;
        case RepeatDirection.Vertical:
            for (int i = 0; i < CheckBoxListControl.Items.Count; i++)
            {
                writer.WriteBeginTag("tr");
                writer.Write(HtmlTextWriter.TagRightChar);
                writer.WriteBeginTag("td");
                writer.Write(HtmlTextWriter.TagRightChar);
                RenderCheckbox(writer, i);
                writer.WriteEndTag("td");
                writer.WriteEndTag("tr");
            }
            break;
    }
}

private void RenderCheckbox(HtmlTextWriter writer, int i)
{
    Image img = new Image();
    Label l = new Label();
    if (CheckBoxListControl.Items[i].Selected)
    {
        img.ImageUrl = Page.ClientScript.GetWebResourceUrl(this.GetType(),
            String.Format("Apress.Extensibility.Adapters.Resources.{0}.png",
            CheckBoxListControl.OnImage));
        l.Text = String.Format("{0} (on) ",
```

```
                CheckBoxListControl.Items[i].Text);
    }
    else
    {
        img.ImageUrl = Page.ClientScript.GetWebResourceUrl(this.GetType(),
            String.Format("Apress.Extensibility.Adapters.Resources.{0}.png",
            CheckBoxListControl.OffImage));
        l.Text = String.Format("{0} (off) ",
            CheckBoxListControl.Items[i].Text);
    }
    img.ToolTip = CheckBoxListControl.Items[i].Value;
    img.RenderControl(writer);
    l.RenderControl(writer);
    }
}
```

A CheckBoxList supports a RenderDirection property, which has several more features not fully supported by this example. To obtain the right render direction, a table is used that either grows to the right by adding <td> tags, or downwards using <tr><td> pairs. The private RenderCheckbox method is used to create the content. To simplify this, built-in controls are employed and their internal Render method is used through the public RenderControl method. This ensures that the other adapters responsible for Image and Label controls will work as expected.

In Listing 9-4, an embedded resource is used, and the properties the custom control exposes are accessed in order to obtain the correct resource. The assembly attributes (WebResourceAttribute) described previously define the embedded resources, which are retrieved by means of the GetWebResourceUrl method.

When building HTML, it's often necessary to write parts of a tag, empty lines, or other characters. The HtmlTextWriter class has several public constant values to support such characters. Table 9-4 explains the characters returned by the constants.

Table 9-4. *Constant Characters and Strings As Defined in HtmlTextWriter*

Constant	Character	Description
DefaultTabString		Represents a single tab character
DoubleQuoteChar	"	Represents the quotation mark (") character
EndTagLeftChars	</	Represents the left angle bracket and slash mark of the closing tag
EqualsChar	=	Represents the equals sign
EqualsDoubleQuoteString	=""	Represents an equals sign with a double quotation mark
SelfClosingChars	/	Represents a space and the self-closing slash mark of a markup tag
SelfClosingTagEnd	/>	Represents the closing slash mark and right angle bracket of a self-closing tag
SemicolonChar	;	Represents a semicolon
SingleQuoteChar	'	Represents an apostrophe
SlashChar	/	Represents a forward slash
SpaceChar		Represents a space character
StyleEqualsChar	:	Represents the style equals character used to set style attributes equal to values
TagLeftChar	<	Represents the opening angle bracket of a markup tag
TagRightChar	>	Represents the closing angle bracket of a markup tag

The code should now run as expected. Figure 9-5 illustrates the output of the preceding example.

Figure 9-5. *A CheckBoxList that displays images*

Although the result may seem unimpressive, my intention was to demonstrate how to modify the render behavior of an existing control. The benefit here is that the other parts of the control that do not affect rendering still function as expected. Developers can choose between using this or another render behavior, depending on their application's needs or device capabilities. Imagine that a very basic client can't render checkboxes, but it can render images. Creating a new CheckBoxList control would require a lot more work than simply editing the adapter.

Why Use HtmlTextWriter?

You may be wondering why the HtmlTextWriter plays such an important role. After all, when building HTML, the StringBuilder is frequently the better and faster alternative. There are several reasons. First, the HtmlTextWriter has a number of useful predefined characters and strings, as shown in Table 9-4. Second, it handles indentation well when formatting HTML line by line. This would require additional code with StringBuilder. Third, it is associated with the output stream, which means that the content is written directly to the output (Response.OutputStream). This is the fastest way to transmit the response to the Web Server.

However, there are some disadvantages to the HtmlTextWriter. If you create your own HtmlTextWriter, you might associate it with a StringWriter/StringBuilder pair in order to retrieve the content. But using the writer exposed by the adapter classes, you can't access the stream with anything but write access, and any attempt to read the content will fail.

Configure the Example

To configure the code, you only need to make an entry in a .browser file. For this example, I define a file called *MyClient.browser* and place it in the default folder for browser definition files, *App_Browser.*

```
<browsers>
  <browser refID="Default">
    <controlAdapters>
      <adapter adapterType="Apress.Extensibility.Adapters.MyCheckBoxListAdapter"
               controlType="Apress.Extensibility.Adapters.MyCheckBoxList" />
    </controlAdapters>
  </browser>
</browsers>
```

This is everything you need. Launch the application and the adapter will start working.

Writing a Custom Page Adapter

A PageAdapter is like a ControlAdapter in that it's the preferred way to change the behavior of a page without altering either markup or code. As explained previously, pages are responsible not only for the rendering process but also for saving view state and for several life cycle events. A typical usage scenario involves the view state behavior under specific circumstances. For example, if a client device has a low-bandwidth connection, sending the view state to the client and back during postback will result in disappointed users.

However, to demonstrate creating a custom page adapter I will tackle a simplified scenario.

Steps for Creating the Example

The PageAdapter functions exactly like the ControlAdapter. You'll need the adapter class and a .browser file in order to configure it. Listing 9-5 shows the code which writes the page's source at the end of the page.

Listing 9-5. *Simple PageAdapter to Append Page Source*

```
public class SourcePageAdapter : PageAdapter
{
    protected override void EndRender(System.Web.UI.HtmlTextWriter writer)
    {
        StreamReader sr = File.OpenText( ➥
                    this.Page.Server.MapPath(this.Page.Request.Url.LocalPath));
        writer.WriteFullBeginTag("pre");
        this.Page.Server.HtmlEncode(sr.ReadToEnd(), writer);
        sr.Close();
        writer.WriteEndTag("pre");
        base.EndRender(writer);
    }
}
```

The writer is used to write the page's content from a StreamReader object. This contains page code read directly from the disk. Figure 9-6 assumes that the page is available.

■**Note** The example writes the content after all regular content, including the closing </html> tag. This results in invalid HTML. However, all common browsers render this, despite the discrepancy.

The configuration activates this for all clients. Imagine a workstation that you have configured for testing purposes. On it you have set the User-agent string manually in order to send a private key to the server. The .browser file recognizes this private key and activates the adapter only for requests from the testing computer. It will be the only client to receive the content rendered with source. Everyone else will see only the conventional page output. You won't need to set anything in *web.config*, or in code, or anywhere else.

■**Caution** Several examples recommend calling the RenderChildren method in order to send the rendered content of a page to a private TextWriter. This would not work with an adapter, as the adapter would be summoned again for the subsequent call, which would lead to an endless loop and eventually to a StackOverflowException.

```
Value 1
Value 2
Value 3
Value 4

<%@ Page Language="C#" AutoEventWireup="true" CodeBehind="Default.aspx.cs" Inherits="WebControlAdapter._Default" %>

<%@ Register Assembly="Apress.Extensibility.Adapters" Namespace="Apress.Extensibility.Adapters"
    TagPrefix="cc1" %>

<!DOCTYPE html PUBLIC "-//W3C//DTD XHTML 1.0 Transitional//EN" "http://www.w3.org/TR/xhtml1/DTD/xhtml1-transitional.dtd">

<html xmlns="http://www.w3.org/1999/xhtml" >
<head runat="server">
    <title></title>
</head>
<body>
    <form id="form1" runat="server">
    <div>
        <cc1:MyCheckBoxList ID="MyCheckBoxList1" runat="server"
                            OffImage="OffImage"
                            OnImage="OnImage"
                            BackColor="Red"
                            ForeColor="Blue">
        </cc1:MyCheckBoxList>
    </div>
    </form>
</body>
</html>
```

Figure 9-6. *The page used for the ControlAdapter example and content exposed by the page adapter*

Listing 9-6 shows another way to play with HtmlTextWriter. Instead of exposing the server-side source, I want expose the HTML sent to the client below the page.

Listing 9-6. *PageAdapter to Append Rendered Page Source*

```
public class ClientSourcePageAdapter : PageAdapter
{

    HtmlTextWriter internalWriter;
    HtmlTextWriter newWriter;
    StringBuilder sb;

    protected override void BeginRender(HtmlTextWriter writer)
    {
        internalWriter = writer;
        sb = new StringBuilder();
        newWriter = new HtmlTextWriter(new StringWriter(sb));
        base.BeginRender(newWriter);
    }

    protected override void Render(HtmlTextWriter writer)
    {
        base.Render(newWriter);
        string html = sb.ToString();
        writer.Write(html);
        writer.WriteBeginTag("pre");
        writer.Write(HtmlTextWriter.SpaceChar);
        writer.WriteAttribute("style", "border:solid 1px blue");
        writer.Write(HtmlTextWriter.TagRightChar);
        writer.WriteEncodedText(html);
        writer.WriteEndTag("pre");
    }

}
```

The original writer is now replaced by a custom one in the BeginRender method. In Render it allows you to access your own writer instance and write the content to a string using ToString of the StringBuilder object. First, the string is written back to the original writer. The remaining part creates a <pre> tag and a border style to place the encoded content in, as shown in Figure 9-7.

```
<!DOCTYPE html PUBLIC "-//W3C//DTD XHTML 1.0 Transitional//EN" "http://www.w3.org/TR/xhtml1/DTD/xhtml1-transitional.dtd">

<html xmlns="http://www.w3.org/1999/xhtml" >
<head><title>
</title></head>
<body>
    <form name="form1" method="post" action="default.aspx" id="form1">
<div>
<input type="hidden" name="__VIEWSTATE" id="__VIEWSTATE" value="/wEPDwUKMTgxNDAyMjYzNBBkZBYCAgMPZBYCAgEQEGQPFgRmAgECAgIDFgQQBQdWYWx1ZSAx
</div>

    <div>

<table><tr><td><img title="Value 1 (on) " src="/WebResource.axd?d=hlgYp1WpD9Bzq1eYBaA1InUqxkwX4SOQ2vKmi1IobJxSB8pZnq3oj_FtxsYFbJDSUGv92

    </div>
    </form>
</body>
</html>
```

Figure 9-7. *The page used for the ControlAdapter example and rendered content exposed by the page adapter*

Both examples are very limited in their capabilities. They show the basic principles as well as the power you get when dealing on a low level with the content. However, keep in mind that changing the render behavior is an option to extend ASP.NET when needed.

■**Caution** Before considering the usage of adapters, the common techniques should be tried first. The complete render framework is complex, and you might experience weird behavior if it is not implemented completely or correctly.

Configure the Examples

To configure the code, you'll just need to make an entry in a .browser file. In the first example, I define a file called *MyClient.browser* and place it in the default folder for browser definition files, *App_Browser*.

```
<browsers>
  <browser refID="Default">
    <controlAdapters>
      <adapter adapterType="Apress.Extensibility.Adapters.SourcePageAdapter"
               controlType="System.Web.UI.Page" />
    </controlAdapters>
  </browser>
</browsers>
```

This is everything you need. Launch the application and the adapter will start working. If you combine the PageAdapter with the ControlAdapter example shown previously, you can put two

<adapter> tags within the same <controlAdapters> section. The only reason to split it into several sections or files is to activate it for different kinds of client devices.

For the second example, simply replace the class name SourcePageAdapter with ClientSourcePageAdapter to activate this.

Summary

In this chapter, you looked at a method of extending a core part of ASP.NET—control rendering. Using adapters, you can assign relationships between a control and its adapter. Adapters can change render behavior, persistence of view state and control state, and the treatment of controls during specific states of their life cycle.

Page adapters are specialized control adapters supporting alternative behavior of the page's render and state persistence processes. Adapters can be used in conjunction with device filters in order to render controls differently for devices that can't handle ordinary HTML. Mobile devices especially suffer when it comes to large view states, complex content with several levels of nested tables, or other content originally designed for powerful machines. Using control adapters allows you to replace render behavior with a lean, device-specific version, without changing application code, page markup, or your custom controls.

Index

▪Special characters

</ (EndTagLeftChars constant), 389
< (TagLeftChar constant), 389
<%$ %> pattern, 181
= (EqualsChar constant), 389
="" (EqualsDoubleQuoteString constant), 389
/> (SelfClosingTagEnd constant), 389
> (TagRightChar constant), 389
" (DoubleQuoteChar constant), 389
/ (SelfClosingChars constant), 389
/ (SlashChar constant), 389
; (SemicolonChar constant), 389
' (SingleQuoteChar constant), 389
: (StyleEqualsChar constant), 389

▪A

ABC mnemonic, 298
access control lists (ACLs), 348
AcquireRequestState pipeline state, 257
actionFlags parameter, 265
adaptive control behavior
    control adapters, 376–379
    default behavior, 374–375
    device-specific filter for adaptive behavior,
        381–384
    overview, 373–374
    page adapters, 379–380
add command, 55
Add method, 52
AddEditorControl method, 227
AddNode method
    SiteMapProvider, 346
    StaticSiteMapProvider, 352
AddOnPreRenderCompleteAsync method,
    141–142
AddUsersToRoles method, 280
AJAX (Asynchronous JavaScript and XML), 325
allowPathInfo attribute, 145
AnonymousAuthenticationModule module,
    109
AnonymousIdentificationModule class, 112
App_Browsers folder, 383
App_GlobalResources folder, 197
App_LocalResources folder, 197
AppDomainAppVirtualPath property, 218
AppDomains
    enumerating, 63–64
    HttpApplication instances, 17
        loading .NET runtime, 10–11
        overview, 60
        unloading all, 62
        unloading specific, 60–61
AppendTrailingSlash property, 358
AppInitialize method, 355
Application collection, 246
application pipeline
    overview, 21–22
    request arrival
        HttpApplication class, 24
        IIS6 versus IIS7, 23–24
        overview, 22–23
        request processing, 24
        request receiving, 23
        response objects, 23
application pool, 7
ApplicationManager class, 23
ApplicationName method
    PersonlizationProvider base class, 330
    Profile Provider class, 311
ApplicationName property
    Membership Provider classes, 279
    Role Provider classes, 281
ApplicationPhysicalPath property, 357
ApplicationPool property, 57
ApplicationVirtualPath property, 357
AppSettingsExpressionBuilder class, 181
ArgumentNullException, 160
.asax extension, 4
.ascx extension, 122
.ashx extension, 4
.asmx extension, 3–4, 122
ASP.NET
    application pipeline
        overview, 21–22
        request arrival, 22–24
    control state, 33
    data binding events, 30–31
    defined, 2
    dynamic control events, 29–30
    IIS7 integrated pipeline, 21
    login control events, 31
    .NET runtime, 9–10, 13
    overview, 1
    page life cycle
        considerations, 29
        events, 27–28

ASP.NET *(continued)*
    Master page, 25
    overview, 25
    page request stages, 26–27
    from view state perspective, 33–43
    request handling
        HttpApplication class, 13–17
        HttpContext class, 13–14
        HttpHandler class, 19
        HttpModule class, 19
        life cycles, 20–21
        .NET runtime, 8
        pipeline, 18–19
        request arrival, 7
        request lifetime, 2–6
    view state
        anti-patterns, 44–52
        overview, 31–33
        role of, 43–44
aspnet_Configurations property, 170
aspnet_isapi.dll, 3
Aspnet_regsql.exe tool, 262
aspnetdb.mdf database, 348
AspNetHostingPermission attribute, 356
.aspx extension, 3–5, 19, 122
Assembly Resource Loader (WebResource.axd),
    122
Asynchronous JavaScript and XML (AJAX), 325
asynchronous operations, threading
    ASP.NET, 77–81
    custom thread pool
        asynchronous handlers, 81–87
        creating, 87–105
    overview, 77
asynchronous pages
    configuring
        default Web Server, 144
        development environment, 144
        IIS7 settings, 144–145
        overview, 143
        using generic handlers, 146
        using IIS Management Console, 145
    overview, 138
    preparing pages for asynchronous opera-
        tion, 138–139
    using public Web Service, 140–141
Attributes property, 347
Authenticate event, 31
AuthenticateRequest event, 273
authentication
    modules, 116–117, 276
    preparing, 333–334
authorization
    modules, 276–277
    techniques, 274
AuthorizationStoreRoleProvider class, 280

AuthorizeRequest event, 273
AutoEventWireup attribute, 27
.axd extension, 4

■B
base classes
    implementing security, 348
    overview, 344–346
    sitemap nodes in code, 347
basePath attribute, 272
BasicAuthenticationModule module, 109
Begin/End pattern, 141–142
BeginMethod method, 142
BeginProcessRequest method, 82, 85
BeginRender method, 393
BeginRender property, 377
BinaryFormatter type, 257
Browser property
    ControlAdapter base class, 377
    HttpRequest class, 374
built-in handlers, 122
built-in providers, 156–157

■C
CacheRefreshInterval property, 281
CacheVaryByHeaders property, 381
CacheVaryByParams property, 381
caching modules, 110, 112
CalculateSHA1 method, 289, 294
CallbackValidator attribute, 176
<!CDATA> section, 324
CertificateMappingAuthenticationModule
        module, 109
CfgExpressionEditor type, 190
CfgExpressionEditorSheet type, 190
CgiModule module, 110
_Change events, 42
change tracking, 39
ChangePassword method, 279
ChangePasswordQuestionAndAnswer method,
    279
CheckBoxList class, 389
child controls, initializing, 48–49
ChildNodes property, 347
Class attribute, 146
classKey parameter, 208
client side-driven Profile provider
    exposing profile settings to AJAX, 325
    JavaScript, 327–328
    overview, 325
    user interface, 326
clientConnectedCheck attribute, 66, 70
ClientState property, 381
CodeBehind attribute, 146
CodeExpression method, 187
CodeMethodInvokeExpression method, 187

CodePrimitiveExpression method, 187
CodeTypeReferenceExpression method, 187
ColorElement class, 178
Combine property, 358
CommitChanges method, 57
CompilerOptions attribute, 146
CompleteRequest method, 117
compression modules, 110
ComVisible attribute, 10
.config (Forbidden Handler), 122
config parameter, 160
<configSections> element, 159
configuration, accessing declaratively
    advanced expressions, 188–189
    creating expression builders, 183–187
    design-time support, 189–190
    expression syntax, 181–183
    extending expression binding syntax, 181
    implementing expression builders with
        design-time support, 190–195
    non-compiled pages, 187–188
    overview, 181
configuration sections
    anatomy of, 174
    attributes, 176
    class model, 175
    defining, 176–179
    overview, 153, 174
    scaffolding, 174
    using, 180
ConfigurationElement class, 174–175
ConfigurationManager class, 180
ConfigurationProperty attribute, 172
ConfigurationSection class, 174–175
ConfigurationValidationModule module, 111
ConnectionStringsExpressionBuilder class, 181
content modules, 109
content parameter, 222
context parameter, 188
control adapters
    CSS-friendly, 385
    device-friendly, 385
    overview, 385
    using, 376–379
    writing custom
        configuring example, 390
        creating example, 385
        example code, 386–390
        HtmlTextWriter, 390
        overview, 385
Control events, 28
control extensibility
    adaptive control behavior
        default behavior, 374–375
        device-specific filter for adaptive behav-
            ior, 381–384

overview, 373–374
    using control adapters, 376–379
    using page adapters, 379–380
control adapters
    CSS-friendly, 385
    device-friendly, 385
    overview, 385
    writing custom, 385–390
overview, 373
page adapters, writing custom, 391–394
Control property
    ControlAdapter base class, 377
    WebControlAdapter, 378
control state, 33, 247–249
ControlAdapter base class, 376, 377
ConvertFromString method, 324
ConvertToString method, 324
cookies, 246, 258–259
cpuMask attribute, 66
CreateChildControls method, 52
CreateChildControls property, 377
CreateDesignTimeLocalResourceWriter
        method, 211
CreateNewStoreData method, 265
CreateRole method, 280
CreateSessionID method, 260
CreateSupportedUserCapabilities method, 330
CreateUninitializedItem method, 265–266
CreateUser method, 279, 290
CreateWorkerRequest method, 12
CSS
    adapters friendly to, 385
    reading dynamic from resource, 131
ctrlId parameter, 222
culture parameter, 222
Cultures.xml file, 220
CurrentCulture property, 212
CurrentNode property, 345
CurrentNotification property, 23
CustomDesignTimeResourceProviderFactory
        type, 209
CustomErrorModule module, 109
CustomLoggingModule module, 111
CustomResourceWriter, 201
CustomThreadPool class, 88

■ D

-d databasename option, 262
data binding events, 30–31
data stores, 154
DataBinding event, 31
DataBound event, 31
DataContract attribute, 292
DataMemberAttribute attribute, 292
DataReader object, 352
DataSourceID property, 28

Debug attribute, 146
debugging
  design-time extensions, 218–219
  modules and handlers
    overview, 146
    using IIS, 147–151
declare prefix, 182
DecryptPassword method, 279
DefaultAuthenticationModule class, 112
DefaultDocumentModule module, 110
DefaultTabString class, 389
DefaultValue attribute, 176
delete command, 55
DeleteInactiveProfiles method, 311
DeleteProfiles method, 311
DeleteRole method, 280
DeleteUser method, 279
Description method, 330
Description property
  Role Provider class, 281
  SiteMapNode, 347
  SiteMapProperty, 345
  WebHandler directive, 146
DeserializationSection method, 160
Deserialize method, 257
deserializing, 252, 312
DesignerHost class, 211
design-time stage, 199
design-time support
  overview, 209
  registering
    debugging, 218–219
    overview, 209–218
DesignTimeResourceProviderFactory base
    class, 209
DetermineInitialScope method, 330
DeterminePostBackMode member, 381
DetermineUserCapabilities method, 330
devenv.exe file, 219
device-friendly adapters, 385
device-specific filter, 381–384
diagnostic modules, 111
Dictionary value, 206
DigestAuthenticationModule module, 109
DirectoryExists method, 370
DirectoryListingModule module, 110
Dispose member, 264
Dispose method, 116–117
Domain Name System (DNS), defined, 3
DoubleQuoteChar constant ("), 389
do-while loop, 207
downloading IIS7 managed modules starter
    kit, 113
DropDownList control, 29
dynamic control events, 29–30

dynamic controls
  attaching, 50–51
  initializing, 51–52
  view state, 39
DynamicCompressionModule module, 110
DynamicMethod method, 372

■ E
ECB (Extension Control Block), 9–10
edit.gif image, 227
EditIndex property, 248
editing resources at runtime
  function of, 219–223
  online editor, creating, 223–242
  overview, 219
EditorAttribute class, 190
embedded resources, 386
enable attribute, 66
Enabled attribute, 332
EnableLocalization property, 345
EnablePasswordReset property, 279
EnablePasswordRetrieval property, 279
EnableSessionState="ReadOnly" attribute, 264
EncryptPassword method, 279
End method, 117
EndRender property, 377
EndRequest method, 86, 264
EndTagLeftChars constant (</), 389
EnsureChildControls class, 28
entry parameter, 189
EqualsChar constant (=), 389
EqualsDoubleQuoteString constant (=""), 389
EvaluateExpression method, 183, 187–188
eventMapping element, 255
EventTime value, 256
ExcludeRange class, 178
executionTimeout attribute, 75, 266
expression builders
  creating, 183–187
  implementing with design-time support
    debugging, 194–195
    overview, 190–194
expression syntax
  declare prefix, 182
  extending, 181
  function, 182–183
  internal process, 181
  overview, 181
<expressionBuilders> element, 182
ExpressionEditorSheet class, 190
ExpressionPrefix parameter, 189
ExpressionValues class, 186
Extension Control Block (ECB), 9–10
extension mapping, 5–6
extensions, ISAPI, 5, 9

■F

FailedRequestsTracingModule module, 111
FastCgiModule module, 110
file operation classes, 357–358
FileAuthorizationModule class, 112
file-based session state persister
    configuring provider, 271–272
    overview, 271
FileCacheModule module, 110
FileCleanupProvider class, 255
FileExists method, 370
FileStream class, 132
FindChildren method, 367
Findfiles method, 367
FindInactiveProfilesByUserName method, 311
FindProfilesByUserName method, 311
FindSiteMapNode method, 346
FindSiteMapNodeFromKey method, 346
FindState method, 330
FindSubDirectories method, 367
FindUsersByEmail method, 279
FindUsersByName method, 279
FindUsersInRole method, 280
FontElement class, 177
Forbidden Handler (.config), 122
forcing defaults, 46
FormsAuthenticationModule class, 112, 276
FromBase64String method, 338

■G

gate keepers, 273
GetAllInactiveProfiles method, 311
GetAllNodes property, 347
GetAllProfiles method, 311
GetAllRoles method, 280
GetAllUsers method, 279
GetAncestor method, 352
GetCacheDependency method, 370
GetCfg method, 186–187
GetChildNodes method, 346
GetCodeExpression method, 182–183, 186
GetCountOfState method, 330
GetCurrentNodeAndHintAncestorNodes
        method, 346
GetCurrentNodeAndHintNeighborhoodNodes
        method, 346
GetDataSourceView property, 347
GetDirectory method, 367, 370
GetDirectory property, 358
GetExplicitResourceString property, 347
GetExtension property, 358
GetFile method, 367, 370
GetFileName property, 358
GetHandler method, 135–136
GetHierarchicalDataSourceView property, 347
GetImplicitResourceString property, 347

GetInvariantResxPathAtDesignTime method,
    215, 217
GetItem method, 258, 264, 265
GetItemExclusive method, 264–265
GetNumberOfInactiveProfiles method, 311
GetNumberOfUsersOnline method, 279, 290
GetObject method, 201, 207
GetParentNode method, 346
GetParentNodeRelativeToCurrentNodeAnd-
        HintDownFromParent method, 346
GetParentNodeRelativeToNodeAndHintDown-
        FromParent method, 346
GetParentSiteMapNode method, 352
GetPassword method, 279
GetPossibleResourceList method, 230
GetPostBackFormReference property, 381
GetPropertyValues method, 311, 324
GetRadioButtonsByGroup property, 381
GetRequests method, 59
GetResources method, 206
GetResourceWriter method, 201
GetResxPath method, 218
GetRolesForUser method, 281
GetRoot method, 352
GetRootNodeCore method, 346
GetRootNodeCoreFromProvider method, 346
GetStandardValues method, 194
GetStandardValuesSupported method, 194
GetStatePersister property, 380–381
GetString method, 352
GetUser method, 279, 285
GetUserNameByEmail method, 279
GetUserProfile method, 324
GetWebResourceUrl method, 389
global resources, 198
global.asax file, 355
GridView property, 248

■H

Handler property, 137
handlers
    advanced usage of, 136–138
    asynchronous pages
        configuring, 146
        overview, 138
        preparing pages for asynchronous opera-
            tion, 138–139
        using public Web Service, 141
    building
        entry point, 125–126
        handlers that don't create content,
            131–133
        image handler, 126–128
        overview, 124
        reading dynamic CSS from resource, 131
        using IHttpHandlerFactory to perform
            URL rewriting, 133–136

handlers *(continued)*
  built-in, 122
  debugging
    overview, 146
    using IIS, 147–151
  defined, 107
  HTTP, 122–124
  overview, 19, 107–108, 122
  tracing, setting up for, 151
HasChildNodes property, 347
Headers property, 23
health monitor, 254–256
HiddenField control, 254
HiddenFieldPageStatePersister base class, 249
HideDisabledControlAdapter class, 378
HierarchicalDataBoundControlAdapter class, 378
HierarchyId column, 349
HierarchyId data type, 348, 352
Hint methods, 346
HintAncestorNodes method, 346
HintNeighborhoodNodes method, 346
HostingEnvironment class, 23, 358
HtmlForm control, 34
HtmlTextWriter class, 374, 389–390
HTTP handlers
  defined, 1
  overview, 122–124
  scenarios for using, 123
HTTP modules, 109
HTTP runtime, 2
HttpApplication class, 13–17, 24, 115
HTTPCacheModule module, 110
HttpContext class, 13–14, 23, 88
HttpHandler class, 19
HttpLoggingModule module, 111
HttpModule class, 19, 115–116
HttpRedirectionModule module, 109
HttpRequest object, 23–24
HttpResponse object, 23
HttpRuntime object, 256
<httpRuntime> tag, 71
HttpStaticObjectsCollection type, 257

IAsyncResult interface, 83, 142
Id property, 63
Identity property, 274
IDesignerHost interface, 210
IDesignTimeResourceWriter interface, 212
Idle property, 63
idleTime attribute, 66
idleTimeout attribute, 69
IFRAME element, 131–133
IHttpAsyncHandler interface, 81, 123
IHttpHandler interface, 5, 123
IHttpHandlerFactory interface, 133–136

IHttpHandlerFactory2 interface, 134
IHttpModule interface, 5, 24
IIS Management Console
  configuring asynchronous pages using, 145
  configuring modules using, 122
IIS6 (Internet Information Services 6)
  versus IIS7, 23–24
  thread usage, 70–71
IIS7 (Internet Information Services 7)
  versus IIS6, 23–24
  integrated pipeline, 21
  modules
    managed, 111–115
    native, 108–111
    overview, 108
  thread usage
    busy server, 73
    configuring ThreadPool, 72–73
    overview, 71–72
  worker process
    AppDomains, 60–64
    basic tasks, 56–57
    configuration backup, 55
    configuring, 64–68
    prerequisites, 54
    retrieving information about, 57–60
    specific tasks, 68–70
    task management, 54–55
IISCertificateMappingAuthenticationModule module, 109
image handler, 126–128
ImageDataDataContext class, 168
ImageProvider class, 171
ImageProviderSection class, 172
impersonation, 277
includeExceptionDetailInFaults attribute, 300
Init event, 27, 29, 39
Init method, 116–117
InitComplete event, 27
Initialize method
  Membership Provider class, 279
  overview, 157, 160–162, 168
  Profile Provider class, 311
  RegisterVirtualPathProviderInternal class, 356
  SiteMapProvider class, 346
InitializeCulture method, 27
InitializeRequest member, 264
InProcSessionStateStore class, 261
instantiation, 34–38
IntegerValidator attribute, 176, 178
internal session state providers
  InProcSessionStateStore class, 261
  OutOfProcSessionStateStore class, 262
  overview, 260–261
  SqlSessionStateStore class, 262–263
internal site map provider, 341–343

internationalization, 197
Internet Information Services 6. *See* IIS6
Internet Information Services 7. *See* IIS7
Internet Service API (ISAPI), 2, 4–5
IPostBackDataHandler interface, 40–42
IpRestrictionModule module, 109
IPrincipal interface, 274
IReadOnlySessionState interface, 136–137
IRequiredSessionState interface, 136
IResourceProvider interface, 212
IsAbsolute property, 358
IsAccessibleToUser method, 346
IsAccessibleToUser property, 347
ISAPI (Internet Service API), 2, 4–5
IsapiFilterModule module, 110
IsapiModule module, 110
ISAPIRuntime class, 10
ISAPIWorkerRequest object, 12–13
ISAPIWorkerRequestInProc class, 13
ISAPIWorkerRequestInProcForIIS7 type, 13
IsAppRelative property, 358
IsApproved property, 295
IsDefaultCollection attribute, 176
IsDescendantOf property, 347
IsDesignerViewLocked property, 212
IsEnabled property, 378
IServiceProvider interface, 210
ISessionIDManager interface, 259
IsInRole method, 274
IsKey attribute, 176
IsLoading property, 212
IsLockedOut property, 295
IsPostBack property, 26–27
IsPostNotification property, 23
IsRequired attribute, 176
IsReusable property, 124
IsUserInRole method, 281
Item property, 347
ItemCreated event, 31
ItemDataBound event, 31
IWebFormsDocumentService interface, 212, 214

■**J**
JavaScript, 327–328

■**K**
Key property, 347

■**L**
Language attribute, 146
life cycles, 20–21. *See also* page life cycle
lifetime
    provider, 161
    request, 2–6
list command, 55
LiteralControl controls, 34

Load event, 28–29
Load method, 254
load page request stage, 26
LoadAdapterControlState property, 377
LoadAdapterViewState property, 377
LoadComplete event, 28
LoadControl class, 371–372
LoadMe function, 240
LoadPersonalizationBlobs method, 330
LoadPersonalizationState method, 330
LoadPostData method, 40–41
LoadProviders method, 165
LoadResource method, 222
localization, 343
lock statement, 161–162
Log Request state, 22
LoggedIn event, 31
logging modules, 111
LoggingIn event, 31
login control events, 31
LoginError event, 31
logLevel attribute, 66
LongValidator attribute, 176

■**M**
machine.config file, 64–65
MakeRelative property, 358
managed modules
    overview, 111–113
    starter kit
        benefits of, 113–115
        downloading, 113
        overview, 113
ManagedEngine module, 111
Map Handler state, 22
MapPath property, 357
markupTextWriterType attribute, 384
Master page life cycle, 25
maxAppDomains attribute, 66
maxconnection attribute, 74–75
MaxInvalidPasswordAttempts property, 279
maxIoThreads attribute, 66, 74
maxWorkerThreads attribute, 66, 74
MeasureString method, 128
Membership providers
    developing
        configuring provider, 308
        configuring services, 298–300
        implementing provider, 300–308
        overview, 282
        testing provider, 308–309
        Web service-driven, 282–298
    extending, 281–282
Membership service, 155–156, 277
MembershipUser class, 306
memoryLimit attribute, 66, 68
MemoryStream object, 130

Menu control, 341–342
MenuAdapter class, 378
MenuItemClick event handler, 333
meta:resourcekey attribute, 223
mexHttpBinding attribute, 299
minFreeThreads attribute, 71, 74
minIoThreads attribute, 66
minLocalRequestFreeThreads attribute, 71, 74
MinRequiredNonAlphanumericCharacters
        property, 279
MinRequiredPasswordLength property, 279
minWorkerThreads attribute, 66, 74
MissHandler method, 207
mode attribute, 276
modules
    building
        checking for specific headers, 117–119
        defining, 115–116
        overview, 115
        writing simple authentication module,
            116–117
    configuring, 120–122
    debugging
        overview, 146
        using IIS, 147–151
    IIS7 architecture
        managed modules, 111–115
        native modules, 108–111
        overview, 108
    interaction between, 119–120
    overview, 18–19, 107–108
modules attribute, 145
Modules property, 120
Monitor method, 162
Multi Threaded Apartment (MTA), 17

N

name attribute, 121
Name method, 330
Name property
    Membership Provider class, 279
    overview, 157
    SiteMapNode, 347
    SiteMapProvider class, 345
NameValueCollection class, 160
native modules, 108–111
NavigateControl method, 225
NavigateUrl property, 347
.NET Reflector, 8
.NET runtime
    handling requests within, 12–13
    loading, 10–11
    overview, 8–9
    processes, 9–10
    threads, 9–10
NextSibling property, 347
NotImplementedException method, 163

O

onError function, 327
OnInit event, 47–48
OnInit method, 376
OnInit property, 377
online editor, creating, 223, 242
OnLoad event, 28, 47
OnLoad property, 377
onLoadSuccess function, 327
OnPreInit event, 49
OnPreRender property, 377
OnUnload property, 377
OperationContract attribute, 283, 285
Options attribute, 176
OutOfProcSessionStateStore class, 262
OutputCacheModule class, 112

P

page adapters
    adaptive control behavior, 379–380
    writing custom
        configuring example, 393–394
        creating example, 391–393
        overview, 391
Page Handler (.aspx), 122
page initialization, 26
page life cycle
    considerations, 29
    events, 27–28
    Master page, 25
    overview, 25
    page request stages, 26–27
    from view state perspective
        initializing, 39
        instantiation, 34–38
        loading postback data, 40–41
        loading step, 42
        loading view state, 39–40
        overview, 33
        raising postback events, 42
        rendering page, 43
        storing view state, 43
page management
    control state, 247–249
    overview, 245
    page state persister, 245–246
    page state provider, 251–256
    view state, 247
Page property, 377
page request stages, 26–27
    load, 26
    overview, 26
    page initialization, 26
    postback event handling, 26
    rendering, 26
    start, 26

unload, 27
validation, 26
page state persister, 245–246
page state provider
    default, 250–251
    developing custom
        analyzing, 252
        data storage, 252
        extending, 254
        health monitor, 254–256
        implementing, 252–254
        overview, 251–252
PageAdapter property, 377
PageHandlerFactory, 107, 133
pageId parameter, 222
PageIndex property, 248
Pagename.resx file, 197
PageStatePersister base class, 249
PageStatePersister property, 251
parentID attribute, 384
ParentNode property, 347
ParentProvider property, 345
ParseExpression method, 182–183, 186, 188
partial keyword, 34
PassportAuthenticationModule, 276
PasswordAttemptWindow property, 280
PasswordFormat property, 280
PasswordStrengthRegularExpression property,
    280
path attribute, 144
path operation classes, 357–358
Path property, 347
Performance Counter, installing, 75–77
persisting
    cheap data, 46–48
    constant data, 46
personalization providers
    authentication, 333–334
    configuring, 339
    creating, 334–339
    implementing, 331–339
    overview, 331
    Portal page, 331–333
    Web Parts
        implementing, 331–339
        overview, 329–331
        testing, 339
PersonalizationState class, 329
PhysicalPath property, 63
pingFrequency attribute, 67, 69
pingTimeout attribute, 67, 69
Portal page, 331–333
PositiveTimespanValidator attribute, 176
postback event handling, 26
precompiled sites, 372
preCondition attribute, 121, 145
PreInit event, 27, 222

PreLoad event, 28
PreRender event, 28
PreviousHandler property, 137
PreviousSibling property, 347
ProcessEvent method, 256
ProcessGuid method, 57
processing pipeline, defined, 1
<processModel> tag, 65, 68, 72, 77
ProcessRequest method, 9, 12, 33, 123, 125, 173
Profile class, 317
profile handling modules, 112
Profile providers
    client side-driven
        exposing profile settings to AJAX, 325
        JavaScript, 327–328
        overview, 325
        user interface, 326
    configuring, 314
    extending
        configuring, 314
        defining profile settings, 312–313
        overview, 310
        Profile service, 310
        serializing and deserializing, 312
        using Profile data, 313
    implementing, 319–325
    overview, 314
    preparation steps, 314–319
Profile service, 155–156, 278, 310
<Profile> element, 325
ProfileAuthenticationOption parameter, 312
ProfileModule class, 112
ProfileService class, 327
PropertyGrid control, 324
propertyType parameter, 189
Protected Configuration service, 155–156
ProtocolSupportModule module, 109
provider element, 255
ProviderBase class, 157, 165–166, 267
ProviderCollection class, 170
ProviderException class, 160
ProviderHelper class, 165
providers
    anatomy of
        configuring, 158–160
        making available, 158
        overview, 157
    built-in
        extending, 156–157
        overview, 156
    configuring, 308
    considerations
        initialization procedure, 160
        lifetime, 161
        overview, 160
        thread safety, 161
    custom provider-based service

providers *(continued)*
    configuring providers, 170–172
    creating provider, 165–170
    creating service, 164–165
    limitations of code samples, 163
    overview, 163
    using service, 172–173
  default, 154–155
  goals of, 154
  implementing, 300–308
  Membership
    developing, 282–309
    extending, 281–282
  overview, 153
  page state
    default, 250–251
    developing custom, 251–256
  personalization
    authentication, 333–334
    configuring, 339
    creating, 334–339
    implementing, 331–339
    overview, 331
    Portal page, 331–333
    Web Parts, 329–339
  Profile
    client side-driven, 325–328
    configuring, 314
    extending, 310–314
    implementing, 319–325
    overview, 314
    preparation steps, 314–319
  resource
    configuring, 208
    extending provider model, 198–199
    implementing, 201–208
    overview, 198
    prerequisites for, 200
    using, 208
  Role
    developing, 282–309
    extending, 281–282
  session state
    internal, 260–263
    overview, 256
    session state service, 256–258
  session state store
    file-based session state persister, 267–272
    handling expired data, 266
    locking session-store data, 266
    overview, 264
    session state module, 264–266
    setting application name, 266
  sitemap
    base classes, 344–348
    internal, 341–343
    localization, 343
    overview, 341, 344
    prerequisites, 344
    reasons to customize, 343
    security, 343
    SQL server-based navigation, 348–353
   testing, 308–309
<providers> section, 319
public Web Service, 140–141

■R

raising postback events, 42
ReadAllText class, 254
ReaderWriterLock class, 133, 162
ReadOnly property, 263, 347
ReferenceManager property, 212
referrers, 117–118
regenerateExpiredSessionId="true" attribute,
  259
RegexStringValidator attribute, 176, 179
RegisterAsyncTask method, 141
registering design-time support
  debugging, 218–219
  overview, 209–218
RegisterRadioButton property, 381
RegisterRequiresControlState method, 248
RegisterVirtualPathProvider property, 357
ReleaseItemExclusive method, 265–266
RemapHandler property, 137–138
RemoteOnly property, 177
RemoveItem method, 258, 265–266
RemoveNode method, 346
RemoveTrailingSlash property, 358
RemoveUsersFromRoles method, 281
Render method, 26, 377
Render property, 378
RenderBeginHyperlink property, 381
RenderBeginTag property, 378
RenderCheckbox method, 389
RenderChildren method, 376
RenderChildren property, 377
RenderContents property, 378
RenderControl method, 374, 389
RenderDirection property, 389
RenderEndHyperlink property, 381
RenderEndTag property, 378
rendering page request stage, 26
RenderPostBackEvent property, 381
request arrival
  ASP.NET, 7
  HttpApplication class, 24
  IIS6 versus IIS7, 23–24
  overview, 22–23
  request processing, 24
  request receiving, 23
  response objects, 23
request handling
  HttpApplication class, 13–17

HttpContext class, 13–14
HttpHandler class, 19
HttpModule class, 19
life cycles, 20–21
.NET runtime
  handling requests within, 12–13
  loading, 10–11
  overview, 8–9
  threads, 9–10
pipeline, 18–19
request arrival, 7
request lifetime
  extension mapping, 5–6
  ISAPI, 4–5
  overview, 2–4
RequestFilteringModule module, 109
requestLimit attribute, 67–68
RequestMonitorModule module, 111
RequestNotification enumeration, 22
requestQueueLimit attribute, 67, 73
requireAccess attribute, 144
RequiresQuestionAndAnswer property, 280
RequiresUniqueEmail property, 280
ResetPassword method, 279
ResetPersonalizationBlob method, 330
ResetPersonalizationState method, 330
ResetState method, 330
ResetUserState method, 331
ResolveSiteMapNode method, 346
resource management principles
  fallback strategy, 197–198
  global resources, 198
  limitations of existing provider, 198
  overview, 197
resource model, extending
  design-time support, 209–219
  editing resources at runtime, 219–242
  overview, 197
  resource management principles, 197–198
  resource provider, programming custom,
    198–208
resource providers
  configuring, 208
  extending provider model, 198–199
  implementing, 201–208
  overview, 198
  prerequisites for, 200
  using, 208
resource reader, 207–208
ResourceExpressionBuilder class, 181
ResourceKey property, 345, 347
ResourceReader class, 201
ResourceReader property, 215
ResourceTuple class, 206
resourceType attribute, 144–145
responseDeadlockInterval attribute, 67, 69
restartQueueLimit attribute, 67

restore command, 55
.resx files, 198–199, 206, 219
resx.gif image, 227
ResXResourceReader class, 208
ResXResourceWriter class, 218
RetrieveImage method, 164–166, 168, 170, 173
Role providers
  developing
    configuring provider, 308
    configuring services, 298–300
    implementing provider, 300–308
    testing providers, 308–309
    Web service-driven, 282–298
  extending, 281–282
Role service, 155–156, 278
RoleExists method, Role Provider classes, 281
RoleManagerModule class, 112
roles attribute, 277
Roles elements, 295
Roles property, 347
RoleService class, 298
RootComponent property, 211
RootNode property, 345, 347
RootProvider property, 345
RowCreated event, 31
RowDataBound event, 31
rules element, 255

■S

-S servername option, 262
Save method, 254, 298
SaveAdapterControlState property, 377
SaveAdapterViewState property, 377
SavePersonalizationBlob method, 331, 338
SavePersonalizationState method, 331
SaveResource method, 222
SaveStateComplete event, 28
ScopeName property, 281
Script resource handler (ScriptResource.axd),
  122
ScriptManager control, 231
scriptProcessor attribute, 144
ScriptResource.axd (Script resource handler),
  122
SectionAttribute attribute, 165, 172
security. *See also* user management
  base classes, 348
  modules, 109, 112
  site map providers, 343
SecurityTrimmingEnabled property, 345, 348
select clause, 64
SelfClosingChars constant (/), 389
SelfClosingTagEnd constant (/>), 389
SemicolonChar constant (;), 389
serialization method, 252
SerializationSection method, 160
Serialize method, 257

serializeAs attribute, 313
serializing, 312
serverErrorMessageFile attribute, 67
ServerManager class, 57
ServerSideIncludeModule module, 110
ServerVariables property, 24
service oriented architectures (SOA), 281
service tier, 283
[ServiceContract] attribute, 283
services, defined, 154
Session collection, 246
session handling modules, 112
session management
    overview, 245
    session state providers
        identifying session, 258–260
        improving session state, 263
        internal, 260
        overview, 256
        session state service, 256–258
    session state store provider
        file-based session state persister, 267–272
        handling expired data, 266
        locking session-store data, 266
        overview, 264
        session state module, 264–266
        setting application name, 266
session state handlers, 136–137
session state providers
    identifying session, 258–260
    improving session state, 263
    internal
        InProcSessionStateStore class, 261
        OutOfProcSessionStateStore class, 262
        overview, 260–261
        SqlSessionStateStore class, 262–263
    overview, 256
    session state service, 256–258
session state service, 155–156, 256–258
session state store providers
    file-based session state persister
        configuring provider, 271–272
        overview, 267–271
    handling expired data, 266
    locking session-store data, 266
    overview, 264
    session state module, 264–266
    setting application name, 266
sessionIDManagerType attribute, 260
SessionPageStatePersister class, 251–252
sessionState element, 271
SessionStateItemCollection type, 257
SessionStateModule class, 112, 264
SessionStateStoreData class, 256
SessionStateStoreProviderBase class, 257
SetAndReleaseItemExclusive method, 265–266
SetItemExpireCallback method, 265–266

SetPropertyValues method, 311
shared resources, 198
shutDownTimeout attribute, 67, 69
Single Threaded Apartment (STA), 17
SingleQuoteChar constant ('), 389
site management
    overview, 341
    sitemap providers
        base classes, 344–348
        custom, 343
        implementing SQL server based naviga-
            tion, 348–353
        internal site map provider, 341–343
        localization, 343
        overview, 341, 344
        prerequisites, 344
        reasons to customize, 343
        security issues, 343
        suggestions for extending example, 354
    VirtualPathProvider
        limitations of, 371–372
        overview, 354
        path and file operation classes, 358
        prerequisites for, 356
        registering, 355–356
        themes, getting from database, 358–371
        using, 355
Site Map service, 155, 156
sitemap providers
    base classes
        implementing security, 348
        overview, 344–346
        sitemap nodes in code, 347
    internal, 341–343
    localization, 343
    prerequisites, 344
    reasons to customize, 343
    security, 343
    SQL server-based navigation
        configuring custom provider, 352–353
        creating provider, 349–352
        overview, 348
        preparing database, 348–349
        testing provider, 353
SiteMapDataSource control, 341–342
SiteMapPath control, 341–342
SiteMapProvider class, 344
SiteMapResolve event, 346
SiteName property, 357
SlashChar constant (/), 389
Sleep call, 16
Sleep method, 83
SOA (service oriented architectures), 281
SortDirection property, 248
SpaceChar constant, 389
SQL server based navigation
    configuring custom provider, 352–353

creating provider, 349–352
overview, 348
preparing database, 348–349
testing provider, 353
SqlPersonalizationProvider class, 329
SqlProfileProvider class, 310
SqlSessionStateStore class, 262–263
-ssadd option, 262
-ssremove option, 263
-sstype c option, 263
-sstype p option, 263
-sstype t option, 263
STA (Single Threaded Apartment), 17
start page request stage, 26
State property, 57
state storage, 247
StateBag class, 39, 41, 50, 247, 252
StateFormatter class, 254
stateless protocol, 245
StaticCompressionModule module, 110
StaticFileModule module, 110
StaticObjects property, 257
StaticSiteMapProvider class, 344
stickiness, 41, 47
storing view state, 43
stress test tool, 79–81
StringValidator attribute, 176, 178–179
StyleEqualsChar constant (:), 389
SubclassTypeValidator attribute, 176
SubStatusCode property, 23
SupportsEvaluate class, 183, 187
.svc extension, 4
System.serviceModel section, 299

■T

TagLeftChar constant (<), 389
TagRightChar constant (>), 389
tagwriter, 383
testing providers, 308–309
TextWriter class, 385
theme parameter, 222
themes, getting from database
configuring path provider, 371
creating VirtualPathProvider, 358–370
overview, 358
prepare project, 358
thread safety, 161
ThreadInfo class, 97, 99
ThreadPool class, 70–73
threads
asynchronous operations
ASP.NET, 77–81
custom thread pool, 81–105
overview, 77
IIS6, 70–71
IIS7, 71–73
.NET runtime, 9–10

overview, 53, 70
tune threading
installing performance counter, 75–77
overview, 73
tasks, 73–75
ThreadWrapper class, 99
TimeExpressionEditor type, 192
TimeExpressionEditorSheet type, 193
timeout attribute, 67–68
TimespanValidator attribute, 176
Title property, 347
ToAbsolute property, 358
ToAppRelative property, 358
TokenCacheModule module, 110
TokenParser class, 186
Trace Handler (trace.axd), 122
tracing, 151
TracingModule module, 111
TransactionDescription property, 211
TransformText property, 381
TreeView control, 341–342
trigger events, 42
tune threading
installing performance counter, 75–77
overview, 73
tasks, 73–75
type attribute, 121, 144–145
Type property, 347
typeConverter attribute, 194, 324
TypeConverterAttribute class, 190

■U

UICulture property, 26
unified request processing pipeline, 21
UniqueID property, 26
Unload event, 28
unload page request stage, 27
unloadFunc() method, 62
UnlockUser method, 279
UpdateUser method, 279, 306
UriCacheModule module, 110
Url property, SiteMapNode, 347
URL rewriting, 133–136
UrlAuthorizationModule class, 109, 112
UrlMappingsModule class, 112
useHostingIdentity attribute, 264
User Control Handler (.ascx), 122
user management
authentication modules, 276
authorization modules, 276–277
interfaces
extensibility issues, 278–281
overview, 277–278
Membership and Role providers
configuring provider, 308
configuring services, 298–300
extending, 281–282

user management *(continued)*
  implementing provider, 300–308
  overview, 282
  testing providers, 308–309
  Web service-driven, 282–298
overview, 273–275
Profile provider, custom
  client side-driven, 325–328
  implementing provider, 319–325
  overview, 314
  preparation steps, 314–319
Profile providers
  configuring, 314
  overview, 310–313
  Profile service, 310
Web Parts personalization providers
  implementing, 331–339
  overview, 329–331
  testing, 339
UserAgent property, 130
userAgent tag, 383
UserData class, 290, 298
username attribute, 67
users attribute, 277

▪**V**

Validate method, 26, 260
ValidateUser method, 279
ValidatingPassword event, 279
validation page request stage, 26
validator.gif image, 227
Value property, 347
verb attribute, 144, 277
view state
  anti-patterns
    attaching dynamic controls, 50–51
    forcing defaults, 46
    initializing child controls, 48–49
    initializing dynamically created controls, 51–52
    overview, 44
    persisting cheap data, 46–48
    persisting constant data, 46
  overview, 31–33
  page life cycle from perspective of
    initializing, 39
    instantiation, 34–38
    loading postback data, 40–41
    loading step, 42
    loading view state, 39–40
    overview, 33
    raising postback events, 42
    rendering page, 43
    storing view state, 43
  role of, 43–44
__VIEWSTATE field, 33, 39, 43
ViewStateDecoder tool, 250

VirtualFile instance, 370
virtualPath parameter, 208
VirtualPath property, 63
VirtualPathProvider class
  limitations of, 371–372
  overview, 354
  path and file operation classes, 357–358
  prerequisites for, 356
  registering, 355–356
  themes, getting from database
    configuring path provider, 371
    creating VirtualPathProvider, 358–370
    overview, 358
    preparing project, 358
  using, 355
VirtualPathProvider property, 357
VirtualPathUtility class, 358
VirtualThemeDirectory class, 360
VirtualThemeFile class, 359

▪**W**

WarningLevel attribute, 146
WAS (Windows Process Activation Service), 54
WCF (Windows Communication Foundation), 282
Web Events service, 155
Web Parts personalization providers
  authentication, 333–334
  configuring, 339
  creating, 334–339
  overview, 329–331
  Portal page, 331–333
  testing, 339
Web Parts service, 155–156
Web Service Handler (.asmx), 122
Web service-driven membership providers, 282–298
Web service-driven role providers, 282–298
web.config section, 314, 325
WebControlAdapter base class, 378
webGarden attribute, 67
WebHandler directive, 146
WebHeartbeatEvent class, 254, 255
webpart.gif image, 227
WebResource.axd (Assembly Resource Loader), 122
web.sitemap XML file, 341
where clause, 60, 62
Windows Communication Foundation (WCF), 282
Windows Management Instrumentation (WMI), 53–54
Windows Process Activation Service (WAS), 54
WindowsAuthenticationModule class, 109, 112, 276
WindowsTokenRoleProvider class, 280

WMI (Windows Management Instrumentation), 53–54
worker process
    AppDomains
        enumerating, 63–64
        overview, 60
        unloading all, 62
        unloading specific, 60–61
    basic tasks, 56–57
    configuration backup, 55
    configuring
        attributes, 65–67
        machine.config file, 64–65
        overview, 64
        processModel tag, 68
    overview, 53
    prerequisites, 54
    retrieving information about
        executing requests, 59–60
        overview, 57
        state of worker process, 57–58
    specific tasks
        checking client connection, 70
        overview, 68
        recycling, 68–69
        shutting down, 69
    task management, 54–55
WorkerProcess object, 57
WorkerProcesses property, 58
WorkRequest class, 102
WriteAllText class, 254
wsHttpBinding class, 299
WSRoleProvider class, 306

■**X**

XmlArrayItem attributes, 293
XmlElement attribute, 290
XmlResourceHelper class, 215
XmlSiteMapProvider provider, 341
XPath expressions, 338

You Need the Companion eBook